Military Strategy and the
Origins of the First World War
REVISED AND EXPANDED EDITION

International Security Readers

Strategy and Nuclear Deterrence (1984)

Military Strategy and the Origins of the First World War (1985)

Conventional Forces and American Defense Policy (1986)

The Star Wars Controversy (1986)

Naval Strategy and National Security (1988)

Military Strategy and the Origins of the First World War, revised and expanded edition (1991)

—published by Princeton University Press

Soviet Military Policy (1989)

Conventional Forces and American Defense Policy, revised edition (1989)

Nuclear Diplomacy and Crisis Management (1990)

The Cold War and After: Prospects for Peace (1991)

—published by The MIT Press

Military Strategy and the Origins of the First World War

AN *International Security* READER

REVISED AND EXPANDED EDITION

EDITED BY

Steven E. Miller
Sean M. Lynn-Jones
and Stephen Van Evera

PRINCETON UNIVERSITY PRESS
PRINCETON, NEW JERSEY

Published by Princeton University Press, 41 William Street, Princeton, New Jersey, 08540

In the United Kingdom: Princeton University Press, Chichester, West Sussex

First Princeton Paperback printing, 1991

Princeton University Press books are printed on acid-free paper, and meet the guidelines for permanence and durability of the Committee on Production Guidelines for Book Longevity of the Council on Library Resources

Michael Howard, "Men Against Fire: Expectations of War in 1914," *IS* 9, no. 1 (Summer 1984); Stephen Van Evera, "The Cult of the Offensive and the Origins of the First World War," *IS* 9, no. 1 (Summer 1984); Jack Snyder, "Civil-Military Relations and the Cult of the Offensive, 1914 and 1984," *IS* 9, no. 1 (Summer 1984); Scott D. Sagan, "1914 Revisited: Allies, Offense, and Instability," *IS* 11, no. 2 (Fall 1986); Jonathan Shimshoni, "Technology, Military Advantage, and World War I: A Case for Military Entrepreneurship," *IS* 15, no. 3 (Winter 1990/91); Sean M. Lynn-Jones, "Detente and Deterrence: Anglo-German Relations, 1911–1914," *IS* 11, no. 2 (Fall 1986); Marc Trachtenberg, "The Meaning of Mobilization in 1914," *IS* 15, no. 3 (Winter 1990/91); Jack S. Levy, "Preferences, Constraints, and Choices in July 1914," *IS* 15, no. 3 (Winter 1990/91); Holger H. Herwig, "Clio Deceived: Patriotic Self-Censorship in Germany After the Great War," *IS* 12, no. 2 (Fall 1987).

ISBN 0-691-02349-2 (rev. ed., pbk.)

Library of Congress Cataloging-in-Publication Data

Military strategy and the origins of the First World War/ edited by
Steven E. Miller, Sean M. Lynn-Jones, and Stephen Van Evera.—Rev. and expanded ed.
p.   cm.—International security readers)
ISBN 0-691-02349-2 (pbk.: acid-free paper)
1. World War, 1914–1918—Causes. 2. Strategy. I. Miller, Steven E. II. Lynn-Jones, Sean M. III. Van Evera, Stephen. IV. Series.
D511.M53   1991
940.3'11—dc20   91-19143

Printed in the United States of America

9   8   7   6

Contents

The Contributors

STEVEN E. MILLER is Director of Studies at the Center for Science and International Affairs, Harvard University, and Editor of *International Security*. He was the journal's Managing Editor, 1981–1984.

SEAN M. LYNN-JONES is Consulting Editor of *International Security* and a Research Fellow at the Center for Science and International Affairs, Harvard University. He was the journal's Managing Editor, 1987–1991.

STEPHEN VAN EVERA is Assistant Professor of Political Science at the Massachusetts Institute of Technology. He was Managing Editor of *International Security*, 1984–1987.

MICHAEL HOWARD is Lovett Professor of Military and Naval History at Yale University.

JACK SNYDER is Professor of Political Science at Columbia University.

SCOTT D. SAGAN is Assistant Professor of Political Science at Stanford University.

JONATHAN SHIMSHONI is the author of *Israel and Conventional Deterrence: Border Warfare from 1953 to 1970*.

MARC TRACHTENBERG is Professor of History at the University of Pennsylvania.

JACK S. LEVY is Professor of Political Science at Rutgers University.

HOLGER H. HERWIG is Professor of History at the University of Calgary.

Acknowledgments

The editors gratefully acknowledge the assistance that has made this book possible. A deep debt is owed to all those at the Center for Science and International Affairs, Harvard University, who have played an editorial role at *International Security*, including Paul Doty, Joseph S. Nye, Jr., Ashton B. Carter, Albert Carnesale, Michael Nacht, Derek Leebaert, Melissa Healy, Lisbeth Tarlow Bernstein, Lynn Page Whittaker, Teresa Pelton Johnson, Mary Ann Wells, Maude Fish, and Lisa Grumbach. Robert Art, John Mearsheimer, and Stephen Walt offered helpful suggestions on the selection of articles for this book. Special thanks go to Julia Slater for her invaluable help in preparing this volume for publication.

Preface | Steven E. Miller
and Sean M. Lynn-
Jones

Though distant in time, the disaster of 1914 continues to haunt the contemporary security debate. Over seventy-five years after the fateful shots rang out in Sarajevo, images from the summer of 1914 remain: escalation from an isolated event in a far corner of Europe to global war, key decisionmakers' apparent loss of control of the situation, diplomacy crowded out by military exigencies, the countdown to an ultimatum's deadline as vast military machines geared up for battle, and the shattering of illusions that war could be short and glorious. These images stay with us because they raise troubling doubts about our ability to conduct affairs of state safely in an international environment plagued by a continuing risk of war. The awful, protracted, often senseless slaughter to capture a few square miles of devastated territory, the introduction of new and more horrible forms of warfare these continue to remind us of the unpredictability of war. Hence the need to study anew, in light of recent research and theoretical perspectives, the outbreak of war in 1914.

The first edition of this volume, published six years ago, helped to stimulate renewed attention to the lessons of the First World War. The editors of this revised and expanded edition have been pleasantly surprised by the attention generated by the book, and by the continuing debate that it has provoked. The present edition reflects the ongoing interest in this subject as well as the editors' continuing belief that the lessons of World War I deserve reexamination.

Why should we study World War I? First, the First World War continues to cast a long shadow over contemporary international politics. On August 3, 1914, British Foreign Secretary Sir Edward Grey stared out the Foreign Office window and said: "The lamps are going out all over Europe; we shall not see them lit again in our lifetime." At a moment when others proclaimed that the troops would be "home by Christmas," Grey's prediction was all too accurate. The war was a cataclysm that shaped the twentieth century. It destroyed the Hapsburg, Ottoman, and Russian Empires, sowed the seeds of the Second World War, killed and maimed the cream of a generation in the trenches of the Western Front, and undermined beliefs in the glory and heroism of war.

Most observers describe the present period of international politics as the "post–Cold War" era, but in many ways our age is better defined as the "post–World War I" era. Barbara Tuchman has written that World

War I "lies like a band of scorched earth" across modern history. Even if the events of 1914 seem remote from contemporary Europe, we should remember that the roots of the Great War were in the ethnic and national strife of the Balkans as multinational empires crumbled, precisely the issue that Europe confronts today. Moreover, many of the central security problems in post–Cold War Europe—the dilemmas of Soviet reform or disintegration, ethnic and boundary disputes in the Balkans, Germany's uncertain role in the center of Europe—were shaped by the First World War and the ensuing peace settlement. Similarly, in the Middle East, most of today's international boundaries were determined following the collapse of the defeated Ottoman Empire at the end of World War I. The postwar Western occupation of Iraq, Jordan, Lebanon, Palestine, and Syria had profound and lasting consequences for the domestic and international politics in that region. Studying the events of the summer of 1914 may at least remind us of the sources of our current problems, and that a major war can have unforeseen effects.

Second, World War I has been the prime source of a powerful metaphor—the blind blunder into horrifying accidental war, the belief that statesmen ordered their armies into battle in ignorance of the military, human, and social disasters to follow. Accurate or not, this version of the 1914 analogy is invoked in support of arguments for caution in a crisis, for conciliatory policies, for maintaining strict civilian control over the military, and for eschewing strategies that require offensive strikes. The consequences of accidental or inadvertent nuclear war would be so catastrophic that we would neglect the lessons of August 1914 only at our peril. On the other hand, if the analogy is misleading or inappropriate, it might lead to disastrous policy failures. We should therefore reexamine the outbreak of World War I to avoid simplistic analogies that could undermine sound analysis and perhaps contribute to future catastrophes.

Finally, the First World War compels our attention because it might contain lessons that would enable us to avoid a recurrence of its carnage and upheaval. As George Kennan asked in his inquiry into the origins of World War I, *The Decline of Bismarck's European Order*: "Must not the generation of 1914 have been the victim of certain massive misunderstandings, invisible, of course, to themselves but susceptible of identification today . . . ? Was there not a possibility that if we could see how they went wrong, if we could identify the tendencies of mass psychology that led them thus astray, we might see where the dangers lay for ourselves in our attempt to come to terms with some of the great problems of public policy of our own day?" Kennan thus captures with his customary eloquence the underlying motivation for this revised and expanded collection of essays. The possibility that there could be another "monstrous miscalculation" makes it imperative that we face the future with the fullest possible comprehension of the mistakes of the past, and that we search the wreckage of that earlier accident for clues about its cause. For those who believe that the 1914 analogy has relevance today, the nine essays collected here provide thoughtful reminders of the dangers to which it alludes.

The first section of this volume explores the argument that the well-spring of disaster in 1914 resided in the unwavering and wholehearted commitment of all the major European militaries to offensive doctrines when in fact prevailing technologies afforded overwhelming defensive advantages. This argument holds that a profound belief in the primacy of the offensive linked the mobilization plans of the major powers to each other, made speed necessary and preemption desirable, limited the opportunities for diplomacy while creating an irresistible dynamic of escalation, and took policy from the hands of the political leaders and put it in those of the generals. By the summer of 1914, all the major continental powers—in particular, France, Germany, and Russia—had adopted offensive military doctrines. In the July Crisis this collective offensive-mindedness resulted in such severe political-military instability that a single assassination in Bosnia triggered a world war.

The first three essays in this section focus on the pernicious effects of this "cult of the offensive." In "Men Against Fire: Expectations of War in 1914," Michael Howard describes *what* European militaries believed about the nature of warfare in the period leading up to the war. He documents their relentless adherence to doctrines which emphasized morale, cavalry charges, bayonet assaults, and offensive spirit at a time when the emergence of rapid-fire weapons, barbed wire, and entrenchments were making such operational inclinations not merely obsolete but suicidal. He provides evidence as well of their willful neglect of the signs that their preferred doctrines had been rendered ineffective by new technologies and tactics. The result was the offensive doctrines, completely at odds with prevailing military reality, that not only contributed to the outbreak of war but spent hundreds of thousands of lives to gain mere yards or miles of strategically meaningless turf.

Jack Snyder, in "Civil-Military Relations and the Cult of the Offensive," seeks to explain *why* European militaries preferred offensive doctrines. He argues that the cause of this intense pursuit of offense in Germany, France, and Russia was a crisis of civil-military relations that led militaries to choose doctrines that enhanced their autonomy and minimized the possibilities for civilian interference, improved their ability to plan, increased their importance in national policy, and created the need for larger and better-funded military forces. By allowing militaries to plan on assuming the initiative, and by making conquest seem feasible, if not easy, and external threats consequently seem great, offensive doctrines served these purposes even though, on the battlefield, they were to prove to be disastrously unsuccessful.

Stephen Van Evera analyzes the *consequences* of Europe's passion for offense in "The Cult of the Offensive and the Origins of the First World War." These effects were, he suggests, almost without exception malignant. Belief in the power of the offensive made expansionist policies seem possible and attractive even if only to make offensive operations by one's opponent more difficult. This belief raised preemptive and preventive war vulnerabilities and opportunities, and placed such a premium on secrecy that civilian leaders were neither fully aware of the plans of their own military nor cognizant that some of the dangers of diplomatic crisis remained hidden. It led also to the creation of ambitious and inflexible war plans, intended to provide a knockout blow, that made speed essential, the crossing of frontiers necessary even as a defensive precaution, and early mobilization imperative. Given the offensive nature of the war plans, mobilization meant war, while failure to mobilize early and quickly was thought likely to be disastrous. All of these factors combined to put great pressure on diplomats, made crises difficult to control, and made diplomatic mistakes both extremely dangerous and difficult to correct. Applying these lessons to the nuclear age, Van Evera argues that Soviet and American decision makers ought to be far more sensitive to the potential dangers of nuclear counterforce doctrines, which are essentially offensive.

The proposition that a cult of the offensive permeated European militaries before 1914 and triggered the catastrophes of the Great War has provoked considerable debate. Since the publication of the first edition of this book, several authors have argued that the First World War was not caused by an unwavering and unthinking commitment to offensive principles. The next two essays criticize the cult of the offensive theory advanced mainly by Snyder and Van Evera.

In "1914 Revisited: Allies, Offense, and Instability," Scott Sagan challenges the claim that a cult of the offensive contributed to the outbreak of the First World War. His essay reconsiders the causes and consequences of offensive doctrines in 1914. Sagan argues that Snyder exaggerates the extent to which military biases led countries to adopt offensive doctrines before the war. In contrast to Snyder and Van Evera, who emphasize the domestic and organizational sources of offensive thinking, Sagan finds strong international and political reasons for offensive strategies. He suggests that the political objectives of countries like France and Russia—to assist potentially vulnerable allies—determined their military doctrines. Only offense would enable them to assist allies. Moreover, Sagan points out that the dominance of the defensive in 1914 is by no means beyond doubt. Germany's Schlieffen Plan, after all, almost succeeded, and on the Eastern front offensives met with considerable success, calling into question whether a technologically based defensive advantage really existed.

Sagan also disputes the extent to which a cult of the offensive created instabilities that contributed to the outbreak of war in the July Crisis. Instead, critical military vulnerabilities of the Entente powers and Belgium—the inability of the Russian army to mobilize rapidly, the lack of permanent defenses at the Belgian railway junction of Liège—not offensive postures, created military incentives for preemptive attacks. Moreover, these sources of instability probably would not have led to war if Britain had made clear its intention to intervene. Such a threat would have deterred Germany, leading to a resolution of the crisis without war.[1]

Jonathan Shimshoni offers a broad challenge to the cult of the offensive school. In "Technology, Military Advantage, and World War I: A Case for Military Entrepreneurship," he questions the very concept of a technologically determined offense-defense balance. Shimshoni argues that innovative, "entrepreneurial" military thinking can use technology

1. For a further debate on these issues, see the exchange of letters by Jack Snyder and Scott Sagan in "Correspondence: The Origins of Offense and the Consequences of Counterforce," *International Security*, Vol. 11, No. 3 (Winter 1986–87), pp. 187–198.

to create and manipulate advantages. The problem in 1914, he suggests, was not that there existed a defensive advantage, but that military leaders failed to devise offensive capabilities that would successfully serve the political goals pursued by their governments. Like Sagan, Shimshoni argues that political and strategic objectives should determine military doctrine. Before 1914, strategic goals dictated offensive doctrines, but the militaries of Europe did not develop offensive operational advantages. Far from being condemned to accept an existing offense/defense balance, military leaders can and should manipulate such advantages through "military entrepreneurship." The course of World War I shows that such innovation was possible. The Germans successfully developed infiltration tactics and the allies learned to mount assaults with tanks. Offensives ultimately ended the war on all fronts.

The next section of this collection deals with the image of World War I as an inadvertent conflict—a catastrophic war that nobody wanted—that has obsessed contemporary strategists. The statesmen who were present during the July Crisis were among the first to lament the apparently inexorable approach of war. As the massive armies moved toward their titanic collisions, German Chancellor Bethmann Hollweg declared: "We have lost control and the landslide has begun." After the war, former British Prime Minister David Lloyd George looked back and claimed that "we all stumbled into war." Many historians have echoed this theme, and it is reflected in some of the essays on offensive doctrines and mobilization plans in this volume.

The image of the origins of the First World War has had a remarkable influence on theories of international politics. Particularly in the United States, the idea that a nuclear war could be the result of inadvertence or miscalculation has drawn inspiration from the apparent lessons of 1914.[2] This image often has been contrasted with that of the coming of the Second World War, which is usually seen as a deliberate war of aggression initiated by Adolf Hitler. The lesson of World War I is said to be: avoid provoking an adversary with excessive strength; that of World War II: avoid encouraging an aggressor with excessive weakness.[3]

2. For recent arguments resting on the accidental war analogy, see Paul Bracken, *The Command and Control of Nuclear Forces* (New Haven: Yale University Press, 1983); and Graham T. Allison, Albert Carnesale, and Joseph S. Nye, Jr., eds., *Hawks, Doves, and Owls: An Agenda for Avoiding Nuclear War* (New York: Norton, 1985).
3. The seminal comparison of the "spiral model" of World War I and the "deterrence model" of World War II is Robert Jervis, *Perception and Misperception in International Politics* (Princeton: Princeton University Press, 1976).

Although many observers still regard the First World War as an inadvertent conflict, recent historical scholarship has examined the degree to which the war was deliberately initiated.[4] This volume includes three essays that reconsider the claim that Europe was dragged into war in 1914 by rigid mobilization schedules, excessive belligerence, and spirals of hostility.

Sean Lynn-Jones examines Anglo-German diplomacy before the war. In "Détente and Deterrence: Anglo-German Relations, 1911–1914," he argues that the war may not have been the result of an inadvertent spiral of escalation caused by undue bellicosity, but the product of a failure of deterrence brought on by excessive conciliation. Britain and Germany actually improved their relations considerably in the years immediately before the war. They cooperated to resolve crises in the Balkans, agreed on how to divide the Portuguese territories in Africa, settled their dispute over the Baghdad railway, and even seemed to reach a tacit understanding about the naval arms race. Perhaps this improvement in London-Berlin ties, however, contributed to the outbreak of war in 1914. The British, believing that the Germans would cooperate to keep the peace, did not make a clear threat to intervene on the side of the Entente. Such a warning might have deterred Germany and prevented war. For their part, the Germans may have exaggerated the prospects for British neutrality, assuming that the Anglo-German détente meant that Britain would not oppose Germany in the July Crisis. Miscalculation thus helped to bring on the war, but it was the result of excessive and mistaken conciliation, not deterrence that turned into provocation. The outbreak of World War I may thus resemble the origins of World War II more closely than is implied by the long-standing 1914 analogy.

Marc Trachtenberg's "The Meaning of Mobilization in 1914" argues that the prevalent belief that World War I was inadvertent is a myth without historical support. After reexamining the July Crisis, Trachtenberg finds that neither the system of interlocking mobilization plans, incentives for preemption, nor pressure from the generals forced the hand of German, Russian, or French statesmen in July 1914. He suggests that key European statesmen—including the Russian leaders—were aware of the implications of mobilization decisions, and deliber-

4. See, in particular, the works of the German historian Fritz Fischer: *Germany's Aims in the First World War* (New York: Norton, 1967); *War of Illusions: German Policies from 1911 to 1914*, trans. Marian Jackson (London: Chatto and Windus, 1975); and *World Power or Decline*, trans. Lancelot L. Farrar, Robert Kimber, and Rita Kimber (New York: Norton, 1975).

ately chose to risk war. War broke out because military and political leaders concluded that political conflicts made it unavoidable. In the final hours of the crisis, German Chancellor Bethmann Hollweg did not lose control, Trachtenberg concludes, but deliberately abdicated control and decided to let war come. The idea that military pressures produced a loss of control that led to war is a myth, Trachtenberg argues, that was propagated for political reasons. It served the interests of the statesmen involved in the crisis, overcame the difficult political problem of assigning war guilt in the interwar period, and later offered a persuasive alternative to the "Munich analogy" that dominated American foreign policy after World War II.

In "Preferences, Constraints, and Choices in July 1914," Jack Levy concludes that the outbreak of World War I should be viewed neither as a case of inadvertent war nor as a failure of crisis management. Levy examines the preferences of each of the important European states and the constraints that shaped their behavior in the July Crisis. In his view, underlying economic, military, diplomatic, political and social forces made war likely in 1914, even though none of the major powers deliberately sought a world war. Germany wanted a local war, yet triggered a general European war. It expected British neutrality, but could not prevent war when it realized that Britain would enter the war on the side of the Entente.[5] Mobilization plans constrained last-minute efforts to avert war, but were not a cause of war themselves.

The final essay in this volume, Holger Herwig's "Clio Deceived: Patriotic Self-Censorship in Germany After the Great War," presents a sobering tale of the dangers of manipulating history for political purposes. Herwig details the German government's remarkable postwar campaign to disprove the thesis that Germany was responsible for the First World War. The Weimar Republic selectively published documents and restricted access to its archives to prevent scholars from understanding Germany's role in 1914. The German Foreign Ministry funded propaganda, obstructed parliamentary investigations, and meddled in academic appointments. This disinformation campaign largely succeeded, advancing the image of the Great War as an inadvertent conflict and distorting understanding of the war's origins inside and outside Germany down to the present day.

5. Levy and Trachtenberg debate the importance of British neutrality to Germany further in an exchange of letters in *International Security*, Vol. 16, No. 1 (Summer 1991). See also the letter from Thomas Christensen in the same issue.

Herwig's study sheds important light on the origins of World War II, as well as the effects of World War I. During the 1920s and 1930s, Nazi propaganda featured an image of an innocent Germany encircled and attacked by a predatory Entente in 1914, and Nazi leaders exploited this image to bolster arguments for German expansion. The efforts to show German innocence outlined by Herwig thus laid the domestic political foundation for Nazi foreign policy, and helped to prime Europe for war in 1939. His story suggests that substantial responsibility for the Second World War lies with the leaders of the Weimar Republic and with the German academics who abetted them in this campaign.

Herwig's essay provides the best reason for reading this book carefully: misunderstanding or distorting history can have tragic consequences. Conclusions drawn from one war can shape diplomacy and military policy for many decades. As the essays in this volume amply demonstrate, there is plenty of room for disagreement over World War I. This fact should inspire caution about the widespread practice of drawing broad conclusions from simple, but possibly misleading or inaccurate, historical analogies. And it should be a reminder of the importance of detailed scholarship and of the difficulty of that essential task, attempting to derive wisdom from history.

*Offensive Military
Doctrines and the
Great War*

Men Against Fire

Expectations of War in 1914

Michael Howard

In 1898 there was published in Paris a six-volume work entitled *La Guerre Future; aux points de vue technique, economique et politique*. This was a translation of a series of articles which had been appearing in Russia, the fruit of collective research but masterminded and written by one of the leading figures in the world of Russian finance and industry, Ivan (or Jean de) Bloch (1836–1902). Sometimes described as "a Polish banker," Bloch was in fact an entrepreneur almost on the scale of the Rothschilds in Western Europe or Carnegie in the United States. He had made his money in railroad promotion, and then turned to investment on a large scale, promoting and sharing in the great boom in the Russian economy of the 1890s. He had written prolifically about the economic problems of the Russian Empire, and was increasingly alarmed by the degree to which they were complicated, then as now, by the military need to keep abreast, in an age of rapidly developing technology, with the wealthier and more advanced states of the West. Having been responsible for organizing the railway supply for the Russian armies in their war with the Ottoman Empire in 1877–78, Bloch had an unusual grasp of military logistics. And he brought to the study of war an entirely new sort of mind, one in which the analytical skills of the engineer, the economist, and the sociologist were all combined. His book was in fact the first work of modern operational analysis, and nothing written since has equalled it for its combination of rigor and scope.

Only the last of the six volumes was translated into English, under the title *Is War Now Impossible?*[1] This volume conveniently summarizes the argument of the entire work, and it was itself summarized by the author in an interview with the English journalist W.T. Stead which is printed as an introduction to the book. Bloch began by stating his conclusions: war between great states was now impossible—or, rather, suicidal. "The dimensions of modern armaments and the organisation of society have rendered its pros-

Michael Howard is Regius Professor of History at Oxford University. This paper was written while he was a Fellow at the Woodrow Wilson International Center for Scholars in Washington, D.C.

1. Jean de Bloch, *Is War Now Impossible? The Future of War in its Technical, Economic and Political Relations* (London and Boston, 1899).

International Security, Summer 1984 (Vol. 9, No. 1) 0162-2889/84/010041-17 $02.50/1

ecution an economic impossibility."[2] This could be almost mathematically demonstrated. The range, accuracy, and rate of fire of modern firearms—rifles lethal at 2000 meters, artillery at 6000—made the "decisive battles" which had hitherto determined the outcome of wars now impossible. Neither the infantry could charge with the bayonet nor cavalry with the saber. To protect themselves against the lethal storm of fire which would be unleashed on the modern battlefield, armies would have to dig themselves in: "the spade will be as indispensable to the soldier as his rifle. . . . That is one reason why it will be impossible for the battle of the future to be fought out rapidly. . . . Battles will last for days, and at the end it is very doubtful whether any decisive victory can be gained."[3]

Thus far Bloch was not breaking new ground. He was only setting out a problem which intelligent officers in all European armies had been studying ever since the experiences of the Franco–Prussian War in 1870 and the Russo–Turkish War in 1877–78 had shown (quite as clearly as, and rather more immediately than, those of the American Civil War) the effect of modern firearms on the battlefield. The introduction of "smokeless powder" in the 1880s, increasing the range and accuracy of all firearms and making possible the near invisibility of their users, would, it was generally agreed, complicate the difficulties of the attack yet further. But even these, it was widely assumed, would not change the fundamental nature of the problem.

The answer, it was believed, lay in the development of the firepower of the assailant, especially of his artillery. The assaulting infantry had to approach closely enough, making all use of cover, to be able to deploy a hail of rifle fire on the defenders' positions. Artillery must cooperate closely, keeping the defenders' heads down with shrapnel and digging them out of their trenches with high explosives. As for machine-guns, these, with their mobility and concentrated firepower, were seen as likely to enhance the power of the attack rather than the defense. "Fire is the supreme argument," declared Colonel Ferdinand Foch in his lectures at the École de Guerre in 1900.[4] "The superiority of fire . . . becomes the most important element of an infantry's fighting value." But the moment would always come when the advance could get no further: "Before it is a zone almost impassable; there remain no covered approaches; a hail of lead beats the ground . . . to flee or

---

2. Ibid., p. xi.
3. Ibid., p. xxviii.
4. Ferdinand Foch, *The Principles of War* (New York, 1918), p. 362.

to charge is all that remains." Foch, and the majority of French thinkers of his time, believed that the charge was still possible and could succeed by sheer dint of numbers: "To charge, but to charge in numbers, therein lies safety. . . . With more guns we can reduce his to silence, and the same is true of rifles and bayonets, if we know how to make use of them all."[5] Others were less sure. The Germans, who still after thirty years had vivid memories of the slaughter of their infantry at Gravelotte, preferred if possible to pin the enemy down by fire from the front but attack from a flank. Nobody was under any illusion, even in 1900, that frontal attack would be anything but very difficult and that success could be purchased with anything short of very heavy casualties. There would probably indeed have been a wide measure of agreement with Bloch's calculation, that a superiority at the assaulting point of 8 to 1 would be necessary to ensure success.[6]

Bloch's War of the Future: Society versus Society

It was in the further conclusions which Bloch deduced from his study of the modern battlefield that he outpaced his contemporaries—not so much because they disagreed with him, but because they had given the problems which he examined virtually no thought at all.

What, asked Bloch, would be the eventual result of the operational dead lock that was likely to develop on the battlefield? "At first there will be increased slaughter—increased slaughter on so terrible a scale as to render it impossible to push the battle to a decisive issue. . . . Then, instead of a war fought out to the bitter end in a series of decisive battles, we shall have to substitute a long period of continually increasing strain upon the resources of the combatants." This, would involve "entire dislocation of all industry and severing of all the sources of supply by which alone the community is enabled to bear the crushing burden. . . . That is the future of war—not fighting, but famine, not the slaying of men but the bankruptcy of nations and the break-up of the whole social organisation."[7] In these circumstances the decisive factors would be "the quality of toughness and capacity for endurance, of patience under privation, of stubborness under reverse or disappointment. That element in the civil population will be, more than

---

5. Ibid., pp. 365–366.
6. Bloch, *Is War Now Impossible?*, p. xxvii.
7. Ibid., p. xvii.

anything else, the deciding factor in modern war. . . . Your soldiers," concluded Bloch grimly, "may fight as they please; the ultimate decision is in the hands of *famine*."[8] And famine would strike first at those proletarian elements which, in advanced industrial societies, were most prone to revolution.

It is important to recognize that Bloch got a great deal wrong. He assumed that the prolonged feeding and administration of the vast armies which rail transport made possible would be far beyond the capacity of the military authorities, and that armies in the field would quickly degenerate into starving and mutinous mobs. He predicted that the care of the sick and wounded would also assume unmanageable proportions, and that on the battlefield the dead and dying would have to be heaped up into macabre barriers to protect the living from enemy fire. As did many professional soldiers, Bloch doubted the capacity of reservists fresh from civil life to stand up to the strain of the battlefield: "it is impossible to rely upon modern armies submitting to sacrifice and deprivation to such an extent as is desired by military theorists who lose sight of the tendencies which obtain in Western society."[9] In fact the efficiency with which armies numbering millions were to be maintained in the field, the success with which the medical services were, with certain grisly exceptions, to rise to the enormous task that confronted them and the stoical endurance displayed by the troops of all belligerent powers in face of hardships worse than Bloch could ever have conceived were perhaps the most remarkable and admirable aspects of the First World War. Bloch, like so many pessimistic prophets (including those of air power a generation later), underestimated the capacity of human societies to adjust themselves to adverse circumstances.

But Bloch also had astonishing insights. The scale of military losses, he pointed out, would depend on the skill of the commanders, and "it must not be forgotten that a considerable number of the higher officers in modern armies have never been under fire"; while among junior officers the rate of casualties would, if they did their job as leaders, be inordinately high. Finally, there was the problem of managing the wartime economy; what were the long-term effects of that likely to be? "If we suppose," Bloch surmised, "that governments will be forced to interfere in the regulation of prices and to support the population, will it be easy after the war to abandon this practise

8. Ibid., p. xlvi.
9. Ibid., p. 30.

and re-establish the old order?"[10] Win or lose, therefore, if war came "the old order" was doomed—by transformation from above if not by revolution from below.

This remarkably accurate blueprint for the war which was to break out in Europe in 1914, last for four and a half years, and end only with the social disintegration of the defeated belligerents and the economic exhaustion of all was the result, not of second-sight, but of meticulous analysis of weapons capabilities, of military organization and doctrine, and of financial and economic data—five fat volumes which still provide a superb source book for any student of the military, technological, and economic condition of Europe at the end of the nineteenth century. Nobody took Bloch's economic arguments and attempted to disprove them. They were just ignored. Why, it may be asked, was so little account taken of them by statesmen and military leaders? Why did they continue on a course which led ineluctably to the destruction of the old order which Bloch so unerringly predicted? The question is one uncomfortably relevant to our own times.

The answer is of course that societies, and the pattern of international relationships, cannot be transformed overnight on the basis of a single prophetic insight, however persuasively it may be argued. Bloch's thinking and influence were indeed two elements in persuading Czar Nicholas II to convoke the first International Peace Conference which met at the Hague in May 1899, and were even more significant in mobilizing public support throughout Europe for that conference's objectives. But the conference was no more than a ripple in the current of international politics. A more immediate problem, as Bloch himself repeatedly pointed out, was that there existed nowhere in Europe bodies charged with the task of thinking about the problems of warfare in any kind of comprehensive fashion, rather than about the narrowly professional questions that concerned the military. As for the military specialists, they were not likely to admit that the problems which faced them were insoluble, and that they would be incapable in the future of conducting wars so effectively and decisively as they had in the past.

Lessons of the Boer War

The force of Bloch's arguments, however, was powerfully driven home when, within a few months of the publication of *La Guerre Future*, there broke

---

10. Ibid., pp. 335, 314.

out in South Africa a war in which for the first time both sides were fully equipped with the new technology—magazine-loading small-bore rifles, quick-firing artillery, machine guns—and things turned out on the battlefield exactly as he had predicted. The British army, moving in close formations and firing by volleys, were unable to get anywhere near an enemy whom they could not even see. At Spion Kop, at Colenso, at the Modder Rover, and at Magersfontein, their frontal attacks were driven back by the Boers with horrifying losses. As the leading British military theorist, Colonel G.F.R. Henderson, who accompanied the army in South Africa, wrote shortly afterwards:

> There was a constant endeavor to make battle conform to the parade ground . . . to depend for success on courage and subordination and to relegate intelligence and individuality to the background . . . the fallacy that a thick firing line in open country can protect itself, outside decisive range, by its own fire, had not yet been exposed. It was not yet realised that the defender, occupying ingeniously constructed trenches and using smokeless powder, is practically invulnerable to both gun and rifle.[11]

Unsympathetic continental observers tended to play down the significance of the South African experience on the grounds that the British army and its commanders were unsuitably trained for confronting a "civilized" adversary, having been spoiled by the easy victories in Egypt and the Sudan. Further, they suggested that the differences in terrain made the lessons to be learned from that war, as they had made those from the American Civil War, irrelevant in the European theater. The British themselves, while unable to deny the unsuitability of their traditional tactics and training to the transformed conditions of warfare, could nonetheless point out that, once they had mastered the necessary techniques, they had been able successfully to go over to the offensive, and had then rapidly won the war. This they had done by pinning down the Boers in their positions by firepower and maneuvering round their flanks with cavalry—cavalry used not in its traditional role for shock on the battlefield, but to develop the kind of strategic mobility which was essential if the problems created by the new power of the defensive

---

11. George F.R. Henderson, *The Science of War* (London, 1905), p. 411. It is ironic to read in an article which Henderson had written shortly before the war: "Neither smokeless powder nor the magazine rifle will necessitate any radical change. If the defense has gained, as has been asserted, by these inventions, the plunging fire of rifled howitzers will add a more than proportional strength to the attack. And if the magazine rifle has introduced a new and formidable element into battle, the moral element still remains the same." Ibid., pp. 159–160.

were to be overcome. When in 1901 Bloch described to an audience at the British Royal United Services Institution how the experience of the British army in South Africa, repeated as it would be in Europe on an enormous scale, precisely illustrated his arguments, his audience was able to point out that in fact Lord Roberts had shown how to combine the tactical advantages of firepower with the strategic advantages of horse-borne mobility to secure precisely those decisive results which Bloch had maintained would, in future, be impossible.[12]

A study of the voluminous military literature of the period shows that between 1900 and 1905 a consensus developed among European strategic thinkers over two points. The first was the strategic importance of cavalry as mobile firepower. If the firepower of the defense made it now impossible for cavalry to assault unshaken infantry—a view which had been reluctantly accepted ever since the disasters of the Franco-Prussian War of 1870—cavalry would now develop their own firepower, enhanced by mobile quick-firing artillery and machine guns, and exploit opportunities on a scale undreamed of since the days of the American Civil War. The South African experience indeed sent back intelligent cavalrymen, especially in England, to studying the Civil War, often for the first time.[13] In the British army, it was laid down that the carbine or rifle would henceforth be "the principal weapon" for cavalry. But for most cavalrymen this was going altogether too far. In no country in Europe was this proudest, most exclusive, most anachronistic of arms prepared to be, as they saw it, downgraded to the role of mounted infantry. That kind of thing could be left to colonial roughriders. Writing as late as 1912, the German general Friedrich von Bernhardi bitterly observed that "The cavalry looks now . . . upon a charge in battle as its paramount duty; it has almost deliberately closed its eyes against the far-reaching changes in warfare. By this it has *itself* barred the way that leads to greater successes."[14] Within the cavalry in every European army therefore a controversy raged which was settled only by the kind of compromise expressed by the British Cavalry Manual of 1907:

---

12. *Journal of the United Services Institution*, Vol. 15, pp. 1316–1344, 1413–1451.
13. G.F.R. Henderson had been writing and lecturing on the American Civil War well before 1899 and Lord Roberts was to acknowledge the influence of those writings on his own operational planning in South Africa. After 1901 the Civil War became the main topic for historical study at the British Army Staff College at Camberley. Jay Luvaas, *The Military Legacy of the Civil War* (Chicago: University of Chicago Press, 1959), p. 229.
14. Friedrich von Bernhardi, *On War Today* (London, 1912), Vol. 1, p. 192.

The essence of the cavalry spirit lies in holding the balance correctly between fire power and shock action . . . it must be accepted as a principle that the rifle, effective as it is, cannot replace the effect produced by the speed of the horse, the magnetism of the charge, and the terror of cold steel.[15]

The mood of the cavalryman on the eve of the First World War is perhaps best captured in an analysis of British military doctrine published in 1914:

Technically the great decisive cavalry charge on the main battlefield is a thing of the past, yet training in shock tactics is claimed by all cavalry authorities to be still essential to the strategic use of the arm, and even on the battlefield shock tactics may, under special conditions, conceivably still be possible, while brilliant opportunities will almost certainly be offered for the employment in perhaps a decisive manner of the power conferred by the combination of mobility with fire action. . . . For whatever tactics are adopted, the desire to take the offensive will always remain the breath of life for cavalry, and where shock action is impossible, the cavalryman must be prepared to expend, rifle in hand, the last man in an advance on foot, if the victory can thus only be achieved.[16]

So training in shock action continued; for even the reformers had to admit that cavalry would have to meet and defeat the enemy's cavalry, presumably in a gigantic mêlée, before it could fulfil its strategic task. "The opening of future wars," wrote von Bernhardi in 1912, "will, therefore, in all likelihood be characterised by great cavalry combats."[17]

So the cavalry continued to practice sword drill; and the infantry continued, for the same reason, to practice bayonet drill. The German writer Wilhelm Balck saw no reason to alter, in the 1911 edition of his huge study of *Tactics*, the doctrine preached in the first edition of 1896:

The soldier should be taught not to shrink from the bayonet attack, but to seek it. If the infantry is deprived of the arme blanche, if the impossibility of bayonet fighting is preached . . . an infantry will be developed which is unsuitable for attack and which moreover lacks a most essential quality, viz. the moral power to reach the enemy's position . . . [And he went on to quote from the Russian General Dragomirov, a well-known fanatic on the subject:] "The bayonet cannot be abolished for the reason, if for no other, that it is the sole and exclusive embodiment of that will-power which alone,

---

15. Quoted by Luvaas, *Military Legacy of the Civil War*, p. 107.
16. Maj. General E.A. Altham, *The Principles of War Historically Illustrated* (London, 1914), p. 92.
17. Bernhardi, *On War Today*, Vol. 2, p. 337.

both in war and in everyday life attains its object, whereas reason only facilitates the achievement of the object."[18]

The British General Staff manuals expressed the same idea slightly differently: "The moral effect of the bayonet is out of all proportion to its material effect, and not the least important of virtues claimed for it is that the desire to use it draws the attacking side on." To deprive the infantry of their bayonets would be like depriving the cavalry of their swords; it "would be to some extent to take away their desire to close."[19]

That brings us to the second point over which a rather more troubled consensus developed among European military thinkers as a consequence of the South African War: the unprecedented difficulty of carrying through frontal attacks, even with substantial artillery support, would now make necessary more extended formations in the attack. On this point also there had been a continuing controversy ever since 1870. The normal formation for the infantry attack, inherited from the Napoleonic era, consisted of three lines. First came the skirmishers in open formation, making maximum use of cover so as to reach positions from which they could bring a concentrated fire on the enemy in order, in cooperation with the artillery, to "win the fire fight." Behind them came the main assault line, normally in close formation under the immediate control of their officers, to assault with the bayonet. Finally came the supports, the immediate tactical reserve.

The German army, remembering the massacres of their infantry in the assault at the battles of Wörth and St. Privat in August 1870, had always inclined to the view that once the attacking infantry came under fire, close formations in the old style would be impossible. The main assault line would itself now have to scatter and edge its way forward to thicken up the skirmishers or extend their line, feeling for an exposed flank. Effectively it was now the skirmishers who bore the brunt of the attack, and success could be achieved only by the dominance of their fire. The bayonet, if used at all, would only gather up the harvest already reaped by the rifle and the gun.[20]

This was the doctrine against which Dragomirov and his disciples everywhere set their faces. It must be admitted that it did present real problems. Once the assaulting troops were scattered and left to themselves, out of range of the officers whose task it was to inspire them and the non-coms

---

18. Wilhelm Balck, *Tactics*, 4th ed. (Fort Leavenworth, 1911), Vol. 1, p. 383.
19. Altham, *Principles of War*, p. 80.
20. Balck, *Tactics*, Vol. 1, p. 373.

whose job it was to frighten them, what incentive would there be for them to go forward in face of enemy fire? Once they went to ground behind cover, would they ever get up again? There were several notorious instances in 1870 when substantial proportions of German assaulting formulations had unaccountably "got lost." Colonel Ardent du Picq, who had been killed in that war and whose posthumously published *Etudes sur le Combat* contain some of the shrewdest observations on troop morale that have ever been written, had described the terrifying isolation of the soldier on a modern battlefield (even before the days of smokeless powder) once he was deprived of the solid support of comrades on either side which had enabled men to face death ever since the days of the Roman legions. "The soldier is unknown even to his comrades; he loses them in the disorientating confusion of battle, where he fights as a lonely individual; solidarity is no longer guaranteed by mutual surveillance."[21] All now depended on the morale and reliability of the smallest units; "by force of circumstances all battles nowadays tend more than ever to become soldiers' battles."[22] How could these lonely frightened men, deprived of the intoxication of drums and trumpets, the support of their comrades, the inspiration of their leaders, find within themselves the courage to die?

The French army, its traditions of martial leadership and close formations for the attack antedating even the Napoleonic era, was particularly reluctant to accept the logic of the new firepower. For a decade after 1870 its leaders had attempted to impose the open tactical formations on their units, but they never really succeeded. By 1884 regulations were again prescribing "the principle of the decisive attack, head held high, unconcerned about casualties." The notorious regulations of 1894 laid it down that attacking units should advance elbow to elbow, not breaking formation to take advantage of cover, but assaulting *en masses* "to the sound of bugles and drums."[23] Stirring stuff, and the French were not alone in preferring it that way. So did the Russians, in spite of their chastening experiences before Plevna in 1877; and so did the British. They also, after a decade of uncertainty inspired by the events of 1870, returned to their old traditions. In the regulations of 1888, wrote Colonel Henderson:

---

21. Charles Ardent du Picq, *Etudes sur le Combat: Combat Antique et Moderne*, (Paris, repr. 1942), p. 110.
22. Ibid., p. 87.
23. Eugene Carrias, *La pensée militaire française* (Paris, 1960), p. 276.

The bayonet has once more reasserted itself. To the second line, relying on cold steel only, as in the days of the Peninsula, is entrusted the duty of bringing the battle to a speedy conclusion. . . . The confusion of the Prussian battles was in a large degree due to their neglect of the immutable principles of tactics and . . . they are a bad model for us to follow. The sagacity of our own people is a surer guide and if, after 1870, we wanted a model, the tactics of the last great war waged by English-speaking soldiers would have served us better.

The Americans on both sides had always launched frontal attacks in close formations, having found that "to prevent the battle degenerating into a protracted struggle between two strongly entrenched armies, and to attain a speedy and decisive result, mere development of fire was insufficient." The lesson was clear: "close order whenever it is possible, extended order only when it is unavoidable."[24]

By 1900 Henderson was a sadder and a wiser man. Events in South Africa had once again shown the world that under fire close order was *not* possible; and the argument that it was good for morale was seen to be ludicrous. "When the preponderant mass suffers enormous losses; when they feel, as others will feel, that other and less costly means of achieving the same end might have been adopted, what will become of their morale? . . . The most brilliant offensive victories," went on Henderson, "are not those which were mere 'bludgeon work' and cost the most blood, but those which were won by surprise, by adroit manoeuvre, by mystifying and misleading the enemy, by turning the ground to the best account, and where the butchers' bill was small."[25] A generation later Henderson's countryman Liddell Hart was to elaborate this insight into an entire philosophy of war, but long before 1914 the British army was to discard this subversive suggestion that discretion might be the better part of valor.

Over the matter of close *versus* open formations for the attack, however, the South African experience was generally seen to be decisive. Even the French high command, while attributing the catastrophes which had overtaken the British entirely to Anglo–Saxon ineptitude, rewrote its regulations in 1904, abandoning the *coude à coude* formations of 1894 and prescribing advance by small groups covering each other by fire—the kind of infantry tactics that were to become general in the Second World War.[26] It is doubtful

24. Henderson, *Science of War*, pp. 135–150.
25. Ibid., pp. 373–375.
26. Carrias, *La pensée militaire française*, p. 290.

however whether these eminently sensible guidelines made any impression on an army which had been thrown, in the aftermath of the Dreyfus case, into a state of administrative confusion verging on anarchy.[27] Certainly the performance of the French infantry in 1914 shows no evidence of it. In any case, such tactics demanded of the ordinary soldier a degree of skill and self-reliance such as neither the French nor any other European army (with the possible exception of the Germans) had hitherto expected, or done anything to inculcate, either in their junior officers or in their other ranks.

And there remained unsolved the nagging, fundamental problem of *morale*—a problem all the greater since a large part of all armies would now be made up of reservists whose moral fiber, it was feared, would have been sapped by the enervating influences of civil life. Concern about the morale of the army was thus generalized, among European military thinkers, into concern about the morale of their nations as a whole; not so much whether they would stand up to the economic attrition which Bloch was almost unique in foreseeing, but whether they could inculcate into their young men that stoical contempt for death which alone would enable them to face, and overcome, the horrors of the assault.[28]

The Russo–Japanese War and the Superiority of the Offensive

It was while this concern was at its height that war broke out between Japan and Russia in the Far East. In February 1904 the Japanese navy launched a surprise attack on the Russian fleet at Port Arthur and, with local command of the sea thus secured, effected amphibious landings on the Korean and Manchurian coasts. It took the Japanese army a year to establish themselves in the disputed province of Manchuria, capturing Port Arthur by land assault and fighting its way north along the railway to capture the main Russian forward base at Mukden in a two-week battle involving altogether over half a million men. It was a war fought on both sides with the latest products of

---

27. Douglas Porch, *The March to the Marne* (Cambridge: Cambridge University Press, 1981), pp. 214–220.
28. "The steadily improving standards of living tend to increase the instinct of self-preservation and to diminish the spirit of self-sacrifice. . . . The fast manner of living at the present day undermines the nervous system, the fanaticism and religious and national enthusiasm of a bygone age are lacking, and finally the physical powers of the human species are also partly diminishing." Balck, *Tactics*, Vol. 1, p. 194. For equally gloomy British assessments see T.H.E. Travers, "Technology, Tactics, and Morale: Jean de Bloch, the Boer War, and British Military Theory 1900–1914," *Journal of Modern History*, Vol. 51, No. 2 (June 1979), pp. 264–286. This article is of seminal importance in showing the connection between tactical doctrine and national morale before 1914.

modern technology: not only magazine rifles and quick-firing field artillery but mobile heavy guns, machine guns, mines, barbed wire, searchlights, telephonic communications and, above all, *trenches*. The Russo–Japanese War proved beyond any doubt that the infantryman's most useful weapon, second only to his rifle, was a spade. Though the war inevitably had unique characteristics—both sides fought at the end of long supply lines, in sparsely inhabited country, which sharply limited the scale of force they could employ—it could not be dismissed, as so many conservative thinkers on the Continent dismissed the Boer War, as a colonial irrelevance. The Russian army was one of the greatest—certainly one of the largest—in Europe. The Japanese had had their armed forces equipped and trained by Europeans, mainly Germans, to the finest European standards. European—and American—military and naval observers with the fighting forces sent back expert reports on the operations, which were digested and mulled over by their general staffs. The British, the French, and the German armies all thought it worth their while to produce multi-volume histories of the Russo–Japanese War, and for the next ten years, until interest was eclipsed by events nearer home, its lessons were analyzed in the most precise detail by pundits writing in military periodicals. It was neither the Boer War nor the American Civil War nor even the Franco–Prussian War that European military specialists had in mind when their armies deployed in 1914: it was the fighting in Manchuria of 1904–5.

As usual, the experts tended to read into the experiences of the war very much what they wanted to find. Conservative cavalrymen observed the failure of the Russian cavalry, trained as it was to the use of the rifle, to achieve anything very much either on the battlefield or off it; absence of "the offensive spirit" making both its raids and its reconnaissance remarkably ineffectual. Reformers noted, on the contrary, how effectively the Japanese had deployed their cavalry in the role of mobile firepower, and the important part it had played at the battle of Mukden. Everyone agreed that artillery, with its accuracy, range, and rate of fire, was now of supreme importance; that it must almost always employ indirect fire; that shrapnel rather than high explosive was its most effective projectile; and that the consumption of ammunition would be enormous. Valuable lessons were learned about supply and communication problems and the need for inconspicuous uniforms; every European army quickly reclothed its armies in various shades of brown or grey, and it was political rather than military conservatism that fatally delayed this reform on the part of the French. But most important of all was the general consensus that infantry assaults with the bayonet, in spite of the South African experience, were still not only possible but necessary. The Japanese had carried them out time and again, and usually with ultimate success.

The Japanese bayonet assaults came, it was true, only at the end of a long and careful advance. They approached whenever possible by night, digging in before dawn, lying up by day, and repeating the process until they could get no further. Then, breaking completely with the European tradition of advancing in extended lines, they dashed forward in small groups of one or two dozen men, each with its own objective, moving rapidly from cover to cover until they were sufficiently close to assault. A French observer described one such scene:

The whole Japanese line is now lit up with the glitter of steel flashing from the scabbard. . . . Once again the officers quit shelter with ringing shouts of "Banzai!" wildly echoed by all the rank and file. Slowly, but not to be denied, they make headway, in spite of the barbed wire, mines and pitfalls, and the merciless hail of bullets. Whole units are destroyed—others take their places; the advancing wave pauses for a moment, but sweeps ever onward. Already they are within a few yards of the trenches. Then, on the Russian side, the long grey line of Siberian Fusiliers forms up in turn, and delivers one last volley before scurrying down the far side of the hill at the double.[29]

The Japanese losses in these assaults were heavy, but they succeeded; and, so argued the European theorists, such tactics would succeed again. "The Manchurian experience," as one British military writer put it, "showed over and over again that the bayonet was in no sense an obsolete weapon. . . . The assault is even of more importance than the attainment of fire mastery which antecedes it. It is the supreme moment of the fight. . . . Upon it the final issue depends. . . . From these glorious examples it may be deduced that no duty, however difficult, should be regarded as impossible by well-trained infantry of good morale and discipline."[30]

It was this "morale and discipline" of the Japanese armed forces that all observers stressed, and they were equally unanimous in stressing that these qualities characterized not only the armed forces but the entire Japanese nation. General Kuropatkin, the commander of the Russian forces, noted ruefully in his memoirs:

---

29. General François de Négrier, *Lessons from the Russo-Japanese War* (London, 1905), p. 69.
30. Altham, *Principles of War*, pp. 295–6, 302.

In the late war . . . our moral strength was less than that of the Japanese; and it was this inferiority, rather than mistakes in generalship, that caused our defeats. . . . The lack of martial spirit, of moral exaltation, and of heroic impulse, affected particularly our stubbornness in battle. In many cases we did not have sufficient resolution to conquer such antagonists as the Japanese.[31]

The same quality gave a representative of Japan's British ally, General Sir Ian Hamilton, almost equal concern:

It is not so much the idea that we have put our money on the wrong horse that now troubles me. . . . But it should cause European statesmen some anxiety when their people seem to forget that there are millions outside the charmed circle of Western Civilisation who are ready to pluck the sceptre from nerveless hands so soon as the old spirit is allowed to degenerate. . . . Providentially Japan is our ally. . . . England has time, therefore—time to put her military affairs in order; time to implant and cherish the military ideal in the hearts of her children; time to prepare for a disturbed and an anxious twentieth century. . . . From the nursery and its toys to the Sunday school and its cadet company, every influence of affection, loyalty, tradition and education should be brought to bear on the next generation of British boys and girls, so as deeply to impress upon their young minds a feeling of reverence and admiration for the patriotic spirit of their ancestors.[32]

Such expressions of admiration for the creed of Bushido are to be found widely scattered in the military and militarist literature of the day. Particularly important for our purposes, however, was the general recognition that the Japanese performance had proved, up to the hilt, the moral and military superiority of *the offensive.* The passive immobility of the Russians, in spite of all the advantages they should have enjoyed from the defense, had in the long run ensured their defeat. It was a conclusion which the military everywhere, after the miasmic doubts engendered by the Boer War, embraced with heartfelt relief. "The defensive is never an acceptable role to the Briton, and he makes little or no study of it," wrote Major General Sir W.G. Knox flatly in 1914.[33] "It was not by dwelling on the idea of passive defense," wrote the Secretary of State for War R.B. Haldane in 1911, "that our fore-

31. General G.N. Kuropatkin, *The Russian Army and the Japanese War* (London, 1909), Vol. 2, p. 80.
32. Major General Sir Ian Hamilton, *A Staff Officer's Scrapbook* (London, 1905), Vol. 1, pp. 10–13.
33. Quoted by Travers, "Technology, Tactics, and Morale."

fathers made our country what it is today."[34] In Germany General von Schlieffen, on retiring as Chief of the General Staff in 1905, held up to his successors the model of the German armies in 1870: "Attacks, and more attacks, ruthless attacks brought it unparalleled losses but also victory and, it is probably true to say, the decision of the campaign."[35] And his successor, the younger von Moltke, acknowledged the heritage: "We have learned the object that you seek to achieve: not to obtain limited successes but to strike great, destructive blows. . . . Your object is the annihilation of the enemy, and all efforts must be directed towards this end."[36]

Nowhere was the lesson more gratefully received, however, than in France. Marshal Joffre, whose offensive operations from 1914 through 1916 are now generally considered to have been a succession of unmitigated disasters, described the French reaction to the Russo–Japanese War in his Memoirs with quite unrepentant frankness. After the Boer War, he wrote,

a whole series of false doctrines . . . began to undermine even such feeble offensive sentiment as had made its appearance in our war doctrines . . . an incomplete study of the events of a single war had led the intellectual elite of our Army to believe that the improvement in firearms and the power of fire action had so increased the strength of the defensive that an offensive opposed to it had lost all virtue.

After the Russo–Japanese War, however,

our young intellectual elite finally shook off the malady of this phraseology which had upset the military world and returned to a more healthy conception of the general conditions prevailing in war.[37]

Joffre admitted that the new passion for the offensive did take on a "somewhat unreasoning character," citing Colonel de Grandmaison's famous lectures of 1911 as an example. "Unreasoning" is the right word. One must always, declared de Grandmaison to his audience,

succeed in combat in doing things which would be *impossible* in cold blood. For instance . . . advancing under fire. . . . We must prepare ourselves for

---

34. R.B. Haldane, Introduction to Sir Ian Hamilton, *Compulsory Service*, 2nd ed. (London, 1911), p. 38.
35. Quoted by Fritz Fischer, *War of Illusions* (New York and London: W. W. Norton, 1975), p. 395.
36. Eugene Carrias, *La pensée militaire allemande* (Paris, 1948), p. 319.
37. Joseph Joffre, *The Personal Memoirs of Marshal Joffre* (London: Harper & Brothers, 1932), Vol. 1, pp. 27ff.

it, and prepare others by cultivating, passionately, everything which bears the mark of the offensive spirit. To take this to excess would probably still not be far enough.[38]

There was nothing in this to indicate the careful use of ground and of mutual fire support which had characterized the actual Japanese tactics—tactics in fact remarkably close to those prescribed in the despised French infantry regulation of 1904. But de Grandmaison was not so much setting out a military doctrine as echoing a national mood—a generalized sense of chauvinistic assertiveness which dominated the French "establishment," civil and military alike, in 1911–12.[39] It was a mood which did much to restore the morale of an army battered and confused after the excesses of the Dreyfus affair, but it could not of itself create the battlefield skills which had also characterized the Japanese army, and without which "the spirit of the offensive" was not so much an assertion of national morale as a generalized death wish. It was in this mood that French officers led the attacks in August–September 1914 which within six weeks produced 385,000 casualties, of which 100,000 were dead.[40]

Bloch died in 1902, but he could have taken much comfort from the experiences of the Russo–Japanese War. Its battles were prolonged, costly, and indecisive. Victory came through attrition; and defeat, for Russia, brought revolution. But Bloch's critics could equally well argue that his major thesis had been disproved. War had been shown to be neither impossible, nor suicidal. It was still a highly effective instrument of policy for a nation which had the courage to face its dangers and the endurance to bear its costs—especially its inevitable and predictable costs in human lives. Those nations which were not prepared to put their destinies to this test, they urged, could expect no mercy in the grim battle for survival which had always characterized human history and which seemed likely, in the coming century, to be waged with ever greater ferocity. It was in this mood, and with these hopes, that the nations of Europe went to war in 1914.

---

38. Quoted in Henri Contamine, *La Revanche 1871–1914* (Paris, 1957), p. 167.
39. Eugene Weber, *The Nationalist Revival in France, 1905–1914* (Berkeley and Los Angeles: University of California Press, 1959), pp. 93–105.
40. Contamine, *La Revanche*, p. 276.

Civil-Military Relations and the Cult of the Offensive, 1914 and 1984

Jack Snyder

Military technology should have made the European strategic balance in July 1914 a model of stability, but offensive military strategies defied those technological realities, trapping European statesmen in a war-causing spiral of insecurity and instability. As the Boer and Russo–Japanese Wars had foreshadowed and the Great War itself confirmed, prevailing weaponry and means of transport strongly favored the defender. Tactically, withering firepower gave a huge advantage to entrenched defenders; strategically, defenders operating on their own territory could use railroads to outmaneuver marching invaders. Despite these inexorable constraints, each of the major continental powers began the war with an offensive campaign. These war plans and the offensive doctrines behind them were in themselves an important and perhaps decisive cause of the war. Security, not conquest, was the principal criterion used by the designers of the plans, but their net effect was to reduce everyone's security and to convince at least some states that only preventive aggression could ensure their survival.

Even if the outbreak of war is taken as a given, the offensive plans must still be judged disasters. Each offensive failed to achieve its ambitious goals and, in doing so, created major disadvantages for the state that launched it. Germany's invasion of Belgium and France ensured that Britain would join the opposing coalition and implement a blockade. The miscarriage of France's ill-conceived frontal attack almost provided the margin of help that the Schlieffen Plan needed. Though the worst was averted by a last-minute railway maneuver, the Germans nonetheless occupied a key portion of France's industrial northeast, making a settlement based on the status quo ante impossible to negotiate. Meanwhile, in East Prussia the annihilation of an over-extended Russian invasion force squandered troops that might have

Robert Jervis, William McNeill, Cynthia Roberts, and Stephen Van Evera provided helpful comments on this paper, which draws heavily on the author's forthcoming book, *The Ideology of the Offensive: Military Decision Making and the Disasters of 1914* (Ithaca, N.Y.: Cornell University Press, 1984).

Jack Snyder is an Assistant Professor in the Political Science Department, Columbia University.

International Security, Summer 1984 (Vol. 9, No. 1) 0162-2889/84/010108-39 $02.50/1

been decisive if used to reinforce the undermanned advance into Austria. In each case, a defensive or more limited offensive strategy would have left the state in a more favorable strategic position.

None of these disasters was unpredictable or unpredicted. It was not only seers like Ivan Bloch who anticipated the stalemated positional warfare. General Staff strategists themselves, in their more lucid moments, foresaw these outcomes with astonishing accuracy. Schlieffen directed a war game in which he defeated his own plan with precisely the railway maneuver that Joffre employed to prevail on the Marne. In another German war game, which actually fell into Russian hands, Schlieffen used the advantage of railway mobility to defeat piecemeal the two prongs of a Russian advance around the Masurian Lakes—precisely the maneuver that led to the encirclement of Sazonov's Second Army at Tannenberg in August 1914. This is not to say that European war planners fully appreciated the overwhelming advantages of the defender; partly they underrated those advantages, partly they defied them. The point is that our own 20/20 hindsight is not qualitatively different from the understanding that was achievable by the historical protagonists.[1]

Why then were these self-defeating, war-causing strategies adopted? Although the particulars varied from country to country, in each case strategic policymaking was skewed by a pathological pattern of civil-military relations that allowed or encouraged the military to use wartime operational strategy to solve its institutional problems. When strategy went awry, it was because a penchant for offense helped the military organization to preserve its autonomy, prestige, and traditions, to simplify its institutional routines, or to resolve a dispute within the organization. As further discussion will show, it was not just a quirk of fate that offensive strategies served these functions. On balance, offense tends to suit the needs of military organizations better than defense does, and militaries normally exhibit at least a moderate preference for offensive strategies and doctrines for that reason. What was special about the period before World War I was that the state of civil-military relations in each of the major powers tended to exacerbate that normal offensive bias, either because the lack of civilian control allowed it to grow

---

1. Gerhard Ritter, *The Schlieffen Plan* (New York: Praeger, 1958), p. 60, note 34; A.A. Polivanov, *Voennoe delo*, No. 14 (1920), p. 421, quoted in Jack Snyder, *The Ideology of the Offensive: Military Decision Making and the Disasters of 1914* (Ithaca: Cornell University Press, 1984), chapter 7.

unchecked or because an abnormal degree of civil-military conflict heightened the need for a self-protective ideology.

In part, then, the "cult of the offensive" of 1914 reflected the endemic preference of military organizations for offensive strategies, but it also reflected particular circumstances that liberated or intensified that preference. The nature and timing of these catalytic circumstances, though all rooted in problems of civil-military relations, were different in each country. Indeed, if war had broken out as late as 1910, the Russian and French armies would both have fought quite defensively.[2]

Germany was the first European power to commit itself to a wildly over-ambitious offensive strategy, moving steadily in this direction from 1891 when Schlieffen became the Chief of the General Staff. The root of this pathology was the complete absence of civilian control over plans and doctrine, which provided no check on the natural tendency of mature military organizations to institutionalize and dogmatize doctrines that support the organizational goals of prestige, autonomy, and the elimination of novelty and uncertainty. Often, as in this case, it is offense that serves these interests best.[3]

France moved in 1911 from a cautious counteroffensive strategy towards the reckless frontal assault prescribed by the *offensive à outrance*. The roots of this doctrine can also be traced to a problem in civil-military relations. The French officer corps had always been wary of the Third Republic's inclination towards shorter and shorter terms of military service, which threatened the professional character and traditions of their organization. Touting the offense was a way to contain this threat, since everyone agreed that an army based on reservists and short-service conscripts would be good only for defense. The Dreyfus Affair and the radical military reforms that followed it heightened the officer corps' need for a self-protective ideology that would justify the essence and defend the autonomy of their organization. The extreme doctrine of the *offensive à outrance* served precisely this function, helping to discredit the defensive, reservist-based plans of the politicized

---

2. One reason that the war did not happen until 1914 was that Russian offensive power did not seriously threaten Germany until about that year. In this sense, the fact that all the powers had offensive strategies in the year the war broke out is to be explained more by their strategies' interactive consequences than by their common origins.

3. Snyder, *Ideology of the Offensive*, chapters 1, 4, and 5. I have profited greatly from the works of Barry Posen, *The Sources of Military Doctrine* (Ithaca: Cornell University Press, 1984), and Stephen Van Evera, "Causes of War" (Ph.D. dissertation, University of California, Berkeley, 1984), who advance similar arguments.

"republican" officers who ran the French military under civilian tutelage until the Agadir crisis of 1911. Given a freer rein in the harsher international climate, General Joffre and the Young Turks around him used the offensive doctrine to help justify a lengthening of the term of service and to reemphasize the value of a more highly professionalized army.[4]

Russia's drift towards increasingly overcommitted offensive plans between 1912 and 1914 was also abetted by the condition of civil-military relations. The problem in this case was the existence of two powerful veto groups within the military, one in the General Staff that favored an offensive against Germany and another centered on the Kiev military district that wanted to attack Austria. Forces were insufficient to carry out both missions, but there was no strong, centralized civilian authority who could or would enforce a rational priority commensurate with Russian means. Lacking firm civilian direction, the two military factions log-rolled the issue, each getting to implement its preferred offensive but with insufficient troops.[5]

It might be argued that these pathologies of civil-military relations are unique to the historical setting of this period. Civilians may have been ignorant of military affairs in a way that has been unequaled before or since. The transition in this period of the officer corps from an aristocratic caste to a specialized profession may have produced a uniquely unfavorable combination of the ill effects of both. Finally, social changes associated with rapid industrialization and urbanization may have provided a uniquely explosive setting for civil-military relations, as class conflicts reinforced civil-military conflicts.[6] Even if this is true, however, the same general patterns may persist but with lesser intensity, and understanding the circumstances that provoke more intense manifestations may help to forestall their recurrence.

Such a recurrence, whether intense or mild, is not a farfetched scenario. As in 1914, today's military technologies favor the defender of the status quo, but the superpowers are adopting offensive counterforce strategies in defiance of these technological constraints. Like machine guns and railroads, survivable nuclear weapons render trivial the marginal advantages to be gained by striking first. In the view of some, this stabilizing effect even neutralizes whatever first-strike advantages may exist at the conventional level, since the fear of uncontrollable escalation will restrain even the first

---

4. Snyder, *Ideology of the Offensive*, chapters 2 and 3. See also Samuel Williamson, *The Politics of Grand Strategy* (Cambridge: Harvard University Press, 1969).
5. Snyder, *Ideology of the Offensive*, chapters 6 and 7. See also A.M. Zaionchkovskii, *Podgotovka Rossii k imperialisticheskoi voine* (Moscow: Gosvoenizdat, 1926).
6. Van Evera, "Causes of War," chapter 7, explores these questions briefly.

steps in that direction. Since the would-be aggressor has the "last clear chance" to avoid disaster and normally cares less about the outcome than the defender does, mutual assured destruction works strongly for stability and the defense of the status quo. In this way, the absolute power to inflict punishment eases the security dilemma. All states possessing survivable second-strike forces can be simultaneously secure.[7]

Even those who are not entirely satisfied by the foregoing line of argument—and I include myself among them—must nevertheless admit the restraining effect that the irrevocable power to punish has had on international politics. Caveats aside, the prevailing military technology tends to work for stability, yet the strategic plans and doctrines of both superpowers have in important ways defied and undermined that basic reality. As in 1914, the danger today is that war will occur because of an erroneous belief that a disarming, offensive blow is feasible and necessary to ensure the attacker's security.

In order to understand the forces that are eroding the stability of the strategic balance in our own era, it may be helpful to reflect on the causes and consequences of the "cult of the offensive" of 1914. In proceeding towards this goal, I will discuss, first, how offensive strategies promoted war in 1914 and, second, why each of the major continental powers developed offensive military strategies. Germany will receive special attention because the Schlieffen Plan was the mainspring tightening the European security dilemma in 1914, because the lessons of the German experience can be more broadly generalized than those of the other cases, and because of the need to correct the widespread view that Germany's military strategy was determined by its revisionist diplomatic aims. After examining the domestic sources of military strategy in Germany, France, and Russia, I will discuss the effect of each state's policies on the civil-military relations and strategies of its neighbors. A concluding section will venture some possible applications of these findings to the study of contemporary Soviet military doctrine.

How Offense Promoted War

Conventional wisdom holds that World War I was caused in part by runaway offensive war plans, but historians and political scientists have been remark-

---

7. The best and most recent expression of this view is Robert Jervis, *The Illogic of American Nuclear Strategy* (Ithaca: Cornell University Press, 1984).

ably imprecise in reconstructing the logic of this process. Their vagueness has allowed critics of arms controllers' obsession with strategic instability to deny that the war resulted from "the reciprocal fear of surprise attack" or from any other by-product of offensive strategy.[8] Stephen Van Evera's contribution to this issue takes a major step towards identifying the manifold ways in which offensive strategies and doctrines promoted war in 1914. I would add only two points to his compelling argument. The first identifies some remaining puzzles about the perception of first-strike advantage in 1914; the second elaborates on Germany's incentive for preventive attack as the decisive way in which offensive military strategy led Europe towards war.

Van Evera cites statements and behavior indicating that European military and political decision-makers believed that the first army to mobilize and strike would gain a significant advantage. Fearing that their own preparations were lagging (or hoping to get a jump on the opponent), authorities in all of the countries felt pressed to take military measures that cut short the process of diplomacy, which might have converged on the solution of a "halt in Belgrade" if given more time. What is lacking in this story is a clear explanation of how the maximum gain or loss of two days could decisively affect the outcome of the campaign.

Planning documents suggest that no one believed that a two-day edge would allow a disarming surprise attack. Planners in all countries guarded against preemptive attacks on troops disembarking at railheads by concentrating their forces out of reach of such a blow. The only initial operation that depended on this kind of preemptive strike against unprepared forces was the German *coup de main* against the Belgian transport bottleneck of Liège. As the July crisis developed, the German General Staff was caused some anxiety by the progress of Belgian preparations to defend Liège, which jeopardized the smooth implementation of the Schlieffen Plan, but Moltke's attitude was not decisively influenced by this incentive to preempt.[9] In any event, it was Russia that mobilized first, and there is little to suggest that preemption was decisive in this case either. Prewar planning documents and

---

8. Even the usually crystal-clear Thomas Schelling is a bit murky on this point. See his *Arms and Influence* (New Haven: Yale University Press, 1966), pp. 221–225. For a critic, see Stephen Peter Rosen, "Nuclear Arms and Strategic Defense," *Washington Quarterly*, Vol. 4, No. 2 (Spring 1981), pp. 83–84.
9. Ulrich Trumpener, "War Premeditated? German Intelligence Operations in July 1914," *Central European History*, Vol. 9, No. 1 (March 1976), p. 80.

staff exercises show that the Russians worried about being preempted, but took sufficient precautions against it. They also indicate that preemption was not particularly feared if Austria was embroiled in the Balkans—precisely the conditions that obtained in July 1914. On the offensive side, however, the incentive to strike first might have been an important factor. Van Evera points out that the difference between the best case (mobilizing first) and the worst case (mobilizing second) was probably a net gain of four days (two gained plus two not lost). Given the Russians' aim of putting pressure on Germany's rear before the campaign in France was decided, four days was not a negligible consideration. To save just two days, the Russians were willing to begin their advance without waiting for the formation of their supply echelons. Thus, time pressure imposed by military exigencies may explain the haste of the crucial Russian mobilization. It should be stressed, however, that it was neither "the reciprocal fear of surprise attack" nor the chance of preempting the opponent's unalerted forces that produced this pressure. Rather, it was the desire to close Germany's window of opportunity against France that gave Russia an incentive to strike first.[10]

A second elaboration of Van Evera's argument, which will be crucial for understanding the following sections of this paper, is that offensive plans not only reflected the belief that states are vulnerable and conquest is easy; they actually caused the states adopting them to *be* vulnerable and consequently fearful. Even the Fischer school, which emphasizes Germany's "grasping for 'World Power'" as the primary cause of the war, admits that Germany's decision to provoke a conflict in 1914 was also due to the huge Russian army increases then in progress, which would have left Germany at Russia's mercy upon their completion in 1917.[11] This impending vulnerabil-

---

10. Russia, 10-i otdel General'nogo shtaba RKKA, *Vostochnoprusskaia operatsiia: sbornik dokumentov* (Moscow: Gosvoenizdat, 1939), especially p. 62, which reproduces a Russian General Staff intelligence estimate dated March 1, 1914. Van Evera's quotations suggest that decision-makers in all countries exhibited more concern about being preempted than seems warranted by actual circumstances. One explanation may be that the military oversold this danger as a way of guarding against the risk of excessive civilian foot-dragging, which was clearly a concern among the French military, at least. Another possibility is that there was a disconnect between the operational level of analysis, where it was obvious that no one could disrupt his opponent's concentration, and the more abstract level of doctrine, where the intangible benefits of "seizing the initiative" were nonetheless considered important. See Snyder, *Ideology of the Offensive*, chapters 2 and 3.
11. The Germans saw the planned 40 percent increase in the size of the Russian standing army as a threat to Germany's physical survival, not just a barrier foreclosing opportunities to expand. This is expressed most clearly in the fear that the power shift would allow Russia to force a

ity, though real enough, was largely a function of the Schlieffen Plan, which had to strip the eastern front in order to amass the forces needed to deal with the strategic conundrums and additional opponents created by the march through Belgium. If the Germans had used a positional defense on the short Franco–German border to achieve economies of force, they could have handled even the enlarged Russian contingents planned for 1917.[12]

In these ways, offensive strategies helped to cause the war and ensured that, when war occurred, it would be a world war. Prevailing technologies should have made the world of 1914 an arms controllers' dream; instead, military planners created a nightmare of strategic instability.

Germany: Uncontrolled Military or Militarized Civilians?

The offensive character of German war planning in the years before World War I was primarily an expression of the professional interests and outlook of the General Staff. Civilian foreign policy aims and attitudes about international politics were at most a permissive cause of the Schlieffen Plan. On balance, the General Staff's all-or-nothing war plan was more a hindrance than a help in implementing the diplomats' strategy of brinkmanship. The reason that the military was allowed to indulge its strategic preferences was not so much that the civilians agreed with them; rather, it was because war planning was considered to be within the autonomous purview of the General Staff. Military preferences were never decisive on questions of the use of force, however, since this was not considered their legitimate sphere. But indirectly, war plans trapped the diplomats by handing them a blunt instrument suitable for massive preventive war, but ill-designed for controlled coercion. The military's unchecked preference for an unlimited offensive strategy and the mismatch between German military and diplomatic strategy were important causes of strategic instability rooted in the problem of civil-military relations. This section will trace those roots and point out some implications relevant to contemporary questions.

The Schlieffen Plan embodied all of the desiderata commonly found in field manuals and treatises on strategy written by military officers: it was an

---

revision of the status quo in the Balkans, leading to Austria's collapse. See especially Fritz Fischer, *War of Illusions: German Policies from 1911 to 1914* (New York: W.W. Norton, 1975; German edition 1969), pp. 377–379, 427.

12. This is argued in Snyder, *Ideology of the Offensive*, chapter 4.

offensive campaign, designed to seize the initiative, to exploit fleeting opportunities, and to achieve a decisive victory by the rapid annihilation of the opponents' military forces. War was to be an "instrument of politics," not in the sense that political ends would restrain and shape military means, but along lines that the General Staff found more congenial: war would solve the tangle of political problems that the diplomats could not solve for themselves. "The complete defeat of the enemy always serves politics," argued General Colmar von der Goltz in his influential book, *The Nation in Arms*. "Observance of this principle not only grants the greatest measure of freedom in the political sphere but also gives widest scope to the proper use of resources in war."[13]

To do this, Schlieffen sought to capitalize on the relatively slow mobilization of the Russian army, which could not bring its full weight to bear until the second month of the campaign. Schlieffen reasoned that he had to use this "window of opportunity" to decisively alter the balance of forces in Germany's favor. Drawing on precedents provided by Moltke's campaigns of 1866 and 1870 as well as his later plans for a two-front war, Schlieffen saw that a rapid decision could be achieved only by deploying the bulk of the German army on one front in order to carry out a grandiose encirclement maneuver. France had to be the first victim, because the Russians might spoil the encirclement by retreating into their vast spaces. With Paris at risk, the French would have to stand and fight. By 1897, Schlieffen had concluded that this scheme could not succeed without traversing Belgium, since the Franco–German frontier in Alsace–Lorraine was too narrow and too easily defended to permit a decisive maneuver. In the mature conception of 1905, most of the German army (including some units that did not yet exist) would march for three or four weeks through Belgium and northern France, encircling and destroying the French army, and then board trains for the eastern front to reinforce the few divisions left to cover East Prussia.

Even Schlieffen was aware that his plan was "an enterprise for which we are too weak."[14] He and his successor, the younger Moltke, understood most of the pitfalls of this maneuver quite well: the gratuitous provocation of new enemies, the logistical nightmares, the possibility of a rapid French rede-

---

13. Gerhard Ritter, *The Sword and the Scepter: The Problem of Militarism in Germany* (Coral Gables: University of Miami Press, 1969; German edition 1954), Vol. 1, p. 196, citing *Das Volk in Waffen* (5th ed., 1889), p. 129.
14. Ritter, *Schlieffen Plan*, p. 66.

ployment to nullify the German flank maneuver, the numerical insufficiency of the Germany army, the tendency of the attacker's strength to wane with every step forward and the defender's to grow, and the lack of time to finish with France before Russia would attack. The General Staff clung to this plan not because they were blind to its faults, but because they thought all the alternatives were worse. To mollify Austria in 1912, they went through the motions of gaming out a mirror-image of the Schlieffen Plan pointed towards the east, concluding that the French would defeat the weak forces left in the Rhineland long before a decision could be reached against Russia.[15] What the General Staff refused to consider seriously after 1890 was the possibility of an equal division of their forces between west and east, allowing a stable defensive against France and a limited offensive with Austria against Russia. (This was the combination that Germany used successfully in 1915 and that the elder Moltke had resigned himself to in the 1890s.)

Around the turn of the century, the General Staff played some war games based on a defensive in the west. These led to the embarrassing conclusion that the French would have great difficulty overwhelming even a modest defensive force. In future years, when games with this premise were played, the German defenders were allotted fewer forces, while Belgians and Dutch were arbitrarily added to the attacking force. Stacking the deck against the defensive appeared not only in war-gaming but also in Schlieffen's abstract expostulations of doctrine. Even some German critics caught him applying a double standard, arbitrarily granting the attacker advantages in mobility, whereas the reality should have been quite the opposite.[16]

In short, German war planning, especially after 1890, showed a strong bias in favor of offensive schemes for decisive victory and against defensive or more limited offensive schemes, even though the latter had a greater prospect of success. This bias cannot be explained away by the argument that Germany would have been at an economic disadvantage in a long war against Russia and hence had to gamble everything on a quick victory. As the actual war showed, this was untrue. More important, Schlieffen hit upon economic rationalizations for his war plan only after it had already been in place for years. Moreover, he actively discouraged serious analysis of wartime economics, deciding *a priori* that the only good war was a short war and that

---

15. Louis Garros, "Préludes aux invasions de la Belgique," *Revue historique de l'armée* (March 1949), pp. 37–38; French archival documents cited in Snyder, *Ideology of the Offensive*, chapter 4.
16. Friedrich von Bernhardi, *On War of Today* (London: Rees, 1912), Vol. 1, p. 44.

the only way to end a war quickly was to disarm the opponent decisively.[17] These conclusions were not in themselves unreasonable, but Schlieffen reached them before he did his analysis and then arranged the evidence in order to justify his preferred strategy.

The explanation for the General Staff's bias in favor of offensive strategy is rooted in the organizational interests and parochial outlook of the professional military. The Germans' pursuit of a strategy for a short, offensive, decisive war despite its operational infeasibility is simply an extreme case of an endemic bias of military organizations. Militaries do not always exhibit a blind preference for the offensive, of course. The lessons of 1914–1918 had a tempering effect on the offensive inclinations of European militaries, for example.[18] Still, exceptions and questionable cases notwithstanding, initial research indicates that militaries habitually prefer offensive strategies, even though everyone from Clausewitz to Trevor Dupuy has proved that the defender enjoys a net operational advantage.[19]

EXPLAINING THE OFFENSIVE BIAS

Several explanations for this offensive bias have been advanced. A number of them are consistent with the evidence provided by the German case. A particularly important explanation stems from the division of labor and the narrow focus of attention that necessarily follows from it. The professional training and duties of the soldier force him to focus on threats to his state's security and on the conflictual side of international relations. Necessarily preoccupied with the prospect of armed conflict, he sees war as a pervasive aspect of international life. Focusing on the role of military means in ensuring the security of the state, he forgets that other means can also be used towards that end. For these reasons, the military professional tends to hold a simplified, zero-sum view of international politics and the nature of war, in which wars are seen as difficult to avoid and almost impossible to limit.

---

17. Lothar Burchardt, *Friedenswirtschaft und Kriegsvorsorge: Deutschlands wirtschaftliche Rüstungsbestrebungen vor 1914* (Boppard am Rhein: Boldt, 1968), pp. 15, 163–164.
18. However, this effect should not be overdrawn. Barry Posen, *Sources of Military Doctrine*, has recently demonstrated that the French collapse in 1940 was due not to a Maginot Line mentality but to the overcommitment of forces to the offensive campaign in Belgium.
19. Possible biases in civilian views on offense and defense have not been studied systematically. For Trevor Dupuy's attempts to analyze quantitatively offensive and defensive operations in World War II, see his *Numbers, Predictions and War* (New York: Bobbs-Merrill, 1979), chapter 7, and other publications of his "HERO" project.

When the hostility of others is taken for granted, prudential calculations are slanted in favor of preventive wars and preemptive strikes. Indeed, as German military officers were fond of arguing, the proper role of diplomacy in a Hobbesian world is to create favorable conditions for launching preventive war. A preventive grand strategy requires an offensive operational doctrine. Defensive plans and doctrines will be considered only after all conceivable offensive schemes have been decisively discredited. Under uncertainty, such discrediting will be difficult, so offensive plans and doctrines will frequently be adopted even if offense is not easier than defense in the operational sense.

The assumption of extreme hostility also favors the notion that decisive, offensive operations are always needed to end wars. If the conflict of interest between the parties is seen as limited, then a decisive victory may not be needed to end the fighting on mutually acceptable terms. In fact, denying the opponent his objectives by means of a successful defense may suffice. However, when the opponent is believed to be extremely hostile, disarming him completely may seem to be the only way to induce him to break off his attacks. For this reason, offensive doctrines and plans are needed, even if defense is easier operationally.

Kenneth Waltz argues that states are socialized to the implications of international anarchy.[20] Because of their professional preoccupations military professionals become "oversocialized." Seeing war more likely than it really is, they increase its likelihood by adopting offensive plans and buying offensive forces. In this way, the perception that war is inevitable becomes a self-fulfilling prophecy.

A second explanation emphasizes the need of large, complex organizations to operate in a predictable, structured environment. Organizations like to work according to a plan that ties together the standard operating procedures of all the subunits into a prepackaged script. So that they can stick to this script at all costs, organizations try to dominate their environment rather than react to it. Reacting to unpredictable circumstances means throwing out the plan, improvising, and perhaps even deviating from standard operating procedures. As Barry Posen points out, "taking the offensive, exercising the initiative, is a way of structuring the battle."[21] Defense, in contrast, is more reactive, less structured, and harder to plan. Van Evera argues that the

---

20. Kenneth N. Waltz, *Theory of International Politics* (Reading, Mass.: Addison-Wesley, 1979).
21. Posen, *Sources of Military Doctrine*, chapter 2.

military will prefer a task that is easier to plan even if it is more difficult to execute successfully.[22] In Russia, for example, regional staffs complained that the General Staff's defensive war plan of 1910 left their own local planning problem too unstructured. They clamored for an offensive plan with specified lines of advance, and in 1912 they got it.[23]

The German military's bias for the offensive may have derived in part from this desire to structure the environment, but evidence on this point is mixed. The elder Moltke developed clockwork mobilization and rail transport plans leading to offensive operations, but he scoffed at the idea that a campaign plan could be mapped out step-by-step from the initial deployment through to the crowning encirclement battle. For him, strategy remained "a system of *ad hoc* expedients . . . , the development of an original idea in accordance with continually changing circumstances."[24] This attitude may help to explain his willingness to entertain defensive alternatives when his preferred offensive schemes began to look too unpromising. The Schlieffen Plan, in contrast, was a caricature of the link between rigid planning and an unvarying commitment to the offensive. Even here, however, there is some evidence that fits poorly with the hypothesis that militaries prefer offense because it allows them to fight according to their plans and standard operating procedures. Wilhelm Groener, the General Staff officer in charge of working out the logistical preparations for the Schlieffen Plan, recognized full well that the taut, ambitious nature of the plan would make it impossible to adhere to normal, methodical supply procedures. Among officers responsible for logistics, "the feeling of responsibility must be so great that in difficult circumstances people free themselves from procedural hindrances and take the responsibility for acting in accordance with common sense."[25] Nonetheless, it is difficult to ignore the argument ubiquitously advanced by European military writers that defense leads to uncertainty, confusion, passivity, and incoherent action, whereas offense focuses the efforts of the army and the mind of the commander on a single, unwavering goal. Even when they understood the uncertainties and improvisations required by offensive operations, as Groener did, they may still have feared the uncertainties of the defensive more. An offensive plan at least gives the illusion of certainty.

22. Van Evera, "Causes of War," chapter 7.
23. Zaionchkovskii, *Podgotovka Rossii k imperialisticheskoi voine*, pp. 244, 277.
24. Quoted by Hajo Holborn, "Moltke and Schlieffen," in Edward M. Earle, ed., *Makers of Modern Strategy* (Princeton: Princeton University Press, 1971), p. 180.
25. Papers of Wilhelm Groener, U.S. National Archives, roll 18, piece 168, p. 5.

Another possibility, however, is that this argument for the offensive was used to justify a doctrine that was preferred primarily on other grounds. French military publicists invoked such reasoning more frequently, for example, during periods of greater threat to traditional military institutions.[26]

Other explanations for the offensive bias are rooted even more directly in the parochial interests of the military, including the autonomy, prestige, size, and wealth of the organization.[27] The German case shows the function of the offensive strategy as a means towards the goal of operational autonomy. The elder Moltke succinctly stated the universal wish of military commanders: "The politician should fall silent the moment that mobilization begins."[28] This is least likely to happen in the case of limited or defensive wars, where the whole point of fighting is to negotiate a diplomatic solution. Political considerations—and hence politicians—have to figure in operational decisions. The operational autonomy of the military is most likely to be allowed when the operational goal is to disarm the adversary quickly and decisively by offensive means. For this reason, the military will seek to force doctrine and planning into this mold.

The prestige, self-image, and material health of military institutions will prosper if the military can convince civilians and themselves that wars can be short, decisive, and socially beneficial. One of the attractions of decisive, offensive strategies is that they hold out the promise of a demonstrable return on the nation's investment in military capability. Von der Goltz, for example, pushed the view that "modern wars have become the nation's way of doing business"—a perspective that made sense only if wars were short, cheap, and hence offensive.[29] The German people were relatively easy to convince of this, because of the powerful example provided by the short, offensive, nation-building wars of 1866 and 1870, which cut through political fetters and turned the officer corps into demigods. This historical backdrop gave the General Staff a mantel of unquestioned authority and legitimacy in operational questions; it also gave them a reputation to live up to. Later, when technological and strategic circumstances challenged the viability of their

---

26. See the argument in Snyder, *Ideology of the Offensive*, chapter 3, citing especially Georges Gilbert, *Essais de critique militaire* (Paris: Librairie de la Nouvelle Revue, 1890), pp. 43, 47–48.
27. Posen and Van Evera, in analyzing organizational interests in this way, have drawn on the categories laid out by Morton Halperin, *Bureaucratic Politics and Foreign Policy* (Washington: Brookings, 1974), chapter 3.
28. Quoted by Bernard Brodie, *War and Politics* (New York: Macmillan, 1973), p. 11.
29. Quoted by Van Evera from Ferdinand Foch, *The Principles of War* (New York: Fly, 1918), p. 37.

formula for a short, victorious war, General Staff officers like Schlieffen found it difficult to part with the offensive strategic formulae that had served their state and organization so effectively. As Posen puts it, offense makes soldiers "specialists in victory," defense makes them "specialists in attrition," and in our own era mutual assured destruction makes them "specialists in slaughter."[30]

THE EVOLUTION OF GERMAN WAR PLANNING

The foregoing arguments could, for the most part, explain the offensive bias of the military in many countries and in many eras. What remains to be explained is why this offensive bias became so dogmatic and extreme in Germany before 1914. The evolution of the General Staff's strategic thinking from 1870 to 1914 suggests that a tendency towards doctrinal dogmatism and extremism may be inherent in mature military organizations that develop under conditions of near-absolute autonomy in doctrinal questions. This evolution, which occurred in three stages, may be typical of the maturation of uncontrolled, self-evaluating organizations and consequently may highlight the conditions in which doctrinal extremism might recur in our own era.[31]

The first stage was dominated by the elder Moltke, who established the basis tenets of the organizational ideology of the German General Staff. These were the inevitability and productive nature of war, the indispensability of preventive war, and the need for an operational strategy that could provide rapid, decisive victories. Moltke was the creator, not a captive of his doctrines and did not implement them in the manner of a narrow technician. He was willing to think in political terms and to make his opinion heard in political matters. This practice had its good and bad sides. On one hand, it allowed him to consider war plans that gave diplomacy some role in ending the war; on the other, it spurred him to lobby for preventive war against France in 1868 and against Russia in 1887. Moltke thought he understood what international politics was all about, but he understood it in a military way. In judging the opportune moment for war, Moltke looked exclusively at military factors, whereas Bismarck focused primarily on preparing domestic and foreign opinion for the conflict.[32]

---

30. Posen, *Sources of Military Doctrine.*
31. Van Evera uses the concept of the self-evaluating organization, drawing on the work of James Q. Wilson.
32. Ritter, *Sword and Scepter*, Vol. 1, pp. 217–218, 245.

Schlieffen, the key figure in the second stage of the General Staff's development, was much more of a technocrat than Moltke. Not a founder, he was a systematizer and routinizer. Schlieffen dogmatized Moltke's strategic precepts in a way that served the mature institution's need for a simple, standardized doctrine to facilitate the training of young officers and the operational planning of the General Staff. In implementing this more dogmatic doctrine, Schlieffen and his colleagues lacked Moltke's ability to criticize fundamental assumptions and tailor doctrine to variations in circumstances. Thus, Moltke observed the defender's increasing advantages and decided reluctantly that the day of the rapid, decisive victory was probably gone, anticipating that "two armies prepared for battle will stand opposite each other, neither wishing to begin battle."[33] Schlieffen witnessed even further developments in this direction in the Russo–Japanese War, but concluded only that the attacker had to redouble his efforts. "The armament of the army has changed," he recognized, "but the fundamental laws of combat remain the same, and one of these laws is that one cannot defeat the enemy without attacking."[34]

Seeing himself as primarily a technician, Schlieffen gave political considerations a lesser place in his work than had Moltke. Again, this had both good and bad consequences. On one hand, Schlieffen never lobbied for preventive war in the way Moltke and Waldersee had, thinking such decisions were not his to make. When asked, of course, he was not reluctant to tell the political authorities that the time was propitious, as he did in 1905. On the other hand, Schlieffen had a more zero-sum, apolitical view of the conduct of warfare than did the elder Moltke. Consequently, his war plans excluded any notion of political limitations on the conduct of war or diplomatic means to end it.[35]

Contrasting the problems of civilian control of the military in stages one and two, we see that the founders' generation, being more "political," chal-

---

33. Helmuth von Moltke, *Die Deutschen Aufmarschpläne, 1871–1890,* Ferdinand von Schmerfeld, ed. (Berlin: Mittler, 1929), p. 122ff.
34. The quotation is from an 1893 comment on an operational exercise, quoted by O. von Zoellner, "Schlieffens Vermächtnis," *Militärwissenschaftliche Rundschau* (Sonderheft, 1938), p. 18, but identical sentiments are expressed in Schlieffen's "Krieg in der Gegenwart," *Deutsche Revue* (1909).
35. Brodie, *War and Politics,* p. 58, reports a perhaps apocryphal statement by Schlieffen that if his plan failed to achieve decisive results, then Germany should negotiate an end to the war. Even if he did say this, the possibility of negotiations had no effect on his war planning, in contrast to that of the elder Moltke.

lenges the political elite on questions of the use of force, but as if in compensation, is more capable of self-evaluation and self-control in its war planning. The technocratic generation, however, is less assertive politically but
also less capable of exercising political judgment in its own work. The founders' assertiveness is the more dramatic challenge to political control, but as
the German case shows, Bismarck was able to turn back the military's direct
lobbying for preventive war, which was outside of the military's legitimate
purview even by the Second Reich's skewed standards of civil-military relations. Much more damaging in the long run was Schlieffen's unobtrusive
militarism, which created the conditions for a preventive war much more
surely than Moltke's overt efforts did.

A third stage, which was just developing on the eve of World War I,
combined the worst features of the two previous periods. Exemplary figures
in this final stage were Erich Ludendorff and Wilhelm Groener, products of
a thoroughgoing socialization to the organizational ideology of the German
General Staff. Groener, describing his own war college training, makes it
clear that not only operational principles but also a militaristic philosophy of
life were standard fare in the school's curriculum. These future functionaries
and leaders of the General Staff were getting an intensive course in the same
kind of propaganda that the Army and Navy Leagues were providing the
general public. They came out of this training believing in the philosophy of
total war, demanding army increases that their elders were reluctant to
pursue and fearing that "weaklings" like Bethmann Hollweg would throw
away the army's glorious victories.[36]

An organizational explanation for this third stage would point to the self-
amplifying effects of the organizational ideology in a mature, self-evaluating
unit. An alternative explanation also seems plausible, however. Geoff Eley,
in his study of right-wing radical nationalism in Wilhelmine Germany, argues
that emerging counterelites used national populist causes and institutions
like the Navy and Army Leagues as weapons aimed at the political monopoly
retained by the more cautious traditional elite, who were vulnerable to criticism on jingoistic issues.[37] This pattern fits the cases of Groener and Ludendorff, who were middle-class officers seeking the final transformation of the

---

36. Helmut Haeussler, *General William Groener and the Imperial German Army* (Madison: The State
Historical Society of Wisconsin, 1962), p. 72.
37. Geoff Eley, *Reshaping the German Right: Radical Nationalism and Political Change after Bismarck*
(New Haven: Yale University Press, 1980).

old Prussian army into a mass organ of total war, which would provide upward mobility for their own kind. German War Ministers, speaking for conservative elements in the army and the state, had traditionally resisted large increases in the size of the army, which would bring more bourgeois officers into the mess and working-class soldiers into the ranks; it would also cost so much that the Junkers' privileged tax status would be brought into question. This alternative explanation makes it difficult to know whether organizational ideologies really tend toward self-amplification or whether extremist variants only occur from some particular motivation, as the French case suggests.

THE MISMATCH BETWEEN MILITARY STRATEGY AND DIPLOMACY

It is sometimes thought that Germany required an unlimited, offensive military strategy because German civilian elites were hell-bent on overturning the continental balance of power as a first step in their drive for "World Power." In this view, the Schlieffen Plan was simply the tool needed to achieve this high-risk, high-payoff goal, around which a national consensus of both military and civilian elites had formed.[38] There are several problems with this view. The first is that the civilians made virtually no input into the strategic planning process. Contrary to the unsupported assertions of some historians, the shift from Moltke's plan for a limited offensive against Russia to Schlieffen's plan for a more decisive blow aimed at France had nothing to do with the fall of Bismarck or the "New Course" in foreign policy. Rather, Schlieffen saw it as a technical change, stemming from an improved Russian ability to defend their forward theater in Poland. Nor was Schlieffen chosen to head the General Staff because of the strategy he preferred. Schlieffen had simply been the next in line as deputy chief under Waldersee, who was fired primarily because he dared to criticize the Kaiser's tactical decisions in a mock battle.[39] Later, when Reich Chancellor von Bülow learned of Schlieffen's intention to violate Belgian neutrality, his reaction was: "if the Chief of Staff, especially a strategic authority such as Schlieffen, believes such a measure to be necessary, then it is the obligation of diplomacy to adjust to it and prepare for it in every possible way."[40] In 1912 Foreign Secretary von

---

38. See, for example, L.L. Farrar, Jr., *Arrogance and Anxiety* (Iowa City: University of Iowa Press, 1981), pp. 23–24.

39. Ritter, *Schlieffen Plan*, pp. 17–37; Norman Rich and M.H. Fisher, eds., *The Holstein Papers* (Cambridge: Cambridge University Press, 1963), Vol. 3, pp. 347, note 1, and 352–353.

40. Ritter, *Schlieffen Plan*, pp. 91–92.

Jagow urged a reevaluation of the need to cross Belgian territory, but a memo from the younger Moltke ended the matter.[41] In short, the civilians knew what Schlieffen was planning to do, but they were relatively passive bystanders in part because military strategy was not in their sphere of competence and legitimate authority, and perhaps also because they were quite happy with the notion that the war could be won quickly and decisively. This optimism alleviated their fear that a long war would mean the destruction of existing social and economic institutions, no matter who won it. The decisive victory promised by the Schlieffen Plan may have also appealed to civilian elites concerned about the need for spectacular successes as a payoff for the masses' enthusiastic participation in the war. Trying to justify the initial war plan from the retrospective vantage point of 1919, Bethmann Hollweg argued that "offense in the East and defense in the West would have implied that we expected at best a draw. With such a slogan no army and no nation could be led into a struggle for their existence."[42] Still, this is a long way from the totally unfounded notion that Holstein and Schlieffen cooked up the Schlieffen Plan expressly for the purpose of bullying France over the Morocco issue and preparing the way for "Welt Politik."[43] The Schlieffen Plan had some appeal for German civilian elites, but the diplomats may have had serious reservations about it, as the Jagow episode suggests. Mostly, the civilians passively accepted whatever operational plan the military deemed necessary.

If German diplomats had devised a military strategy on their own, it is by no means certain that they would have come up with anything like the Schlieffen Plan. This all-or-nothing operational scheme fit poorly with the diplomatic strategy of expansion by means of brinkmanship and controlled, coercive pressure, which they pursued until 1914. In 1905, for example, it is clear that Bülow, Holstein, and Wilhelm II had no inclination to risk a world war over the question of Morocco.

"The originators of *Weltpolitik* looked forward to a series of small-scale, marginal foreign policy successes," says historian David Kaiser, "not to a major war."[44] Self-deterred by the unlimited character of the Schlieffen Plan,

---

41. Fischer, *War of Illusions*, p. 390.
42. Konrad Jarausch, *The Enigmatic Chancellor* (New Haven: Yale University Press, 1973), p. 195.
43. This is implied by Martin Kitchen, *The German Officer Corps* (Oxford: Oxford University Press, 1968), p. 104, and Imanuel Geiss, *German Foreign Policy, 1871–1914* (London: Routledge & Kegan Paul, 1976), pp. 101–103.
44. David E. Kaiser, "Germany and the Origins of the First World War," *Journal of Modern History*, Vol. 55, No. 3 (September 1983), p. 448.

they had few military tools that they could use to demonstrate resolve in a competition in risk-taking. The navy offered a means for the limited, demonstrative use of force, namely the dispatch of the gunboat *Panther* to the Moroccan port of Agadir, but the army was an inflexible tool. At one point in the crisis, Schlieffen told Bülow that the French were calling up reservists on the frontier. If this continued, Germany would have to respond, setting off a process that the Germans feared would be uncontrollable.[45] Thus, the German military posture and war plan served mainly to deter the German diplomats, who did not want a major war even though Schlieffen told them the time was favorable. They needed limited options, suitable for coercive diplomacy, not unlimited options, suitable for preventive war. With the Schlieffen Plan, they could not even respond to the opponent's precautionary moves without setting off a landslide toward total war.

This mismatch between military and diplomatic strategy dogged German policy down through 1914. Bethmann Hollweg described his strategy in 1912 as one of controlled coercion, sometimes asserting German demands, sometimes lulling and mollifying opponents to control the risk of war. "On all fronts we must drive forward quietly and patiently," he explained, "without having to risk our existence."[46] Bethmann's personal secretary, Kurt Riezler, explained this strategy of calculated risk in a 1914 volume, *Grundzüge der Weltpolitik*. A kind of cross between Thomas Schelling and Norman Angell, Riezler explained that wars were too costly to actually fight in the modern, interdependent, capitalist world. Nonetheless, states can still use the threat of war to gain unilateral advantages, forcing the opponent to calculate whether costs, benefits, and the probability of success warrant resorting to force. His calculations can be affected in several ways. Arms-racing can be used, *á la* Samuel Huntington, as a substitute for war—that is, a bloodless way to show the opponent that he would surely lose if it came to a fight. Brinkmanship and bluffing can be used to demonstrate resolve; *faits accomplis* and salami tactics can be used to shift the onus for starting the undesired war onto the opponent. But, Riezler warns, this strategy will not work if one is greedy and impatient to overturn the balance of power. Opponents will fight if they sense that their vital interests are at stake. Consequently, "victory

---

45. Holstein to Radolin, June 28, 1905, in *Holstein Papers*, Vol. 4, p. 347.
46. Jarausch, *Enigmatic Chancellor*, pp. 110–111.

belongs to the steady, tenacious, and gradual achievement of small successes
. . . without provocation."[47]

Although this may have been a fair approximation of Bethmann's thinking in 1912, the theory of the calculated risk had undergone a major transformation by July 1914. By that time, Bethmann wanted a major diplomatic or military victory and was willing to risk a continental war—perhaps even a world war—to achieve it. *Fait accompli* and onus-shifting were still part of the strategy, but with a goal of keeping Britain out of the war and gaining the support of German socialists, not with a goal of avoiding war altogether.

The Schlieffen Plan played an important role in the transformation of Bethmann's strategy and in its failure to keep Britain neutral in the July crisis. Riezler's diary shows Bethmann's obsession in July 1914 with Germany's need for a dramatic victory to forestall the impending period of vulnerability that the Russian army increases and the possible collapse of Austria–Hungary would bring on.[48] As I argued earlier, the Schlieffen Plan only increased Germany's vulnerability to the Russian buildup, stripping the eastern front and squandering forces in the vain attempt to knock France out of the war. In this sense, it was the Schlieffen Plan that led Bethmann to transform the calculated-risk theory from a cautious tool of coercive diplomacy into a blind hope of gaining a major victory without incurring an unwanted world war.

Just as the Schlieffen Plan made trouble for Bethmann's diplomacy, so too German brinkmanship made trouble for the Schlieffen Plan. The Russian army increases, provoked by German belligerence in the 1909 Bosnian crisis and Austrian coercion of the Serbs in 1912, made the German war plan untenable.[49] The arms-racing produced by this aggressive diplomacy was not a "substitute for war"; rather, it created a window of vulnerability that helped to cause the war. Thus, Riezler (and Bethmann) failed to consider how easily a diplomatic strategy of calculated brinkmanship could set off a chain of uncontrollable consequences in a world of military instability.

---

47. Andreas Hillgruber, *Germany and the Two World Wars* (Cambridge: Harvard University Press, 1981), pp. 22–24; J.J. Ruedorffer (pseud. for Kurt Riezler), *Grundzüge der Weltpolitik in der Gegenwart* (Berlin: Deutsche Verlags-Anstalt, 1914), especially pp. 214–232; quotation from Jarausch, *Enigmatic Chancellor*, pp. 143–144.

48. Jarausch, *Enigmatic Chancellor*, p. 157.

49. P.A. Zhilin, "Bol'shaia programma po usileniiu russkoi armii," *Voenno-istoricheskii zhurnal*, No. 7 (July 1974), pp. 90–97, shows the connection between the 1913 increases and the Balkan crisis of 1912. He also shows that this project, with its emphasis on increasing the standing army and providing rail lines to speed its concentration, was directly connected to the offensive character of Russia's increasingly overcommitted, standing-start, short-war campaign plan.

Even the transformed version of the calculated-risk theory, implemented in July 1914, was ill-served by the Schlieffen Plan. If Bethmann had had eastern-oriented or otherwise limited military options, all sorts of possibilities would have been available for defending Austria, bloodying the Russians, driving a wedge between Paris and St. Petersburg, and keeping Britain neutral. In contrast, the Schlieffen Plan cut short any chance for coercive diplomacy and ensured that Britain would fight. In short, under Bethmann as well as Bülow, the Schlieffen Plan was hardly an appropriate tool underwriting the brinkmanship and expansionist aims of the civilian elite. Rather, the plan was the product of military organizational interests and misconceptions that reduced international politics to a series of preventive wars. The consequences of the all-or-nothing war plan were, first, to reduce the coercive bargaining leverage available to German diplomats, and second, to ensnare German diplomacy in a security dilemma that forced the abandonment of the strategy of controlled risks. Devised by military officers who wanted a tool appropriate for preventive war, the Schlieffen Plan trapped Germany in a situation where preventive war seemed like the only safe option.

In summary, three generalizations emerge from the German case. First, military organizations tend to exhibit a bias in favor of offensive strategies, which promote organizational prestige and autonomy, facilitate planning and adherence to standard operating procedures, and follow logically from the officer corps' zero-sum view of international politics. Second, this bias will be particularly extreme in mature organizations which have developed institutional ideologies and operational doctrines with little civilian oversight. Finally, the destabilizing consequences of an inflexible, offensive military strategy are compounded when it is mismatched with a diplomatic strategy based on the assumption that risks can be calculated and controlled through the skillful fine-tuning of threats.

France: Civil-Military Truce and Conflict

France before the Dreyfus Affair exemplifies the healthiest pattern of civil-military relations among the European states, but after Dreyfus, the most destructive. In the former period civilian defense experts who understood and respected the military contained the latent conflict between the professional army and republican politicians by striking a bargain that satisfied the main concerns of both sides. In this setting, the use of operational doctrine as a weapon of institutional defense was minimal, so plans and doctrine were a moderate combination of offense and defense. After the Dreyfus watershed, the truce broke. Politicians set out to "republicanize" the army, and the officer corps responded by developing the doctrine of *offensive à outrance*, which helped to reverse the slide towards a military system based overwhelmingly on reservists and capable only of defensive operations.[50]

The French army had always coexisted uneasily with the Third Republic. Especially in the early years, most officers were Bonapartist or monarchist in their political sentiments, and Radical politicians somewhat unjustifiably feared a military coup against Parliament in support of President MacMahon, a former Marshal. The military had its own fears, which were considerably more justified. Responding to constituent demands, republican politicians gradually worked to reduce the length of military service from seven to three years and to break down the quasi-monastic barriers insulating the regiment from secular, democratic trends in French society at large. Military professionals, while not averse to all reform, rightly feared a slippery slope towards a virtual militia system, in which the professional standing army would degenerate into a school for the superficial, short-term training of France's decidedly unmilitary youth. War college professors and military publicists like Georges Gilbert, responding to this danger, began by the 1880s to promote an offensive operational doctrine, which they claimed could only be implemented by well-trained, active-duty troops.[51]

This explosive situation was well managed by nationalist republican leaders like Léon Gambetta, leader of the French national resistance in the second phase of the Franco–Prussian War, and especially Charles de Freycinet, organizer of Gambetta's improvised popular armies. As War Minister in the 1880s and 1890s, Freycinet defused military fears and won their acceptance of the three-year service. He backed the military on questions of matériel, autonomy in matters of military justice, and selection of commanders on the basis of professional competence rather than political acceptability. At the same time, he pressed for more extensive use of the large pool of reservist manpower that was being created by the three-year conscription system, and the military was reasonably accommodating. In this context of moderate civil-military relations, war plans and doctrine were also moderate. Henri Bonnal's

50. Presenting somewhat contrasting views of French civil-military relations during this period are Douglas Porch, *March to the Marne: The French Army, 1871–1914* (Cambridge: Cambridge University Press, 1981) and David B. Ralston, *The Army of the Republic: The Place of the Military in the Political Evolution of France, 1871–1914* (Cambridge: M.I.T. Press, 1967).
51. See, for example, Gilbert, *Essais*, p. 271.

"defensive-offensive" school was the Establishment doctrine, reflected in the cautious, counteroffensive war plans of that era.[52]

Freycinet and other republican statesmen of the militant neo-Jacobin variety cherished the army as the instrument of revanche and as a truly popular institution, with roots in the *levée en masse* of the Wars of the Revolution. Though he wanted to democratize the army, Freycinet also cared about its fighting strength and morale, unlike many later politicians who were concerned only to ease their constituents' civic obligations. His own moderate policies, respectful of military sensitivities but insistent on key questions of civilian control, elicited a moderate response from military elites, whose propensity to develop a self-protective organizational ideology was thus held in check.

The deepening of the Dreyfus crisis in 1898 rekindled old fears on both sides and destroyed the system of mutual respect and reassurance constructed by Freycinet. The military's persistence in a blatant miscarriage of justice against a Jewish General Staff officer accused of espionage confirmed the republicans' view of the army as a state within the state, subject to no law but the reactionary principles of unthinking obedience and blind loyalty. When conservatives and monarchists rallied to the military's side, it made the officer corps appear (undeservedly) to be the spearhead of a movement to overthrow the Republic. Likewise, attacks by the Dreyfusards confirmed the worst fears of the military. Irresponsible Radicals were demanding to meddle in the army's internal affairs, impeaching the integrity of future wartime commanders, and undermining morale. Regardless of Dreyfus's guilt or innocence, the honor of the military had to be defended for the sake of national security.

The upshot of the affair was a leftward realignment of French politics. The new Radical government appointed as War Minister a young reformist general, Louis André, with instructions to "republicanize" the army. André, aided by an intelligence network of Masonic Lodges, politicized promotions and war college admissions, curtailed officers' perquisites and disciplinary powers, and forced Catholic officers to participate in inventorying church property. In 1905, the term of conscription was reduced to two years, with reservists intended to play a more prominent role in war plans, field exercises, and the daily life of the regiment.

---

52. Charles de Freycinet, *Souvenirs, 1878–1893* (New York: Da Capo, 1973).

In this hostile environment, a number of officers—especially the group of "Young Turks" around Colonel Loyzeaux de Grandmaison—began to reemphasize in extreme form the organizational ideology propounded earlier by Gilbert. Its elements read like a list of the errors of Plan 17: *offensive à outrance*, mystical belief in group *élan* achieved by long service together, denigration of reservists, and disdain for reactive war plans driven by intelligence estimates. Aided by the Agadir Crisis of 1911, General Joffre and other senior figures seeking a reassertion of professional military values used the Young Turks' doctrine to scuttle the reformist plans of the "republican" commander in chief, Victor Michel, and to hound him from office. Michel, correctly anticipating the Germans' use of reserve corps in the opening battles and the consequent extension of their right wing across northern Belgium, had sought to meet this threat by a cordon defense, making intensive use of French reservists. Even middle-of-the-road officers considered ruinous the organizational changes needed to implement this scheme. It was no coincidence that Grandmaison's operational doctrine provided a tool for attacking Michel's ideas point-by-point, without having to admit too blatantly that it was the institutional implications of Michel's reservist-based plan that were its most objectionable aspect.[53] Having served to oust Michel in 1911, the Grandmaison doctrine also played a role (along with the trumped-up scenario of a German standing-start attack) in justifying a return to the three-year term of service in 1913. The problem was that this ideology, so useful as a tool for institutional defense, became internalized by the French General Staff, who based Plan 17 on its profoundly erroneous tenets.

Obviously, there is much that is idiosyncratic in the story of the *offensive à outrance*. The overlapping of social and civil-military cleavages, which produced an unusually intense threat to the "organizational essence" and autonomy of the French army, may have no close analog in the contemporary era. At a higher level of abstraction, however, a broadly applicable hypothesis may nonetheless be gleaned from the French experience. That is, doctrinal bias is likely to become more extreme whenever strategic doctrine can be used an an ideological weapon to protect the military organization from threats to its institutional interests. Under such circumstances, doctrine be-

---

53. An internal General Staff document that was highly critical of Michel's scheme stated: "It is necessary only to remark that this mixed force would require very profound changes in our regulations, our habits, our tactical rules, and the organization of our staffs." Cited in Snyder, *Ideology of the Offensive*, chapter 3.

comes unhinged from strategic reality and responds primarily to the more pressing requirements of domestic and intragovernmental politics.

Russia: Institutional Pluralism and Strategic Overcommitment

Between 1910 and 1912, Russia changed from an extremely cautious defensive war plan to an overcommitted double offensive against both Germany and Austria. The general direction of this change can be easily explained in terms of rational strategic calculations. Russia's military power had increased relative to Germany's, making an offensive more feasible, and the tightening of alliances made it more obvious that Germany would deploy the bulk of its army against France in the first phase of the fighting, regardless of the political circumstances giving rise to the conflict. Russian war planners consequently had a strong incentive to invade Germany or Austria during the "window of opportunity" provided by the Schlieffen Plan. Attacking East Prussia would put pressure on Germany's rear, thus helping France to survive the onslaught; attacking the Austrian army in Galicia might decisively shift the balance of power by knocking Germany's ally out of the war, while eliminating opposition to Russian imperial aims in Turkey and the Balkans.[54]

What is harder to explain is the decision to invade both Germany and Austria, which ensured that neither effort would have sufficient forces to achieve its objectives. At a superficial level the explanation for this failure to set priorities is simple enough: General Yuri Danilov and the General Staff in St. Petersburg wanted to use the bulk of Russia's forces to attack Germany, while defending against Austria; General Mikhail Alekseev and other regional commanders wanted to attack Austria, leaving a weak defensive screen facing East Prussia. Each faction had powerful political connections and good arguments. No higher arbiter could or would choose between the contradictory schemes, so a *de facto* compromise allowed each to pursue its preferred offensive with insufficient forces. At this level, we have a familiar tale of bureaucratic politics producing an overcommitted, Christmas-tree "resultant."[55]

---

54. Apart from Zaionchkovskii, the most interesting work on Russian strategy is V.A. Emets, *Ocherki vneshnei politiki Rossii v period pervoi mirovoi voiny: vzaimootnosheniia Rossii s soiuznikami po voprosam vedeniia voiny* (Moscow: Nauka, 1977).
55. On the characteristics of compromised policy, see Warner Schilling, "The Politics of National Defense: Fiscal 1950," in Schilling et al., *Strategy, Politics, and Defense Budgets* (New York: Columbia University Press, 1962), pp. 217–218.

At a deeper level, however, several puzzles remain. One is that "where you sat" bureaucratically was only superficially related to "where you stood" on the question of strategy. Alekseev was the Chief-of-Staff-designate of the Austrian front, so had an interest in making his turf the scene of the main action. But Alekseev had always preferred an Austria-first strategy, even when he had been posted to the General Staff in St. Petersburg. Similarly, Danilov served under General Zhilinskii, the Chief of Staff who negotiated a tightening of military cooperation with France after 1911, so his bureaucratic perspective might explain his adoption of the Germany-first strategy that France preferred. But Danilov's plans had always given priority to the German front, even in 1908–1910 when he doubted the reliability and value of France as an ally.[56] Thus, this link between bureaucratic position and preferred strategy was mostly spurious.

Bureaucratic position does explain why Alekseev's plan attracted wide support among military district chiefs of staff, however. These regional planners viewed the coming war as a problem of battlefield operations, not grand strategy. Alekseev's scheme was popular with them, because it proposed clear lines of advance across open terrain. Danilov's plans, in contrast, were a source of frustration for the commanders who would have to implement them. His defensive 1910 plan perplexed them, because it offered no clear objectives.[57] His 1913 plan for an invasion of East Prussia entailed all sorts of operational difficulties that local commanders would have to overcome: inordinate time pressure, the division of the attacking force by the Masurian Lakes, and the defenders' one-sided advantages in rail lines, roads, fortifications, and river barriers.

Nonetheless, the main differences between Danilov and Alekseev were intellectual, not bureaucratic.[58] Danilov was fundamentally pessimistic about Russia's ability to compete with modern, efficient Germany. He considered Russia too weak to indulge in imperial dreams, whether against Austria or Turkey, arguing that national survival required an absolute priority be given to containing the German danger. In 1910, this pessimism was expressed in his ultra-defensive plan, based on the fear that Russia would have to face Germany virtually alone. By 1913–1914, Danilov's pessimism took a different form. The improved military balance, the tighter alliance with France after

---

56. Zaionchkovskii, *Podgotovka Rossii k imperialisticheskoi voine*, pp. 184–190.
57. Ibid., pp. 206–207.
58. See Schilling, "Politics of National Defense," for this distinction.

Agadir, and telling criticism from Alekseev convinced Danilov that a porcupine strategy was infeasible politically and undesirable strategically. Now his nightmare was that France would succumb in a few weeks, once again leaving backward Russia to face Germany virtually alone. To prevent this, he planned a hasty attack into East Prussia, designed to draw German forces away from the decisive battle in France.

Alekseev was more optimistic about Russian prospects, supporting imperial adventures in Asia and anticipating that a "sharp rap" would cause Austria to collapse. Opponents of Danilov's Germany-first strategy also tended to argue that a German victory against France would be Pyrrhic. Germany would emerge from the contest bloodied and lacking the strength or inclination for a second round against Russia. A Russo–German condominium would ensue, paving the way for Russian hegemony over the Turkish Straits and in the Balkans.[59]

Available evidence is insufficient to explain satisfactorily the sources of these differing views. Personality differences may explain Danilov's extreme pessimism and Alekseev's relative optimism, but this begs the question of why each man was able to gain support for his view. What evidence exists points to idiosyncratic explanations: Danilov's plan got support from Zhilinskii (it fit the agreements he made with Joffre), the commander-designate of the East Prussian front (it gave him more troops), and the General Staff apparatus (a military elite disdainful of and pessimistic about the rabble who would implement their plans). Alekseev won support from operational commanders and probably from Grand Duke Nikolai Nikolaevitch, the future commander-in-chief and a quintessential optimist about Russian capabilities and ambitions. The War Minister, the Czar, and the political parties seem to have played little role in strategic planning, leaving the intramilitary factions to logroll their own disputes.[60]

Perhaps the most important question is why the outcome of the logrolling was not to scale down the aims of both offensives to fit the diminished forces available to each. In particular, why did Danilov insist on an early-start, two-pincer advance into East Prussia, when the weakness of each pincer made them both vulnerable to piecemeal destruction? Why not wait a few days

---

59. *Documents diplomatiques français (1871–1914)*, Series 2, Vol. XII, p. 695, and other sources cited in Snyder, *Ideology of the Offensive*, chapter 7.
60. Norman Stone, *The Eastern Front, 1914–1917* (New York: Scribner's, 1975), chapter 1, presents some speculations about factional alignments, but evidence is inconclusive in this area.

until each pincer could be reinforced by late-arriving units, or why not advance only on one side of the lakes? The answer seems to lie in Danilov's extreme fears about the viability of the French and his consequent conviction that Russian survival depended on early and substantial pressure on the German rear. This task was a necessity, given his outlook, something that had to be attempted whether available forces were adequate or not. Trapped by his pessimism about Russia's prospects in the long run, Danilov's only way out was through unwarranted optimism about operational prospects in the short run. Like most cornered decision-makers, Danilov saw the "necessary" as possible.

This is an important theme in the German case as well. Schlieffen and the younger Moltke demonstrated an ability to be ruthlessly realistic about the shortcomings of their operational plans, but realism was suppressed when it would call into question their fundamental beliefs and values. Schlieffen's qualms about his war plan's feasibility pervade early drafts, but disappear later on, without analytical justification. He entertained doubts as long as he thought they would lead to improvements, but once he saw that no further tinkering would resolve the plan's remaining contradictions, he swept them under the rug. The younger Moltke did the same thing, resorting to blithe optimism only on make-or-break issues, like the seizure of Liège, where a realistic assessment of the risks would have spotlighted the dubiousness of *any* strategy for rapid, decisive victory. Rather than totally rethink their strategic assumptions, which were all bound up with fundamental interests and even personal characteristics, all of these strategists chose to see the "necessary" as possible.[61]

Two hypotheses emerge from the Russian case. The first points to bureaucratic logrolling as a factor that is likely to exacerbate the normal offensive bias of military organizations. In the absence of a powerful central authority, two factions or suborganizations will each pursue its own preferred offensive despite a dramatic deficit of available forces. Thus, offensives that are moderately ambitious when considered separately become extremely overcommitted under the pressure of scarce resources and the need to logroll with

---

61. Groener, writing in the journal *Wissen und Wehr* in 1927, p. 532, admitted that it had been mere "luck" that an "extremely important" tunnel east of Liège was captured intact by the Germans in August 1914. Ritter, *Schlieffen Plan*, p. 166, documents Moltke's uncharacteristic optimism about quickly seizing Liège and avoiding the development of a monumental logistical bottleneck there. In the event, the Belgians actually ordered the destruction of their bridges and rail net, but the orders were not implemented systematically.

other factions competing for their allocation. The German case showed how the lack of civilian control can produce doctrinal extremism when the military is united; the Russian case shows how lack of civilian control can also lead to extreme offensives when the military is divided.

The second hypothesis, which is supported by the findings of cognitive theory, is that military decision-makers will tend to overestimate the feasibility of an operational plan if a realistic assessment would require forsaking fundamental beliefs or values.[62] Whenever offensive doctrines are inextricably tied to the autonomy, "essence," or basic worldview of the military, the cognitive need to see the offensive as possible will be strong.

External Influences on Strategy and Civil-Military Relations

The offensive strategies of 1914 were largely domestic in origin, rooted in bureaucratic, sociopolitical, and psychological causes. To some extent, however, external influences exacerbated—and occasionally diminished—these offensive biases. Although these external factors were usually secondary, they are particularly interesting for their lessons about sources of leverage over the destabilizing policies of one's opponents. The most important of these lessons—and the one stressed by Van Evera elsewhere in this issue— is that offense tends to promote offense and defense tends to promote defense in the international system.

One way that offense was exported from one state to another was by means of military writings. The French discovered Clausewitz in the 1880s, reading misinterpretations of him by contemporary German militarists who focused narrowly on his concept of the "decisive battle." At the same time, reading the retrograde Russian tactician Dragomirov reinforced their home-grown overemphasis on the connection between the offensive and morale. Russian writings later reimported these ideas under the label of *offensive à outrance*, while borrowing from Germany the short-war doctrine. Each of Europe's militaries cited the others in parroting the standard lessons drawn from the Russo–Japanese War: offense was becoming tactically more difficult but was still advantageous strategically. None of this shuffling and sharing of rationales for offense was the initial cause of anyone's offensive bias. Everyone was exporting offense to everyone else; no one was just receiving.

---

62. Irving Janis and Leon Mann, *Decision Making* (New York: Free Press, 1977).

Its main effect was mutual reinforcement. The military could believe (and argue to others) that offense must be advantageous, since everyone else said so, and that the prevalence of offensive doctrines was somebody else's fault.[63]

The main vehicle for exporting offensive strategies was through aggressive policies, not offensive ideas. The aggressive diplomacy and offensive war plans of one state frequently encouraged offensive strategies in neighboring states both directly, by changing their strategic situation, and indirectly, by changing their pattern of civil-military relations. German belligerence in the Agadir crisis of 1911 led French civilians to conclude that war was likely and that they had better start appeasing their own military by giving them leaders in which they would have confidence. This led directly to Michel's fall and the rise of Joffre, Castelnau, and the proponents of the *offensive à outrance*. German belligerence in the Bosnian crisis of 1908–1909 had a similar, if less direct effect on Russia. It convinced Alekseev that a limited war against Austria alone would be impossible, and it put everyone in a receptive mood when the French urged the tightening of the alliance in 1911.[64] Before Bosnia, people sometimes thought in terms of a strategic modus vivendi with Germany; afterwards, they thought in terms of a breathing spell while gaining strength for the final confrontation. Combined with the Russians' growing realization of the probable character of the German war plan, this led inexorably to the conclusions that war was coming, that it could not be limited, and that an unbridled offensive was required to exploit the window of opportunity provided by the Schlieffen Plan's westward orientation. Caught in this logic, Russian civilians who sought limited options in July 1914 were easily refuted by Danilov and the military. Completing the spiral, the huge Russian arms increases provoked by German belligerence allowed the younger Moltke to argue persuasively that Germany should seek a pretext for preventive war before those increases reached fruition in 1917. This recommendation was persuasive only in the context of the Schlieffen Plan, which made Germany look weaker than it really was by creating needless enemies and wasting troops on an impossible task. Without the Schlieffen Plan, Germany would not have been vulnerable in 1917.

In short, the European militaries cannot be blamed for the belligerent diplomacy that set the ball rolling towards World War I. Once the process began, however, their penchant for offense and their quickness to view war

---

63. Snyder, *Ideology of the Offensive*, chapters 2 and 3.
64. Ibid., chapter 7, citing Zaionchkovskii, pp. 103, 350, and other sources.

as inevitable created a slide towards war that the diplomats did not foresee.[65] The best place to intervene to stop the destabilizing spiral of exported offense was, of course, at the beginning. If German statesmen had had a theory of civil-military relations and of the security dilemma to help them calculate risks more accurately, their choice of a diplomatic strategy might have been different.

If offense gets exported when states adopt aggressive policies, it also gets exported when states try to defend themselves in ways that are indistinguishable from preparations for aggression.[66] In the 1880s, the Russians improved their railroads in Poland and increased the number of troops there in peacetime, primarily in order to decrease their vulnerability to German attack in the early weeks of a war. The German General Staff saw these measures as a sign that a Russian attack was imminent, so counseled launching a preventive strike before Russian preparations proceeded further. Bismarck thought otherwise, so the incident did not end in the same way as the superficially similar 1914 case. Several factors may account for the difference: Bismarck's greater power over the military, his lack of interest in expansion for its own sake, and the absence of political conditions that would make war seem inevitable to anyone but a General Staff officer. Perhaps the most important difference, however, was that in 1914 the younger Moltke was anticipating a future of extreme vulnerability, whereas in 1887 the elder Moltke was anticipating a future of strategic stalemate. Moltke, planning for a defense in the west in any event, believed that the Germans could in the worst case hold out for 30 years if France and Russia forced war upon them.[67]

Although states can provoke offensive responses by seeming too aggressive, they can also invite offensive predation by seeming too weak. German hopes for a rapid victory, whether expressed in the eastward plan of the 1880s or the westward Schlieffen Plan, always rested on the slowness of Russia's mobilization. Likewise, Germany's weakness on the eastern front, artificially created by the Schlieffen Plan, promoted the development of offensive plans in Russia. Finally, Belgian weakness allowed the Germans to

---

65. Isabel V. Hull, *The Entourage of Kaiser Wilhelm II, 1888–1918* (New York: Cambridge University Press, 1982), discusses the effect on the Kaiser of his military aides' incessant warnings that war was inevitable.
66. Robert Jervis, "Cooperation under the Security Dilemma," *World Politics*, Vol. 31, No. 2 (January 1978), pp. 199–210.
67. Barbara Tuchman, *The Guns of August* (1962; rpt., New York: Dell, 1971), p. 38; see also *Aufmarschpläne*, pp. 150–156, for Moltke's last war plan of February 1888.

retain their illusions about decisive victory by providing an apparent point of entry into the French keep.

States who want to export defense, then, should try to appear neither weak nor aggressive. The French achieved this in the early 1880s, when a force posture heavy on fortifications made them an unpromising target and an ineffective aggressor. In the short run, this only redirected Moltke's offensive toward a more vulnerable target, Russia. But by 1888–1890, when Russia too had strengthened its fortifications and its defensive posture in Poland generally, Moltke was stymied and became very pessimistic about offensive operations. Schlieffen, however, was harder to discourage. When attacking Russia became unpromising, he simply redirected his attention towards France, pursuing the least unpromising offensive option. For hard core cases like Schlieffen, one wonders whether any strategy of non-provocative defense, no matter how effective and non-threatening, could induce abandoning the offensive.

Soviet Strategy and Civil-Military Relations

In 1914, flawed civil-military relations exacerbated and liberated the military's endemic bias for offensive strategies, creating strategic instability despite military technologies that aided the defender of the status quo. Some of the factors that produced this outcome may have been peculiar to that historical epoch. The full professionalization of military staffs had been a relatively recent development, for example, and both civilians and military were still groping for a satisfactory *modus vivendi*. After the First World War, military purveyors of the "cult of the offensive" were fairly well chastened except in Japan, where the phenomenon was recapitulated. Our own era has seen nothing this extreme, but more moderate versions of the military's offensive bias are arguably still with us. It will be worthwhile, therefore, to reiterate the kinds of conditions that have intensified this bias in the past in order to assess the likelihood of their recurrence.

First, offensive bias is exacerbated when civilian control is weak. In Germany before 1914, a long period of military autonomy in strategic planning allowed the dogmatization of an offensive doctrine, rooted in the parochial interests and outlook of the General Staff. In Russia, the absence of firm, unified civilian control fostered logrolling between two military factions, compounding the offensive preferences exhibited by each. Second, offensive bias grows more extreme when operational doctrine is used as a weapon in civil-military disputes about domestic politics, institutional arrangements, or other nonstrategic issues. The French *offensive à outrance*, often dismissed as some mystical aberration, is best explained in these terms.

Once it appears, an acute offensive bias tends to be self-replicating and resistant to disconfirming evidence. Offensive doctrinal writings are readily transmitted across international boundaries. More important, offensive strategies tend to spread in a chain reaction, since one state's offensive tends to create impending dangers or fleeting opportunities for other states, who must adopt their own offensives to forestall or exploit them. Finally, hard operational evidence of the infeasibility of an offensive strategy will be rationalized away when the offensive is closely linked to the organization's "essence," autonomy, or fundamental ideology.

I believe that these findings, derived from the World War I cases, resonate strongly with the development of Soviet nuclear strategy and with certain patterns in the U.S.–Soviet strategic relationship. At a time when current events are stimulating considerable interest in the state of civil-military relations in the Soviet Union, the following thoughts are offered not as answers but as questions that researchers may find worth considering.

Soviet military doctrine, as depicted by conventional wisdom, embodies all of the desiderata typically expressed in professional military writings throughout the developed world since Napoleon. Like Schlieffen's doctrine, it stresses offense, the initiative, and decisive results through the annihilation of the opponent's ability to resist. It is suspicious of political limitations on violence based on mutual restraint, especially in nuclear matters. Both in style and substance, Sidorenko reads like a throwback to the military writers of the Second Reich, warning that "a forest which has not been completely cut down grows up again."[68] The similarity is not accidental. Not only does offense serve some of the same institutional functions for the Soviet military as it did for the German General Staff, but Soviet doctrine is to some degree their lineal descendant. "In our military schools," a 1937 Pravda editorial averred, "we study Clausewitz, Moltke, Schlieffen, and Ludendorff."[69] Soviet nuclear doctrine also parallels pre-1914 German strategy in that both cut against the grain of the prevailing technology. The Soviets have never been

---

68. Quoted by Benjamin Lambeth, "Selective Nuclear Options and Soviet Strategy," in Johan Holst and Uwe Nerlich, *Beyond Nuclear Deterrence* (New York: Crane, Russak, 1977), p. 92.
69. Raymond Garthoff, *Soviet Military Doctrine* (Glencoe, Ill.: Free Press, 1953), p. 56.

in a position to achieve anything but disaster by seizing the initiative and striving for decisive results; neither was Schlieffen.

There are also parallels in the political and historical circumstances that permitted the development of these doctrines. The Soviet victories in World War II, like the German victories in 1866 and 1870, were nation-building and regime-legitimating enterprises that lent prestige and authority to the military profession, notwithstanding Stalin's attempt to check it. This did not produce a man on horseback in either country, nor did it allow the military to usurp authority on questions of the use of force. But in both cases the military retained a monopoly of military operational expertise and was either never challenged or eventually prevailed in practical doctrinal disputes. In the German case, at least, it was military autonomy on questions of operational plans and doctrine that made war more likely; direct lobbying for preventive strikes caused less trouble because it was clearly illegitimate.

While many accounts of the origins of Soviet nuclear strategy acknowledge the effect of the professional military perspective, they often lay more stress on civilian sources of offensive, warfighting doctrines: for example, Marxism–Leninism, expansionist foreign policy goals, and historical experiences making Russia a "militarized society." Political leaders, in this view, promote or at least accept the military's warfighting doctrine because it serves their foreign policy goals and/or reflects a shared view of international politics as a zero-sum struggle. Thus, Lenin is quoted as favoring a preemptive first strike, Frunze as linking offense to the proletarian spirit. The military principle of annihilation of the opposing armed force is equated with the Leninist credo of *kto kogo.*[70]

Although this view may capture part of the truth, it fails to account for recurrent statements by Soviet political leaders implying that nuclear war is unwinnable, that meaningful damage limitation cannot be achieved through superior warfighting capabilities, and that open-ended expenditures on strategic programs are wasteful and perhaps pointless. These themes have been voiced in the context of budgetary disputes (not just for public relations purposes) by Malenkov, Khrushchev, Brezhnev, and Ustinov. To varying degrees, all of these civilian leaders have chafed at the cost of open-ended warfighting programs and against the redundant offensive capabilities de-

---

70. Herbert Dinerstein, *War and the Soviet Union* (New York: Praeger, 1962), pp. 210–211; Garthoff, *Soviet Military Doctrine*, pp. 65, 149.

manded by each of several military suborganizations. McNamara discovered in the United States that the doctrine of mutual assured destruction, with its emphasis on the irrelevance of marginal advantages and the infeasibility of counterforce damage-limitation strategies, had great utility in budgetary debates. Likewise, recent discussions in the Soviet Union on the feasibility of victory seem to be connected with the question of how much is enough. Setting aside certain problems of nuance and interpretation, a case can be made that the civilian leadership, speaking through Defense Minister Ustinov, has been using strategic doctrine to justify slowing down the growth of military spending. In the context of arguments about whether the Reagan strategic buildup will really make the Soviet Union more vulnerable, Ustinov has quite clearly laid out the argument that neither superpower can expect to gain anything by striking first, since both have survivable retaliatory forces and launch-on-warning capabilities. Thus, Ustinov has been stressing that the importance of surprise is diminishing and that "preemptive nuclear strikes are alien to Soviet military doctrine." Ogarkov, the Chief of the General Staff, has been arguing the opposite on all counts: the U.S. buildup is truly threatening, the international scene is akin to the 1930s, the surprise factor is growing in importance, damage limitation is possible (though "victory" is problematic), and consequently the Soviet Union must spare no expense in preparing to defend itself.[71]

This is somewhat reminiscent of the French case in World War I, in which civilians and the military were using doctrinal arguments as weapons in disputes on other issues. Two related dangers arise in such situations. The first is that doctrinal argumentation and belief, responding to political and organizational necessity, lose their anchoring in strategic realities and become dogmatic and extremist. The second is that a spiral dynamic in the political dispute may carry doctrine along with it. That is, the harder each side fights to prevail on budgetary or organizational questions, the more absolute and unyielding their doctrinal justifications will become. In this regard, it would be interesting to see whether the periods in which Soviet military spokesmen

---

71. Citations to the main statements by Ogarkov and Ustinov can be found in Dan L. Strode and Rebecca V. Strode, "Diplomacy and Defense in Soviet National Security Policy," *International Security*, Vol. 8, No. 2 (Fall 1983), pp. 91–116. Quotation from William Garner, *Soviet Threat Perceptions of NATO's Eurostrategic Missiles* (Paris: Atlantic Institute for International Affairs, 1983), p. 69, citing *Pravda*, July 25, 1981. I have benefitted from discussions of the Ogarkov and Ustinov statements with Lawrence Caldwell, Stephen Coffey, Clifford Kupchan, and Cynthia Roberts, who advanced a variety of interpretations not necessarily similar to my own.

were arguing hardest that "victory is possible" coincided with periods of sharp budgetary disputes.

Even if some of the above is true, the pattern may be a weak one in comparison with the French case. Ustinov is more like Freycinet than André, and marginal budgetary issues do not carry the same emotional freight as the threats to organizational "essence" mounted in the Dreyfus aftermath. Still, if we consider that the Soviet case couples some of the autonomy problems of the German case with some of the motivational problems of the French case, a volatile mixture may be developing.

Another civil-military question is whether Soviet military doctrine is mismatched with Soviet diplomacy. On the surface, it may seem that the awe-inspiring Soviet military machine and its intimidating offensive doctrine are apt instruments for supporting a policy of diplomatic extortion. It may, however, pose the same problem for Soviet statesmen that the Schlieffen Plan did for Bülow and Bethmann. Soviet leaders may be self-deterred by the all-or-nothing character of their military options.[72] Alternatively, if the Soviets try to press ahead with a diplomacy based on the "Bolshevik operational code" principles of controlled pressure, limited probes, and controlled, calculated risks, they may find themselves trapped by military options that create risks which cannot be controlled.

These problems may not arise, however, since the Soviets seem to have turned away from Khrushchev's brinkmanship diplomacy. In the Brezhnev era, Soviet doctrine on the political utility of nuclear forces stressed its role as an umbrella deterring intervention against "progressive" political change.[73] Insofar as limited options and "salami tactics" are more clearly indispensable for compellent than for deterrent strategies, this would help to solve the Soviet diplomats' mismatch problem. The "last clear chance" to avoid disaster would be shifted onto the United States. This solution to the diplomats'

---

72. Increased Soviet attention to the "conventional option" since the late 1960s would seem to have mitigated this problem, but in fact it may have compounded it. Military interest in preparing for a conventional phase and acquiring capabilities for escalation dominance in the theater may derive more from obvious organizational motives than from a fundamental change in the military's mind-set of "inflexible over-response." In Soviet thinking, limitations seem to be based less on mutual restraint than on NATO's willingness to see its theater nuclear forces destroyed during the conventional phase. This raises the nightmarish possibility that the Soviet leadership could embark on war thinking that it had a conventional option, whereas in fact unrestrained conventional operations and preemptive incentives at the theater nuclear level would lead to rapid escalation.

73. Coit Blacker, "The Kremlin and Detente: Soviet Conceptions, Hopes, and Expectations," in Alexander George, ed., *Managing U.S.–Soviet Rivalry* (Boulder: Westview, 1983), pp. 122–123.

problem might cause problems for the military's budget rationale, however, since strategic parity should be sufficient to carry out a strictly deterrent function.

The German case suggests that extremism in strategic thinking may depend a great deal on institutionalization and dogmatization of doctrine in the mature military organization. If Roman Kolkowicz's "traditionalists" are equated with the Moltke generation and his "modernist" technocrats with the Schlieffen generation, do we find a parallel in the dogmatization of doctrine? Benjamin Lambeth argues that Soviet doctrine is quite flexible and creative, but so was Schlieffen on questions of how to implement his strategic tenets under changing conditions.[74] Creativity within the paradigm of decisive, offensive operations may coexist with utter rigidity towards options that would require a change in the basic paradigm. For example, the Soviet ground forces adapted creatively to improvements in precision-guided munitions (PGMs) that seemed to threaten the viability of their offensive doctrine; they did not consider, however, that PGMs might offer an opportunity to give up their fundamentally offensive orientation. As for the third phase of organizational evolution, are there any parallels to Ludendorff or Groener among younger Soviet officers? Are they forging links to Russian nationalists, whose social base Alexander Yanov describes in ways that are strongly reminiscent of Eley's account of the ultranationalist German right?[75]

Any discussion of the extremist potential of Soviet strategy must consider the strong reality constraint imposed by the mutual-assured-destruction relationship. Despite the reckless rhetoric of some junior officers, it seems clear that when the head of the Strategic Rocket Forces said in 1967 that "a sudden preemptive strike cannot give [the aggressor] a decisive advantage," he knew that launch-on-warning and the hardening of silos made this true for both sides.[76] And today Ogarkov does not deny that a scot-free victory is impossible. But despite this, the theme of damage limitation remains strong in Soviet military thinking, and we should remember those World War I strategists who saw the "necessary" as possible, no matter how realistically they did their operational calculations.

---

74. Lambeth, "Selective Nuclear Options"; Kolkowicz, The Soviet Military and the Communist Party (Princeton: Princeton University Press, 1967).
75. Alexander Yanov, Detente after Brezhnev (Berkeley: Institute of International Studies, University of California, 1977).
76. Garner, Soviet Threat Perceptions, p. 69.

Finally, how have the policies of the United States affected the development of civil-military relations and strategic doctrine in the U.S.S.R.? Some analysts argue that the Ogarkov–Ustinov debates ended in May 1983 with Ustinov's capitulation, at least on the level of rhetoric. Although leadership politics may have been a factor, a more important reason may have been the Reagan "Star Wars" speech and the Reagan defense program generally.[77] Echoing the developments in France in 1911, rising levels of external threat may have helped the military to win the doctrinal argument and achieve its institutional aims in the underlying issues tied to the doctrinal dispute. This episode may also be seen as the latest round of a process of exporting and re-importing warfighting strategies. The impact of Soviet counterforce doctrines on the American strategic debate in the 1970s is obvious; now the fruits of our conversion are perhaps being harvested by Ogarkov in Soviet debates on military budgets and operational policies.

Whatever the precise reality of current civil-military relations in the Soviet Union, patterns revealed by the World War I cases suggest that the Soviet Union manifests several "risk factors" that could produce an extreme variant of the military's endemic offensive bias. The historical parallel further suggests that the actions of rival states can play an important role in determining how these latent risks unfold. Aggressive policies were liable to touch off these latent dangers, but vulnerability also tended to encourage the opponent to adopt an offensive strategy. Postures that were both invulnerable and non-provocative got the best results, but even these did not always dissuade dogmatic adherents to the "cult of the offensive." Although Soviet persistence in working the problems of conventional and nuclear offensives does recall the dogged single-mindedness of a Schlieffen, nuclear weapons pose a powerful reality constraint for which no true counterpart existed in 1914. Consequently, if the twin dangers of provocation and vulnerability are avoided, there should be every hope of keeping Soviet "risk factors" under control. The current drift of the strategic competition, however, makes that not a small "if. "

---

77. Setting these debates into the context of U.S.–Soviet relations are Lawrence T. Caldwell and Robert Legvold, "Reagan Through Soviet Eyes," *Foreign Policy*, No. 52 (Fall 1983), pp. 3–21.

The Cult of the Offensive and the Origins of the First World War

Stephen Van Evera

During the decades before the First World War a phenomenon which may be called a "cult of the offensive" swept through Europe. Militaries glorified the offensive and adopted offensive military doctrines, while civilian elites and publics assumed that the offense had the advantage in warfare, and that offensive solutions to security problems were the most effective.

This article will argue that the cult of the offensive was a principal cause of the First World War, creating or magnifying many of the dangers which historians blame for causing the July crisis and rendering it uncontrollable. The following section will first outline the growth of the cult of the offensive in Europe in the years before the war, and then sketch the consequences which international relations theory suggests should follow from it. The second section will outline consequences which the cult produced in 1914, and the final section will suggest conclusions and implications for current American policy.

The Cult of the Offensive and International Relations Theory

THE GROWTH OF THE CULT

The gulf between myth and the realities of warfare has never been greater than in the years before World War I. Despite the large and growing advantage which defenders gained against attackers as a result of the invention of rifled and repeating small arms, the machine gun, barbed wire, and the development of railroads, Europeans increasingly believed that attackers would hold the advantage on the battlefield, and that wars would be short and "decisive"—a "brief storm," in the words of the German Chancellor,

I would like to thank Jack Snyder, Richard Ned Lebow, Barry Posen, Marc Trachtenberg, and Stephen Walt for their thoughtful comments on earlier drafts of this paper.

Stephen Van Evera is a Research Fellow at the Center for Science and International Affairs, Harvard University.

International Security, Summer 1984 (Vol. 9, No. 1) 0162-2889/84/010058-50 $02.50/1

Bethmann Hollweg.[1] They largely overlooked the lessons of the American Civil War, the Russo–Turkish War of 1877–78, the Boer War, and the Russo–Japanese War, which had demonstrated the power of the new defensive technologies. Instead, Europeans embraced a set of political and military myths which obscured both the defender's advantages and the obstacles an aggressor would confront. This mindset helped to mold the offensive military doctrines which every European power adopted during the period 1892–1913.[2]

In Germany, the military glorified the offense in strident terms, and inculcated German society with similar views. General Alfred von Schlieffen, author of the 1914 German war plan, declared that "Attack is the best defense," while the popular publicist Friedrich von Bernhardi proclaimed that "the offensive mode of action is by far superior to the defensive mode," and that "the superiority of offensive warfare under modern conditions is greater than formerly."[3] German Chief of Staff General Helmuth von Moltke also endorsed "the principle that the offensive is the best defense," while General August von Keim, founder of the Army League, argued that "Germany ought to be armed for attack," since "the offensive is the only way of insuring victory."[4] These assumptions guided the Schlieffen Plan, which envisaged rapid and decisive attacks on Belgium, France, and Russia.

---

1. Quoted in L.L. Farrar, Jr., "The Short War Illusion: The Syndrome of German Strategy, August–December 1914," *Militaergeschictliche Mitteilungen*, No. 2 (1972), p. 40.
2. On the origins of the cult of the offensive, see Jack Lewis Snyder, "Defending the Offensive: Biases in French, German, and Russian War Planning, 1870–1914" (Ph.D. dissertation, Columbia University, 1981), forthcoming as a book from Cornell University Press in 1984; Snyder's essay in this issue; and my "Causes of War" (Ph.D. dissertation, University of California, Berkeley, 1984), chapter 7. On the failure of Europeans to learn defensive lessons from the wars of 1860–1914, see Jay Luvaas, *The Military Legacy of the Civil War: The European Inheritance* (Chicago: University of Chicago Press, 1959); and T.H.E. Travers, "Technology, Tactics, and Morale: Jean de Bloch, the Boer War, and British Military Theory, 1900–1914," *Journal of Modern History*, Vol. 51 (June 1979), pp. 264–286. Also relevant is Bernard Brodie, *Strategy in the Missile Age* (Princeton: Princeton University Press, 1965), pp. 42–52.
    A related work which explores the sources of offensive and defensive doctrines before World War II is Barry R. Posen, *The Sources of Military Doctrine: France, Britain, and Germany Between the World Wars* (Ithaca: Cornell University Press, 1984), pp. 47–51, 67–74, and passim.
3. Gerhard Ritter, *The Schlieffen Plan: Critique of a Myth*, trans. Andrew and Eva Wilson, with a Foreword by B.H. Liddell Hart (London: Oswald Wolff, 1958; reprint ed., Westport, Conn.: Greenwood Press, 1979), p. 100; and Friedrich von Bernhardi, *How Germany Makes War* (New York: George H. Doran Co., 1914), pp. 153, 155.
4. Imanuel Geiss, ed., *July 1914: The Outbreak of the First World War: Selected Documents* (New York: W.W. Norton, 1967), p. 357; and Wallace Notestein and Elmer E. Stoll, eds., *Conquest and Kultur: Aims of the Germans in Their Own Words* (Washington, D.C.: U.S. Government Printing Office, 1917), p. 43. Similar ideas developed in the German navy; see Holger H. Herwig, *Politics*

In France, the army became "Obsessed with the virtues of the offensive," in the words of B.H. Liddell Hart, an obsession which also spread to French civilians.[5] The French army, declared Chief of Staff Joffre, "no longer knows any other law than the offensive. . . . Any other conception ought to be rejected as contrary to the very nature of war,"[6] while the President of the French Republic, Clément Fallières, announced that "The offensive alone is suited to the temperament of French soldiers. . . . We are determined to march straight against the enemy without hesitation."[7] Emile Driant, a member of the French chamber of deputies, summarized the common view: "The first great battle will decide the whole war, and wars will be short. The idea of the offense must penetrate the spirit of our nation."[8] French military doctrine reflected these offensive biases.[9] In Marshall Foch's words, the French army adopted "a single formula for success, a single combat doctrine, namely, the decisive power of offensive action undertaken with the resolute determination to march on the enemy, reach and destroy him."[10]

Other European states displayed milder symptoms of the same virus. The British military resolutely rejected defensive strategies despite their experience in the Boer War which demonstrated the power of entrenched defenders against exposed attackers. General W.G. Knox wrote, "The defensive is never an acceptable role to the Briton, and he makes little or no study of it," and General R.C.B. Haking argued that the offensive "will win as sure as there is a sun in the heavens."[11] The Russian Minister of War, General V.A. Sukhomlinov, observed that Russia's enemies were directing their armies "towards guaranteeing the possibility of dealing rapid and decisive blows.

of Frustration: The United States in German Naval Planning, 1889–1941 (Boston: Little, Brown & Co., 1976), pp. 42–66.

5. B.H. Liddell Hart, *Through the Fog of War* (New York: Random House, 1938), p. 57.

6. In 1912, quoted in John Ellis, *The Social History of the Machine Gun* (New York: Pantheon, 1975), pp. 53–54.

7. Barbara Tuchman, *The Guns of August* (New York: Dell, 1962), p. 51.

8. In 1912, quoted in John M. Cairns, "International Politics and the Military Mind: The Case of the French Republic, 1911–1914," *The Journal of Modern History*, Vol. 25, No. 3 (September 1953), p. 282.

9. On the offensive in French prewar thought, see B.H. Liddell Hart, "French Military Ideas before the First World War," in Martin Gilbert, ed., *A Century of Conflict, 1850–1950* (London: Hamilton Hamish, 1966), pp. 135–148.

10. Richard D. Challener, *The French Theory of the Nation in Arms, 1866–1939* (New York: Columbia University Press, 1955), p. 81. Likewise, Joffre later explained that Plan XVII, his battle plan for 1914, was less a plan for battle than merely a plan of "concentration. . . . I adopted no preconceived idea, other than a full determination to take the offensive with all my forces assembled." Theodore Ropp, *War in the Modern World*, rev. ed. (New York: Collier, 1962), p. 229.

11. In 1913 and 1914, quoted in Travers, "Technology, Tactics, and Morale," p. 275.

. . . We also must follow this example."[12] Even in Belgium the offensive found proponents: under the influence of French ideas, some Belgian officers favored an offensive strategy, proposing the remarkable argument that "To ensure against our being ignored it was essential that we should attack," and declaring that "We must hit them where it hurts."[13]

Mythical or mystical arguments obscured the technical dominion of the defense, giving this faith in the offense aspects of a cult, or a mystique, as Marshall Joffre remarked in his memoirs.[14] For instance, Foch mistakenly argued that the machine gun actually strengthened the offense: "Any improvement of firearms is ultimately bound to add strength to the offensive. . . . Nothing is easier than to give a mathematical demonstration of that truth." If two thousand men attacked one thousand, each man in both groups firing his rifle once a minute, he explained, the "balance in favor of the attack" was one thousand bullets per minute. But if both sides could fire ten times per minute, the "balance in favor of the attacker" would increase to ten thousand, giving the attack the overall advantage.[15] With equally forced logic, Bernhardi wrote that the larger the army the longer defensive measures would take to execute, owing to "the difficulty of moving masses"; hence, he argued, as armies grew, so would the relative power of the offense.[16]

British and French officers suggested that superior morale on the attacking side could overcome superior defensive firepower, and that this superiority in morale could be achieved simply by assuming the role of attacker, since offense was a morale-building activity. One French officer contended that "the offensive doubles the energy of the troops" and "concentrates the thoughts of the commander on a single objective,"[17] while British officers declared that "Modern [war] conditions have enormously increased the value of moral quality," and "the moral attributes [are] the primary causes of all great success."[18] In short, mind would prevail over matter; morale would triumph over machine guns.

---

12. In 1909, quoted in D.C.B. Lieven, *Russia and the Origins of the First World War* (New York: St. Martin's Press, 1983), p. 113.
13. See Tuchman, *Guns of August*, pp. 127–131.
14. Marshall Joffre, *Mémoires du Maréchel Joffre* (Paris: Librarie Plon, 1932), p. 33. Joffre speaks of "le culte de l'offensive" and "d'une 'mystique de l'offensive'" of "le caractère un peu irraisonné."
15. Ropp, *War in the Modern World*, p. 218.
16. Ibid., p. 203. See also Bernhardi, *How Germany Makes War*, p. 154.
17. Captain Georges Gilbert, quoted in Snyder, "Defending the Offensive," pp. 80–81.
18. The *Field Service Regulations* of 1909 and Colonel Kiggell, quoted in Travers, "Technology, Tactics, and Morale," pp. 273, 276–277.
Even when European officers recognized the new tactical power of the defense, they often

Europeans also tended to discount the power of political factors which would favor defenders. Many Germans believed that "bandwagoning" with a powerful state rather than "balancing" against it was the guiding principle in international alliance-formation.[19] Aggressors would gather momentum as they gained power, because opponents would be intimidated into acquiescence and neutrals would rally to the stronger side. Such thinking led German Chancellor Bethmann Hollweg to hope that "Germany's growing strength . . . might force England to realize that [the balance of power] principle had become untenable and impracticable and to opt for a peaceful settlement with Germany,"[20] and German Secretary of State Gottlieb von Jagow to forecast British neutrality in a future European war: "We have not built our fleet in vain," and "people in England will seriously ask themselves whether it will be just that simple and without danger to play the role of France's guardian angel against us."[21] German leaders also thought they might frighten Belgium into surrender: during the July crisis Moltke was "counting on the possibility of being able to come to an understanding [with Belgium] when the Belgian Government realizes the seriousness of the situation."[22] This ill-founded belief in bandwagoning reinforced the general belief that conquest was relatively easy.

The belief in easy conquest eventually pervaded public images of international politics, manifesting itself most prominently in the widespread application of Darwinist notions to international affairs. In this image, states competed in a decisive struggle for survival which weeded out the weak and ended in the triumph of stronger states and races—an image which assumed a powerful offense. "In the struggle between nationalities," wrote former

---

resisted the conclusion that the defender would also hold the strategic advantage. Thus Bernhardi wrote that while "the defense as a form of fighting is stronger than the attack," it remained true that "in the conduct of war as a whole the offensive mode of action is by far superior to the defensive mode, especially under modern conditions." Bernhardi, *How Germany Makes War*, p. 155. See also Snyder, "Defending the Offensive," pp. 152–154, 253–254; and Travers, "Technology, Tactics, and Morale," passim.

19. On these concepts, see Kenneth N. Waltz, *Theory of International Politics* (Reading, Mass.: Addison–Wesley, 1979), pp. 125–127; and Stephen M. Walt, "The Origins of Alliances" (Ph.D. dissertation, University of California, Berkeley, 1983).

20. December 2, 1914, quoted in Fritz Fischer, *War of Illusions: German Policies from 1911 to 1914*, trans. Marian Jackson, with a Foreword by Alan Bullock (New York: W.W. Norton, 1975), p. 69.

21. February 1914, quoted in Geiss, *July 1914*, p. 25. For more examples, see Fischer, *War of Illusions*, pp. 133, 227; and Wayne C. Thompson, *In the Eye of the Storm: Kurt Riezler and the Crises of Modern Germany* (Iowa City: University of Iowa Press, 1980), p. 120.

22. August 3, quoted in Bernadotte E. Schmitt, *The Coming of the War: 1914*, 2 vols. (New York: Charles Scribner's Sons, 1930), Vol. 2, p. 390n.

German Chancellor Bernhard von Bülow, "one nation is the hammer and the other the anvil; one is the victor and the other the vanquished. . . . it is a law of life and development in history that where two national civilisations meet they fight for ascendancy."[23] A writer in the London *Saturday Review* portrayed the Anglo–German competition as "the first great racial struggle of the future: here are two growing nations pressing against each other . . . all over the world. One or the other has to go; one or the other will go."[24] This Darwinist foreign policy thought reflected and rested upon the implicit assumption that the offense was strong, since "grow or die" dynamics would be impeded in a defense-dominant world where growth could be stopped and death prevented by self-defense.

CONSEQUENCES OF OFFENSE-DOMINANCE

Recent theoretical writing in international relations emphasizes the dangers that arise when the offense is strong relative to the defense.[25] If the theory outlined in these writings is valid, it follows that the cult of the offensive was a reason for the outbreak of the war.

Five major dangers relevant to the 1914 case may develop when the offense is strong, according to this recent writing. First, states adopt more aggressive

---

23. Prince Bernhard von Bülow, *Imperial Germany*, trans. Marie A. Lewenz (New York: Dodd, Mead & Co., 1915), p. 291. On international social Darwinism, see also H.W. Koch, "Social Imperialism as a Factor in the 'New Imperialism,'" in H.W. Koch, ed., *The Origins of the First World War* (London: Macmillan, 1972), pp. 329–354.

24. Joachim Remak, *The Origins of World War I, 1871–1914* (Hinsdale, Ill.: Dryden Press, 1967), p. 85. Likewise the British Colonial Secretary, Joseph Chamberlain, declared that "the tendency of the time is to throw all power into the hands of the greater empires," while the "minor kingdoms" seemed "destined to fall into a secondary and subordinate place. . . ." In 1897, quoted in Fischer, *War of Illusions*, p. 35.

25. See Robert Jervis's pathbreaking article, "Cooperation under the Security Dilemma," *World Politics*, Vol. 30, No. 2 (January 1978), pp. 167–214; and Chapter 3 of my "Causes of War." Also relevant are George H. Quester, *Offense and Defense in the International System* (New York: John Wiley & Sons, 1977); John Herz, "Idealist Internationalism and the Security Dilemma," *World Politics*, Vol. 2, No. 2 (January 1950), pp. 157, 163; and Herbert Butterfield, *History and Human Relations* (London: Collins, 1950), pp. 19–20. Applications and elaborations include: Shai Feldman, *Israeli Nuclear Deterrence* (New York: Columbia University Press, 1982); idem, "Superpower Security Guarantees in the 1980's," in *Third World Conflict and International Security, Part II*, Adelphi Paper No. 167 (London: International Institute for Strategic Studies, 1981), pp. 34–44; Barry R. Posen, "Inadvertent Nuclear War? Escalation and NATO's Northern Flank," *International Security*, Vol. 7, No. 2 (Fall 1982), pp. 28–54; Jack Lewis Snyder, "Perceptions of the Security Dilemma in 1914," in Robert Jervis and Richard Ned Lebow, eds., *Perceptions and Deterrence*, forthcoming in 1985; and Kenneth N. Waltz, *The Spread of Nuclear Weapons: More May Be Better*, Adelphi Paper No. 171 (London: International Institute for Strategic Studies, 1981). Of related interest is John J. Mearsheimer, *Conventional Deterrence* (Ithaca: Cornell University Press, 1983).

foreign policies, both to exploit new opportunities and to avert new dangers which appear when the offense is strong. Expansion is more tempting, because the cost of aggression declines when the offense has the advantage. States are also driven to expand by the need to control assets and create the conditions they require to secure themselves against aggressors, because security becomes a scarcer asset. Alliances widen and tighten as states grow more dependent on one another for security, a circumstance which fosters the spreading of local conflicts. Moreover, each state is more likely to be menaced by aggressive neighbors who are governed by the same logic, creating an even more competitive atmosphere and giving states further reason to seek security in alliances and expansion.

– Second, the size of the advantage accruing to the side mobilizing or striking first increases, raising the risk of preemptive war.[26] When the offense is strong, smaller shifts in ratios of forces between states create greater shifts in their relative capacity to conquer territory. As a result states have greater incentive to mobilize first or strike first, if they can change the force ratio in their favor by doing so. This incentive leads states to mobilize or attack to

---

26. In a "preemptive" war, either side gains by moving first; hence, one side moves to exploit the advantage of moving first, or to prevent the other side from doing so. By contrast, in a "preventive" war, one side foresees an adverse shift in the balance of power, and attacks to avoid a more difficult fight later.

"Moving first" in a preemptive war can consist of striking first *or mobilizing* first, if mobilization sets in train events which cause war, as in 1914. Thus a war is preemptive if statesmen attack because they believe that it pays to strike first; or if they mobilize because they believe that it pays to mobilize first, even if they do not also believe that it pays to strike first, if mobilizations open "windows" which spur attacks for "preventive" reasons, or if they produce other effects which cause war. Under such circumstances war is caused by preemptive actions which are not acts of war, but which are their equivalent since they produce conditions which cause war.

A preemptive war could also involve an attack by one side and mobilization by the other—for instance, one side might mobilize to forestall an attack, or might attack to forestall a mobilization, as the Germans apparently attacked Liège to forestall Belgian preparations to defend it (see below). Thus four classes of preemption are possible: an attack to forestall an attack, an attack to forestall a mobilization, a mobilization to forestall an attack, or a mobilization to forestall a mobilization (such as the Russian mobilizations in 1914).

The size of the incentive to preempt is a function of three factors: the degree of secrecy with which each side could mobilize its forces or mount an attack; the change in the ratio of forces which a secret mobilization or attack would produce; and the size and value of the additional territory which this changed ratio would allow the attacker to conquer or defend. If secret action is impossible, or if it would not change force ratios in favor of the side moving first, or if changes in force ratios would not change relative ability to conquer territory, then there is no first-strike or first-mobilization advantage. Otherwise, states have some inducement to move first.

On preemption, see Thomas C. Schelling, *Arms and Influence* (New Haven: Yale University Press, 1966), pp. 221–259; and idem, *Strategy of Conflict* (New York: Oxford University Press, 1963), pp. 207–254.

seize the initiative or deny it to adversaries, and to conceal plans, demands, and grievances to avoid setting off such a strike by their enemies, with deleterious effects on diplomacy.

Third, "windows" of opportunity and vulnerability open wider, forcing faster diplomacy and raising the risk of preventive war. Since smaller shifts in force ratios have larger effects on relative capacity to conquer territory, smaller prospective shifts in force ratios cause greater hope and alarm, open bigger windows of opportunity and vulnerability, and enhance the attractiveness of exploiting a window by launching a preventive attack.

Fourth, states adopt more competitive styles of diplomacy—brinkmanship and presenting opponents with *faits accomplis*, for instance—since the gains promised by such tactics can more easily justify the risks they entail. At the same time, however, the risks of adopting such strategies also increase, because they tend to threaten the vital interests of other states more directly. Because the security of states is more precarious and more tightly interdependent, threatening actions force stronger and faster reactions, and the political ripple effects of *faits accomplis* are larger and harder to control.

Fifth, states enforce tighter political and military secrecy, since national security is threatened more directly if enemies win the contest for information. As with all security assets, the marginal utility of information is magnified when the offense is strong; hence states compete harder to gain the advantage and avoid the disadvantage of disclosure, leading states to conceal their political and military planning and decision-making more carefully.

The following section suggests that many of the proximate causes of the war of 1914 represent various guises of these consequences of offense-dominance: either they were generated or exacerbated by the assumption that the offense was strong, or their effects were rendered more dangerous by this assumption. These causes include: German and Austrian expansionism; the belief that the side which mobilized or struck first would have the advantage; the German and Austrian belief that they faced "windows of vulnerability"; the nature and inflexibility of the Russian and German war plans and the tight nature of the European alliance system, both of which spread the war from the Balkans to the rest of Europe; the imperative that "mobilization meant war" for Germany; the failure of Britain to take effective measures to deter Germany; the uncommon number of blunders and mistakes committed by statesmen during the July crisis; and the ability of the Central powers to evade blame for the war. Without the cult of the offensive these problems probably would have been less acute, and their effects would have posed smaller risks. Thus the cult of the offensive was a mainspring driving many of the mechanisms which brought about the First World War.

The Cult of the Offensive and the Causes of the War

GERMAN EXPANSION AND ENTENTE RESISTANCE

Before 1914 Germany sought a wider sphere of influence or empire, and the war grew largely from the political collision between expansionist Germany and a resistant Europe. Germans differed on whether their empire should be formal or informal, whether they should seek it in Europe or overseas, and whether they should try to acquire it peacefully or by violence, but a broad consensus favored expansion of some kind. The logic behind this expansionism, in turn, rested on two widespread beliefs which reflected the cult of the offensive: first, that German security required a wider empire; and second, that such an empire was readily attainable, either by coercion or conquest. Thus German expansionism reflected the assumption that conquest would be easy both for Germany and for its enemies.

Prewar statements by German leaders and intellectuals reflected a pervasive belief that German independence was threatened unless Germany won changes in the status quo. Kaiser Wilhelm foresaw a "battle of Germans against the Russo–Gauls for their very existence," which would decide "the existence or non-existence of the Germanic race in Europe,"[27] declaring: "The question for Germany is to be or not to be."[28] His Chancellor, Bethmann Hollweg, wondered aloud if there were any purpose in planting new trees at his estate at Hohenfinow, near Berlin, since "in a few years the Russians would be here anyway."[29] The historian Heinrich von Treitschke forecast that "in the long run the small states of central Europe can not maintain themselves,"[30] while other Germans warned, "If Germany does not rule the world . . . it will disappear from the map; it is a question of either or," and "Germany will be a world power or nothing."[31] Similarly, German military officers predicted that "without colonial possessions [Germany] will suffocate in her small territory or else will be crushed by the great world powers" and

27. In 1912, quoted in Thompson, *Eye of the Storm*, p. 42.
28. In 1912, quoted in Fischer, *War of Illusions*, p. 161.
29. V.R. Berghahn, *Germany and the Approach of War in 1914* (London: Macmillan, 1973), p. 186.
30. In 1897, quoted in Notestein and Stoll, *Conquest and Kultur*, p. 21.
31. Houston Chamberlain and Ernest Hasse, quoted in Fischer, *War of Illusions*, pp. 30, 36.

foresaw a "supreme struggle, in which the existence of Germany will be at stake. . . ."[32]

Germans also widely believed that expansion could solve their insecurity: "Room; they must make room. The western and southern Slavs—or we! . . . Only by growth can a people save itself."[33] German expansionists complained that German borders were constricted and indefensible, picturing a Germany "badly protected by its unfavorable geographic frontiers. . . ."[34] Expansion was the suggested remedy: "Our frontiers are too narrow. We must become land-hungry, must acquire new regions for settlement. . . ."[35] Expanded borders would provide more defensible frontiers and new areas for settlement and economic growth, which in turn would strengthen the German race against its competitors: "the continental expansion of German territory [and] the multiplication on the continent of the German peasantry . . . would form a sure barrier against the advance of our enemies. . . ."[36] Such utterances came chiefly from the hawkish end of the German political spectrum, but they reflected widely held assumptions.

Many Germans also failed to see the military and political obstacles to expansion. The Kaiser told departing troops in early August, "You will be home before the leaves have fallen from the trees,"[37] and one of his generals predicted that the German army would sweep through Europe like a bus full of tourists: "In two weeks we shall defeat France, then we shall turn round, defeat Russia and then we shall march to the Balkans and establish order there."[38] During the July crisis a British observer noted the mood of "supreme confidence" in Berlin military circles, and a German observer reported that the German General Staff "looks ahead to war with France with great confidence, expects to defeat France within four weeks. . . ."[39] While some

---

32. *Nauticus*, in 1900, quoted in Berghahn, *Germany and the Approach of War in 1914*, p. 29; and Colmar von der Goltz, quoted in Notestein and Stoll, *Conquest and Kultur*, p. 119.
33. Otto Richard Tannenberg, in 1911, quoted in Notestein and Stoll, *Conquest and Kultur*, p. 53.
34. Crown Prince Wilhelm, in 1913, quoted in ibid., p. 44. Likewise Walter Rathenau complained of German "frontiers which are too long and devoid of natural protection, surrounded and hemmed in by rivals, with a short coastline. . . ." In July 1914, quoted in Fischer, *War of Illusions*, p. 450.
35. Hermann Vietinghoff-Scheel, in 1912, quoted in William Archer, ed., *501 Gems of German Thought* (London: T. Fisher Unwin, 1916), p. 46.
36. Albrecht Wirth, in 1901, quoted in Notestein and Stoll, *Conquest and Kultur*, p. 52.
37. Quoted in Tuchman, *Guns of August*, p. 142.
38. Von Loebell, quoted in Fischer, *War of Illusions*, p. 543.
39. The English Military Attaché, quoted in Luigi Albertini, *The Origins of the War of 1914*, 3 vols., trans. and ed. Isabella M. Massey (London: Oxford University Press, 1952–57; reprint ed.,

German military planners recognized the tactical advantage which defenders would hold on the battlefield, most German officers and civilians believed they could win a spectacular, decisive victory if they struck at the right moment.

Bandwagon logic fed hopes that British and Belgian opposition to German expansion could be overcome. General Moltke believed that "Britain is peace loving" because in an Anglo–German war "Britain will lose its domination at sea which will pass forever to America"[40]; hence Britain would be intimidated into neutrality. Furthermore, he warned the Belgians, "Small countries, such as Belgium, would be well advised to rally to the side of the strong if they wished to retain their independence," expecting Belgium to follow this advice if Germany applied enough pressure.[41]

Victory, moreover, would be decisive and final. In Bülow's words, a defeat could render Russia "incapable of attacking us for at least a generation" and "unable to stand up for twenty-five years," leaving it "lastingly weakened,"[42] while Bernhardi proposed that France "must be annihilated once and for all as a great power."[43]

Thus, as Robert Jervis notes: "Because of the perceived advantage of the offense, war was seen as the best route both to gaining expansion and to avoiding drastic loss of influence. There seemed to be no way for Germany merely to retain and safeguard her existing position."[44] The presumed power of the offense made empire appear both feasible and necessary. Had Germans recognized the real power of the defense, the notion of gaining wider empire would have lost both its urgency and its plausibility.

Security was not Germany's only concern, nor was it always a genuine one. In Germany, as elsewhere, security sometimes served as a pretext for expansion undertaken for other reasons. Thus proponents of the "social imperialism" theory of German expansion note that German elites endorsed imperialism, often using security arguments, partly to strengthen their do-

Westport, Conn.: Greenwood Press, 1980), Vol. 3, p. 171; and Lerchenfeld, the Bavarian ambassador in Berlin, quoted in Fischer, *War of Illusions*, p. 503.

40. In 1913, quoted in Fischer, *War of Illusions*, p. 227.

41. In 1913, quoted in Albertini, *Origins of the War*, Vol. 3, p. 441. See also Bernhardi's dismissal of the balance of power, in Friedrich von Bernhardi, *Germany and the Next War*, trans. Allen H. Powles (New York: Longmans, Green & Co., 1914), p. 21.

42. In 1887, quoted in Fischer, *War of Illusions*, p. 45.

43. In 1911, quoted in Tuchman, *Guns of August*, p. 26.

44. Jervis, "Cooperation under the Security Dilemma," p. 191.

mestic political and social position.[45] Likewise, spokesmen for the German military establishment exaggerated the threat to Germany and the benefits of empire for organizationally self-serving reasons. Indeed, members of the German elite sometimes privately acknowledged that Germany was under less threat than the public was being told. For example, the Secretary of State in the Foreign Office, Kiderlen-Wächter, admitted, "If we do not conjure up a war into being, no one else certainly will do so," since "The Republican government of France is certainly peace-minded. The British do not want war. They will never give cause for it. . . ."[46]

Nevertheless, the German public believed that German security was precarious, and security arguments formed the core of the public case for expansion. Moreover, these arguments proved persuasive, and the chauvinist public climate which they created enabled the elite to pursue expansion, whatever elite motivation might actually have been. Indeed, some members of the German government eventually felt pushed into reckless action by an extreme chauvinist public opinion which they felt powerless to resist. Admiral von Müller later explained that Germany pursued a bellicose policy during the July crisis because "The government, already weakened by domestic disunity, found itself inevitably under pressure from a great part of the German people which had been whipped into a high-grade chauvinism by Navalists and Pan-Germans."[47] Bethmann Hollweg felt his hands tied by an expansionist public climate: "With these idiots [the Pan-Germans] one cannot conduct a foreign policy—on the contrary. Together with other factors they will eventually make any reasonable course impossible for us."[48] Thus the search for security was a fundamental cause of German conduct, whether or not the elite was motivated by security concerns, because the elite was

45. Examples are: Arno Mayer, "Domestic Causes of the First World War," in Leonard Krieger and Fritz Stern, eds., *The Responsibility of Power* (New York: Macmillan, 1968), pp. 286–300; Berghahn, *Germany and the Approach of War*; Fischer, *War of Illusions*, pp. 257–258; and Imanuel Geiss, *German Foreign Policy, 1871–1914* (Boston: Routledge & Kegan Paul, 1976). A criticism is Marc Trachtenberg, "The Social Interpretation of Foreign Policy," *Review of Politics*, Vol. 40, No. 3 (July 1978), pp. 341–350.
46. In 1910, quoted in Geiss, *German Foreign Policy*, p. 126.
47. Admiral von Müller, quoted in Fritz Stern, *The Failure of Illiberalism* (London: Allen & Unwin, 1972), p. 94.
48. In 1909, quoted in Konrad H. Jarausch, *The Enigmatic Chancellor: Bethmann Hollweg and the Hubris of Imperial Germany* (New Haven: Yale University Press, 1973), p. 119. See also ibid., p. 152; and Geiss, *German Foreign Policy*, pp. 135–137. As Jules Cambon, French ambassador to Germany, perceptively remarked: "It is false that in Germany the nation is peaceful and the government bellicose—the exact opposite is true." In 1911, quoted in Jarausch, *Enigmatic Chancellor*, p. 125.

allowed or even compelled to adopt expansionist policies by a German public which found security arguments persuasive.

The same mixture of insecurity and perceived opportunity stiffened resistance to German expansion and fuelled a milder expansionism elsewhere in Europe, intensifying the conflict between Germany and its neighbors. In France the nationalist revival and French endorsement of a firm Russian policy in the Balkans were inspired partly by a growing fear of the German threat after 1911,[49] partly by an associated concern that Austrian expansion in the Balkans could shift the European balance of power in favor of the Central Powers and thereby threaten French security, and partly by belief that a war could create opportunities for French expansion. The stiffer French "new attitude" on Balkan questions in 1912 was ascribed to the French belief that "a territorial acquisition on the part of Austria would affect the general balance of power in Europe and as a result touch the particular interests of France"—a belief which assumed that the power balance was relatively precarious, which in turn assumed a world of relatively strong offense.[50] At the same time some Frenchmen looked forward to "a beautiful war which will deliver all the captives of Germanism,"[51] inspired by a faith in the power of the offensive that was typified by the enthusiasm of Joffre's deputy, General de Castelnau: "Give me 700,000 men and I will conquer Europe!"[52]

Russian policy in the Balkans was driven both by fear that Austrian expansion could threaten Russian security and by hopes that Russia could destroy its enemies if war developed under the right conditions. Sazonov saw a German–Austrian Balkan program to "deliver the Slavonic East, bound hand and foot, into the power of Austria–Hungary," followed by the German seizure of Constantinople, which would gravely threaten Russian security by placing all of Southern Russia at the mercy of German power.[53] Eventually a "German Khalifate" would be established, "extending from the banks of the Rhine to the mouth of the Tigris and Euphrates," which would reduce

---

49. See Eugen Weber, *The Nationalist Revival in France, 1905–1914* (Berkeley and Los Angeles: University of California Press, 1968), passim; and Snyder, "Defending the Offensive," pp. 32–33.
50. By the Russian ambassador to Paris, A.P. Izvolsky, quoted in Schmitt, *Coming of the War*, Vol. 1, p. 21.
51. *La France Militaire*, in 1913, quoted in Weber, *Nationalist Revival in France*, p. 127.
52. In 1913, quoted in L.C.F. Turner, *Origins of the First World War* (London: Edward Arnold, 1970), p. 53.
53. Serge Sazonov, *Fateful Years, 1909–1916* (London: Jonathan Cape, 1928), p. 179. See also Schmitt, *Coming of the War*, Vol. 1, p. 87.

"Russia to a pitiful dependence upon the arbitrary will of the Central Powers."[54] At the same time some Russians believed these threats could be addressed by offensive action: Russian leaders spoke of the day when "the moment for the downfall of Austria–Hungary arrives,"[55] and the occasion when "The Austro-Hungarian ulcer, which today is not yet so ripe as the Turkish, may be cut up."[56] Russian military officers contended that "the Austrian army represents a serious force. . . . But on the occasion of the first great defeats all of this multi-national and artificially united mass ought to disintegrate."[57]

In short, the belief that conquest was easy and security scarce was an important source of German–Entente conflict. Without it, both sides could have adopted less aggressive and more accommodative policies.

THE INCENTIVE TO PREEMPT

American strategists have long assumed that World War I was a preemptive war, but they have not clarified whether or how this was true.[58] Hence two questions should be resolved to assess the consequences of the cult of the offensive: did the states of Europe perceive an incentive to move first in 1914, which helped spur them to mobilize or attack? If so, did the cult of the offensive help to give rise to this perception?

The question of whether the war was preemptive reduces to the question of why five principal actions in the July crisis were taken. These actions are: the Russian preliminary mobilization ordered on July 25–26; the partial Russian mobilization against Austria–Hungary ordered on July 29; the Russian

---

54. Sazonov, *Fateful Years*, pp. 191, 204.
55. Izvolsky, in 1909, quoted in Schmitt, *Coming of the War*, Vol. 1, p. 129.
56. Sazonov, in 1913, quoted in ibid., p. 135.
57. *Sbornik glavnogo upravleniia general'nogo shtaba,* the secret magazine of the Russian general staff, in 1913, quoted in William C. Fuller, "The Russian Empire and Its Potential Enemies" (manuscript, 1980), p. 21.

British resistance was also driven by security concerns: during the July crisis the London *Times* warned that "the ruin of France or the Low Countries would be the prelude to our own," while other interventionists warned that Antwerp in German hands would be a "pistol pointed at the heart of England," and that the German threat to France and the Low Countries created "a deadly peril for ourselves." The *Times* on August 4, quoted in Geoffrey Marcus, *Before the Lamps Went Out* (Boston: Little, Brown, 1965), p. 305; and the *Pall Mall Gazette* and James Gavin, on July 29 and August 2, quoted in ibid., pp. 243, 268.
58. Suggesting that World War I was preemptive are: Herman Kahn, *On Thermonuclear War*, 2nd ed. (New York: The Free Press, 1969), pp. 359–362; Schelling, *Arms and Influence*, pp. 223–224; Jervis, "Cooperation under the Security Dilemma," pp. 191–192; Quester, *Offense and Defense*, pp. 110–111; Richard Ned Lebow, *Between Peace and War: The Nature of International Crisis* (Baltimore, Md.: The Johns Hopkins University Press, 1981), pp. 238–242.

full mobilization ordered on July 30; French preliminary mobilization measures ordered during July 25–30; and the German attack on the Belgian fortress at Liège at the beginning of the war. The war was preemptive if Russia and France mobilized preemptively, since these mobilizations spurred German and Austrian mobilization, opening windows which helped cause war. Thus while the mobilizations were not acts of war, they caused effects which caused war. The war was also preemptive if Germany struck Liège preemptively, since the imperative to strike Liège was one reason why "mobilization meant war" to Germany.

The motives for these acts cannot be determined with finality; testimony by the actors is spotty and other direct evidence is scarce. Instead, motives must be surmised from preexisting beliefs, deduced from circumstances, and inferred from clues which may by themselves be inconclusive. However, three pieces of evidence suggest that important preemptive incentives existed, and helped to shape conduct. First, most European leaders apparently believed that mobilization by either side which was not answered within a very few days, or even hours, could affect the outcome of the war. This judgment is reflected both in the length of time which officials assumed would constitute a militarily significant delay between mobilization and offsetting counter-mobilization, and in the severity of the consequences which they assumed would follow if they mobilized later than their opponents.

Second, many officials apparently assumed that significant mobilization measures and preparations to attack could be kept secret for a brief but significant period. Since most officials also believed that a brief unanswered mobilization could be decisive, they concluded that the side which mobilized first would have the upper hand.

Third, governments carried out some of their mobilization measures in secrecy, suggesting that they believed secret measures were feasible and worthwhile.

THE PERCEIVED SIGNIFICANCE OF SHORT DELAYS. Before and during the July crisis European leaders used language suggesting that they believed a lead in ordering mobilization of roughly one to three days would be significant. In Austria, General Conrad believed that "every day was of far-reaching importance," since "any delay might leave the [Austrian] forces now assembling in Galicia open to being struck by the full weight of a Russian offensive in the midst of their deployment."[59] In France, Marshall Joffre warned the

---

59. July 29, quoted in Albertini, *Origins*, Vol. 2, p. 670.

French cabinet that "any delay of twenty-four hours in calling up our reservists" once German preparations began would cost France "ten to twelve miles for each day of delay; in other words, the initial abandonment of much of our territory."[60] In Britain, one official believed that France "cannot possibly delay her own mobilization for even the fraction of a day" once Germany began to mobilize.[61]

In Germany, one analyst wrote that "A delay of a single day . . . can scarcely ever be rectified."[62] Likewise Moltke, on receiving reports of preparations in France and Russia during the July crisis, warned that "the military situation is becoming from day to day more unfavorable for us," and would "lead to fateful consequences for us" if Germany did not respond.[63] On July 30 he encouraged Austria to mobilize, warning that "every hour of delay makes the situation worse, for Russia gains a start."[64] On August 1, the Prussian ministry of war was reportedly "very indignant over the day lost for the mobilization" by the German failure to mobilize on July 30.[65] The German press drove home the point that if mobilization by the adversary went unanswered even briefly, the result could be fatal, one German newspaper warning that "Every delay [in mobilizing] would cost us an endless amount of blood" if Germany's enemies gained the initiative; hence "it would be disastrous if we let ourselves be moved by words not to carry on our preparations so quickly. . . ."[66]

---

60. July 29, from Marshall Joffre, *The Personal Memoirs of Marshall Joffre*, 2 vols., trans. T. Bentley Mott (New York: Harper & Brothers, 1932), Vol. 1, p. 125.
61. Eyre Crowe, on July 27, quoted in Geiss, *July 1914*, p. 251.
62. Kraft zu Hohenlohe-Ingelfingen, in 1898, quoted in Ropp, *War in the Modern World*, p. 203.
63. To Bethmann Hollweg, on July 29, quoted in Geiss, *July 1914*, p. 284.
64. Quoted in Schmitt, *Coming of the War*, Vol. 2, p. 196.
65. Ibid., p. 265n.
66. The *Reinisch-Westfälische Zeitung*, July 31, quoted in Jonathan French Scott, *The Five Weeks* (New York: John Day Co., 1927), p. 146.
Likewise after the war General von Kluck, who commanded the right wing of the German army in the march on Paris, claimed that if the German army had been mobilized and deployed "three days earlier, a more sweeping victory and decisive result would probably have been gained" against France, and Admiral Tirpitz complained that German diplomats had given Britain and Belgium several crucial days warning of the German attack on July 29, which "had an extraordinarily unfavorable influence on the whole course of the war." A delay of "only a few days" in the preparation of the British expeditionary force "might have been of the greatest importance to us." Schmitt, *Coming of the War*, Vol. 2, p. 148n.; and Albertini, *Origins*, Vol. 3, p. 242n.
A more relaxed opinion was expressed by the Prussian war minister, General Falkenhayn, who seemed to feel that it would be acceptable if German mobilization "follows two or three days later than the Russian and Austrian," since it "will still be completed more quickly than theirs." Schmitt, *Coming of the War*, Vol. 2, p. 147. However, he also expressed himself in favor

Thus time was measured in small units: "three days," "day to day," "a single day," "the fraction of a day," or even "every hour." Moreover, the consequences of conceding the initiative to the adversary were thought to be extreme. The Russian Minister of Agriculture, Alexander Krivoshein, warned that if Russia delayed its mobilization "we should be marching toward a certain catastrophe,"[67] and General Janushkevich warned the Russian foreign minister that "we were in danger of losing [the war] before we had time to unsheath our sword" by failing to mobilize promptly against Germany.[68] General Joffre feared that France would find itself "in an irreparable state of inferiority" if it were outstripped by German mobilization.[69] And in Germany, officials foresaw dire consequences if Germany conceded the initiative either in the East or the West. Bethmann Hollweg explained to one of his ambassadors that if German mobilization failed to keep pace with the Russian, Germany would suffer large territorial losses: "East Prussia, West Prussia, and perhaps also Posen and Silesia [would be] at the mercy of the Russians."[70] Such inaction would be "a crime against the safety of our fatherland."[71]

Germans also placed a high value on gaining the initiative at Liège, since Liège controlled a vital Belgian railroad junction, and German forces could not seize Liège with its tunnels and bridges intact unless they surprised the Belgians. As Moltke wrote before the war, the advance through Belgium "will hardly be possible unless Liège is in our hands . . . the possession of Liège is the *sine qua non* of our advance." But seizing Liège would require "meticulous preparation and surprise" and "is only possible if the attack is made at once, before the areas between the forts are fortified," "immediately" after the declaration of war.[72] In short, the entire German war plan would be ruined if Germany allowed Belgium to prepare the defense of Liège.

This belief that brief unanswered preparations and actions could be decisive reflected the implicit assumption that the offense had the advantage. Late mobilization would cost Germany control of East and West Prussia only

of preemption at other junctures. See ibid., p. 297; and Berghahn, *Germany and the Approach of War*, p. 203.

67. To Sazonov, July 30, quoted in Geiss, *July 1914*, p. 311.
68. To Sazonov, July 30, quoted in Albertini, *Origins*, Vol. 2, p. 566.
69. August 1, Poincaré reporting Joffre's view, quoted in Albertini, *Origins*, Vol. 3, p. 100.
70. August 1, quoted in Schmitt, *Coming of the War*, Vol. 2, p. 264.
71. August 1, quoted in Albertini, *Origins*, Vol. 3, p. 167.
72. Ritter, *The Schlieffen Plan*, p. 166. On the Liège attack, see also Snyder, "Defending the Offensive," pp. 203, 285–287.

if Russian offensive power were strong, and German defensive power were weak; mobilizing late could only be a "crime against the safety" of Germany if numerically superior enemies could destroy it; lateness could only confront Russia with "certain catastrophe" or leave it in danger of "losing before we have time to unsheath our sword" if Germany could develop a powerful offensive with the material advantage it would gain by preparing first; and lateness could only condemn France to "irreparable inferiority" if small material inferiority translated into large territorial losses. Had statesmen understood that in reality the defense had the advantage, they also would have known that the possession of the initiative could not be decisive, and could have conceded it more easily.

WAS SECRET PREPARATION BELIEVED FEASIBLE? The belief that delay could be fatal would have created no impulse to go first had European leaders believed that they could detect and offset their opponents' preparations immediately. However, many officials believed that secret action for a short time was possible. Russian officials apparently lacked confidence in their own ability to detect German or Austrian mobilization, and their decisions to mobilize seem to have been motivated partly by the desire to forestall surprise preparation by their adversaries. Sazonov reportedly requested full mobilization on July 30 partly from fear that otherwise Germany would "gain time to complete her preparations in secret."[73] Sazonov offers confirmation in his memoirs, explaining that he had advised mobilization believing that "The perfection of the German military organization made it possible by means of personal notices to the reservists to accomplish a great part of the work quietly." Germany could then "complete the mobilization in a very short time. This circumstance gave a tremendous advantage to Germany, but we could counteract it to a certain extent by taking measures for our own mobilization in good time."[74]

Similar reasoning contributed to the Russian decision to mobilize against Austria on July 29. Sazonov explains that the mobilization was undertaken in part "so as to avoid the danger of being taken unawares by the Austrian

---

73. Paleologue's diary, quoted in Albertini, *Origins*, Vol. 2, p. 619.
74. Sazonov, *Fateful Years*, pp. 202–203. The memorandum of the day of the Russian foreign ministry for July 29 records that Russian officials had considered whether Germany seriously sought peace, or whether its diplomacy "was only intended to lull us to sleep and so to postpone the Russian mobilization and thus gain time wherein to make corresponding preparations." Quoted in Geiss, *July 1914*, pp. 296–297.

preparations."[75] Moreover, recent experience had fuelled Russian fears of an Austrian surprise: during the Balkan crisis of 1912, the Russian army had been horrified to discover that Austria had secretly mobilized in Galicia, without detection by Russian intelligence; and this experience resolved the Russian command not to be caught napping again. In one observer's opinion, "the experience of 1912 . . . was not without influence as regards Russia's unwillingness to put off her mobilization in the July days of 1914."[76]

Top Russian officials also apparently believed that Russia could itself mobilize secretly, and some historians ascribe the Russian decision to mobilize partly to this erroneous belief. Luigi Albertini writes that Sazonov did not realize that the mobilization order would be posted publicly and that, accordingly, he "thought Russia could mobilize without Germany's knowing of it immediately."[77] Albertini reports that the German ambassador caused "real stupefaction" by appearing at the Russian ministry for foreign affairs with a red mobilization poster on the morning of mobilization,[78] and concludes that the "belief that it was possible to proceed to general mobilization without making it public may well have made Sazonov more inclined to order it."[79]

Contemporary accounts confirm that the Russian leadership believed in their own ability to mobilize in secret. The memorandum of the Russian Ministry for Foreign Affairs records that Sazonov sought to "proceed to the general mobilization as far as possible secretly and without making any public announcement concerning it," in order "To avoid rendering more acute our relations with Germany."[80] And in informing his government of Russian preliminary mobilization measures which began on July 26, the French ambassador indicated Russian hopes that they could maintain secrecy: "Secret preparations will, however, commence already today,"[81] and "the military districts of Warsaw, Vilna and St. Petersburg are secretly making preparations."[82] His telegram informing Paris of Russian general mobilization ex-

---

75. Sazonov, *Fateful Years*, p. 188.
76. A.M. Zayonchovsky, quoted in Lieven, *Russia and the Origins of the First World War*, p. 149.
77. Albertini, *Origins*, Vol. 2, p. 624.
78. Ibid., quoting Taube who quoted Nolde.
79. Ibid., p. 573. See also p. 584, suggesting that "Sazonov was such a greenhorn in military matters as to imagine the thing could be done, and was only convinced of the contrary when on 31 July he saw the red notices, calling up reservists, posted up in the streets of St. Petersburg." This point "provides the key to many mysteries" (p. 624).
80. For July 31, in Geiss, *July 1914*, p. 326.
81. Paleologue, July 25, in Albertini, *Origins*, Vol. 2, p. 591.
82. Paleologue, July 26, in ibid., p. 592.

plained that "the Russian government has decided to proceed secretly to the first measures of general mobilization."[83]

Like their Russian counterparts, top French officials also apparently feared that Germany might mobilize in secret, which spurred the French to their own measures. Thus during the July crisis General Joffre spoke of "the concealments [of mobilization] which are possible in Germany,"[84] and referred to "information from excellent sources [which] led us to fear that on the Russian front a sort of secret mobilization was taking place [in Germany]."[85] In his memoirs, Joffre quotes a German military planning document acquired by the French government before the July crisis, which he apparently took to indicate German capabilities, and which suggested that Germany could take "quiet measures . . . in preparation for mobilization," including "a discreet assembly of complementary personnel and materiel" which would "assure us advantages very difficult for other armies to realize in the same degree."[86] The French ambassador to Berlin, Jules Cambon, also apparently believed that Germany could conduct preliminary mobilization measures in secret, became persuaded during the July crisis that it had in fact done this, and so informed Paris: "In view of German habits, [preliminary measures] can be taken without exciting the population or causing indiscretions to be committed. . . ."[87] For their part the Germans apparently did not believe that they or their enemies could mobilize secretly, but they did speak in terms suggesting that Germany could surprise the Belgians: German planners referred to the *"coup de main"* at Liège and the need for "meticulous preparation and surprise."[88]

To sum up, then, French policymakers feared that Germany could mobilize secretly; Russians feared secret mobilization by Germany or Austria, and hoped Russian mobilization could be secret; while Central Powers planners

83. Ibid., p. 620.
84. August 1, quoted in Joffre, *Personal Memoirs*, p. 128.
85. July 29, quoted in ibid., p. 120.
86. Ibid., p. 127.
87. Cambon dispatch to Paris, July 21, quoted in ibid., p. 119. Joffre records that Cambon's telegram, which mysteriously did not arrive in Paris until July 28, convinced him that "for seven days at least the Germans had been putting into effect the plan devised for periods of political tension and that our normal methods of investigation had not revealed this fact to us. Our adversaries could thus reach a condition of mobilization that was almost complete," reflecting Joffre's assumption that secret German measures were possible.
88. Moltke, quoted in Ritter, *The Schlieffen Plan*, p. 166.

saw less possibility for preemptive mobilization by either side, but hoped to mount a surprise attack on Belgium.[89]

DID STATESMEN ACT SECRETLY? During the July crisis European statesmen sometimes informed their opponents before they took military measures, but on other occasions they acted secretly, suggesting that they believed the initiative was both attainable and worth attaining, and indicating that the desire to seize the initiative may have entered into their decisions to mobilize. German leaders warned the French of their preliminary measures taken on July 29,[90] and their pre-mobilization and mobilization measures taken on July 31;[91] and they openly warned the Russians on July 29 that they would mobilize if Russia conducted a partial mobilization.[92] Russia openly warned Austria on July 27 that it would mobilize if Austria crossed the Serbian frontier,[93] and then on July 28 and July 29 openly announced to Germany and Austria its partial mobilization of July 29,[94] and France delayed full mobilization until after Germany had taken the onus on itself by issuing ultimata to Russia and France. However, Russia, France, and Germany tried

89. During the July crisis, adversaries actually detected signs of most major secret mobilization activity in roughly 6–18 hours, and took responsive decisions in 1–2 days. Accordingly, the maximum "first mobilization advantage" which a state could gain by forestalling an adversary who otherwise would have begun mobilizing first was roughly 2–4 days. Orders for Russian preliminary mobilization measures were issued in sequential telegrams transmitted between 4:00 p.m. on July 25 and 3:26 a.m. on July 26; Berlin received its first reports of these measures early on July 26; and at 4:00 p.m. on July 27 the German intelligence board concluded that Russian premobilization had in fact begun, for a lag of roughly one and one-half to two days between the issuance of orders and their definite detection. Sidney B. Fay, *The Origins of the World War*, 2 vols., 2nd ed. rev. (New York: Free Press, 1966), Vol. 2, pp. 310–315; and Ulrich Trumpener, "War Premeditated? German Intelligence Operations in July 1914," *Central European History*, Vol. 9 (1976), pp. 67–70. Full Russian mobilization was ordered at 6:00 p.m. on July 30, first rumors reached Berlin very late on July 30, more definite but inconclusive information was received around 7:00 a.m. July 31, reliable confirmation was received at 11:45 a.m., and German preliminary mobilization was ordered at 1:00 p.m., for a lag of roughly 20 hours. Fay, *Origins of the World War*, Vol. 2, p. 473; Schmitt, *Coming of the War*, Vol. 2, pp. 211–212, 262–265; and Trumpener, "War Premeditated?," pp. 80–83. French preliminary measures were begun on July 25, expanded on July 26, further expanded on July 27, and remained substantially undetected on July 28. Secondary sources do not clarify when Germany detected French preliminary measures, but it seems that German discovery lagged roughly two days behind French actions. Schmitt, *Coming of the War*, Vol. 2, pp. 17–19; Joffre, *Personal Memoirs*, pp. 115–118; and Trumpener, "War Premeditated?," pp. 71–73. As for Liège, it was not captured as quickly as German planners had hoped, but was not properly defended when the Germans arrived, and was taken in time to allow the advance into France.
90. Albertini, *Origins*, Vol. 2, p. 491.
91. Schmitt, *Coming of the War*, Vol. 2, pp. 267–268.
92. Ibid., p. 105.
93. Albertini, *Origins*, Vol. 2, p. 529.
94. Ibid., pp. 549, 551; and Geiss, *July 1914*, pp. 262, 278, 299.

to conceal four of the five major preemptive actions of the crisis: the Russians hid both their preliminary measures of July 25–26 and their general mobilization of July 30, the French attempted to conceal their preliminary mobilization measures of July 25–29, and the Germans took great care to conceal their planned *coup de main* against Liège. Thus states sometimes conceded the initiative, but sought it at critical junctures.

Overall, evidence suggests that European leaders saw some advantage to moving first in 1914: the lags which they believed significant lay in the same range as the lags they believed they could gain or forestall by mobilizing first. These perceptions probably helped spur French and Russian decisions to mobilize, which in turn helped set in train the German mobilization, which in turn meant war partly because the Germans were determined to preempt Liège. Hence the war was in some modest measure preemptive.

If so, the cult of the offensive bears some responsibility. Without it, statesmen would not have thought that secret mobilization or preemptive attack could be decisive. The cult was not the sole cause of the perceived incentive to preempt; rather, three causes acted together, the others being the belief that mobilization could briefly be conducted secretly, and the systems of reserve manpower mobilization which enabled armies to multiply their strength in two weeks. The cult had its effect by magnifying the importance of these other factors in the minds of statesmen, which magnified the incentive to preempt which these factors caused them to perceive. The danger that Germany might gain time to complete preparations in secret could only alarm France and Russia if Germany could follow up these preparations with an effective offensive; otherwise, early secret mobilization could *not* give "a tremendous advantage" to Germany, and such a prospect would not require a forestalling response. Sazonov could have been tempted to mobilize secretly only if early Russian mobilization would forestall important German gains, or could provide important gains for Russia, as could only have happened if the offense were powerful.

"WINDOWS" AND PREVENTIVE WAR

Germany and Austria pursued bellicose policies in 1914 partly to shut the looming "windows" of vulnerability which they envisioned lying ahead, and partly to exploit the brief window of opportunity which they thought the summer crisis opened. This window logic, in turn, grew partly from the cult of the offensive, since it depended upon the implicit assumption that the offense was strong. The shifts in the relative sizes of armies, economies, and alliances which fascinated and frightened statesmen in 1914 could have cast such a long shadow only in a world where material advantage promised decisive results in warfare, as it could only in an offense-dominant world.

The official communications of German leaders are filled with warnings that German power was in relative decline, and that Germany was doomed unless it took drastic action—such as provoking and winning a great crisis which would shatter the Entente, or directly instigating a "great liquidation" (as one general put it).[95] German officials repeatedly warned that Russian military power would expand rapidly between 1914 and 1917, as Russia carried out its 1913–1914 Great Program, and that in the long run Russian power would further outstrip German power because Russian resources were greater.[96] In German eyes this threat forced Germany to act. Secretary of State Jagow summarized a view common in Germany in a telegram to one of his ambassadors just before the July crisis broke:

Russia will be ready to fight in a few years. Then she will crush us by the number of her soldiers; then she will have built her Baltic fleet and her strategic railways. Our group in the meantime will have become steadily weaker. . . . I do not desire a preventive war, but if the conflict should offer itself, we ought not to shirk it.[97]

Similarly, shortly before Sarajevo the Kaiser reportedly believed that "the big Russian railway constructions were . . . preparations for a great war which could start in 1916" and wondered "whether it might not be better to attack than to wait."[98] At about the same time Chancellor Bethmann Hollweg declared bleakly, "The future belongs to Russia which grows and grows and becomes an even greater nightmare to us,"[99] warning that "After the completion of their strategic railroads in Poland our position [will be] untenable."[100] During the war, Bethmann confessed that the "window" argument

---

95. Von Plessen, quoted in Isabell V. Hull, *The Entourage of Kaiser Wilhelm II, 1888–1918* (New York: Cambridge University Press, 1982), p. 261. Thus Bethmann summarized German thinking when he suggested on July 8 that the Sarajevo assassination provided an opportunity either for a war which "we have the prospect of winning" or a crisis in which "we still certainly have the prospect of maneuvering the Entente apart. . . ." Thompson, *In the Eye of the Storm*, p. 75.
96. The Russian program planned a 40 percent increase in the size of the peacetime Russian army and a 29 percent increase in the number of officers over four years. Lieven, *Russia & the Origins of the First World War*, p. 111.
97. July 18, quoted in Schmitt, *Coming of the War*, Vol. 1, p. 321.
98. June 21, quoted in Fischer, *War of Illusions*, p. 471, quoting Max Warburg.
99. July 7, quoted in ibid., p. 224, quoting Riezler.
100. July 7, quoted in Jarausch, "The Illusion of Limited War," p. 57. Likewise on July 20, he expressed terror at Russia's "growing demands and colossal explosive power. In a few years

had driven German policy in 1914: "Lord yes, in a certain sense it was a preventive war," motivated by "the constant threat of attack, the greater likelihood of its inevitability in the future, and by the military's claim: today war is still possible without defeat, but not in two years!"[101]

Window logic was especially prevalent among the German military officers, many of whom openly argued for preventive war during the years before the July crisis. General Moltke declared, "I believe a war to be unavoidable and: the sooner the better" at the infamous "war council" of December 8, 1912,[102] and he expressed similar views to his Austrian counterpart, General Conrad, in May 1914: "to wait any longer meant a diminishing of our chances; as far as manpower is concerned, one cannot enter into a competition with Russia,"[103] and "We [the German Army] are ready, the sooner the better for us."[104] During the July crisis Moltke remarked that "we shall never hit it again so well as we do now with France's and Russia's expansion of their armies incomplete," and argued that "the singularly favorable situation be exploited for military action."[105] After the war Jagow recalled a conversation with Moltke in May 1914, in which Moltke had spelled out his reasoning:

In two–three years Russia would have completed her armaments. The military superiority of our enemies would then be so great that he did not know how we could overcome them. Today we would still be a match for them. In his opinion there was no alternative to making preventive war in order to defeat the enemy while we still had a chance of victory. The Chief of General Staff therefore proposed that I should conduct a policy with the aim of provoking a war in the near future.[106]

Other members of the German military shared Moltke's views, pressing for preventive war because "conditions and prospects would never become

she would be supreme—and Germany her first lonely victim." Quoted in Lebow, *Between Peace and War*, p. 258n.

101. Jarausch, "The Illusion of Limited War," p. 48. Likewise Friedrich Thimme quoted Bethmann during the war: "He also admits that our military are quite convinced that they could still be victorious in the war, but that in a few years time, say in 1916 after the completion of Russia's railway network, they could not. This, of course, also affected the way in which the Serbian question was dealt with." Quoted in Volker R. Berghahn and Martin Kitchen, eds., *Germany in the Age of Total War* (Totowa, N.J.: Barnes and Noble, 1981), p. 45.

102. Fischer, *War of Illusions*, p. 162.

103. Berghahn, *Germany and the Approach of War*, p. 171.

104. Geiss, *German Foreign Policy*, p. 149.

105. Berghahn, *Germany and the Approach of War*, p. 203.

106. Quoted in J.C.G. Röhl, ed., *From Bismarck to Hitler: The Problem of Continuity in German History* (London: Longman, 1970), p. 70.

better."[107] General Gebstattel recorded the mood of the German leadership on the eve of the war: "Chances better than in two or three years hence and the General Staff is reported to be confidently awaiting events."[108] The Berlin *Post*, a newspaper which often reflected the views of the General Staff, saw a window in 1914: "at the moment the state of things is favorable for us. France is not yet ready for war. England has internal and colonial difficulties, and Russia recoils from the conflict because she fears revolution at home. Ought we to wait until our adversaries are ready?" It concluded that Germany should "prepare for the inevitable war with energy and foresight" and "begin it under the most favorable conditions."[109]

German leaders also saw a tactical window of opportunity in the political constellation of July 1914, encouraging them to shut their strategic window of vulnerability. In German eyes, the Sarajevo assassination created favorable conditions for a confrontation, since it guaranteed that Austria would join Germany against Russia and France (as it might not if war broke out over a colonial conflict or a dispute in Western Europe), and it provided the Central powers with a plausible excuse, which raised hopes that Britain might remain neutral. On July 8, Bethmann Hollweg reportedly remarked, "If war comes from the east so that we have to fight for Austria–Hungary and not Austria–Hungary for us, we have a chance of winning."[110] Likewise, the German ambassador to Rome reportedly believed on July 27 that "the present moment is extraordinarily favorable to Germany,"[111] and the German ambassador to London even warned the British Prime Minister that "there was some feeling in Germany . . . that trouble was bound to come and therefore it would be better not to restrain Austria and let trouble come now, rather than later."[112]

The window logic reflected in these statements is a key to German conduct in 1914: whether the Germans were aggressive or restrained depended on

---

107. Leuckart's summary of the views of the General Staff, quoted in Geiss, *July 1914*, p. 69. For more on advocacy of preventive war by the German army, see Martin Kitchen, *The German Officer Corps, 1890–1914* (Oxford: Clarendon Press, 1968), pp. 96–114; and Hull, *Entourage of Kaiser Wilhelm II*, pp. 236–265.
108. August 2, quoted in Fischer, *War of Illusions*, p. 403.
109. February 24, 1914, in Schmitt, *Coming of the War*, Vol. 1, p. 100n.; and Fischer, *War of Illusions*, pp. 371–272.
110. Jarausch, "Illusion of Limited War," p. 58. Earlier Bülow had explained why the Agadir crisis was an unsuitable occasion for war in similar terms: "In 1911 the situation was much worse. The complication would have begun with Britain; France would have remained passive, it would have forced us to attack and then there would have been no *causus foederis* for Austria . . . whereas Russia was obliged to join in." In 1912, quoted in Fischer, *War of Illusions*, p. 85.
111. Schmitt, *Coming of the War*, Vol. 2, p. 66n.
112. Ibid., Vol. 1, p. 324, quoting Lichnowsky, on July 6.

whether at a given moment they thought windows were open or closed. Germany courted war on the Balkan question after Sarajevo because window logic led German leaders to conclude that war could not be much worse than peace, and might even be better, if Germany could provoke the right war under the right conditions against the right opponents. German leaders probably preferred the status quo to a world war against the entire Entente, but evidence suggests that they also preferred a continental war against France and Russia to the status quo—as long as Austria joined the war, and as long as they could also find a suitable pretext which they could use to persuade the German public that Germany fought for a just cause. This, in turn, required that Germany engineer a war which engaged Austrian interests, and in which Germany could cast itself as the attacked, in order to involve the Austrian army, to persuade Britain to remain neutral, and to win German public support. These window considerations help explain both the German decision to force the Balkan crisis to a head and German efforts to defuse the crisis after it realized that it had failed to gain British neutrality. The German peace efforts after July 29 probably represent a belated effort to reverse course after it became clear that the July crisis was not such an opportune war window after all.

Window logic also helped to persuade Austria to play the provocateur for Germany. Like their German counterparts, many Austrian officials believed that the relative strength of the central powers was declining, and saw in Sarajevo a rare opportunity to halt this decline by force. Thus the Austrian War Minister, General Krobatin, argued in early July that "it would be better to go to war immediately, rather than at some later period, because the balance of power must in the course of time change to our disadvantage," while the Austrian Foreign Minister, Count Berchtold, favored action because "our situation must become more precarious as time goes on,"[113] warning that unless Austria destroyed the Serbian army in 1914, it would face "another attack [by] Serbia in much more unfavorable conditions" in two or three years.[114] Likewise, the Austrian foreign ministry reportedly believed that, "if Russia would not permit the localization of the conflict with Serbia, the present moment was more favorable for a reckoning than a later one would be";[115] General Conrad believed, "If it comes to war with Russia—as

---

113. July 7, quoted in Geiss, *July 1914*, pp. 81, 84.
114. July 31, quoted in Schmitt, *Coming of the War*, Vol. 2, p. 218.
115. Ibid., Vol. 1, p. 372, quoting Baron von Tucher on July 18.

it must some day—today is as good as any other day";[116] and the Austrian ambassador to Italy believed an Austro–Serbian war would be "a piece of real good fortune," since "for the Triple Alliance the present moment is more favorable than another later."[117]

Thus the First World War was in part a "preventive" war, launched by the Central powers in the belief that they were saving themselves from a worse fate in later years. The cult of the offensive bears some responsibility for that belief, for in a defense-dominated world the windows which underlie the logic of preventive war are shrunken in size, as the balance of power grows less elastic to the relative sizes of armies and economies; and windows cannot be shut as easily by military action. Only in a world taken by the cult of the offensive could the window logic which governed German and Austrian conduct have proved so persuasive: Germans could only have feared that an unchecked Russia could eventually "crush us by the numbers of her soldiers," or have seen a "singularly favorable situation" in 1914 which could be "exploited by military action" if material superiority would endow the German and Russian armies with the ability to conduct decisive offensive operations against one another. Moltke claimed he saw "no alternative to making preventive war," but had he believed that the defense dominated, better alternatives would have been obvious.

The cult of the offensive also helped cause the arms race before 1914 which engendered the uneven rates of military growth that gave rise to visions of windows. The German army buildup after 1912 was justified by security arguments: Bethmann Hollweg proclaimed, "For Germany, in the heart of Europe, with open boundaries on all sides, a strong army is the most secure guarantee of peace," while the Kaiser wrote that Germany needed "More ships and soldiers . . . because our existence is at stake."[118] This buildup provoked an even larger Russian and French buildup, which created the windows which alarmed Germany in 1914.[119] Thus the cult both magnified

---

116. In October 1913, quoted in Gerhard Ritter, *The Sword and the Scepter: The Problem of Militarism in Germany*, 4 vols., trans. Heinz Norden (Coral Gables, Fla.: University of Miami Press, 1969–73), Vol. 2, p. 234. Likewise the *Militärisch Rundschau* argued for provoking war: "Since we shall have to accept the contest some day, let us provoke it at once." On July 15, 1914, quoted in Schmitt, *Coming of the War*, Vol. 1, p. 367. For more on preventive war and the Austrian army, see Ritter, *Sword and the Scepter*, Vol. 2, pp. 227–239.
117. Count Merey, July 29, quoted in Albertini, *Origins*, Vol. 2, p. 383.
118. Both in 1912, quoted in Jarausch, *Enigmatic Chancellor*, p. 95; and Fischer, *War of Illusions*, p. 165.
119. On the motives for the Russian buildup, see P.A. Zhilin, "Bol'shaia programma po usileniiu russkoi armii," *Voenno-istoricheskii zhurnal*, No. 7 (July 1974), pp. 90–97.

the importance of fluctuations in ratios of forces and helped to fuel the arms race which fostered them.

THE SCOPE AND INFLEXIBILITY OF MOBILIZATION PLANS

The spreading of World War I outward from the Balkans is often ascribed to the scope and rigidity of the Russian and German plans for mobilization, which required that Russia must also mobilize armies against Germany when it mobilized against Austria–Hungary, and that Germany also attack France and Belgium if it fought Russia. Barbara Tuchman writes that Europe was swept into war by "the pull of military schedules," and recalls Moltke's famous answer when the Kaiser asked if the German armies could be mobilized to the East: "Your Majesty, it cannot be done. The deployment of millions cannot be improvised. If Your Majesty insists on leading the whole army to the East it will not be an army ready for battle but a disorganized mob of armed men with no arrangements for supply."[120] Likewise, Herman Kahn notes the "rigid war plan[s]" of 1914, which "were literally cast in concrete,"[121] and David Ziegler notes the influence of military "planning in advance," which left "no time to improvise."[122]

The scope and character of these plans in turn reflected the assumption that the offense was strong. In an offense-dominant world Russia would have been prudent to mobilize against Germany if it mobilized against Austria–Hungary; and Germany probably would have been prudent to attack Belgium and France at the start of any Russo–German war. Thus the troublesome railroad schedules of 1914 reflected the offense-dominant world in which the schedulers believed they lived. Had they known that the defense was powerful, they would have been drawn towards flexible plans for limited deployment on single frontiers; and had such planning prevailed, the war might have been confined to Eastern Europe or the Balkans.

Moreover, the "inflexibility" of the war plans may have reflected the same offensive assumptions which determined their shape. Russian and German soldiers understandably developed only options which they believed prudent to exercise, while omitting plans which they believed would be dangerous to implement. These judgments in turn reflected their own and their adver-

---

120. Tuchman, *Guns of August*, pp. 92, 99.
121. Kahn, *On Thermonuclear War*, pp. 359, 362.
122. David W. Ziegler, *War, Peace and International Politics* (Boston: Little, Brown, 1977), p. 25.

saries' offensive ideas. Options were few because these offensive ideas seemed to narrow the range of prudent choice.

Lastly, the assumption of offense-dominance gave preset plans greater influence over the conduct of the July crisis, by raising the cost of improvisation if statesmen insisted on adjusting plans at the last minute. Russian statesmen were told that an improvised partial mobilization would place Russia in a "extremely dangerous situation,"[123] and German civilians were warned against improvisation in similar terms. This in turn reflected the size of the "windows" which improvised partial mobilizations would open for the adversary on the frontier which the partial mobilization left unguarded, which in turn reflected the assumption that the offense was strong (since if defenses were strong a bungled mobilization would create less opportunity for others to exploit). Thus the cult of the offensive gave planners greater power to bind statesmen to the plans they had prepared.

RUSSIAN MOBILIZATION PLANS. On July 28, 1914, Russian leaders announced that partial Russian mobilization against Austria would be ordered on July 29. They took this step to address threats emanating from Austria, acting partly to lend emphasis to their warnings to Austria that Russia would fight if Serbia were invaded, partly to offset Austrian mobilization against Serbia, and partly to offset or forestall Austrian mobilization measures which they believed were taking place or which they feared might eventually take place against Russia in Galicia.[124] However, after this announcement was made, Russian military officers advised their civilian superiors that no plans for partial mobilization existed, that such a mobilization would be a "pure improvisation," as General Denikin later wrote, and that sowing confusion in the Russian railway timetables would impede Russia's ability to mobilize later on its northern frontier. General Sukhomlinov warned the Czar that "much time would be necessary in which to re-establish the normal conditions for any further mobilization" following a partial mobilization, and General Yanushkevich flatly told Sazonov that general mobilization "could not be put into operation" once partial mobilization began.[125] Thus Russian lead-

---

123. By Generals Yanushkevich and Sukhomlinov, according to Sazonov, quoted in Albertini, *Origins*, Vol. 2, p. 566. See also M.F. Schilling, "Introduction," in *How the War Began*, trans. W. Cyprian Bridge, with a Foreword by S.D. Sazonov (London: Allen & Unwin, 1925), pp. 16, 63.
124. On the Russian decision, see Schmitt, *Coming of the War*, Vol. 2, pp. 85–87, 94–101; and Albertini, *Origins*, Vol. 2, pp. 539–561.
125. Anton I. Denikin, *The Career of a Tsarist Officer: Memoirs, 1872–1916*, trans. Margaret Patoski (Minneapolis: University of Minnesota Press, 1975), p. 222; Albertini, *Origins*, Vol. 2, p. 559; Schilling, *How the War Began*, p. 16.

ers were forced to choose between full mobilization or complete retreat, choosing full mobilization on July 30.

The cult of the offensive set the stage for this decision by buttressing Russian military calculations that full mobilization was safer than partial. We have little direct evidence explaining why Russian officers had prepared no plan for partial mobilization, but we can deduce their reasoning from their opinions on related subjects. These suggest that Russian officers believed that Germany would attack Russia if Russia fought Austria, and that the side mobilizing first would have the upper hand in a Russo–German war (as I have outlined above). Accordingly, it followed logically that Russia should launch any war with Austria by preempting Germany.

Russian leaders had three principal reasons to fear that Germany would not stand aside in an Austro–Russian conflict. First, the Russians were aware of the international Social Darwinism then sweeping Germany, and the expansionist attitude toward Russia which this worldview engendered. One Russian diplomat wrote that Germany was "beating all records of militarism" and "The Germans are not . . . wholly without the thought of removing from Russia at least part of the Baltic coastline in order to place us in the position of a second Serbia" in the course of a campaign for "German hegemony on the continent."[126] Russian military officers monitored the bellicose talk across the border with alarm, one intelligence report warning: "In Germany at present, the task of gradually accustoming the army and the population to the thought of the inevitability of conflict with Russia has begun," noting the regular public lectures which were then being delivered in Germany to foster war sentiment.[127]

Second, the Russians were aware of German alarm about windows and the talk of preventive war which this alarm engendered in Germany. Accordingly, Russian leaders expected that Germany might seize the excuse offered by a Balkan war to mount a preventive strike against Russia, especially since a war arising from the Balkans was a "best case" scenario for Germany, involving Austria on the side of Germany as it did. Thus General Yanushkevich explained Russia's decision to mobilize against Germany in 1914: "We knew well that Germany was ready for war, that she was longing

---

126. G.N. Trubetskoy, in 1909, quoted in Lieven, *Russia & the Origins of the First World War*, p. 96.
127. The Kiev District Staff, February 23, 1914, quoted in Fuller, "The Russian Empire and Its Potential Enemies," p. 17.

for it at that moment, because our big armaments program was not yet completed . . . and because our war potential was not as great as it might be." Accordingly, Russia had to expect war with Germany: "We knew that war was inevitable, not only against Austria, but also against Germany. For this reason partial mobilization against Austria alone, which would have left our front towards Germany open . . . might have brought about a disaster, a terrible disaster."[128] In short, Russia had to strike to preempt a German preventive strike against Russia.

Third, the Russians knew that the Germans believed that German and Austrian security were closely linked. Germany would therefore feel compelled to intervene in any Austro–Russian war, because a Russian victory against Austria would threaten German safety. German leaders had widely advertised this intention: for instance, Bethmann Hollweg had warned the Reichstag in 1912 that if the Austrians "while asserting their interests should against all expectations be attacked by a third party, then we would have to come resolutely to their aid. And then we would fight for the maintenance of our own position in Europe and in defense of our future and security."[129] And in fact this was precisely what happened in 1914: Germany apparently decided to attack on learning of Russian *partial* mobilization, before Russian full mobilization was known in Germany.[130] This suggests that the role of "inflexible" Russian plans in causing the war is overblown—Russian full mobilization was sufficient but not necessary to cause the war; but it also helps explain why these plans were drawn as they were, and supports the view that some of the logic behind them was correct, given the German state of mind with which Russia had to contend.

---

128. Albertini, *Origins*, Vol. 2, p. 559. See also Fuller, "The Russian Empire and Its Potential Enemies," p. 16.
129. In 1912, quoted in Stern, *Failure of Illiberalism*, p. 84. Likewise the Kaiser explained that security requirements compelled Germany to defend Austria: "If we are forced to take up arms it will be to help *Austria*, not only to defend ourselves against Russia but against the Slavs in general and to remain *German*. . . ." In 1912, quoted in Fischer, *War of Illusions*, pp. 190–191, emphasis in original. The German White Book also reflected this thinking, declaring that the "subjugation of all the Slavs under Russian sceptre" would render the "position of the Teutonic race in Central Europe untenable." August 3, 1914, quoted in Geiss, *German Foreign Policy*, p. 172.
130. See Schmitt, *Coming of the War*, Vol. 2, pp. 198–199; and Albertini, *Origins*, Vol. 3, pp. 7, 17–27; also Vol. 2, p. 485n. As Jagow plainly told the Russians on July 29: "If once you mobilize against Austria, then you will also take serious measures against us. . . . We are compelled to proclaim mobilization against Russia. . . ." Schmitt, *Coming of the War*, Vol. 2, p. 140.

In sum, Russians had to fear that expansionist, preventive, and alliance concerns might induce Germany to attack, which in turn reflected the German assumption that the offense was strong. The Russian belief that it paid to mobilize first reflected the effects of the same assumption in Russia. Had Europe known that the defense dominated, Russians would have had less reason to fear that an Austro–Russian war would spark a German attack, since the logic of expansionism and preventive war would presumably have been weaker in Germany, and Germany could more easily have tolerated some reduction in Austrian power without feeling that German safety was also threatened. At the same time, Russian soldiers would presumably have been slower to assume that they could improve their position in a Russo–German war by mobilizing preemptively. In short, the logic of general mobilization in Russia largely reflected and depended upon conclusions deduced from the cult of the offensive, or from its various manifestations. Without the cult of the offensive, a partial southern mobilization would have been the better option for Russia.

It also seems probable that the same logic helped persuade the Russian General Staff to eschew planning for a partial mobilization. If circumstances argued against a partial mobilization, they also argued against planning for one, since this would raise the risk that Russian civilians might actually implement the plan. This interpretation fits with suggestions that Russian officers exaggerated the difficulties of partial mobilization in their representations to Russian civilians.[131] If Russian soldiers left a partial mobilization option undeveloped because they believed that it would be dangerous to exercise, it follows that they also would emphasize the difficulty of improvising a southern option, since they also opposed it on other grounds.

GERMAN MOBILIZATION PLANS. The Schlieffen Plan was a disastrous scheme which only approached success because the French war plan was equally foolish: had the French army stood on the defensive instead of lunging into Alsace–Lorraine, it would have smashed the German army at the French frontier. Yet General Schlieffen's plan was a sensible response to the offense-

---

131. See L.C.F. Turner, "The Russian Mobilization in 1914," *Journal of Contemporary History*, Vol. 3, No. 1 (January 1968), pp. 72–74. But see also Lieven, *Russia and the Origins of the First World War*, pp. 148–150.
   Likewise, German soldiers exaggerated the difficulties of adapting to eastward mobilization, as many observers note, e.g., Tuchman, *Guns of August*, p. 100, and Lebow, *Between Peace and War*, p. 236.

dominant world imagined by many Germans. The plan was flawed because it grew from a fundamentally flawed image of warfare.

In retrospect, Germany should have retained the later war plan of the elder Moltke (Chief of Staff from 1857 to 1888), who would have conducted a limited offensive in the east against Russia while standing on the defensive in the west.[132] However, several considerations pushed German planners instead toward Schlieffen's grandiose scheme, which envisioned a quick victory against Belgium and France, followed by an offensive against Russia.

First, German planners assumed that France would attack Germany if Germany fought Russia, leaving Germany no option for a one-front war. By tying down German troops in Poland, an eastern war would create a yawning window of opportunity for France to recover its lost territories, and a decisive German victory over Russia would threaten French security by leaving France to face Germany alone. For these reasons they believed that France would be both too tempted and too threatened to stand aside. Bernhardi, among others, pointed out "the standing danger that France will attack us on a favorable occasion, as soon as we find ourselves involved in complications elsewhere."[133] The German declaration of war against France explained that France might suddenly attack from behind if Germany fought Russia; hence, "Germany cannot leave to France the choice of the moment" at which to attack.[134]

Second, German planners assumed that "window" considerations required a German offensive against either France or Russia at the outset of any war against the Entente. German armies could mobilize faster than the combined Entente armies; hence, the ratio of forces would most favor Germany at the beginning of the war. Therefore, Germany would do best to force an early decision, which in turn required that it assume the offensive, since otherwise its enemies would play a waiting game. As one observer explained, Germany

132. Assessing the Schlieffen Plan are Ritter, *The Schlieffen Plan,* and Snyder, "Defending the Offensive," pp. 189–294.
133. Bernhardi, quoted in Anon., *Germany's War Mania* (London: A.W. Shaw, 1914), p. 161.
134. Albertini, *Origins,* Vol. 3, p. 194. Moreover, these fears reflected views found in France. When Poincaré was asked on July 29 if he believed war could be avoided, he reportedly replied: "It would be a great pity. We should never again find conditions better." Albertini, *Origins,* Vol. 3, p. 82n. Likewise, in 1912 the French General Staff concluded that a general war arising from the Balkans would leave Germany "at the mercy of the Entente" because Austrian forces would be diverted against Serbia, and "the Triple Entente would have the best chances of success and might gain a victory which would enable the map of Europe to be redrawn." Turner, *Origins,* p. 36. See also the opinions of Izvolsky and Bertie in Schmitt, *Coming of the War,* Vol. 1, pp. 20–21, and Vol. 2, p. 349n.

"has the speed and Russia has the numbers, and the safety of the German Empire forbade that Germany should allow Russia time to bring up masses of troops from all parts of her wide dominions."[135] Germans believed that the window created by these differential mobilization rates was big, in turn, because they believed that both Germany and its enemies could mount a decisive offensive against the other with a small margin of superiority. If Germany struck at the right time, it could win easily—Germans hoped for victory in several weeks, as noted above—while if it waited it was doomed by Entente numerical superiority, which German defenses would be too weak to resist.

Third, German planners believed that an offensive against France would net them more than an offensive against Russia, which explains the western bias of the Schlieffen Plan. France could be attacked more easily than Russia, because French forces and resources lay within closer reach of German power; hence, as Moltke wrote before the war, "A speedy decision may be hoped for [against France], while an offensive against Russia would be an interminable affair."[136] Moreover, France was the more dangerous opponent not to attack, because it could take the offensive against Germany more quickly than Russia, and could threaten more important German territories if Germany left its frontier unguarded. Thus Moltke explained that they struck westward because "Germany could not afford to expose herself to the danger of attack by strong French forces in the direction of the Lower Rhine," and Wegerer wrote later that the German strike was compelled by the need to protect the German industrial region from French attack.[137] In German eyes these considerations made it too dangerous to stand on the defensive in the West in hopes that war with France could be avoided.

Finally, German planners believed that Britain would not have time to bring decisive power to bear on the continent before the German army overran France. Accordingly, they discounted the British opposition which their attack on France and Belgium would elicit: Schlieffen declared that if the British army landed, it would be "securely billeted" at Antwerp or "arrested" by the German armies,[138] while Moltke said he hoped that it would

---

135. Goschen, in Schmitt, *Coming of the War*, Vol. 2, p. 321.
136. Moltke, in General Ludendorff, *The General Staff and its Problems*, trans. F.A. Holt (New York: E.P. Dutton, n.d.), Vol. 1, p. 61.
137. Geiss, *July 1914*, p. 357; and Alfred von Wegerer, *A Refutation of the Versailles War Guilt Thesis*, trans. Edwin H. Zeydel (New York: Alfred A. Knopf, 1930), p. 310.
138. Ritter, *Schlieffen Plan*, pp. 71, 161–162; and Geiss, *German Foreign Policy*, p. 101. See also Ritter, *Schlieffen Plan*, p. 161. But see also Moltke quoted in Turner, *Origins of the World War*, p. 64.

land so that the German army "could take care of it."[139] In accordance with their "bandwagon" worldview, German leaders also hoped that German power might cow Britain into neutrality; or that Britain might hesitate before entering the war, and then might quit in discouragement once the French were beaten—Schlieffen expected that, "If the battle [in France] goes in favor of the Germans, the English are likely to abandon their enterprise as hopeless"—which led them to further discount the extra political costs of attacking westward.[140]

Given these four assumptions, an attack westward, even one through Belgium which provoked British intervention, was the most sensible thing for Germany to do. Each assumption, in turn, was a manifestation of the belief that the offense was strong. Thus while the Schlieffen Plan has been widely criticized for its political and military naiveté, it would have been a prudent plan had Germans actually lived in the offense-dominant world they imagined. Under these circumstances quick mobilization would have in fact given them a chance to win a decisive victory during their window of opportunity, and if they had failed to exploit this window by attacking, they would eventually have lost; the risk of standing on the defense in the West in hopes that France would not fight would have been too great; and the invasion of France and Belgium would have been worth the price, because British power probably could not have affected the outcome of the war.

Thus the belief in the power of the offense was the linchpin which held Schlieffen's logic together, and the main criticisms which can be levelled at the German war plan flow from the falsehood of this belief. German interests would have been better served by a limited, flexible, east-only plan which conformed to the defensive realities of 1914. Moreover, had Germany adopted such a plan, the First World War might well have been confined to Eastern Europe, never becoming a world war.

"MOBILIZATION MEANS WAR"

"Mobilization meant war" in 1914 because mobilization meant war to Germany: the German war plan mandated that special units of the German standing army would attack Belgium and Luxemburg immediately after mobilization was ordered, and long before it was completed. (In fact Germany

---

139. Ritter, *Sword and the Scepter*, Vol. 2, p. 157.
140. Ritter, *The Schlieffen Plan*, p. 163. See also Bethmann Hollweg, quoted in Fischer, *War of Illusions*, pp. 169, 186–187.

invaded Luxemburg on August 1, the same day on which it ordered full mobilization.) Thus Germany had no pure "mobilization" plan, but rather had a "mobilization and attack" plan under which mobilizing and attacking would be undertaken simultaneously. As a result, Europe would cascade into war if any European state mobilized in a manner which eventually forced German mobilization.

This melding of mobilization and attack in Germany reflected two decisions to which I have already alluded. First, Germans believed that they would lose their chance for victory and create a grave danger for themselves if they gave the Entente time to mobilize its superior numbers. In German eyes, German defenses would be too weak to defeat this superiority. As one German apologist later argued, "Germany could never with success have warded off numerically far superior opponents by means of a defensive war against a mobilized Europe" had it mobilized and stood in place. Hence it was "essential for the Central Powers to begin hostilities as soon as possible" following mobilization.[141] Likewise, during the July crisis, Jagow explained that Germany must attack in response to Russian mobilization because "we are obliged to act as fast as possible before Russia has the time to mobilize her army."[142]

Second, the German war plan depended on the quick seizure of Liège. Germany could only secure Liège quickly if German troops arrived before Belgium prepared its defense, and this in turn depended on achieving surprise against Belgium. Accordingly, German military planners enshrouded the planned Liège attack in such dark secrecy that Bethmann Hollweg, Admiral Tirpitz, and possibly even the Kaiser were unaware of it.[143] They also felt compelled to strike as soon as mobilization was authorized, both because Belgium would strengthen the defenses of Liège as a normal part of the Belgian mobilization which German mobilization would engender, and because otherwise Belgium eventually might divine German intentions towards Liège and focus upon preparing its defense and destroying the critical bridges and tunnels which it controlled.

---

141. Von Wegerer, *Refutation*, pp. 307–309.
142. August 4, quoted in Alfred Vagts, *Defense and Diplomacy* (New York: Kings Crown Press, 1956), p. 306. Likewise Bethmann Hollweg explained that, if Russia mobilized, "we could hardly sit and talk any longer because we have to strike immediately in order to have any chance of winning at all." Fischer, *War of Illusions*, p. 484.
143. Albertini, *Origins*, Vol. 2, p. 581; Vol. 3, pp. 195, 250, 391; Ritter, *Sword and the Scepter*, Vol. 2, p. 266; and Fay, *Origins*, Vol. 1, pp. 41–42.

Both of these decisions in turn reflected German faith in the power of the offense, and were not appropriate to a defense-dominant world. Had Germans recognized the actual power of the defense, they might have recognized that neither Germany nor its enemies could win decisively even by exploiting a fleeting material advantage, and decided instead to mobilize without attacking. The tactical windows that drove Germany to strike in 1914 were a mirage, as events demonstrated during 1914–1918, and Germans would have known this in advance had they understood the power of the defense. Likewise, the Liège *coup de main* was an artifact of Schlieffen's offensive plan; if the Germans had stuck with the elder Moltke's plan, they could have abandoned both the Liège attack and the compulsion to strike quickly which it helped to engender.

BRINKMANSHIP AND FAITS ACCOMPLIS

Two *faits accomplis* by the Central powers set the stage for the outbreak of the war: the Austrian ultimatum to Serbia on July 23, and the Austrian declaration of war against Serbia on July 28. The Central powers also planned to follow these with a third *fait accompli*, by quickly smashing Serbia on the battlefield before the Entente could intervene. These plans and actions reflected the German strategy for the crisis: "*fait accompli* and then friendly towards the Entente, the shock can be endured," as Kurt Riezler had summarized.[144]

This *fait accompli* strategy deprived German leaders of warning that their actions would plunge Germany into a world war, by depriving the Entente of the chance to warn Germany that it would respond if Austria attacked Serbia. It also deprived diplomats of the chance to resolve the Austro–Serbian dispute in a manner acceptable to Russia. Whether this affected the outcome of the crisis depends on German intentions—if Germany sought a pretext for a world war, then this missed opportunity had no importance, but if it preferred the status quo to world war, as I believe it narrowly did, then the decision to adopt *fait accompli* tactics was a crucial step on the road to war.

---

144. July 8, quoted in John A. Moses, *The Politics of Illusion: The Fischer Controversy in German Historiography* (London: George Prior, 1975), p. 39. Austria declared war on Serbia, as one German diplomat explained, "in order to forestall any attempt at mediation" by the Entente; and the rapid occupation of Serbia was intended to "confront the world with a '*fait accompli*.'" Tschirschky, in Schmitt, *Coming of the War*, Vol. 2, p. 5; and Jagow, in Albertini, *Origins*, Vol. 2, p. 344; see also pp. 453–460.

Had Germany not done so, it might have recognized where its policies led before it took irrevocable steps, and have drawn back.

The influence of the cult of the offensive is seen both in the German adoption of this *fait accompli* strategy and in the disastrous scope of the results which followed in its train. Some Germans, such as Kurt Riezler, apparently favored brinkmanship and *fait accompli* diplomacy as a means of peaceful expansion.[145] Others probably saw it as a means to provoke a continental war. In either case it reflected a German willingness to trade peace for territory, which reflected German expansionism—which in turn reflected security concerns fuelled by the cult of the offensive. Even those who saw *faits accomplis* as tools of peaceful imperialism recognized their risks, believing that necessity justified the risk. Thus Riezler saw the world in Darwinistic terms: "each people wants to grow, expand, dominate and subjugate others without end . . . until the world has become an organic unity under [single] domination."[146] *Faits accomplis* were dangerous tools whose adoption reflected the dangerous circumstances which Germans believed they faced.

The cult of the offensive also stiffened the resistance of the Entente to the Austro–German *fait accompli*, by magnifying the dangers they believed it posed to their own security.[147] Thus Russian leaders believed that Russian security would be directly jeopardized if Austria crushed Serbia, because they valued the power which Serbia added to their alliance, and because they feared a domino effect, running to Constantinople and beyond, if Serbia were overrun. Sazonov believed that Serbian and Bulgarian military power was a vital Russian resource, "five hundred thousand bayonets to guard the Balkans" which "would bar the road forever to German penetration, Austrian invasion."[148] If this asset were lost, Russia's defense of its own territories would be jeopardized by the German approach to Constantinople: Sazonov warned the Czar, "First Serbia would be gobbled up; then will come Bulgaria's turn, and then we shall have her on the Black Sea." This would be

---

145. On Riezler's thought, see Moses, *Politics of Illusion*, pp. 27–44; and Thompson, *In the Eye of the Storm*.
146. Quoted in Moses, *Politics of Illusion*, pp. 28, 31. Likewise during the war Riezler wrote that unless Germany gained a wider sphere of influence in Europe "we will in the long run be crushed between the great world empires . . . Russia and England." Thompson, *In the Eye of the Storm*, p. 107.
147. I am grateful to Jack Snyder for this and related observations.
148. Schmitt, *Coming of the War*, Vol. 1, p. 131n. See also Lieven, *Russia and the Origins of the First World War*, pp. 40–41, 99–100, 147.

"the death-warrant of Russia" since in such an event "the whole of southern Russia would be subject to [Germany]."[149]

Similar views could be found in France. During the July crisis one French observer warned that French and Serbian security were closely intertwined, and the demise of Serbia would directly threaten French security:

To do away with Serbia means to double the strength which Austria can send against Russia: to double Austro–Hungarian resistance to the Russian Army means to enable Germany to send some more army corps against France. For every Serbian soldier killed by a bullet on the Morava one more Prussian soldier can be sent to the Moselle. . . . It is for us to grasp this truth and draw the consequences from it before disaster overtakes Serbia.[150]

These considerations helped spur the Russian and French decisions to begin military preparations on July 25, which set in train a further sequence of events: German preliminary preparations, which were detected and exaggerated by French and Russian officials, spurring them on to further measures, which helped spur the Germans to their decision to mobilize on July 30. The effects of the original *fait accompli* rippled outward in ever-wider circles, because the reactions of each state perturbed the safety of others—forcing them to react or preempt, and ultimately forcing Germany to launch a world war which even it preferred to avoid.

Had Europe known that, in reality, the defense dominated, these dynamics might have been dampened: the compulsion to resort to *faits accomplis*, the scope of the dangers they raised for others, and the rippling effects engendered by others' reactions all would have been lessened. States still might have acted as they did, but they would have been less pressured in this direction.

PROBLEMS OF ALLIANCES: UNCONDITIONALITY AND AMBIGUITY

Two aspects of the European alliance system fostered the outbreak of World War I and helped spread the war. First, both alliances had an unconditional, offensive character—allies supported one another unreservedly, regardless of whether their behavior was defensive or provocative. As a result a local war would tend to spread throughout Europe. And second, German leaders were not convinced that Britain would fight as an Entente member, which

---

149. Fay, *Origins*, Vol. 2, p. 300; Sazonov, *Fateful Years*, p. 179; Schmitt, *Coming of the War*, Vol. 1, p. 87.
150. J. Herbette, July 29, in Albertini, *Origins*, Vol. 2, p. 596.

encouraged Germany to confront the Entente. In both cases the cult of the offensive contributed to the problem.

UNCONDITIONAL ("TIGHT") ALLIANCES. Many scholars contend that the mere existence of the Triple Alliance and the Triple Entente caused and spread the war. Sidney Fay concluded, "The greatest single underlying cause of the War was the system of secret alliance," and Raymond Aron argued that the division of Europe into two camps "made it inevitable that any conflict involving two great powers would bring general war."[151] But the problem with the alliances of 1914 lay less with their existence than with their nature. A network of defensive alliances, such as Bismarck's alliances of the 1880s, would have lowered the risk of war by facing aggressors with many enemies, and by making status quo powers secure in the knowledge that they had many allies. Wars also would have tended to remain localized, because the allies of an aggressor would have stood aside from any war that aggressor had provoked. Thus the unconditional nature of alliances rather than their mere existence was the true source of their danger in 1914.

The Austro–German alliance was offensive chiefly and simply because its members had compatible aggressive aims. Moreover, German and Russian mobilization plans left their neighbors no choice but to behave as allies by putting them all under threat of attack. But the Entente also operated more unconditionally, or "tightly," because Britain and France failed to restrain Russia from undertaking mobilization measures during the July crisis. This was a failure in alliance diplomacy, which in turn reflected constraints imposed upon the Western allies by the offensive assumptions and preparations with which they had to work.

First, they were hamstrung by the offensive nature of Russian military doctrine, which left them unable to demand that Russia confine itself to defensive preparations. All Russian preparations were inherently offensive, because Russian war plans were offensive. This put Russia's allies in an "all or nothing" situation—either they could demand that Russia stand unprepared, or they could consent to provocative preparations. Thus the British ambassador to St. Petersburg warned that Britain faced a painful decision, to "choose between giving Russia our active support or renouncing her friendship."[152] Had Russia confined itself to preparing its own defense, it

---

151. Fay, *Origins*, Vol. 1, p. 34; and Raymond Aron, *The Century of Total War* (Boston: Beacon Press, 1955), p. 15.
152. Buchanan, in Fay, *Origins*, Vol. 2, p. 379.

would have sacrificed its Balkan interests by leaving Austria free to attack Serbia, and this it would have been very reluctant to do. However, the British government was probably willing to sacrifice Russia's Balkan interests to preserve peace;[153] what Britain was unable to do was to frame a request to Russia which would achieve this, because there was no obvious class of defensive activity that it could demand. Edward Grey, the British Foreign Secretary, wrote later:

I felt impatient at the suggestion that it was for me to influence or restrain Russia. I could do nothing but express pious hopes in general terms to Sazonov. If I were to address a direct request to him that Russia should not mobilize, I knew his reply: Germany was much more ready for war than Russia; it was a tremendous risk for Russia to delay her mobilization. . . . I did most honestly feel that neither Russian nor French mobilization was an unreasonable or unnecessary precaution.[154]

One sees in this statement a losing struggle to cope with the absence of defensive options. Russia was threatened, and must mobilize. How could Britain object?

Britain and France were also constrained by their dependence upon the strength and unity of the Entente for their own security, which limited their ability to make demands on Russia. Because they feared they might fracture the Entente if they pressed Russia too hard, they tempered their demands to preserve the alliance. Thus Poincaré wrote later that France had been forced to reconcile its efforts to restrain Russia with the need to preserve the Franco–Russian alliance, "the break up of which would leave us in isolation at the mercy of our rivals."[155] Likewise Winston Churchill recalled that "the one thing [the Entente states] would not do was repudiate each other. To do this might avert the war for the time being. It would leave each of them to face the next crisis alone. They did not dare to separate."[156] These fears were probably overdrawn, since Russia had no other option than alliance with the other Entente states, but apparently they affected French and British behavior.[157] This in turn reflected the assumption in France and Britain that the security of the Entente members was closely interdependent.

153. See Geiss, *July 1914*, p. 176; and Albertini, *Origins*, Vol. 2, p. 295.
154. Albertini, *Origins*, Vol. 2, p. 518.
155. Ibid., p. 605.
156. Winston Churchill, *The Unknown War* (New York: Charles Scribner's Sons, 1931), p. 103.
157. Thus Grey later wrote that he had feared a "diplomatic triumph on the German side and humiliation on the other as would smash the Entente, and if it did not break the Franco–Russian

French leaders also felt forced in their own interests to aid Russia if Russia embroiled itself with Germany, because French security depended on the maintenance of Russian power. This in turn undermined the French ability to credibly threaten to discipline a provocative Russia. Thus the British ambassador to Paris reflected French views when he cabled that he could not imagine that France would remain quiescent during a Russo–German war, because "If [the] French undertook to remain so, the Germans would first attack [the] Russians and, if they defeated them, they would then turn round on the French."[158] This prospect delimited French power to restrain Russian conduct.

Third, British leaders were unaware that German mobilization meant war, hence that peace required Britain to restrain Russia from mobilizing first, as well as attacking. As a result, they took a more relaxed view of Russian mobilization than they otherwise might, while frittering away their energies on schemes to preserve peace which assumed that war could be averted even after the mobilizations began.[159] This British ignorance reflected German failure to explain clearly to the Entente that mobilization did indeed mean war—German leaders had many opportunities during the July crisis to make this plain, but did not do so.[160] We can only guess why Germany was silent, but German desire to avoid throwing a spotlight on the Liège operation probably played a part, leading German soldiers to conceal the plan from German civilians, which led German civilians to conceal the political implications of the plan from the rest of Europe.[161] Thus preemptive planning threw a shroud of secrecy over military matters, which obscured the mechanism that would unleash the war and rendered British statesmen less able

---

alliance, would leave it without spirit, a spineless and helpless thing." Likewise during July 1914 Harold Nicolson wrote: "Our attitude during the crisis will be regarded by Russia as a test and we must be careful not to alienate her." Schmitt, *Coming of the War*, Vol. 2, pp. 38, 258.

158. Bertie, on August 1, in Schmitt, *Coming of the War*, Vol. 2, p. 349n.

159. Geiss, *July 1914*, pp. 198, 212–213, 250–251; Albertini, *Origins*, Vol. 2, pp. 330–336.

160. See Albertini, *Origins*, Vol. 2, pp. 479–481; Vol. 3, pp. 41–43, 61–65. Albertini writes that European leaders "had no knowledge of what mobilization actually was . . . what consequences it brought with it, to what risks it exposed the peace of Europe. They looked on it as a measure costly, it is true, but to which recourse might be had without necessarily implying that war would follow." This reflected German policy: Bethmann's ultimatum to Russia "entirely omitted to explain that for Germany to mobilize meant to begin war," and Sazonov gathered "the distinct impression that German mobilization was not equivalent to war" from his exchanges with German officials. Vol. 2, p. 479; Vol. 3, pp. 41–43.

161. Kautsky and Albertini suggest that the German deception was intended to lull the Russians into military inaction, but it seems more likely that they sought to lull the Belgians. Albertini, *Origins*, Vol. 3, p. 43.

to wield British power effectively for peace by obscuring what it was that Britain had to do.

Lastly, the nature of German war plans empowered Russia to involve France, and probably Britain also, in war, since Germany would be likely to start any eastern war by attacking westward, as Russian planners were aware. Hence France and Britain would probably have to fight for Russia even if they preferred to stand aside, because German planners assumed that France would fight eventually and planned accordingly, and the plans they drew would threaten vital British interests. We have no direct evidence that Russian policies were emboldened by these considerations, but it would be surprising if they never occurred to Russian leaders.

These dynamics reflected the general tendency of alliances toward tightness and offensiveness in an offense-dominant world. Had Europe known that the defense had the advantage, the British and French could have more easily afforded to discipline Russia in the interest of peace, and this might have affected Russian calculations. Had Russia had a defensive military strategy, its allies could more easily and legitimately have asked it to confine itself to defensive preparations. Had British leaders better understood German war plans, they might have known to focus their efforts on preventing Russian mobilization. And had German plans been different, Russian leaders would have been more uncertain that Germany would entangle the Western powers in eastern wars, and perhaps proceeded more cautiously.

The importance of the failure of the Western powers to restrain Russia can be exaggerated, since Russia was not the chief provocateur in the July crisis. Moreover, too much can be made of factors which hamstrung French restraint of Russia, since French desire to prevent war was tepid at best, so French inaction probably owed as much to indifference as inability. Nevertheless, Russian mobilization was an important step toward a war which Britain, if not France, urgently wanted to prevent; hence, to that extent, the alliance dynamics which allowed it helped bring on the war.

THE AMBIGUITY OF BRITISH POLICY. The British government is often accused of causing the war by failing to warn Germany that Britain would fight. Thus Albertini concludes that "to act as Grey did was to allow the catastrophe to happen,"[162] and Germans themselves later argued that the British had led them on, the Kaiser complaining of "the grossest deception" by the British.[163]

---

162. Ibid., Vol. 2, p. 644.
163. Ibid., p. 517. See also Tirpitz, quoted in ibid., Vol. 3, p. 189.

The British government indeed failed to convey a clear threat to the Germans until after the crisis was out of control, and the Germans apparently were misled by this. Jagow declared on July 26 that "we are sure of England's neutrality," while during the war the Kaiser wailed, "If only someone had told me beforehand that England would take up arms against us!"[164] However, this failure was not entirely the fault of British leaders; it also reflected their circumstances. First, they apparently felt hamstrung by the lack of a defensive policy option. Grey voiced fear that if he stood too firmly with France and Russia, they would grow too demanding, while Germany would feel threatened, and "Such a menace would but stiffen her attitude."[165]

Second, British leaders were unaware of the nature of the German policy to which they were forced to react until very late, which left them little time in which to choose and explain their response. Lulled by the Austro–German *fait accompli* strategy, they were unaware until July 23 that a crisis was upon them. On July 6, Arthur Nicolson, undersecretary of the British foreign office, cheerfully declared, "We have no very urgent and pressing question to preoccupy us in the rest of Europe."[166] They also were apparently unaware that a continental war would begin with a complete German conquest of Belgium, thanks to the dark secrecy surrounding the Liège operation. Britain doubtless would have joined the war even if Germany had not invaded Belgium, but the Belgian invasion provoked a powerful emotional response in Britain which spurred a quick decision on August 4. This reaction suggests that the British decision would have been clearer to the British, hence to the Germans, had the nature of the German operation been known in advance.

Thus the British failure to warn Germany was due as much to German secrecy as to British indecision. Albertini's condemnation of Grey seems unfair: governments cannot easily take national decisions for war in less than a week in response to an uncertain provocation. The ambiguity of British policy should be recognized as an artifact of the secret styles of the Central powers, which reflected the competitive politics and preemptive military doctrines of the times.

WHY SO MANY "BLUNDERS"?
Historians often ascribe the outbreak of the war to the blunders of a mediocre European leadership. Barbara Tuchman describes the Russian Czar as having

---

164. Ibid., Vol. 2, p. 429; and Tuchman, *Guns of August*, p. 143. See also Albertini, *Origins*, Vol. 2, pp. 514–527, 643–650; and Jarausch, "Illusion of Limited War."
165. Albertini, *Origins*, Vol. 2, p. 631; and Schmitt, *Coming of the War*, Vol. 2, p. 90.
166. Schmitt, *Coming of the War*, Vol. 1, pp. 417–418.

"a mind so shallow as to be all surface," and Albertini refers to the "untrained, incapable, dull-witted Bethmann-Hollweg," the "mediocrity of all the personages" in the German government, and the "short-sighted and unenlightened" Austrians. Ludwig Reiners devotes a chapter to "Berchtold's Blunders"; Michael Howard notes the "bland ignorance among national leaders" of defense matters; and Oron Hale claims that "the men who directed international affairs in 1914 were at the lowest level of competence and ability in several decades."[167]

Statesmen often did act on false premises or fail to anticipate the consequences of their actions during the July crisis. For instance, Russian leaders were initially unaware that a partial mobilization would impede a later general mobilization;[168] they probably exaggerated the military importance of mobilizing against Austria quickly;[169] they falsely believed Germany would acquiesce to their partial mobilization; they probably exaggerated the significance of the Austrian bombardment of Belgrade;[170] they falsely believed a general Russian mobilization could be concealed from Germany; and they mobilized without fully realizing that for Germany "mobilization meant war."[171]

German leaders encouraged Russia to believe that Germany would tolerate a partial Russian mobilization, and failed to explain to Entente statesmen that mobilization meant war, leading British and Russian leaders to assume that it did not.[172] They also badly misread European political sentiment, hoping that Italy, Sweden, Rumania, and even Japan would fight with the Central powers, and that Britain and Belgium would stand aside.[173] For their part, Britain and Italy failed to warn Germany of their policies; and Britain acquiesced to Russian mobilization, apparently without realizing that Russian mobilization meant German mobilization, which meant war. Finally, intelli-

---

167. Tuchman, *Guns of August*, p. 78; Albertini, *Origins*, Vol. 2, pp. 389, 436; Vol. 3, p. 253; Ludwig Reiners, *The Lamps Went Out in Europe* (New York: Pantheon, 1955), pp. 112–122; Howard quoted in Schelling, *Arms and Influence*, p. 243; and Oron J. Hale, *The Great Illusion: 1900–1914* (New York: Harper & Row, 1971), p. 285.
168. Albertini, *Origins*, Vol. 2, pp. 295–296.
169. See Turner, *Origins of the First World War*, pp. 92–93; Albertini, *Origins*, Vol. 2, p. 409; Vol. 3, pp. 230–231; but see also Lieven, *Russia and the Origins of the First World War*, pp. 148–149.
170. Reiners, *Lamps Went Out in Europe*, p. 135; and Albertini, *Origins*, Vol. 2, p. 553.
171. Albertini, *Origins*, Vol. 2, p. 574, 579–581; Vol. 3, pp. 56, 60–65.
172. Ibid., Vol. 2, pp. 332, 479–482, 485, 499–500, 550; Vol. 3, pp. 41–43, 61–65; Geiss, *July 1914*, pp. 245, 253, 266.
173. See Albertini, *Origins*, Vol. 2, pp. 334, 673, 678; Vol. 3, p. 233; Geiss, *July 1914*, pp. 226, 255, 302, 350–353; Schmitt, *Coming of the War*, Vol. 1, pp. 72–74, 322; Vol. 2, pp. 52–55, 149, 390n. Also relevant is Albertini, *Origins*, Vol. 2, pp. 308–309, 480, 541.

gence mistakes on both sides made matters worse. Russian leaders exaggerated German and Austrian mobilization measures, some German reports exaggerated Russian mobilizations, and French officials exaggerated German measures, which helped spur both sides to take further measures.[174]

What explains this plethora of blunders and accidents? Perhaps Europe was unlucky in the leaders it drew, but conditions in 1914 also made mistakes easy to make and hard to undo. Because secrecy was tight and *faits accomplis* were the fashion, facts were hard to acquire. Because windows were large and preemption was tempting, mistakes provoked rapid, dramatic reactions that quickly made the mistake irreversible. Statesmen seem like blunderers in retrospect partly because the international situation in 1914 was especially demanding and unforgiving of error. Historians castigate Grey for failing to rapidly take drastic national decisions under confusing and unexpected circumstances in the absence of domestic political consensus, and criticize Sazonov for his shaky grasp of military details on July 28 which no Russian civilian had had in mind five days earlier. The standard implicit in these criticisms is too stiff—statecraft seldom achieves such speed and precision. The blame for 1914 lies less with the statesmen of the times than with the conditions of the times and the severe demands these placed on statesmen.

BLAMECASTING

The explosive conditions created by the cult of the offensive made it easier for Germany to spark war without being blamed, by enabling that country to provoke its enemies to take defensive or preemptive steps which confused the question of responsibility for the war. German advocates of preventive war believed that Germany had to avoid blame for its outbreak, to preserve British neutrality and German public support for the war. Moreover, they seemed confident that the onus for war *could* be substantially shifted onto their opponents. Thus Moltke counselled war but warned that "the attack must be started by the Slavs,"[175] Bethmann Hollweg decreed that "we must

---

174. See generally Lebow, *Between Peace and War*, pp. 238–242; and Albertini, *Origins*, Vol. 3, pp. 67–68. For details on Russia see Albertini, *Origins*, Vol. 2, pp. 499, 545–546, 549, 566–567, 570–571, 576; Schmitt, *Coming of the War*, Vol. 2, pp. 97–98, 238, 244n.; Schilling, *How the War Began*, pp. 61–62; and Sazonov, *Fateful Years*, pp. 193, 199–200, 202–203. For details on France, see Joffre, *Personal Memoirs*, Vol. 1, pp. 117–128; and Albertini, *Origins*, Vol. 2, p. 647; Vol. 3, p. 67. On Germany see Trumpener, "War Premeditated?," pp. 73–74; Albertini, *Origins*, Vol. 2, pp. 529, 560, 637; Vol. 3, pp. 2–3, 6–9; and Geiss, *July 1914*, pp. 291–294.
175. In 1913, in Albertini, *Origins*, Vol. 2, p. 486.

give the impression of being forced into war,"[176] and Admiral von Müller summarized German policy during the July crisis as being to "keep quiet, letting Russia put herself in the wrong, but then not shying away from war."[177] "It is very important that we should appear to have been provoked" in a war arising from the Balkans, wrote Jagow, for "then—but probably only then—Britain can remain neutral."[178] And as the war broke out, von Müller wrote, "The mood is brilliant. The government has succeeded very well in making us appear as the attacked."[179]

These and other statements suggest an official German hope that German responsibility could be concealed. Moreover, whatever the source of this confidence, it had a sound basis in prevailing military conditions, which blurred the distinction between offensive and defensive conduct, and forced such quick reactions to provocation that the question of "who started it?" could later be obscured. Indeed, the German "innocence campaign" during and after the war succeeded for many years partly because the war developed from a rapid and complex chemistry of provocation and response which could easily be misconstrued by a willful propagandist or a gullible historian.[180] Defenders seemed like aggressors to the untrained eye, because all defended quickly and aggressively. Jack Snyder rightly points out elsewhere in this issue that German war plans were poorly adapted for the strategy of brinkmanship and peaceful expansion which many Germans pursued until 1914, but prevailing European military arrangements and beliefs also facilitated the deceptions in which advocates of preventive war believed Germany had to engage.

---

176. On July 27, 1914, in Fischer, *War of Illusions*, p. 486.
177. On July 27, in J.C.G. Röhl, "Admiral von Müller and the Approach of War, 1911–1914," *Historical Journal*, Vol. 12, No. 4 (1969), p. 669. In the same spirit, Bernhardi (who hoped for Russian rather than British neutrality) wrote before the war that the task of German diplomacy was to spur a French attack, continuing: "[W]e must not hope to bring about this attack by waiting passively. Neither France nor Russia nor England need to attack in order to further their interests. . . . [Rather] we must initiate an active policy which, without attacking France, will so prejudice her interests or those of England that both these States would feel themselves compelled to attack us. Opportunities for such procedures are offered both in Africa and in Europe. . . ." Bernhardi, *Germany and the Next War*, p. 280.
178. In 1913, in Fischer, *War of Illusions*, p. 212.
179. Röhl, "Admiral von Müller," p. 670.
180. On this innocence campaign, see Imanuel Geiss, "The Outbreak of the First World War and German War Aims," in Walter Laqueur and George L. Mosse, eds., *1914: The Coming of the First World War* (New York: Harper and Row, 1966), pp. 71–78.

Conclusion

The cult of the offensive was a major underlying cause of the war of 1914, feeding or magnifying a wide range of secondary dangers which helped pull the world to war. The causes of the war are often catalogued as an unrelated grab-bag of misfortunes which unluckily arose at the same time; but many shared a common source in the cult of the offensive, and should be recognized as its symptoms and artifacts rather than as isolated phenomena.

The consequences of the cult of the offensive are illuminated by imagining the politics of 1914 had European leaders recognized the actual power of the defense. German expansionists then would have met stronger arguments that empire was needless and impossible, and Germany could have more easily let the Russian military buildup run its course, knowing that German defenses could still withstand Russian attack. All European states would have been less tempted to mobilize first, and each could have tolerated more preparations by adversaries before mobilizing themselves, so the spiral of mobilization and counter-mobilization would have operated more slowly, if at all. If armies mobilized, they might have rushed to defend their own trenches and fortifications, instead of crossing frontiers, divorcing mobilization from war. Mobilizations could more easily have been confined to single frontiers, localizing the crisis. Britain could more easily have warned the Germans and restrained the Russians, and all statesmen could more easily have recovered and reversed mistakes made in haste or on false information. Thus the logic that led Germany to provoke the 1914 crisis would have been undermined, and the chain reaction by which the war spread outward from the Balkans would have been very improbable. In all likelihood, the Austro–Serbian conflict would have been a minor and soon-forgotten disturbance on the periphery of European politics.

This conclusion does not depend upon how one resolves the "Fischer controversy" over German prewar aims; while the outcome of the Fischer debate affects the *way* in which the cult caused the war, it does not affect the importance which the cult should be assigned. If one accepts the Fischer–Geiss–Röhl view that German aims were very aggressive, then one emphasizes the role of the cult in feeding German expansionism, German window thinking, and the German ability to catalyze a war while concealing responsibility for it by provoking a preemption by Germany's adversaries. If one believes that Germany was less aggressive, then one focuses on the role of the incentive to preempt in spurring the Russian and French decisions to mobilize, the nature of Russian and German mobilization plans, the British failure to restrain Russia and warn Germany, the scope and irreversibility of the effects of the Austro–German *fait accompli*, and the various other blunders of statesmen.[181] The cult of the offensive would play a different role in the history as taught by these two schools, but a central role in both.

The 1914 case thus supports Robert Jervis and other theorists who propose that an offense-dominant world is more dangerous, and warns both superpowers against the offensive ideas which many military planners in both countries favor. Offensive doctrines have long been dogma in the Soviet military establishment, and they are gaining adherents in the United States as well. This is seen in the declining popularity of the nuclear strategy of "assured destruction" and the growing fashionability of "counterforce" nuclear strategies,[182] which are essentially offensive in nature.[183]

The 1914 case bears directly on the debate about these counterforce strategies, warning that the dangers of counterforce include but also extend far beyond the well-known problems of "crisis instability" and preemptive war. If the superpowers achieved disarming counterforce capabilities, or if they believed they had done so, the entire political universe would be disturbed. The logic of self-protection in a counterforce world would compel much of the same behavior and produce the same phenomena that drove the world to war in 1914—dark political and military secrecy, intense competition for resources and allies, yawning windows of opportunity and vulnerability, intense arms-racing, and offensive and preemptive war plans of great scope and violence. Smaller political and military mistakes would have larger and less reversible consequences. Crises would be harder to control, since military

---

181. A useful review of the debate about German aims is Moses, *Politics of Illusion*.

182. On the growth of offensive ideas under the Reagan Administration, see Barry R. Posen and Stephen Van Evera, "Defense Policy and the Reagan Administration: Departure from Containment," *International Security*, Vol. 8, No. 1 (Summer 1983), pp. 24–30. On counterforce strategies, a recent critical essay is Robert Jervis, *The Illogic of American Nuclear Strategy* (Ithaca: Cornell University Press, 1984).

183. "Counterforce" forces include forces which could preemptively destroy opposing nuclear forces before they are launched, forces which could destroy retaliating warheads in flight towards the attacker's cities, and forces which could limit the damage which retaliating warheads could inflict on the attacker's society if they arrived. Hence, "counterforce" weapons and programs include highly accurate ICBMs and SLBMs (which could destroy opposing ICBMs) *and* air defense against bombers, ballistic missile defense for cities, and civil defense. Seemingly "defensive" programs such as the Reagan Administration's ballistic missile defense ("Star Wars") program and parallel Soviet ballistic missile defense programs are in fact *offensive* under the inverted logic of a MAD world. See Posen and Van Evera, "Defense Policy and the Reagan Administration," pp. 24–25.

alerts would open and close larger windows, defensive military preparations would carry larger offensive implications, and smaller provocations could spur preemptive attack. Arms control would be harder to achieve, since secrecy would impede verification and treaties which met the security requirements of both sides would be harder to frame, which would circumscribe the ability of statesmen to escape this frightful world by agreement.

"Assured destruction" leaves much to be desired as a nuclear strategy, and the world of "mutual assured destruction" ("MAD") which it fosters leaves much to be desired as well. But 1914 warns that we tamper with MAD at our peril: any exit from MAD to a counterforce world would create a much more dangerous arrangement, whose outlines we glimpsed in the First World War.

1914 Revisited

Allies, Offense, and Instability

Scott D. Sagan

$\mathbf{T}$he origins of the First World War continue to be of great interest today because there are a number of striking similarities between the events of 1914 and contemporary fears about paths by which a nuclear war could begin. July 1914 was a brinksmanship crisis, resulting in a war that everyone was willing to risk but that no one truly wanted. During the crisis, the political leaderships' understanding of military operations and control over critical war preparations were often tenuous at best. In 1914, the perceived incentives to strike first, once war was considered likely, were great, and the rapidity and inflexibility of offensive war plans limited the time available to diplomats searching for an acceptable political solution to the crisis. In a world in which the possibility of massive nuclear retaliation has made the deliberate, premeditated initiation of nuclear war unlikely, there is widespread concern that a repetition of the Sarajevo scenario may occur: an apparently insignificant incident sparking—through a dangerous mixture of miscalculations, inadvertent escalation, and loss of control over events—a tragic and unintended war.[1] Indeed, for a student of the July crisis, even specific phrases in the current nuclear debate can be haunting: what former Secretary of Defense Harold Brown meant to be a comforting metaphor, that the Soviet Union would never risk its society on "a cosmic throw of the dice," is less reassuring to those who recall German Chancellor Theobald von Bethmann–Hollweg's statement, "If the iron dice are now to be rolled, may God help us," made just hours before Germany declared war against Russia on August 1, 1914.[2]

I would like to thank Robert Art, Stanley Hoffmann, Jack Levy, and Edward Rhodes for their helpful comments on earlier drafts of this paper.

Scott D. Sagan is a Lecturer in the Government Department, Harvard University.

---

1. Recent discussions of nuclear strategy that utilize the 1914 analogy include Graham T. Allison, Albert Carnesale, and Joseph S. Nye, Jr., eds., *Hawks, Doves, and Owls* (New York: Norton, 1985), especially pp. 210–217; Paul J. Bracken, *The Command and Control of Nuclear Forces* (New Haven: Yale University Press, 1983), pp. 222–223, 239–240; and Miles Kahler, "Rumors of War: The 1914 Analogy," *Foreign Affairs*, Vol. 58, No. 2 (Winter 1979–80).
2. Harold Brown, *Department of Defense Annual Report for Fiscal Year 1979* (Washington, D.C.: U.S. Government Printing Office, 1978), p. 63; and Karl Kautsky, ed., *Outbreak of the World War:*

International Security, Fall 1986 (Vol. 11, No. 2)
© 1986 by the President and Fellows of Harvard College and of the Massachusetts Institute of Technology.

Prior to 1914, the general staffs of each of the European great powers had designed elaborate and inflexible offensive war plans, which were implemented in a series of mobilizations and countermobilizations at the end of the July crisis. In August, all the continental powers took the offensive: the Germans attacked across Belgium and Luxembourg into France; the French army launched a massive assault against German positions in Alsace–Lorraine; and the Russian army, although not yet fully mobilized, immediately began simultaneous offenses against Germany and Austria–Hungary. In retrospect, the war plans of the great powers had disastrous political and military consequences. The negative political consequences were seen at the cabinet meetings during the July crisis, for the pressures to begin mobilization and launch offensives promptly, according to the military timetables, contributed greatly to the dynamic of escalation and the political leaderships' loss of freedom of action. In Berlin, for example, as Bethmann–Hollweg frankly admitted to the Prussian Ministry of State, once the Russians began to mobilize, "control had been lost and the stone had started rolling."[3] The military consequences were seen on the battlefield. Each of the major offensive campaigns was checked or repulsed with enormous costs: some 900,000 men were missing, taken prisoner, wounded, or dead by the end of 1914.[4]

Historians and political scientists have long sought to understand why the great powers all had offensive military doctrines when the military technology of 1914—barbed wire, machine guns, and railroads—appears to have favored the defense. The popular explanation is that European soldiers and statesmen blithely ignored the demonstrations of defensive firepower in the American Civil War and the Russo–Japanese War and simply believed that the next European war would be like the last (an offensive victory as in the Franco–Prussian war), but that has never been satisfactory. For, in fact, numerous European military observers were in the United States from 1861–65 and in Manchuria during the 1904–5 conflict. Observer reports were widely distributed, the German, French, and British armies sponsored multivolume official histories of the Russo–Japanese War, and throughout the period prior to 1914 prolonged and heated debates raged in European military journals

---

German Documents (New York: Oxford University Press, 1924), No. 553, p. 441. (Hereinafter, *German Documents*.)
3. *German Documents*, No. 456, p. 382.
4. The estimate is from Michael Howard, "Men Against Fire: The Doctrine of the Offensive in 1914," in Peter Paret, ed., *The Makers of Modern Strategy from Machiavelli to the Nuclear Age* (Princeton: Princeton University Press, 1986), p. 510.

about the relative effectiveness of offensive and defensive tactics and strategies.[5]

Recent scholarship has suggested a new explanation which, using organization theory, emphasizes the degree to which the organizational interests of the professional military are advanced by offensive military doctrines, regardless of whether offensives are recommended by perceived national interests or prevailing technology.[6] Jack Snyder and Stephen Van Evera have found, in the 1914 case, an extreme example of this phenomenon: the "cult of the offensive."[7] This new explanation for the origins of the First World War is becoming widely accepted, and no one has challenged its validity.[8]

This essay reviews the organizational theory arguments and their "cult of the offensive" application to the events of 1914. It concludes that this approach seriously misrepresents the *causes* of the offensive doctrines of 1914 and, therefore, the underlying causes of the war. By focusing on the organizational interests of the professional military, the "cult of the offensive" theory has overlooked the more fundamental causes of the World War I offensive doctrines: the political objectives and alliance commitments of the great powers.

This essay also argues that the "cult of the offensive" theory misrepresents the *consequences* of the 1914 offensive military doctrines. Although offensive

---

5. These writings are reviewed in ibid.; and Michael Howard, "Men Against Fire: Expectations of War in 1914," in Steven E. Miller, ed., *Military Strategy and the Origins of the First World War: An International Security Reader* (Princeton: Princeton University Press, 1985), pp. 41–57. Also see T.H.E. Travers, "The Offensive and the Problem of Innovation in British Military Thought 1870–1915," *Journal of Contemporary History*, Vol. 13 (1978), pp. 531–553; Travers, "Technology, Tactics, and Morale: Jean de Bloch, The Boer War, and British Military Theory, 1900–1914," *Journal of Modern History*, Vol. 51, No. 2 (June 1979), pp. 264–286; and Jay Luvaas, *The Military Legacy of the Civil War: The European Inheritance* (Chicago: University of Chicago Press, 1959).

6. See Barry R. Posen, *The Sources of Military Doctrine: France, Britain and Germany Between the World Wars* (Ithaca: Cornell University Press, 1984), and Stephen Van Evera, "Causes of War" (Ph.D. dissertation, University of California, Berkeley, 1984), especially chapter 7.

7. Jack Snyder, "Civil–Military Relations and the Cult of the Offensive, 1914 and 1984" and Stephen Van Evera, "The Cult of the Offensive and the Origins of the First World War," both in Miller, *Military Strategy and the Origins of the First World War*. Also see Snyder, *The Ideology of the Offensive: Military Decision Making and the Disasters of 1914* (Ithaca: Cornell University Press, 1984); and Van Evera, "Why Cooperation Failed in 1914," *World Politics*, Vol. 38, No. 1 (October 1985), pp. 97–98.

8. See Allison et al., *Hawks, Doves, and Owls*, p. 212; Robert Axelrod and Robert O. Keohane, "Achieving Cooperation under Anarchy: Strategies and Institutions," *World Politics*, Vol. 38, No. 1 (October 1985), pp. 230–231; Richard Ned Lebow, "The Soviet Offensive in Europe: The Schlieffen Plan Revisited?," *International Security*, Vol. 9, No. 4 (Spring 1985), pp. 52–53, 68–69; Jack S. Levy, "Organizational Routines and the Causes of War," *International Studies Quarterly*, in press; and Steven E. Miller, "Introduction: The Great War and the Nuclear Age," in Miller, *Military Strategy and the Origins of the First World War*, p. 3.

military doctrines were necessary, they were not sufficient to cause the strategic instability witnessed in the July crisis; the critical preemptive incentives and pressures to move quickly felt by the German General Staff would not have been so strong without specific military vulnerabilities of the Entente powers and Belgium. In addition, even given the German offensive doctrine and war plans, it appears likely that Berlin would have been deterred in 1914 if the British government had issued a clear and credible threat to intervene in a continental war early in the July crisis. Furthermore, while the "cult of the offensive" theory correctly identifies the problem of offensive instability during the July crisis, it ignores the critical strategic dangers that would have resulted if European statesmen had adopted purely defensive strategies in 1914. These conclusions are, finally, of more than historical interest, for they suggest that the explicit lessons that the "cult of the offensive" theorists offer for contemporary American deterrent strategy are quite misleading.

Offenses, Military Biases, and the Security Dilemma

International relations theory posits the existence of a common security dilemma between sovereign states and has stressed the pernicious impact of offensive military forces and doctrines in exacerbating the problem.[9] The security dilemma exists when actions taken by one state solely for the purposes of increasing its own security simultaneously threaten another state, decreasing its security. This dilemma can be vicious "even in the extreme case in which all states would like to freeze the status quo," when two conditions exist: first, when defensive weapons and strategies cannot be distinguished from offensive ones and, second, when offensive military operations are considered easier than defensive operations.[10] Such conditions are said to produce a number of dangers. When offense is easier, or when one cannot differentiate between offenses and defenses, "unnecessary" arms races are made more likely. Under such conditions, the incentives to launch preventive wars are increased whenever the balance of power is shifting in favor of an adversary. Likewise, when war is considered likely, preemptive

---

9. Robert Jervis, "Cooperation under the Security Dilemma," *World Politics*, Vol. 30, No. 2 (January 1978), pp. 167–214. Also see George H. Quester, *Offense and Defense in the International System* (New York: John Wiley and Sons, 1977); Van Evera, "Causes of War," chapter 3; and Jack S. Levy, "The Offensive/Defensive Balance of Military Technology: A Theoretical and Historical Analysis," *International Studies Quarterly*, Vol. 28 (1984), pp. 219–238.
10. Jervis, "Cooperation under the Security Dilemma," pp. 167, 186–187.

incentives are increased to the degree that striking the first offensive blow is considered advantageous compared to waiting to be attacked.

Earlier work on the subject focused largely on the effect of military technology on the offensive/defensive balance, and many arms control negotiations have sought to promote "stability" by identifying and limiting offensive weapons and promoting defensive ones.[11] This approach's assumption, that status quo powers will pursue defensive, "stabilizing" military capabilities if possible, is challenged by the new "cult of the offensive" literature which emphasizes that military organizations display a strong preference for offensive forces and doctrines, even if the predominant military technology favors defense.

Five related and reinforcing explanations are offered for the military's bias in favor of the offense. First, offensive doctrines enhance the power and size of military organizations.[12] Offenses are usually technologically more complex and quantitatively more demanding than defenses. They often require larger forces, longer range weapons, and more extensive logistic capabilities. Since military organizations, like other organizations, seek to enhance their own size and wealth, as a rule, they will prefer offenses. Second, offensive doctrines tend to promote military autonomy. As Jack Snyder explains, "The operational autonomy of the military is most likely to be allowed when the operational goal is to disarm the adversary quickly and decisively by offensive means."[13] Not only are defensive operations, because they tend to be less complex, easier for civilian leaders to understand, but defenses also can lead to prolonged conflict on one's own soil, increasing the likelihood of civilian interference. In addition, offensive doctrines may require professional armies, rather than more "civilianized" conscripted armies. Third, offenses enhance the prestige and self-image of military officers. Defensive operations are often seen as passive, less challenging, and less glorious. As Barry Posen puts it, offenses can make soldiers "specialists in victory," while defenses merely turn them into "specialists in attrition."[14]

---

11. Ibid., pp. 186–214. For related works see Quester, *Offense and Defense in the International System*; Marion W. Boggs, *Attempts to Define and Limit "Aggressive" Armament in Diplomacy and Strategy* (Columbia, Mo.: University of Missouri, 1941); and B.H. Liddell Hart, "Aggression and the Problem of Weapons," *The English Review*, July 1932, pp. 71–78.

12. Posen, *Sources of Military Doctrine*, p. 49.

13. Snyder, "Civil–Military Relations and the Cult of the Offensive," p. 121; see also Posen, *Sources of Military Doctrine*, pp. 49–50.

14. Posen, *Sources of Military Doctrine*, p. 49. A recent examination of the causes of the persistence of offensive tactics on the part of the Confederacy emphasizes the influence of Southern culture's romantic notions of soldierly honor. See Grady McWhiney and Perry D. Jamieson, *Attack and*

The fourth explanation offered for the military's offensive bias is that offenses structure military campaigns in favorable ways. Taking the initiative helps ensure that your standard scenario and operations plans, instead of the enemy's, dominate at least in the initial battles of a war.[15] This advantage of offensive operations has been repeated in statements of the "principle of the initiative" in military manuals at least since Jomini's maxim of 1807:

The general who takes the initiative knows what he is going to do; he conceals his movements, surprises and crushes an extremity or weak point. The general who waits is beaten at one point before he learns of the attack.[16]

The fifth explanation emphasizes the effect that military officers' training and duties have on their beliefs about the need for decisive military operations that tend to be offensive in nature. Officers, it is argued, are necessarily preoccupied with the possibility of war; they tend to see the adversary as extremely hostile and war as a natural, indeed often an inevitable, part of international politics. Such beliefs lead them to favor preventive wars or preemptive strikes when necessary and decisive operations when possible. "Seeing war more likely than it really is," Snyder concludes, "[military professionals] increase its likelihood by adopting offensive plans and buying offensive forces."[17]

The 1914 Cult of the Offensive

Jack Snyder and Stephen Van Evera have found, in the origins of the First World War, the most extreme example of what can go wrong if the endemic military bias in favor of offensive doctrines is allowed to determine a state's strategy. Why did all the continental powers immediately launch offensives at the outburst of war? Snyder argues, "The offensive strategies of 1914 were largely domestic in origin, rooted in bureaucratic, sociopolitical, and psychological causes."[18] In France, the offensive nature of Plan XVII is seen as the

---

Die: Civil War Military Tactics and Southern Heritage (University, Ala.: University of Alabama Press, 1982).
15. Posen, *Sources of Military Doctrine*, pp. 47–48. It should be noted, however, that this advantage need not be a military bias, as the civilian leadership as well as the military would favor it.
16. Antoine-Henri Jomini, "L'art de la guerre," *Pallas: Eine Zeitschrift für Staats und Kreigs Kunst*, Vol. 1 (1808), pp. 32–40, as quoted in John I. Alger, *The Quest for Victory: The History of the Principles of War* (Westport, Conn.: Greenwood Press, 1982), p. 22.
17. Snyder, "Civil–Military Relations and the Cult of the Offensive," p. 119.
18. Ibid., p. 137.

result of the professional military's use of offensive doctrine as a defense of its institutional interests. After the Dreyfus affair, political leaders sought to "republicanize" the French military, hoping to create an army based largely on reservists and capable of conducting only defensive operations. The French military countered this threat to its institutional "essence," Snyder explains, by adopting the *offensive à outrance* doctrine which required the discipline and élan that only a professional standing army's long training and service together could provide.[19] The offensive strategy of the Schlieffen Plan, according to Snyder, was adopted in Germany because of the Prussian General Staff's bias in favor of decisive operations and because an offensive strategy promoted their power, prestige, and autonomy. In Russia, the ambitious war plans calling for offensive operations against both Germany and Austria–Hungary were adopted because the absence of a strong central political authority enabled each of the conflicting military factions, one favoring an offense against Germany and the other supporting an offense against Austria–Hungary, to pursue its own preferred campaign. Because a realistic assessment of the chances of success would have threatened their fundamental beliefs, Russian military leaders resorted to what Snyder calls "needful thinking," believing that both "necessary" offensives could succeed when objective assessment would have shown that they would fail.[20] The conclusion is clear:

Strategic instability in 1914 was caused not by military technology, which favored the defender and provided no first-strike advantage, but by offensive war plans that defied technological constraints. The lesson here is that doctrines can be destabilizing even when weapons are not, since doctrine may be more responsive to the organizational needs of the military than to the implications of the prevailing weapon technology.[21]

While Snyder has focused on the causes of the "cult of the offensive," Van Evera's work concentrates on its consequences; his detailed analysis of the July crisis goes considerably further than earlier work on this subject in identifying precisely how the military plans of the European powers contrib-

---

19. Ibid., pp. 129–133; and Snyder, *Ideology of the Offensive*, chapters 2 and 3. For a different argument, stressing that offensive doctrine was adopted so that the morale of patriotic French recruits could compensate for superior German material strength, see Douglas Porch, *The March to the Marne: The French Army, 1871–1914* (Cambridge: Cambridge University Press, 1981), chapter 11.
20. Snyder, "Civil–Military Relations and the Cult of the Offensive," pp. 125–129, 133–137; and Snyder, *Ideology of the Offensive*, chapters 4–7.
21. Snyder, *Ideology of the Offensive*, pp. 10–11.

uted to strategic instability in 1914.[22] He finds the "cult of the offensive" to be the "mainspring" driving the numerous mechanisms that led the great powers to war and illustrates his argument by imagining what 1914 would have looked like had military and civilian leaders not had such strong beliefs about the efficacy of offenses. The expansionist aims of Germany, the perceived incentives for preventive war and preemptive strikes, and the dynamics of rapid escalation in the crisis could have all been avoided, Van Evera argues, had European leaders "recognized the actual power of the defense":

German expansionists then would have met stronger arguments that empire was needless and impossible, and Germany could have more easily let the Russian military buildup run its course, knowing that German defenses could still withstand Russian attack. All European states would have been less tempted to mobilize first, and each could have tolerated more preparations by adversaries before mobilizing themselves, so the spiral of mobilization and counter-mobilization would have operated more slowly, if at all.[23]

Van Evera even concludes that the First World War might not have broken out at all if leaders had understood the strength of defenses: "If armies [had] mobilized, they might have rushed to defend their own trenches and fortifications, instead of crossing frontiers. . . ." Indeed, "In all likelihood, the Austro–Serbian conflict would have been a minor and soon-forgotten disturbance on the periphery of European politics."[24]

An Alternative Explanation: Strategic Interests and Alliance Commitments

Snyder's work has identified a number of ways in which the organizational interests of the military can affect strategic doctrine, and Van Evera's writings have persuasively demonstrated the alarming consequences that specific aspects of the offensive war plans of 1914 had on the political leadership's ability to control events during the July crisis. But their "cult of the offensive" analysis greatly exaggerates the degree to which the offensive doctrines in 1914 were caused by military-motivated biases or misperceptions of the of-

22. Van Evera, "The Cult of the Offensive and the Origins of the First World War." Also see Levy, "Organizational Routines and the Causes of War." For earlier interpretations, see Herman Kahn, *On Thermonuclear War* (Princeton: Princeton University Press, 1960), pp. 357–375; and Thomas Schelling's discussion of "the dynamics of mutual alarm" in Schelling, *Arms and Influence* (New Haven: Yale University Press, 1966), pp. 221–244.
23. Van Evera, "The Cult of the Offensive and the Origins of the First World War," p. 105.
24. Ibid. For a similar argument, that the European armies should have been "rushing to their own trenches rather than the enemy's territory" in 1914, see Jervis, "Cooperation under the Security Dilemma," p. 191.

fense/defense balance. Moreover, by focusing exclusively on the problems of the 1914 offensive military doctrines, they have overlooked the negative consequences that would have resulted if the great powers had adopted purely defensive military doctrines.

Three related problems exist with the "cult of the offensive" theory explanation. First, the theory exaggerates the probability that critical offensive military operations would fail. This theory is perhaps the strongest in explaining the French military's *offensive à outrance* doctrine, which even Field Marshall Joffre admitted was influenced by "le culte de l'offensive."[25] But it was not this French offensive doctrine that produced the dynamic of rapid escalation during the July crisis. For the French, a decision to mobilize was not a decision to attack Germany, and the Paris government specifically ordered its army not to move within 10 kilometers of the German border upon general mobilization.[26] Instead, the most critical offensive war plan in 1914 was that of Germany, for it was the German military's perceived need to mobilize quickly to implement the Schlieffen Plan's preemptive attack on Liège and attack in the West before Russian mobilization was complete that caused the crisis to move beyond control.

With 20-20 hindsight, however, it is too easy to argue that the German offensive plan for conquest was doomed to fail. Thus, when Snyder writes of the *"vain attempt* to knock France out of the war" and complains that the German General Staff "could not accept that a future war *would inevitably take the form of an inglorious, unproductive stalemate,"* he assumes that the historical outcome, the defeat of the Schlieffen Plan, was the only one possible.[27] Similarly, when Van Evera writes, "Had statesmen understood that in reality the defense had the advantage, they also would have known that *the possession of the initiative could not be decisive"* or that "German expansionists then would have met stronger arguments that empire was *needless and impossible,"* he assumes that the outcome of the war was a foregone conclusion.[28]

In fact, the Schlieffen Plan came very close to succeeding and the Germans almost did win the short war they had expected to fight. The French, who call the decisive battle outside Paris "the Miracle of the Marne," have a better

---

25. As quoted by Van Evera, "The Cult of the Offensive and the Origins of the First World War," p. 61, fn. 14.
26. See Luigi Albertini, *The Origins of the War of 1914* (London: Oxford University Press, 1957), Vol. 3, pp. 66–111.
27. Snyder, "Civil–Military Relations and the Cult of the Offensive," p. 128; and Snyder, *Ideology of the Offensive,* p. 17. Emphasis added.
28. Van Evera, "The Cult of the Offensive and the Origins of the First World War," pp. 75, 105. Emphasis added.

sense of the probability of German victory than do those who assume that the German attack was bound to fail. It would be beyond the scope of this article to reexamine the long-standing debate among military analysts and historians on whether Moltke's timidity and poor judgment ruined what could have been a major German victory in September 1914. A number of major participants and historians have maintained that the German offense would have succeeded if Moltke had moved more vigorously and had not weakened the strength of the attacking right wing by moving forces to defend Alsace–Lorraine; others have countered that, even if the Germans had won an overwhelming victory at the Marne, the French would not have capitulated and a stalemate would still have developed.[29] Defense-advocates have maintained that the Germans came close to an offensive victory only because the French launched their offensive Plan XVII.[30] Others have stressed, however, that knowledge that the French would attack in Alsace–Lorraine was the underlying premise of the Schlieffen Plan. The subtlety of the German offense was that, as Liddell Hart put it, "it would operate like a revolving door—the harder the French pushed on one side, the more sharply would the other swing around and strike their back."[31]

The key point for this critique of "cult of the offensive" theory is not how this counterfactual debate is resolved, but rather that it exists at all. For it demonstrates that the theory's assumption, that only gross misperceptions

---

29. Among participants, General von Kluck, who commanded the right wing, and Admiral Tirpitz both maintained that, had the German attack started a few days earlier, victory would have been much more likely. More recently, L.C.F. Turner has argued that the plan "offered a real prospect of forcing a decision in the West and avoiding the agonizing trench war deadlock" if it had been executed as Schlieffen had designed. Gordon A. Craig and Walter Goerlitz agree that the plan would have achieved "an overwhelming initial success" if carried out in its original form, but they maintain, as do Martin Van Creveld and Richard Ned Lebow, that the French and British could have made a German success on the Marne a Pyrrhic victory by continuing the war even if the Germans won the battle and Paris fell. It should be noted, however, that the Germans have attacked France three times since 1815: twice they took Paris and France eventually capitulated; once they failed and the French kept fighting. Von Kluck and Tirpitz quoted in Van Evera, "The Cult of the Offensive and the Origins of the First World War," p. 77, fn. 66. See also Turner, "The Significance of the Schlieffen Plan," in Paul M. Kennedy, ed., *The War Plans of the Great Powers 1880–1914* (Boston: Allen & Unwin, 1979), pp. 203–204; Gordon A. Craig, *The Politics of the Prussian Army, 1640–1945* (London: Oxford University Press, 1955), p. 280; Walter Goerlitz, *History of the German General Staff* (New York: Praeger 1953), p. 135; Martin Van Creveld, *Supplying War: Logistics from Wallenstein to Patton* (Cambridge: Cambridge University Press, 1977), p. 116; and Lebow, "The Soviet Offensive in Europe," pp. 62–65.
30. Snyder, *Ideology of the Offensive*, p. 9.
31. B.H. Liddell Hart, "Foreward" to Gerhard Ritter, *The Schlieffen Plan: Critique of a Myth* (London: Oswald Wolff, 1958), p. 6; see also Turner, "The Significance of the Schlieffen Plan," p. 204.

of the offensive/defensive balance can explain why offensive strategies were chosen in 1914, is questionable. In addition, it should be remembered that Schlieffen was acutely aware of the danger of frontal attacks against fortified positions, which was precisely why the German plan emphasized an enveloping attack on the French flanks.[32] Thus, although the professional military's excessive faith in "the offensive spirit" is likely to have played a role in the fruitless British and French frontal assaults along the Western Front during the war,[33] the "cult" explanation is far less persuasive in the case of the offensive Schlieffen Plan, which is what caused the dynamic of escalation in the July crisis.

The second major problem with the "cult of the offensive" explanation is that it ignores the fundamental issue of the military balances. After all, what do the terms used in this literature, "offense-dominance" and "defense-dominance," really mean? Robert Jervis's definition, that offense has the advantage when "it is easier to destroy the other's army and take its territory than it is to defend one's own" is problematic, because it has been generally recognized since Clausewitz that defense is almost always "easier" in land warfare because of advantages of cover and the capability to choose and prepare terrain and fortify positions.[34] This is why military analysts usually think in terms of the force ratios—the required superiority of the offensive forces (2:1, 3:1, etc.) in order to achieve victory—rather than in all-or-nothing terms such as "offense-dominance" or "defense-dominance."

By focusing on the effects of military technology on the "offense/defense balance," the "cult of the offensive" theory fails to consider adequately the quantity or quality of military forces opposed to one another in a particular territorial campaign. How "defense-dominant" was the world of 1914? Certainly the range and rate of fire of small-caliber magazine rifles, machine guns, and field artillery strongly favored the defensive. And yet, even if one assumes that the historical outcome of 1914–1918 was the likely one, it is

---

32. Ritter, *The Schlieffen Plan*, pp. 50–51.
33. Michael Howard argues, however, that "the worst losses were those due not to faulty doctrine but to inefficiency, inexperience, and the sheer organizational problems of combining fire and movement on the requisite scale." Howard, "Men Against Fire: The Doctrine of the Offensive in 1914," p. 526.
34. Jervis, "Cooperation under the Security Dilemma," p. 187. For an excellent review of literature on the offense/defense balance, see Levy, "The Offensive/Defensive Balance of Military Technology." Also see Jack Snyder, "Perceptions of the Security Dilemma in 1914," in Robert Jervis, Richard Ned Lebow, and Janice Gross Stein (with contributions from Patrick M. Morgan and Jack L. Snyder), *Psychology and Deterrence* (Baltimore: Johns Hopkins University Press, 1985), pp. 157–160.

doubtful that defenses were so dominant or advantageous as to make all states simultaneously secure if they had maintained defensive military doctrines.

The point is best made by imagining what would have happened if individual armies had rejected offensive doctrines and had, as Stephen Van Evera and Robert Jervis recommend, "rushed to their trenches" instead of others' territory. Serbia did, after all, adopt what was essentially a defensive strategy and was eventually conquered by the overwhelming forces of the Central Powers.[35] What if the French had no offensive plans but had "rushed to their trenches," staying completely on the defensive in 1914? The outcome of the war in the East suggests that the Central Powers could have defeated the Russians even more soundly if there had been no Western Front. If the Germans, after defeating the Russians, had turned and quickly attacked the French, would the technology of 1914 have proven the "dominance" of the defense? One can, of course, only speculate on such a question, but the near victory of the German offensive in 1918 against the French, a fully mobilized and deployed British army, and the arriving Americans suggests that a massive German offensive against the French alone (or the French and the small British Expeditionary Force) would have stood a strong chance of success.

This leads to the third problem. The "cult of the offensive" argument, by focusing primarily upon narrow issues of military planning, ignores the critical role of the states' political objectives in determining their military doctrines. Here I am not referring to the expansionist war aims of Germany and the other great powers, for, as Jack Snyder correctly notes, the desire to annex territory had its most important influence on decision-making *after* the war began, and the doctrinal decisions of the military officers who prepared the prewar offensive war plans in France, Germany, and Russia were not strongly influenced by such territorial ambitions.[36] Yet, the "cult of the offensive" argument overlooks a key point: offensive military doctrines are needed not only by states with expansionist war aims, but also by states that have a strong interest in protecting an exposed ally. Unless sufficient capability to protect an ally at the point of attack exists, "protector" powers require

---

35. For a brief review of the campaigns in Serbia, see Trevor N. Dupuy and Molly R. Mayo, *Campaigns in Southern Europe* (New York: Franklin Watts, 1967), pp. 9–20, 38–46.
36. Snyder, *Ideology of the Offensive*, pp. 19–20. Snyder does make an exception for Russia: the Russian offensive plans against Austria–Hungary were influenced by ambitions in the Balkans as well as military operational considerations. It should also be noted that Austria–Hungary, because of its punitive policy toward Serbia, required an offensive doctrine.

offensive strategies even if their goals are defensive in nature. This consideration is often recognized with respect to extended deterrence today; it also, however, lay at the heart of the offensive doctrines of 1914.

Thus, the Russians needed an offensive capability against Austria–Hungary, in order to be able to prevent the Austrians from attacking Serbia with overwhelming offensive superiority.[37] The French required offensive capabilities against Germany in order to support Russia. Germany needed an offense to protect Austria–Hungary if Russia launched an attack against Germany's ally. Particular conditions of the military balance in 1914—the slowness of the Russian mobilization and what General von Falkenhayn called "the almost unlimited power of the Russians to evade a final decision by arms"[38] due to its vast territory—resulted in the German plan to attempt to knock France out of the war first. This further complicated the issue, for the German offensive plans against France resulted in both a Russian need for an offensive against Germany and even Austrian plans to attack Russia as a "relief offensive" to give Moltke more time to defeat the French.

This need for offensive capabilities to provide support for allies can be seen as the root cause of the offensive war plans of the great powers. This argument does not mean that motivated biases, due to organizational or psychological factors, had no influence whatsoever on military doctrine prior to 1914. It does suggest that the states' strategic interests were dominant. For example, minor powers, such as Belgium and Serbia, may have had military cults of the offensive, but they did *not* have offensive military doctrines or war plans when war broke out in 1914.[39] In contrast, the great powers required offensive military doctrines because of their alliance com-

---

37. That the initial Austrian offensive against Serbia failed should be seen as a success of the Russian strategy, and not as proof that the Russians misperceived the offense/defense balance in the Balkans. The Austrian attack failed because Conrad was forced to send the Second Army north into Galicia instead of attacking Serbia in the south because of Russian intervention. See Norman Stone, "Moltke and Conrad: Relations between the Austro–Hungarian and German General Staffs, 1909–1914," in Kennedy, *The War Plans of the Great Powers, 1880–1914*, pp. 222–251.

38. General Erich von Falkenhayn, *The German General Staff and its Decisions, 1914–1916* (Freeport, N.Y.: Books for Libraries Press, 1971 reprint), p. 16.

39. As Van Evera notes, some Belgian officers proposed that Belgium attack Germany at the outbreak of war. Van Evera, "The Cult of the Offensive and the Origins of the First World War," p. 61; and Van Evera, "Why Cooperation Failed in 1914," p. 84. It is important to note, however, that the "temerity of such an operation" was immediately pointed out by the Belgian Chief of Staff, and Belgium pursued a defensive strategy despite such "cult of the offensive" influences. The best discussion is Albertini, *The Origins of the War of 1914*, Vol. 3, pp. 455–463, quoting Antonin Selliers de Moranville, *Contribution à l'histoire de la guerre mondiale 1914–19* (Paris, 1933), pp. 163–164.

mitments. This connection between alliance commitments and offensive doctrine was well understood in the years preceding the First World War. The Franco–Russian military convention, written in 1892, specified:

> If France is attacked by Germany or by Italy with Germany's support, Russia will bring all her available forces to bear against Germany. If Russia is attacked by Germany or by Austria with Germany's support, France will bring all her available forces to bear against Germany. . . . These troops will proceed to launch a vigorous and determined offensive, so that Germany will be forced to give battle in the East and West simultaneously.[40]

The spectre of Germany being able to defeat the French or the Russians in a piecemeal fashion haunted the allies before 1914: Joffre states that he replaced the more defensive-oriented Plan XVI with the offensive Plan XVII when he took office in part because the former failed to take into account "an eventuality which was altogether likely, namely, that the Germans might return to the old Von Moltke plan of an immediate offensive directed against the Russians." Foreign Minister Poincaré promised the Russians in 1912 that France would launch an immediate offensive against Germany if war broke out and demanded that the Russians give similar assurances in writing. Furthermore, the French and Russian General Staffs specifically rejected the possibility of war being "conducted defensively" and confirmed the need for immediate offenses in their joint meetings in 1911, 1912, and 1913.[41]

Similarly, the Russian initial offensive against the Germans in 1914 demonstrates "wishful thinking" due to faith in the offensive less than the critical need to stop Germany from amassing its forces against France alone. According to Joffre, in 1912 Grand Duke Nicholas "fully understood the necessity of the Russian Army taking the offensive rapidly, whatever the risks such an attitude might seem to involve; for it was essential to bring some relief to our front at any price. . . ."[42] Thus, in the summer of 1914 Russian Foreign Minister Sazonov and the military commanders of the East Prussian front believed that a hasty offensive against Germany might indeed fail, but that, as Sazonov reportedly argued, "we have no right to leave our Ally in

---

40. Georges Michon, *The Franco–Russian Alliance* (New York: Macmillan, 1929), p. 54.
41. *The Personal Memoirs of Joffre* (New York: Harper and Brothers, 1932), Vol. 1, p. 20; Jan Karl Tannenbaum, "French Estimates of Germany's Operational War Plans," in Ernest R. May, ed., *Knowing One's Enemies: Intelligence Assessment Before the Two World Wars* (Princeton: Princeton University Press, 1984), pp. 167–168; Michon, *The Franco–Russian Alliance*, p. 54; and L.C.F. Turner, "The Russian Mobilization in 1914," in Kennedy, *The War Plans of the Great Powers*, pp. 256–258.
42. *The Personal Memoirs of Joffre*, Vol. 1, p. 59.

danger, and it is our duty to attack at once, notwithstanding the indubitable risk of the operation as planned."[43] The Chief of Staff of the Russian field army also stressed this point, telling his troops to attack Germany "by virtue of the same inter-allied obligations" that were demonstrated by the French offensive.[44]

The logic of the strategic situation was similarly understood in Germany. Offenses were required to support Austria–Hungary, albeit an offensive against France first, to be followed by the combined attack on Russia. When confronted with Austrian complaints that German offense in the West would leave them unprotected, Schlieffen responded that "the fate of Austria will be decided not on the Bug but on the Seine," a line that Moltke repeated to Conrad in February 1913.[45] The need for offensive action to protect Germany's ally was also the central argument of Moltke's urgent memorandum to Bethmann-Hollweg on July 29, 1914, written after Moltke learned that Russia had instituted only *partial* mobilization against Austria–Hungary:

> If Germany is not to be false to her word and permit her ally to suffer annihilation at the hands of Russian superiority, she, too, must mobilize. And that would bring about the mobilization of the rest of Russia's military districts as a result.[46]

The German threat to Russia—that it would soon be forced to mobilize, which meant war, which meant the Schlieffen Plan's offensive, if Russia did not stop the *partial* mobilization against Austria–Hungary—underscores the importance of the alliance commitment in Berlin's calculations.[47] Moreover, it was the long-standing belief of the Russian military, which these threats reinforced in 1914, that the Germans would not passively tolerate Russian preparations for war against Austria–Hungary, which had led them to plan for and then in 1914 to insist upon, not a partial mobilization on the Austrian front, but rather a full mobilization against both Central Powers.[48] This

43. As quoted in Nicolas N. Golovine, *The Russian Army in the World War* (New Haven: Yale University Press, 1931), p. 213.
44. Norman Stone, *The Eastern Front, 1914–1917* (New York: Scribner, 1975), p. 48.
45. See Stone, "Moltke and Conrad: Relations between the Austro–Hungarian and German General Staffs, 1909–1914," pp. 224, 232.
46. The Grand General Staff to the Imperial Chancellor, July 29, 1914, *German Documents*, No. 349, p. 307.
47. See ibid., Nos. 342, 343, 401, and 490. It should be added, however, that both Bethmann-Hollweg and Jagow originally misled the Russians on this issue. See ibid., No. 219; and Albertini, *The Origins of the War of 1914*, Vol. 2, pp. 481–485 and Vol. 3, pp. 220–221.
48. As General Kokovtzov put it, arguing against *partial* mobilization in 1912: "no matter what

decision was critical, for once the full mobilization of the Russian army began, Bethmann-Hollweg called off the attempt to avert war by having Austro–Hungarian forces "Halt in Belgrade." Thus, the alliance system—or more properly, the strategic interests the great powers had in maintaining their alliance partners—led not only to the offensive doctrines of 1914 but even to one of the specific conditions that contributed to the dynamic of rapid mobilization and counter-mobilization that constrained last minute efforts to prevent the outbreak of war.

The failure of the "cult of the offensive" theory to examine the influence of alliances on military doctrines is significant. While the theory has done a service by highlighting a number of the risks and instabilities that can result from offensive doctrines, it has ignored the risks and instabilities that result from purely defensive military strategies. For states with a security interest in preserving an exposed ally, offensive forces and strategies are necessary. Defensive military doctrines may not produce the same degree of preventive war or preemptive war incentives, but they can undercut extended deterrence by denying a government sufficient capability to protect its allies. As France discovered in 1938 and 1939, when the lack of offensive capabilities against Germany enabled Hitler to conquer France's East European allies in a piecemeal manner, a purely defensive military doctrine can also prove strategically disastrous.

The Balance and British Intervention

If the European powers required offensive military doctrines to support their alliance commitments in 1914, does this suggest an added dimension of tragedy to the events of that summer? Did the offensive war plans, required to support alliance commitments, nevertheless inevitably produce the strategic instability that caused the July crisis to spiral out of control? The answer is, in my opinion, no. For the destabilizing consequences of the German war plans, which Van Evera skillfully analyzes, were *not* the result of the mere *offensive nature* of German military doctrine, but rather of *specific vulnerabilities*

---

we chose to call the projected measures, a mobilization remained a mobilization, to be countered by our adversaries with actual war." Quoted in Turner, "The Russian Mobilization in 1914," p. 255. For detailed examinations of the interaction of mobilization plans, see Van Evera, "The Cult of the Offensive and the Origins of the First World War," pp. 85–94; and Ulrich Trumpener, "War Premeditated? German Intelligence Operations in July 1914," *Central European History*, Vol. 9, No. 1 (March 1976).

in the military posture of Germany's adversaries. In other words, the German General Staff's perceived incentives to mobilize rapidly and start the war with a prompt and massive offensive campaign were the result of a number of weaknesses in the Entente and Belgium's military position.

Three specific factors were critical in the July crisis. The first was the inability of the Russian army to mobilize rapidly. Although Berlin required an offensive capability against Russia, to take pressure off Austria–Hungary if that state were attacked, it was the German General Staff's belief that it could knock France out of the war in the West, before the Russians were able to mount a full-strength attack in the East, that produced the Schlieffen Plan's emphasis on rapid mobilization and attacks through Luxembourg and Belgium. Without this particular aspect of the military balance (the weaker France exposed to military defeat while Russia was mobilizing), the German offensive might well have focused on Russia, with fewer incentives to move quickly and less perceived need to turn a war in the East immediately into a continental conflagration.[49]

The second factor was the lack of permanent Belgian defenses at the critical railway junction at Liège. The German General Staff understood that failure to take Liège with its tunnels and bridges intact would mean disaster for the Schlieffen Plan. As Moltke noted prior to the war, the advance through Belgium "will hardly be possible unless Liège is in our hands. . . . the possession of Liège is the *sine qua non* of our advance." Such a *coup de main* would only be possible, however, "if the attack is made at once, before the forts are fortified."[50] Without this preemptive opportunity, again, German incentives to mobilize and attack quickly would have been reduced.

The third critical factor contributing to instability in July 1914 was the uncertainty concerning British intentions to intervene in a continental war if Germany attacked France. Throughout the July crisis, the German government received sufficiently contradictory intelligence about London's intentions as to be highly uncertain about British intervention. Although Ambassador Lichnowsky did report Foreign Minister Grey's warning on July 29 that Britain could not remain uninvolved in a continental war, Prince Heinrich of Prussia had just reported on July 28 that King George V had explicitly told

---

49. Snyder and Van Evera both appear to accept this point. See Snyder, "Civil Military Relations and the Cult of the Offensive," p. 109; and Van Evera, "The Cult of the Offensive and the Origins of the First World War," p. 90.
50. Ritter, *The Schlieffen Plan*, p. 166. As quoted in Van Evera, "The Cult of the Offensive and the Origins of the First World War," p. 74.

him that the British government "shall try all we can to keep out of this and shall remain neutral." Moreover, on August 1, Lichnowsky reported that Grey had suggested that Britain would not only remain neutral, but would guarantee French neutrality if Germany fought in the East but refrained from attacking France. The resulting common assessment in Berlin was expressed well by the report of the Bavarian minister to Berlin: "England's attitude is mysterious."[51]

Sir Edward Grey's failure to present a clear and credible threat of British intervention early in the July crisis and the specific preemptive aspects of Germany's offensive war plans caused by the slow Russian mobilization and the Liège bottleneck are linked together as an immediate cause of the First World War. Bethmann-Hollweg began his belated effort to prevent the imminent war—by pressuring Austria–Hungary into stopping its advance into Serbia once Belgrade had been taken—only after Grey warned Berlin that Britain would not remain neutral in a continental conflict. The available evidence suggests that, while the Kaiser and the Chancellor were willing to precipitate a continental war, they wanted to avoid a world war with England fighting on the side of the allies. But Bethmann-Hollweg had precious little time to forge a difficult diplomatic solution at the last minute, for the military preparations of the Central Powers' adversaries were increasing rapidly. During the night of July 30, he called off the "Halt in Belgrade" effort upon being informed by the General Staff that the "military preparations of our neighbors especially in the east" prevented any further delays in German mobilization.[52] The General Staff had, by 11 p.m., not only received initial indications that Russian general mobilization had begun, but also was in-

51. On the contradictory warnings and Grey's "neutrality offer," see *German Documents*, Nos. 368, 374, 562, 574, 578, 607, and 613. Numerous historians have accepted at face value Grey's explanation that Lichnowsky's reports were due to the German Ambassador's "misunderstanding" Grey's offer. But this explanation is discredited by the fact that Grey raised the prospect of British neutrality in a German–Russian war in a telegram on August 1 to British Ambassador Bertie in Paris. See G.P. Gooch and Harold Temperley, eds., *British Documents on the Origins of the War* (hereinafter *British Documents*), Vol. 11, No. 419, 426, and 453. The best treatment of these incidents is Albertini, *The Origins of the War of 1914*, Vol. 2, pp. 429, 517, 687–688 and Vol. 3, pp. 380–386. Also see Harry F. Young, "The Misunderstanding of August 1, 1914," *The Journal of Modern History*, Vol. 48, No. 4 (December 1976), pp. 644–665. The final quotation from Minister at Berlin to President of Ministerial Council, July 31, 1914, *German Documents*, Supplement 4, No. 27, pp. 634–635.
52. *German Documents*, No. 451, p. 378. The best discussion remains Albertini, *The Origins of the War of 1914*, Vol. 3, pp. 1–65. It is important to note, however, that Bethmann-Hollweg had agreed, under pressure from Moltke, that a decision on German mobilization would be made no later than noon on July 31. Thus, even if the Czar had not ordered *general* mobilization on the night of July 30, the time available to reach a diplomatic "Halt in Belgrade" settlement would have been limited.

formed that the Belgians' preparations to defend Liège and destroy the critical bridges across the Meuse were under way.[53] Military necessity had taken over.

These events were not preordained, however, and should not lead to the conclusion that the outbreak of war was inevitable. A number of possible contingencies could have produced a very different result. *If* Grey had given a clear warning earlier, *if* the Czar had further delayed Russian mobilization against Austria and then Germany, and *if* the German offensive war plans had not been able to depend upon a preemptive *coup de main* against Liège and the decisive battle in France before Russian mobilization was completed in the East, *then* it is possible, just possible, that Bethmann-Hollweg would have had the time and the courage necessary to apply sufficient pressure on Vienna to accept the "Halt in Belgrade." And if this had occurred, 1914 might today appear as only another one of a series of Balkan crises that almost led to a world war.

Any analysis of 1914 that emphasizes the British failure to issue a credible warning to Germany must contend with Richard Ned Lebow's provocative thesis that the members of the Berlin government were so psychologically committed to believing in British neutrality that they utilized common defense mechanisms—such as denial, selective attention, and wishful thinking—to ignore the otherwise clear British intention to intervene. As Lebow has argued, the German miscalculation "ought to be recognized as a German problem for which there is no plausible external explanation":

Given Britain's commitment to Belgium, her enduring interest in the balance of power on the continent, her prior support of France in two crises with Germany and the obvious political reasons that constrained her from speaking out, it should have been apparent to all but the most unsophisticated observer of British politics that no inferences about British intentions could be drawn from her reluctance to commit herself publicly to the defense of France.[54]

This view emphasizing the psychologically motivated bias of the German leadership is not, however, convincing. It overlooks the fact that the leadership in other nations, even those with the opposite interests and motivated biases, held beliefs similar to the Germans about the likelihood of British

---

53. Trumpener, "War Premeditated?," pp. 79–83.
54. Richard Ned Lebow, *Between Peace and War* (Baltimore: Johns Hopkins University Press, 1981), pp. 130–131.

intervention. Government officials in France,[55] Russia,[56] and Great Britain itself[57] were uncertain that London would join its allies against Germany. Indeed, Sir Edward Grey himself later recalled his own pessimistic assessment during the week preceeding the British decision to intervene:

[If] war came, the interest of Britain required that we should not stand aside, while France fought alone in the West, but must support her. I knew it to be *very doubtful* whether the Cabinet, Parliament, and country would take this view on the outbreak of war, and through the whole of this week I had in view the *probable contingency that we should not decide at the critical moment to support France.*[58]

Finally, it is worth noting that the German military, as opposed to the Kaiser and Bethmann-Hollweg, did not bank on British neutrality. Moltke assumed, as did Schlieffen, that London would attempt to send the British Expeditionary Force (BEF) to the continent in support of France.[59] From the military perspective, the critical question was how to *delay* the British decision for as long as possible, in order to increase the likelihood that British military assistance would arrive too late to influence significantly the campaign in

55. Joffre judged British intervention as highly uncertain and did not, in Plan XVII, assume the British army's support. Samuel R. Williamson, "Joffre Shapes French Strategy, 1911–1913," in Kennedy, *The War Plans of the Great Powers, 1880–1914*, p. 146. Also see pp. 137–145. French cabinet member Alexander Millerand similarly noted, "In the event of war, the English soldiers ask only to fight. The machine is ready to go: will it be unleashed? Complete uncertainty. The cabinet is vulnerable in its domestic policies (Home Rule), very uncertain in foreign policy, not knowing what it wants to do." Quoted in Porch, *March to the Marne*, p. 228.
56. For example, Foreign Minister Sazonov told the Russian Council of Ministers on July 24, 1914 that risking a continental war was dangerous "since it is not known what attitude Great Britain would take in the matter." As quoted in D.C.B. Lieven, *Russia and the Origins of the First World War* (New York: St. Martin's Press, 1983), p. 142, citing Bark Ms. 7, pp. 7–13 (Columbia University, Bakhmetev Archive).
57. Lloyd George, Churchill, and Buchanan all expressed skepticism over the likelihood of British intervention. See John Grigg, *Lloyd George: From Peace to War 1912–1916* (Berkeley and Los Angeles: University of California Press, 1985), p. 140; Winston S. Churchill, *The World Crisis*, Vol. 1 (New York: Scribner, 1923), p. 211; and Maurice Paléologue, *An Ambassador's Memoirs*, trans. F.A. Holt (New York: Octagon Books, 1972), Vol. 1, p. 32. Also see Sir George Buchanan, *My Mission to Moscow* (Boston: Little, Brown, 1923), pp. 210–211; and *British Documents*, Vol. 11, No. 101. Buchanan had been informed in April by Sir Arthur Nicolson, Permanent Secretary of the Foreign Office, that the dispatch of a British expeditionary force in the event of war was "extremely remote." Nicolson to Sir George Buchanan, April 7, 1914, as quoted in Cameron Hazlehurst, *Politicians at War, July 1914 to May 1915* (London: Jonathan Cape, 1971), p. 88, fn 2.
58. Grey of Fallodon, *Twenty–Five Years* (New York: Frederick A. Stokes Co., 1925), p. 302.
59. Gerhard Ritter, *The Schlieffen Plan*, pp. 57, 61–63, 68–69; Albertini, *The Origins of the War of 1914*, Vol. 3, p. 239. For an argument that Bethmann-Hollweg shared this view, see Karl Dietrich Erdmann, "War Guilt 1914 Reconsidered: A Balance of New Research," in H.W. Koch, ed., *The Origins of the First World War: Great Power Rivalry and German War Aims*, 2nd ed. (London: Macmillan, 1984), pp. 363–364.

France.[60] This question of timing is important,[61] for it provided yet another incentive for the German General Staff to call for prompt mobilization and offensive action during the closing moments of the July crisis.

To summarize, what caused the perceived incentives in Berlin to mobilize quickly and rapidly launch an offensive campaign? What were the root causes in 1914 of what would today be called "crisis instability"? Certainly, if the German General Staff had designed a purely defensive strategy, there would have been less pressure to mobilize and strike quickly. Yet, even if the Germans had maintained an offensive doctrine to protect Austria–Hungary, as I believe was necessary, the incentives to mobilize and attack promptly might have been severely dampened if the French had not been exposed to a "knockout blow" while the slow Russian mobilization was taking place and if Liège had not been vulnerable to the *coup de main*. Finally, if the British early in the crisis had clearly and credibly placed their forces into the balance on the side of the Entente, it is at least possible that Bethmann-Hollweg and the Kaiser would have been able to restrain their Austrian ally, pulling back from the brink of war and seeking a diplomatic solution to the crisis. Churchill put the argument best: "An open alliance, if it could have peacefully been brought about on an earlier date, would have exercised a deterring effect on the German mind, or at least would have altered their military calculations."[62]

Across the Nuclear Divide: Offense Without Instability?

This article has emphasized the degree to which the political objectives of the European powers determined the offensive nature of their military doc-

---

60. This was the view that Admiral Tirpitz later expressed: "a delay of even a few days in the preparation of the English expeditionary force and its transport to France might have been of the greatest importance to us." Tirpitz, Document II, p. 13, as quoted in Albertini, *The Origins of the War of 1914*, Vol. 3, p. 242, fn. 2.

61. Lebow, unfortunately, does not deal with this issue of delaying British intervention and overlooks the importance of "timing" in his assessments. Indeed, as an example of wishful thinking, Lebow, citing an article by Konrad Jarausch, states that Bethmann-Hollweg assured the Kaiser on July 23 that "it was *impossible* that England would enter the fray." This is, however, a misquotation as Jarausch states that Bethmann-Hollweg told the Kaiser, "it is *improbable* that England will *immediately* enter the fray." The original German sentence reads: "Dass dies sofort geschieht, namentlich, dass England sich gleich zum Eingreifen entschliesst, is nicht anzunehmen." Lebow, *Between Peace and War*, p. 132 (emphasis added); Konrad Jarausch, "The Illusion of Limited War: Chancellor Bethmann Hollweg's Calculated Risk," *Central European History*, Vol. 2, No. 1 (March 1969), p. 62 (emphasis added); Bethmann-Hollweg an Wedel, July 23, 1914, *DD* 125 in Imanuel Geiss, *Julikrise und Kriegsausbruch 1914* (Hannover: Verlang für Litteratur und Aeitgeschehnen GMBH, 1963), Vol. 1, No. 235, p. 305.

62. Churchill, *The World Crisis*, Vol. 1, p. 217.

trines prior to the First World War. Although the "cult of the offensive" theory is correct to note that the professional military glorified the offensive in 1914, it exaggerates the influence of such motivated military biases on the development of offensive doctrines. Continental powers that had territorial ambitions or a strong interest in protecting allies—Austria–Hungary, Germany, France, and Russia—had offensive military doctrines; smaller states that lacked such interests—Belgium and Serbia—had defensive doctrines in August 1914. The "cult" literature has also correctly emphasized the destabilizing consequences of the specific offensive war plans during the July crisis. But it has misplaced its emphasis by blaming the "offensive" nature of the prewar military doctrines, rather than the specific conditions that produced the "destabilizing" characteristics of Moltke's operational plan— the need for prompt mobilization, the immediate attack on Liège, and the plan to knock France out of the war before Russian mobilization was complete—for the lack of "crisis stability" seen in July 1914. These different interpretations of the origins of the First World War are illustrated, in simplified form, in Figure 1.

These models, however, lead not only to different explanations for 1914, but also to different lessons for U.S. strategy today. The "cult of the offensive" theory has led its proponents to argue against all offensive military doctrines today, which they view as destabilizing, and in favor of defensive military

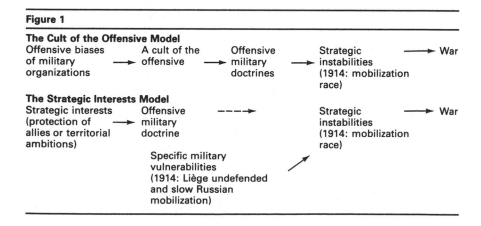

Figure 1

The Cult of the Offensive Model

| Offensive biases of military organizations | → | A cult of the offensive | → | Offensive military doctrines | → | Strategic instabilities (1914: mobilization race) | → | War |

The Strategic Interests Model

| Strategic interests (protection of allies or territorial ambitions) | → | Offensive military doctrine | - - -→ | | | Strategic instabilities (1914: mobilization race) | → | War |

Specific military vulnerabilities (1914: Liège undefended and slow Russian mobilization)

doctrines. At the nuclear level, as Van Evera writes, 1914 "warns us that we tamper with MAD at our peril":

The 1914 case . . . warns both superpowers against the offensive ideas which many military planners in both countries favor. Offensive doctrines have long been dogma in the Soviet military establishment, and they are gaining adherents in the United States as well. This is seen in the declining popularity of the nuclear strategy of "assured destruction" and the growing fashionability of "counterforce" nuclear strategies, which are essentially offensive in nature.[63]

The debate over counterforce vs. countercity targeting is, of course, a familiar one, and there is no need to review all the arguments yet once again. It is important, nevertheless, to draw attention to the different "lessons" suggested by the contrasting views of 1914. Because of the assumption that offensive doctrines are caused by the biases of the professional military, the "cult of the offensive" literature calls for senior civilian authorities to review war plans and reject all counterforce strategies.[64] While civilian review of and central control over U.S. nuclear strategy is essential, this article suggests that there have been strong political and strategic reasons why *civilian* authorities in Washington have preferred counterforce targeting. In particular, it would suggest that the perceived need for counterforce options to enhance the credibility of NATO's first-use threat, which is required for extended deterrence, has been an important factor contributing to U.S. counterforce strategy. Strong evidence for this view can be found in the recently declassified 1961 Draft Memorandum for the President in which Secretary of Defense Robert McNamara specifically rejected "a 'minimum deterrence' posture . . . in which, after a Soviet attack, we would have a capability to destroy most of Soviet urban society, but . . . would not have a capability to counterattack against Soviet military forces."[65] "We should reject the 'minimum deterrence extreme,'" McNamara reported to President Kennedy, "for the following reasons:

---

63. Van Evera, "The Cult of the Offensive and the Origins of the First World War," pp. 106–107.
64. Ibid.; and Posen, *Sources of Military Doctrine*, pp. 241, 244.
65. Draft September 23, 1961, Appendix I to Memorandum for the President, Subject: Recommended Long Range Nuclear Delivery Forces 1963–1967, p. 4. OSD FOI (declassified with deletions).

a. Deterrence may fail, or war may break out for accidental or unintended reasons, and if it does, a capability to counter-attack against high-priority Soviet military targets can make a major contribution to the objectives of limiting damage and terminating the war on acceptable terms;

b. *By reducing to a minimum the possibility of a US nuclear attack in response to Soviet aggression against our Allies, a 'minimum deterrence' posture would weaken our ability to deter such Soviet attacks.*"[66]

Of course, as this document suggests, extended deterrence has not been the only reason for counterforce targeting. Civilian authorities have also approved capabilities and plans to attack Soviet military forces to enhance deterrence by denying Soviet war aims and to limit damage to the United States if deterrence fails. The "cult" literature suggests that all nuclear counterforce plans are highly destabilizing. The perspective on 1914 offered here—emphasizing the degree to which instability in the July crisis was caused by German incentives to mobilize and launch their offenses *quickly* before Liège was fortified and the Russian mobilization completed—leads neither to such a blanket condemnation of counterforce nor to an acceptance of assured destruction targeting. If future U.S. counterforce capabilities and plans are carefully designed to threaten Soviet military and leadership targets, without posing a credible threat of a disarming first strike, it would be possible to avoid throwing out the baby of crisis stability with the bathwater of MAD. This is not the place to examine in detail what such a U.S. second-strike counterforce posture would entail, but clearly U.S. strategic vulnerabilities would have to be reduced as well as U.S. offensive capabilities constrained. Specifically, efforts to reduce the vulnerability of the U.S. ICBM force and the fragility of U.S. command and control are a high priority to enhance deterrence and stability, by reducing both Soviet incentives to strike first and American pressures to launch promptly. In addition, a retaliatory counterforce posture—designed to threaten hardened Soviet leadership targets and disrupt and destroy Soviet follow-on attacks, launch failures, reserves, and reloads—requires fewer counterforce warheads than are needed for a credible first-strike capability and could place increased reliance on slowly arriving weapons (gravity bombs and cruise missiles) for many important missions.

At a more general level, Snyder argues that the disastrous consequences of 1914 suggest that a status quo power should "compete with one hand—its offensive hand—tied behind its back":

---

66. Ibid. Emphasis added.

In practical terms, this means that the status quo state must keep up its end of the power competition but do so by deploying defensive forces, forces that dissuade without the threat of escalation and create no first-strike advantage for either side. Moreover, it must avoid commitments and alliances that can be defended only by destabilizing means.[67]

Yet, for the foreseeable future, as long as the United States has a strong interest in maintaining extended deterrence—that is, as long as the NATO alliance continues to be in the United States' political, strategic, and moral interests—it will be necessary to have offensive military capabilities even if NATO has defensive political objectives. For unless NATO's conventional capability could be increased to offset traditional Warsaw Pact conventional superiority, extended deterrence will require "the threat of escalation." Again, as the French discovered when Hitler conquered their allies in 1938 and 1939, purely "defensive" doctrines can also be strategically destabilizing. This point is an important one, for it is often overlooked not only by the "cult of the offensive" theorists, but also by the most enthusiastic supporters of strategic defense today: if President Reagan's dream of making nuclear weapons impotent and obsolete ever becomes a reality for both superpowers, it will be essential that other means of protecting Western Europe from Soviet conventional superiority be found.

A review of the "lessons of the past" cannot illuminate all of our current defense problems nor provide specific answers to questions of how much counterforce is enough or whether a first-use policy or conventional retaliation policy is most advisable for NATO. Still, in the final analysis, if 1914 is a potent reminder of the strategic instabilities that offensive military doctrines can produce, the events of the late 1930s send an equally strong message about the dangers of purely defensive doctrines for states with extended deterrent interests. Thus, at the abstract level, the lesson is clear enough: the United States must confront both problems and avoid, not only a modern cult of the offensive, but also any potential cult of the defense.

---

67. Snyder, "Perceptions of the Security Dilemma in 1914," p. 179.

Technology, Military Advantage, and World War I

Jonathan Shimshoni

A Case for Military Entrepreneurship

In formulating the military dimension of grand strategy, statesmen face a crucial decision: should they adopt an offensive or a defensive doctrine?[1] How most effectively can one approach this question? Should leaders first assess the technological state of the art, to see whether it favors offense or defense, and adapt their doctrines and grand strategies accordingly? Or should they determine independently their best grand strategy, and expect or direct that their military leaders will create the necessary supportive military advantage, be it offensive, defensive, or both?

The answer depends on where one believes military advantage comes from. The "bottom-up" approach posits that there is—at any given moment—a ubiquitous technological condition that determines, exogenous to the actors, whether offense or defense has the advantage. The "top-down" alternative recommends that advantages are manufactured and destroyed by the

I would like to thank Barry Posen, Steven Miller, Edward Rhodes, Stephen Van Evera, and John Mearsheimer for their comments on earlier drafts of this paper. I am also grateful to Samuel Huntington and Harvard University's Center for International Affairs for their assistance, and am most indebted to Barry Posen, Jack Ruina, and the entire staff at MIT's Center for International Studies for their financial and scholarly support. As ever, my mother Rose Shimshoni provided critical assistance.

Jonathan Shimshoni, the author of Israel and Conventional Deterrence: Border Warfare from 1953 to 1970 *(Cornell University Press, 1988), received his doctorate in public and international affairs from Princeton University. This article was written while he was a Visiting Scholar at MIT's Center for International Studies, and an Associate of Harvard's Center for International Affairs.*

1. *Grand strategy* is a state's overall "theory of how it can best 'cause' security for itself." Barry R. Posen, *The Sources of Military Doctrine: France, Britain and Germany Between the World Wars* (Ithaca: Cornell University Press, 1984), p. 13. Such a theory should be supported by a *military doctrine*, which is the national military organization's applied theory of victory. Military doctrine integrates and institutionalizes the principles of force organization and operation at all levels. In this article, I focus on the higher-level operational principles, such as offense or defense, and at a slightly more detailed level, on doctrines such as "elastic defense" or "blitzkrieg." The *operational level* refers to the operations of large units (corps and armies, for example) in pursuit of goals that serve strategic aims. This notion applies doctrinal principle (e.g., blitzkrieg) in the execution of specific war plans. See also Edward N. Luttwak, *Strategy: The Logic of War and Peace* (Cambridge, Mass.: Belknap/Harvard University Press, 1987), chaps. 6 and 7.

International Security, Winter 1990/91 (Vol. 15, No. 3)
© 1990 by the President and Fellows of Harvard College and of the Massachusetts Institute of Technology.

actors themselves, endogenously. If the first be true, as many authors have argued, then indeed a leader's job is to diagnose and *adapt;* if the second, as I argue in this essay, then he must analyze and *create.*

Jack Snyder writes of World War I that:

Military technology should have made the European strategic balance in July 1914 a model of stability, but offensive military strategies defied those technological realities, trapping European statesmen in a war-causing spiral of insecurity and instability. As the Boer and Russo-Japanese Wars had foreshadowed and The Great War itself confirmed, prevailing weaponry and means of transport strongly favored the defender. . . . Why then were these self-defeating [offensive] war-causing strategies adopted?[2]

This passage reflects one prominent response to this essay's central questions. Snyder, not alone in the security field, is really arguing the following: (1) military technology in 1914 created an overall and system-wide defensive advantage, and therefore (2) a central failing of decision-makers at the time was the adoption of offensive military doctrines and strategies despite this diagnosis.[3]

This offense/defense balance approach is flawed. I argue that, while technology is important to warfare (and advantages surely exist), the first does

---

2. Jack Snyder, "Civil-Military Relations and the Cult of the Offensive, 1914 and 1984," in Steven E. Miller, ed., *Military Strategy and the Origins of the First World War: An* International Security *Reader* (Princeton: Princeton University Press, 1985), pp. 108–109.
3. There is much support for this approach, or slight variations on it, in the security literature. Most prominent are George H. Quester, *Offense and Defense in the International System* (New York: Wiley, 1977); Robert Jervis, "Cooperation Under the Security Dilemma," *World Politics*, Vol. 30, No. 2 (January 1978), pp. 187–214. The approach is directly tied to World War I by Snyder, "Civil-Military Relations"; and by Stephen Van Evera, "The Cult of the Offensive and the Origins of the First World War"; both in Miller, *Military Strategy and the Origins of the First World War,* pp. 108–146, pp. 58–107. The notion that grand strategy should rest on a perceived (though not only technologically determined) offense/defense balance is applied well by Stephen M. Walt, "The Case for Finite Containment: Analyzing U.S. Grand Strategy," *International Security*, Vol. 14, No. 1 (Summer 1989), pp. 5–49, esp. pp. 22–30. Much of the motivation for this literature has been the desire to prevent unintended escalation, or spiraling, to avoid World War III. See Bernard Brodie, *Strategy in the Missile Age* (Princeton: Princeton University Press, 1965), pp. 42–70; and the essays in Miller, *Military Strategy and the Origins of the First World War.* One direction taken by a number of intellectuals and political leaders has been to seek technological fixes by de-escalation or confidence-building measures, such as non-offensive defense in Europe. See, for example, Jack Snyder, "Limiting Offensive Conventional Forces: Soviet Proposals and Western Options," *International Security*, Vol. 12, No. 4 (Spring 1988), pp. 48–77; David Gates, "Area Defence Concepts: The West German Debate," *Survival*, Vol. 29, No. 4 (July/August 1987), pp. 301–317; and the entire September 1988 issue of *Bulletin of the Atomic Scientists.* For a critical survey of much of the technologically-motivated offense/defense balance literature, see Jack S. Levy, "The Offensive/Defensive Balance of Military Technology: A Theoretical and Historical Analysis," *International Studies Quarterly*, Vol. 28, No. 2 (June 1984), pp. 219–238.

not mechanically determine the second. Advantages, rather, are driven by the interaction of technology with doctrine and war plans. Most importantly, all three factors and the manner of their interaction are endogenous, motivated and manipulated by decision-makers. Thus, advantage is not an inherited product of nature; it is manufactured, or created. Furthermore, one should not expect a group of states to enjoy one particular advantage throughout the system. At a given moment some will enjoy an offensive, and others a defensive, advantage. Even a single state may enjoy simultaneously different advantages on different fronts, or on the same front at different moments, or as doctrine, war plans, or technological applications change.[4]

Therefore, instead of resting the choice of doctrine and grand strategy on an assessment of technology, decision makers should choose grand strategy as their point of departure. With the chosen grand strategy as their guide, policymakers should pursue an explicitly entrepreneurial course in which they manipulate, develop, and exploit available technology through doctrine and war plans in order to create the necessary advantages in light of the adversary's behavior. Such imaginative and competitive manipulation of resources I call "military entrepreneurship."

Offense/defense balance theorists have found natural pasture in World War I. As Snyder's passage suggests, the Great War does seem to be an overwhelming demonstration of the price to be paid when the technological dictates are not heeded. The technology of the time—railroads, machine guns, barbed wire—apparently created an immutable defensive advantage. Pursuit of offense by all the actors in 1914, despite the state of technology did, it appears, create a quagmire of futile attacks. Therefore, I reexamine the evidence of 1914–18 for the light it sheds on both the positive and prescriptive questions posed in this article.

In fact, the World War I experience actually undermines the offense/defense balance line of argument, and supports a rather strong indictment of

---

4. For other critical assessments of such theory see John J. Mearsheimer, *Conventional Deterrence* (Ithaca: Cornell University Press, 1983), pp. 24–28. See also Steven E. Miller, "Technology and War," *Bulletin of the Atomic Scientists*, Vol. 41, No. 1 (December 1985); Bernard Brodie, "Technological Change, Strategic Doctrine, and Political Outcomes," in Klaus Knorr, ed., *Historical Dimensions of National Security Problems* (Lawrence: University Press of Kansas, 1976); Colin Gray, "New Weapons and the Resort to Force," *International Journal*, Vol. 30, No. 2 (Spring 1975). For "improvements" or qualifications, see Stephen Van Evera, "Causes of War" (Ph.D. dissertation, University of California at Berkeley, 1984), p. 78; Jack Snyder, *The Ideology of the Offensive: Military Decision Making and the Disasters of 1914* (Ithaca: Cornell University Press, 1984), pp. 20–21.

the European policy makers—not for being misguided believers, but rather for being poor entrepreneurs: having decided that offense was required for reasons of grand strategy, they were neither inventive nor revolutionary in *creating* an offensive advantage. They believed that "the necessary was possible," instead of *making* it so. This was their sin.

My discussion unfolds as follows: First I examine the logical underpinnings of the offense/defense balance approach. Second, I suggest the alternative analysis of military advantage and the role of entrepreneurship in its creation. Third, I offer an analysis of World War I as a massive failure of military entrepreneurship. Finally, I offer some observations on why, despite its importance to warriors, military entrepreneurship is a rare phenomenon.

Technology and the Offense/Defense Balance: A Critique

.At times explicitly, and in any event implicitly, the theory that the offense/ defense balance is technologically motivated posits the following: In a given period there is a state of technology that creates a prevalent system-wide advantage for either offense or defense. By taking account of the available weaponry, an observer can deduce (*a priori*) whether an offensive or a defensive doctrine (and grand strategy) would be best.[5] Logically, this approach rests upon two premises.

First, regarding the nature of operations and their relationship to strategy, offense/defense balance theory presumes that offense and defense are separate and different phenomena, each imposing different requirements on technology. A further presumption is that, if the balance is to be a guide to doctrine and strategy, then whatever appears to promote tactical or operational offensive or defensive superiority must do so at the strategic level as well. In turn, this implies the existence of a useful universal yardstick with which to measure advantage, one that rests on the relative ease of offensive or defensive operations.

---

5. The idea that an effect is systemic is a main organizing theme of Quester, *Offense and Defense*, and is an important underpinning of Snyder "Civil-Military Relations"; and Van Evera, "The Cult of the Offensive." It is a prevalent notion, often incorporated "in passing"; for example, see Robert Gilpin, *War and Change in World Politics* (Cambridge: Cambridge University Press, 1981), pp. 59–63. On this general point see Levy, "Offensive/Defensive Balance," p. 227. Stephen Walt suggests that the prevailing balance be used as a guide in formulating strategy, in "The Case for Finite Containment," pp. 10, 22–30, as do Van Evera, "Cult of the Offensive," especially pp. 105–107, and Snyder, "Civil-Military Relations," pp. 108–112, 140–146.

The second premise concerns the characteristics, distribution, and effects of technology. Holding the gross distribution of military assets equal or constant, the qualitative nature of prevailing technology is believed to determine the advantage, one way or the other.[6] For this to work, it must be true that specific technological assets (or sets of assets) favor offense or defense, that this characteristic is inherent to the weapons and independent of the users, and that this effect is universal throughout the international system in question.

Both sets of beliefs or assumptions are wrong, as I argue in the next section.

OPERATIONS AND STRATEGY

Perhaps at the lowest tactical level there is sense in differentiating between offensive actions aimed to traverse, dislodge, and capture, and defensive actions whose purpose is to stand pat and prevent this from happening. We might think of such actions as modules of operation. However, at any level above this, operations are composed of accumulations of modules, and such discrimination becomes impossible. Military operations are composed of both offensive and defensive components—in parallel, series, or both.[7] As J.F.C. Fuller wrote: "the art of fighting depends upon the closest combination of the offensive and defensive, so closely as does the structure of a building depend upon bricks and mortar."[8] Often operations require sequential ordering of tactical offense and defense: in 1973 the Egyptian (strategically offensive) plan rested on an initial attack, capture of territory, and then defense against Israeli counterattacks. The Israeli (strategically defensive) plan required operational defense, mobilization, and then counterattack. Even more characteristic is the simultaneous execution of offensive and defensive actions. Defense of one's flanks while pursuing offensive operations is an old and trusted principle of warfare. The success of the Schlieffen Plan

---

6. Quester, *Offense and Defense*, p. 3. The attempts to make technologically-based distinctions at the World Disarmament Conference (Geneva, 1932) are of interest. See Marion W. Boggs, *Attempts to Define and Limit "Aggressive" Armament in Diplomacy and Strategy*, University of Missouri Studies XVI, No. 1 (1941); Levy "Offensive/Defensive Balance," pp. 225–226.
7. On the inseparability of offense and defense, see Ariel Levite, *Offense and Defense in Israeli Military Doctrine* (Boulder, Colo.: Westview Press, 1990), chap. 4. On Clausewitz's view that these two forms are necessarily integrated in warfare, see Raymond Aron, *Clausewitz: Philosopher of War*, trans. by Christine Booker and Norman Stone (Englewood Cliffs, N.J.: Prentice Hall, 1985), chap. 6. On Mao Tse Tung's view that offense and defense are complementary, see Samuel B. Griffith, "Introduction," to Sun Tzu, *The Art of War*, trans. by Samuel B. Griffith (Oxford: Oxford University Press, 1963), p. 53.
8. Major-General J.F.C. Fuller, *Armoured Warfare* (London: Eyr and Spottiswoode, 1943), p. 120.

(1914) depended on secure flanks for all the attacking armies, and the entire plan entailed an offensive on the right and defense on the left.

The terms "offense" and "defense" may conjure up specific rather stereotypical images of each, providing the illusion that one might successfully map given technologies into each form of war. One classic distinction has been the fire-power vs. mobility dichotomy. This view portrays defense as static, maximized by fire-power technologies, and offense as mobile and dynamic, made possible by maneuver technologies.[9] However, this oversimplifies matters; there really are no generic defense and offense, though there are some prototypical approaches or doctrines. Significantly, the variance among defensive (or offensive) doctrines is as great as the differences between the two classes of operations. Operational offense may be pursued by attrition, blitzkrieg, or a "limited aims strategy." It may be "baited," allowing the enemy to commit first and then exploiting his demonstrated weaknesses, or by initiated surprise. Operational defense may also take several basic forms: in-depth or forward; static, elastic, or mobile; with or without spoiling attacks; or attrition.[10] Each of these possibilities places different demands on technology; however, either defense and offense can be designed to stress fire-power or maneuver technologies, or both in various combinations.[11]

Although the aim here is to assess the systemic *strategic* advantage (offense or defense) on the basis of the *operational* advantage, the analysis so far suggests that the nature of operations severely muddles any attempt to label an operational advantage on the basis of technology, much less characterize the international system as having a universal advantage, in either direction. Thus, lacking a firm foothold at the operational level, we are unlikely to leap safely to the strategic level.

---

9. See Van Evera, "Causes of War," pp. 102–106; Levy, "Offensive/Defensive Balance," pp. 225, 226; Gunilla Hesolf, "New Technology Favors Defense," *Bulletin of the Atomic Scientists*, Vol. 44, No. 7 (September 1988), p. 42; Boggs, *Attempts to Define "Aggressive" Armament*, passim.

10. For discussions of various types of offensive and defensive operations, see B.H. Liddell Hart, *Thoughts on War* (London: Faber and Faber, 1943), chaps. 16, 17; Mearsheimer, *Conventional Deterrence*, pp. 30–58.

11. The tank has generally been viewed as the epitome of offensive technology, and artillery the mainstay of defense. This is, however, a much over-simplified classification. Tanks do provide maneuver, serving attackers well but also defenders, as the German defense in the east in World War II, and the Israeli defense of the Golan Heights in 1973, amply demonstrate. Artillery mainly provides concentrated fire, which can support friendly maneuver forces (in defense and offense), or protect the flanks of attacking or defending forces. Note Mearsheimer's argument that massive firepower is central to blitzkrieg: *Conventional Deterrence*, chap. 7. For varied opinions regarding the possible contribution and effects of tanks, see Mearsheimer, *Conventional Deterrence*, pp. 25, 26, 34; Snyder, *Ideology of the Offensive*, p. 29; Boggs, *Attempts to Define "Aggressive" Armament*, pp. 47–48.

Furthermore, introducing the strategic level delivers the *coup de grâce* to the idea of a universal yardstick of advantage, even at the operational level. There is little sense in assessing an operational advantage without reference to each state's war aims, as it is the latter that define operational requirements.[12]

Imagine, for example, that Hitler's 1941 objectives in Russia had been much more modest. Might this have guaranteed offensive success? What if Sadat had had a much more extensive purpose in 1973—say the destruction of the Israel Defense Forces (IDF) and forceful recapture of the Sinai. Would we now be asserting the advantage of the defense in that case? The point here is twofold. First, the actual operational advantage (or prospects for success) may be heavily influenced by the extent or definition of grand-strategic war aims. Second, in order to assess an operational advantage one must first ask: Advantage in doing *what?*

TECHNOLOGY

One could argue that the impact of technology is so powerful that it has a leveling effect, washing out the variance suggested in the discussion of operations and strategy. And perhaps in the realm of nuclear weapons and confrontation this is so: it may be a MAD world (with a defensive advantage) no matter what mere earthlings do.[13] But certainly in the world of conventional weapons, the distribution of technology is critical; so is how it is used.

Most importantly, technology is either merely ideas (or capabilities), or, if applied, piles of machinery and equipment in warehouses and on parking lots. Only when technology is developed, manufactured, and put to use does it make a difference. *People* do these things, and they do them differently. Therefore, the impact of technology is by nature inequitable.

An important characteristic of technological application is that small differences matter a lot. Offense/defense balance theorists often correctly iden-

---

12. It is in this sense that Jervis's definition of the offensive/defensive balance will not do. In "Cooperation Under the Security Dilemma," p. 187, he writes that, "when we say the offense has the advantage, we simply mean that it is easier to destroy the other's army and take its territory than it is to defend one's own." But we fight to win specific goals, not simply to *fight*. Therefore the question must be, "is it easier to win?" That question requires a definition of "winning" that is nation-specific and situation-specific.

13. "MAD," mutual assured destruction, refers to the condition in which nuclear powers have invulnerable capability to retaliate; thus all nuclear attacks are deterred. For analyses of MAD arguing that it is defense-dominant, see Shai Feldman, *Israeli Nuclear Deterrence: A Strategy for the 1980s* (New York: Columbia University Press, 1982), chap. 1; Van Evera, "Causes of War," chap. 13.

tify a prominent and ubiquitous technology in a state system—such as "machine guns and barbed wire," "tanks," "artillery," "surface-to-air missiles," or "precision guided munitions." But the effect of the technological variance possible within each such category is large enough to justify much finer differentiation. A NATO artillery force composed of multiple-launch rocket systems (MLRS) firing cluster bomb munitions, Seek-Search-and-Destroy Armor (SADARM)[14] and scatterable mines, and self-propelled guns firing laser-guided munitions, is not comparable to a Soviet artillery force employing regular rocket launchers, some self-propelled guns, and mostly towed howitzers, all firing high explosive (HE) shells. Furthermore, it is not single weapons with which we make war, but rather systems of interdependent hardware. The probability that two states would create identical systems and sets of systems, and then purchase them in similar proportions, is virtually nil.

Even if this purely technological variance could be controlled, and assets were somehow distributed evenly in quantity and quality, technological *impact* would remain—almost by definition—heterogeneous in nature. The operational effect of weapons depends greatly on their interaction with a whole host of factors, some controlled by decision-makers, and others not. The most outstanding factors not subject to leaders' authority are political culture and geography. The former determines the ability to concentrate energy for war at the (macro) national level, and the ability to operate weapons and systems at the personal or small unit (micro) level. An early example is the energy for imperial expansion generated by Mohammed's ability to make of so many tribes a people united by ideology and purpose. They possessed no special technological advantage, but their political culture made them a formidable war-making force.[15] In modern times, the Israelis have had a considerable advantage in confronting their Arab neighbors because of social-cultural differences. Israeli society, steeped in western liberalism, educated, industrialized, and urban, has an advantage in deploying, using, and maintaining sophisticated mechanical and electronic tools of war, and in operating

---

14. For analysis of the special contributions of these technologies, see U.S. Congress, Office of Technology Assessment, *Technologies for NATO's Follow-On Forces Attack Concept—Special Report*, OTA-ISC-312 (Washington, D.C.: U.S. Government Printing Office, July 1986).
15. William H. McNeill, *The Pursuit of Power: Technology, Armed Force and Society Since A.D. 1000* (Chicago: University of Chicago Press, 1982), p. 21. For other European examples, see Gilpin, *War and Change*, p. 63; Michael Howard, *War in European History* (Oxford: Oxford University Press, 1976), pp. 55–58.

with the small-unit independence and overall coordination necessary for modern warfare, both offensive and defensive.[16]

The geography and topography of states in a system, similarly beyond decision-makers' control, heavily influences the demands on, and effects of, technological assets.[17] Armor could produce positive results for the Germans when, early in World War II, they confronted the shallow and finite fronts of Northern France and the Polish theater. But in the nearly infinite expanses of Russia these same tanks ultimately "got lost" and could produce no decisive results.[18] In the same war, the Germans discovered that aircraft well-suited for the short-range missions of short duration required in the Battle of France were later unsuitable for the Battle of Britain across the Channel.[19]

In contrast, doctrine and war plans are directly subject to leaders' control. These have considerable impact on the utility and efficacy of technological assets. Examples abound of protagonists who succeeded in maximizing their "bang for the buck" by purely doctrinal means, and achieved superiority without resorting to technological manipulation. The German blitzkrieg of World War II essentially applied existing armored assets in a new and concentrated manner instead of the accepted infantry-centered approach of the time. Thus, similar armored fleets of the Allies and Germans had very different operational effect. The counterpart in classical times was the Greek phalanx, which concentrated existing infantry into a form previously unaccepted, and was unstoppable.[20] At sea, in both World Wars, the organization

---

16. See Dan Horowitz, "Flexible Responsiveness and Military Strategy: The Case of the Israeli Army," *Policy Sciences*, Vol. 1, No. 2 (Summer 1970). On the role of relative administrative skill in producing military power, see Klaus Knorr, *The Power of Nations: The Political Economy of International Relations* (New York: Basic Books, 1975), pp. 63–67. On the inability of certain societies to apply the same doctrines as other societies, see Howard, *War in European History*, pp. 78–79.

17. On the importance of geography, see Posen, *The Sources of Military Doctrine*, pp. 39, 50–51, 65–67; Sun Tzu, *The Art of War*, pp. 64, 118, 127–128; and Mearsheimer, *Conventional Deterrence*, pp. 43–44.

18. On the problems for blitzkrieg in the east, see Larry H. Addington, *The Blitzkrieg Era and the German General Staff, 1865–1941* (New Brunswick: Rutgers University Press, 1971), pp. 192–193, 209, 216; Martin Van Creveld, *Supplying War: Logistics from Wallenstein to Patton* (Cambridge: Cambridge University Press, 1977), chap. 5. Note that Michael Howard argues that in World War I, cavalry became obsolete quickly in the dense Western Theatre, yet remained effective in the expansive East. *War in European History*, p. 104.

19. Posen, *Sources of Military Doctrine*, p. 97.

20. Often the critical point of leverage is purely organizational. Examples include: Le Tellier's establishment (in the seventeenth century) of a large civil bureaucracy to administer the logistics of the French army; invention of the "division" by the French in the eighteenth century; invention of the Great General Staff in nineteenth century Prussia. See Howard, *War in European*

of Allied ships into convoys gave these defenseless machines a defensive advantage. In World War II, existing air power was wedded to existing naval technology and used in a manner that revolutionized the power and projection of naval forces.

The specific war plan that leaders choose to execute brings technology and doctrine together in a manner that greatly influences military advantage. For example, destruction of Arab air forces on the ground on June 5, 1967, was not a technological feat, nor was the strategic surprise effected by the German attack through the Ardennes on May 10, 1940. Both are examples of how specific plans can amplify the effect of technology so that although it is equitably distributed, its impact may be completely skewed.

IN SUMMARY: TECHNOLOGY DOES NOT DETERMINE ADVANTAGE

What this analysis suggests is that there is no good way to diagnose an offensive or defensive advantage by observing the prevailing technology, much less to use such a measurement to recommend an overall doctrine or strategy. Indeed, the analyst who would attempt to measure an advantage cannot himself really escape reference to specific developments, production, and doctrinal application of weapons—explicitly or not—and should therefore expect to be just as surprised after the fact as adversaries often are. We remember, uncomfortably perhaps, that American technological analysis did not predict the outcome of the Vietnam War accurately. With similar discomfort Allied analysts of the 1930s must have looked back at their pre-war predictions that the technology of the time (armor included) would create a defensive advantage in the war to come.[21]

All of this does not mean that there are no offensive or defensive advantages, merely that a state system is unlikely to enjoy a single characteristic one, be it defensive or offensive. Furthermore, a single state in the system may simultaneously enjoy an offensive advantage on one front and not on another; it may have a defensive advantage at one level of strategic goal yet not on another; it may have an offensive advantage given one operational plan yet not another; or with one doctrine and not another.

History, pp. 64–65, 100–101; McNeill, *Pursuit of Power*, pp. 162–163; and Dallas J. Irvine, "The Origin of Capital Staff," *Journal of Modern History*, Vol. 10, No. 2 (June 1938), pp. 161–173.
21. See John J. Mearsheimer, *Liddell Hart and the Weight of History* (Ithaca: Cornell University Press, 1988), chap. 6; Brian Bond and Martin Alexander, "Liddell Hart and De Gaulle: The Doctrines of Limited Liability and Mobile Defense," in Peter Paret, ed., *Makers of Modern Strategy: From Machiavelli to the Nuclear Age* (Princeton: Princeton University Press, 1986), p. 612.

I also do not argue that technology is not a central pillar of warfare, for surely we fight with "things." But it is a bad foundation on which to build a theory of military advantage, for it is but one of a number of factors that, by interacting, create advantages or disadvantages. Advantages, then, are not exogenously determined for political-military leaders, but rather created by them, as they manipulate the factors that they can: technology, doctrine, and war plans.

Advantage and Entrepreneurship

Various threads of the critique of the offense/defense balance paradigm pull together to create an alternative approach to military advantage. From this critique, what have we learned about military advantage? First, it must serve a grand strategic goal, or purpose. Second, it must be or may be created or engineered. Third, in producing it, leaders must take account of factors outside their control, adapt to these, and concentrate on manipulating three basic elements within their control: doctrine, war plans, and technology. Fourth, "advantage" is relative to an opponent and fleeting, and therefore creating it is a never-ending competitive enterprise, as I discuss in the concluding paragraphs of this article. This characteristic is perhaps the most significant. I argue that there is room for true entrepreneurship in this competitive process, and that the military advantage normally goes to the more entrepreneurial state.

How does a military entrepreneur think about, and go about creating, advantage? As Barry Posen suggests, the point of departure should be at the top, starting from balance of power considerations. States do (or should) determine their military solutions in response to their strategic environment and in pursuit of grand strategic goals. Potential enemies, alliances, and the distribution of power constitute the strategic environment; also important are geography and topography, and socio-cultural constraints on (or advantages in) the use and application of force. Always remembering that "advantage" is a relative notion, a central piece of the analysis must be devoted to one's opponents—their environment, their capabilities, their military doctrine. Armed with goals and this analysis, military leaders must find a way to execute the strategy. This entails the construction or creation of an integrated system of technology, doctrine, and war plans.[22] As they turn to

---

22. A clear discussion of the need to bring current strategic doctrine and organization into line

implementation, military leaders may discover that the goals as defined are not militarily achievable. In this case there is room for another iteration, perhaps requiring the redefinition of grand strategic goals, or some other manipulation at the strategic level. However, even after such reiteration, the problem of finding a solution is in the military leaders' lap.

The framework just described encapsulates the *modus operandi* of a competitive state in search of advantage. However, this process is not, in itself, necessarily entrepreneurial, for states, like corporations, may choose to engage either in regular competition or in the entrepreneurial variety. What is the difference? "The reasonable man adapts himself to the world; the unreasonable one persists in trying to adapt the world to himself," wrote George Bernard Shaw. "Therefore, all progress depends on the unreasonable man." This "lack of reason" is entrepreneurship. Joseph Schumpeter argues that economic progress results, not from the small adjustments that competitive firms routinely make in response to changes in their markets, but by the great innovative leaps made by individuals. Reasonable firms seek out and adjust to existing equilibria, trying to do their best around them. But truly entrepreneurial firms engage in a process of "creative destruction," which promotes them (and capitalism generally), as they seek economic advantage via "the new consumers' goods, the new methods of production or transportation, the new markets, the new forms of industrial organization."[23] Significantly, because firms live in a competitive environment, this process is endless, infinitely iterative. To stay ahead, a firm must be permanently entrepreneurial, for an advantage created today should be the prime target of other competitive entrepreneurial firms tomorrow,[24] and will decay if not nourished constantly.

---

with emerging technology—in particular with precision guided munitions (PGMs)—can be found in Steven Canby, *The Alliance and Europe*, Part IV: *Military Doctrine and Technology*, Adelphi Paper No. 109 (London: International Institute of Strategic Studies [IISS], 1974/75); see also Richard Burt, *New Weapons Technologies: Debate and Directions*, Adelphi Paper No. 126 (London: IISS, 1976).

23. Joseph A. Schumpeter, *Capitalism, Socialism and Democracy*, 3rd ed. (New York: Harper and Row, 1950), chap. seven. On the idea of drastic versus marginal change (in this case as a result of technological innovation), see Nathan Rosenberg, "The Impact of Technological Innovation: A Historical View," in Ralph Landau and Nathan Rosenberg, eds., *The Positive Sum Strategy: Harnessing Technology for Economic Growth* (Washington, D.C.: National Academy Press, 1986). On the entrepreneur as someone who engages in "purposeful innovation" away from the status quo and the present equilibrium, see Peter F. Drucker, *Innovation and Entrepreneurship: Practice and Principles* (New York: Harper and Row, 1985), esp. chap. 1.

24. Drucker, *Innovation and Entrepreneurship*, chap. 12. On the problems of staying ahead, see Michael E. Porter, *Competitive Advantage: Creating and Sustaining Superior Performance* (New York: Free Press, 1985), esp. chap. 5.

I recommend that national leaders approach military advantage within this "entrepreneurship" paradigm.[25] A military entrepreneur must constantly ask two questions that entail difficult leaps of imagination: Given the environmental analysis discussed earlier, (1) what would war look like if fought today, and (2) how can I "engineer" the next war away from (1) so as to maximize my relative advantages and bypass those of my competitors? The second leap is the essence of military entrepreneurship. In the broad sense it represents a constant search for surprise, and captures the dynamic nature of military competition as potential opponents seek to overcome each other's advantages and create their own.

Within this framework, technology (doctrine) and applications (war plans) interact in a cyclical manner, in the quest for integration. On one hand, currently available technology should influence the principles and techniques chosen for the application of force. On the other hand, the way one wishes to fight should create demand for particular technological development and innovation. In the short run effective military leaders will innovate in applications; in the long run they will innovate in research, developments, and the acquisition of technological assets.

The entrepreneurs' desire to create advantage by departure from the norm dictates a particular approach to, or attitude towards, the evidence upon which to base their "leaps." As in most areas of international relations, much of the data for analysis are historical events. While leaders may normally be tempted (mistakenly) to see in previous military encounters (and especially their outcomes) indications of where technological and overall advantage lie—an arrow pointing in the direction of desirable adaptation—the military entrepreneur would use the historical record more analytically. For him battles of the past will not be repeated—he will not expect them to, nor will he let them be; he should use their record warily, to suggest problems, opportunities, potential avenues to solutions, and routes to advantage—an arrow towards consistently rejuvenated theories of victory.[26]

---

25. A trap critical to avoid is the belief that entrepreneurial behavior is somehow reserved for the small business just starting up. Entrepreneurship is a state of mind, or an approach, and has been crucial to the long-term success of such "small" businesses as Johnson and Johnson or IBM. See Drucker, *Innovation and Entrepreneurship*, chap. 13. See Tom Peters, *Thriving on Chaos: Handbook for a Management Revolution* (New York: Harper and Row, 1988), Section III, on how to make and keep large organizations innovative.

26. For discussions of the utility and correct (and incorrect) uses of historical evidence in general and for strategic analysis, see David Hackett Fischer, *Historians' Fallacies: Towards a Logic of Historical Thought* (New York: Harper and Row, 1970), p. 258; see chap. 9 on the use and misuse

In the Battle of France, entrepreneur met "reasonable" competitor and won.[27] For grand-strategic reasons the Germans required a quick offensive decision in France. Facing general technological parity (in quality and quantity) with his opponents in the West, Hitler created an offensive advantage by integrating all three pillars: technology, doctrine, and war planning. Technology was modified to some extent—notably the production of close support aircraft instead of heavy bombers—yet for the most part, existing weapons were used. They were integrated into a revolutionary blitzkrieg doctrine, and all brought to maximum effect through a war plan (Operation Yellow) that maximized strategic surprise. In looking back at the historical record of World War I, the Germans identified severe problems for offensive operations; as effective entrepreneurs, they concentrated on creating a new war, not in adapting to the old one.

The German approach worked exceptionally well because it confronted an opponent conceptually locked in the old equilibrium. The French, like the British, had learned in World War I that tanks and aircraft were important, so they bought lots of them between the wars. However, they imagined a future war as a replay of the previous one, and so failed to produce an innovative and integrated system with which to confront the Germans.[28]

Probably the best recent example of military entrepreneurship is the Egyptian preparation for the 1973 War. The overall grand-strategic goal, never disputed in Egypt,[29] was offensive in nature and called for the reacquisition of the Sinai Peninsula. However, military analysis and the experience of 1967–70 indicated that the Israelis would enjoy a defensive advantage regardless of possible Egyptian efforts and innovations, should the Egyptians attempt to reconquer the Sinai. The military balance of power dictated a

---

of analogy. See also Mearsheimer, *Liddell Hart and the Weight of History*, p. 219. For discussions of Clausewitz's views on theory and history, and his use of analogy. See Aron, *Clausewitz*, chap. 8; and Michael Howard, *Clausewitz* (Oxford: Oxford University Press, 1983), pp. 30–31.
27. On the differential preparation for the Battle of France and descriptions of the results, see Mearsheimer, *Conventional Deterrence*, chaps. 3, 4: Posen, *Sources of Military Doctrine*, chaps. 3, 4, 6; and Addington, *Blitzkrieg Era*, chap. 5.
28. The Battle of Britain witnessed similar asymmetry, but with the roles reversed: the British prepared in a skillful entrepreneurial style, while the Germans did not. See Posen, *Sources of Military Doctrine*, pp. 94–102 and chap. 5; and Liddell Hart, *History of World War Two* (New York: Putnam, 1971), chap. 8.
29. On the process of Egyptian planning, see Lieutenant General Saad el-Shazly, *The Crossing of the Suez* (San Francisco: American Mideast Research, 1980), chaps. 1–5; and Hassan el-Badri, Taha el-Magdoub, and Mohammed Dia el-Din Zohdy, *The Ramadan War, 1973* (Dunn Loring, Va.: T.N. Dupuy, 1978), Part I.

number of adjustments of grand strategy: (1) grand strategic offense would be pursued through the political instability created by limited military offense, followed by defense; (2) an ally (Syria) would be mobilized to improve the overall balance of power; and (3) the Egyptian economy and population would be mobilized to an unprecedented extent in order to establish the required balance.

Now with a military mission, Egyptian military entrepreneurship turned to the task of creating the necessary advantages. The Egyptians drew on their unhappy historical experience with the Israelis just as an entrepreneur should: not as proof of Israeli superiority, but rather as indicative of where Egypt should seek opportunities to create advantages. Thus, undisputed Israeli superiority in the execution of high technology and mobile armored warfare drove the Egyptians to pursue a doctrine of low-technology, infantry-intensive, and static operations, incorporating massive use of anti-tank guided missiles (ATGMs) and infantry instead of armor. Israeli overall superiority in the air led the Egyptians to pursue local instead of general air superiority, through the use of surface-to-air missiles (SAMs) instead of aircraft. For the specific missions required by their plan and doctrine—such as the Canal crossing and breaching of the sand ramparts—the Egyptians equipped their forces with rubber boats, ladders, and water cannons. On the ground, a very large regular Egyptian army stood opposite the IDF, whose main force was reserves. Together with the Canal barrier, this made it possible for Egypt to complete its preparation while avoiding direct friction, enabling the Egyptians to achieve both strategic and operational surprise. These aspects of the war plan were crucial to Egyptian success.

East of the Canal the Israelis performed a traditional, non-entrepreneurial analysis. Based on known technologies, traditional doctrines, and what seemed to be reasonable war plans, it was clear to them that an operational and hence strategic defensive advantage existed.[30] They were thinking in the offense/defense balance paradigm. They were wrong.

In sum, then, the Egyptians integrated technology, war plans, and doctrine in a system that created an advantage by purposefully departing from the historical equilibrium. The Israelis failed to prepare and plan in a similar manner. In the final showdown, the traditional "true believers" could not stop the dynamic entrepreneurs.

---

30. For Israeli failures in preparation, see Chaim Herzog, *The War of Atonement: October 1973* (Boston: Little, Brown, 1975), chaps. 1–4, 18.

World War I and Military Entrepreneurship

For offense/defense balance theorists, World War I is keystone evidence, and at first glance does seem to lend almost incontestable support for their paradigm. Nevertheless, I think it provides even better support for a theory of military entrepreneurship; it is a best case through which to test entrepreneurship precisely because it seems to be so supportive of the former approach. Offense/defense balance theorists argue thus: The Great War provides excellent illustrations (a) of strategic choice that attempts to "buck" the prevailing (defensive) advantage, and (b) of the extreme price exacted as a result of such poor choice. War resulted from a system-wide choice of offense, and was waged in a futile and costly manner, because this choice was wrong. In early twentieth-century Europe, "true believers" chose offense despite clear historical evidence that the defense was dominant. They failed in their analysis; the result was the cream of an entire generation slain and buried, a continent laid waste, for nought. Therefore, concludes the argument, they should have chosen defensive strategies and doctrines. I agree—up to a point.

I concur with the depiction of European leadership and agree that in 1914—at least to some extent—there may have been a defensive advantage. But I differ sharply with the offense/defense theorists' view that this advantage dictated the entire course of the war. European leaders did prepare poorly for war, took sloppy account of technology and historical evidence, and armed themselves with cults and myths instead of analytically derived integrated and innovative systems for victory. In short, they were true believers and not entrepreneurs, and if there was a defensive advantage it was for this reason: they did not *create* offensive capabilities. Examination of the actual conduct of the war suggests that operational offense was possible, and was even achieved in such unlikely arenas as the Western Front when leaders put their minds to it in an imaginative manner. The viability of offense, demonstrated in the war, together with the gloomy picture of how war was prepared for, points to an alternative conclusion: if offensive strategy and operations were required for grand-strategic reasons, European leaders should have gone about producing an offensive advantage in an entrepreneurial manner.

In this section, first I examine the war itself, to demonstrate whether, in fact, the defensive advantage was strong, system-wide, and immutable in the 1914–18 period; whether effective offensive action was possible; whether any offensive advantage was created during the war where the defense had been dominant; and whether there was room for entrepreneurship.

Having shown that entrepreneurship could have made a difference, I then examine the pre-war period to see how the problems exposed as the war began followed from stagnant, non-competitive, and non-innovative preparation.

CONDUCT OF THE WAR

Focusing in from the grand strategic level may have a sobering effect on the confidence with which one so readily labels the First World War as an instance of defense-dominance. It would be fair to ask: just who exactly *won*, or achieved their war aims, through the defense? It would hardly do to score the Allies with success, when they had to spend four years in national attrition or total war, having surrendered Belgium and a good proportion of France's most productive territory. In fact no country gained its strategic purpose through defense, and this assessment is true regardless of what one makes of the relative operational advantage of offense and defense. If strategic goals are the yardstick of advantage, then one cannot ignore the fact that the two critical German fronts were pacified by *offensive* operations. The Germans effectively knocked Russia out of the war through a series of offensives in 1915–16. In the west the Allies brought the war to a close through the offensive of the "last hundred days," in summer 1918.

The common identification of a *strategic* defensive advantage in 1914, based on an *operational* defensive advantage, stems from the extensive reach of grand strategic goals. Imagine our assessment of German offensives, had the Schlieffen Plan called for *limited* offensive victories followed by negotiated settlement, much as the elder Moltke had envisaged.[31] The limited (and possibly near total) victory of the Schlieffen offensive in France, and the effective neutralization of Russia in 1915–16 by German attack, were decisive enough that a more moderate grand strategy might have had us today believing in the offensive advantage in World War I.

For years there was a defensive advantage on the Western Front; one could hardly argue with this observation. But if we put off—for just a moment— discussion of this sad phenomenon, even a cursory look through World War I reveals plenty of operational offense that worked, and worked well. The

---

31. Addington, *Blitzkrieg Era*, pp. 10–12.

two most critical and decisive strategic defensive successes in the opening days of the war were achieved by offensive operations. These were the Battle of the Marne in the west and the Battle of Tannenberg in the east. At Tannenberg the German Eighth Army defeated two numerically superior attacking Russian armies through offensive maneuvers at all levels.[32] At the Marne, the defensive "miracle" was effected by an unexpected allied attack on the flank of the German First Army and through a critical seam between the German First and Second Armies.[33] The eastern theatres witnessed a number of other successful operational offenses: the German offensive in Poland (1915), Russia's Brusilov Offensive into Galicia and the Carpathians (1916); and the Austro-German conquest of Romania (1916).[34]

Even on the Western Front, especially as the war progressed into its second half, much of the defensive success rested on offensive activity. From 1916, and especially after the Battle of the Somme, German defensive doctrine changed from stereotypically static to elastic defense-in-depth. It rested on the principle of surrendering territory purposefully in order to set the attacker up for counterattack.[35] When traditional British offense met the new German elastic defense at Arras (April 1917), the result was an overwhelming German success. Similar results obtained at the infamous Nivelle offensive of April–May 1917, failure of which led to the temporary disintegration of the French army.[36] Later, in 1918, the Allies learned how to use motorized and mechanized units to counterattack the flanks of successful penetrations of the

---

32. James E. Edmonds, *A Short History of World War I* (Oxford: Oxford University Press, 1951), pp. 50–52; B.H. Liddell Hart, *The Real War 1914–1918* (Boston: Little, Brown, 1930), pp. 103–114; Barbara W. Tuchman, *The Guns of August* (New York: Bantam, 1976), chap. 16; and Norman Stone, *The Eastern Front 1914–1917* (New York: Scribner's, 1975), chap. 3.
33. Edmonds, *A Short History of World War I*, pp. 41–49; Liddell Hart, *The Real War 1914–1918*, pp. 82–102; and Tuchman, *Guns of August*, chaps. 20–22.
34. For descriptions of these operations, see Edmonds, *A Short History of World War I*, pp. 31–33, 50–52, 64–68, 99–103, 172–176, 197–201; Geoffrey Jukes, *Carpathian Disaster: Death of an Army* (New York: Ballantine, 1971), chap. 6; and Liddell Hart, *The Real War 1914–1918*, pp. 103–114, 131–134, 224–226, 261–266.
35. Timothy T. Lupfer, *Dynamics of Doctrine: The Changes in German Tactical Doctrine During the First World War*, Leavenworth Papers No. 4 (Fort Leavenworth, Kansas: U.S. Army Command and General Staff College, July 8, 1981), pp. 1–36; Tim Travers, *The Killing Ground: The British Army, the Western Front, and the Emergence of Modern Warfare, 1900–1918* (London: Allen and Unwin, 1987), pp. 257–259; and Liddell Hart, *The Real War 1914–1918*, pp. 197–198, 242, 321–329, 342–343, 390. For descriptions of the Somme, see ibid, pp. 227–248; Travers, *Killing Ground*, pp. 127–199.
36. Liddell Hart, *The Real War 1914–1918*, pp. 321–329; Edmonds, *A Short History of World War I*, chaps. 19, 20.

German spring offensive, thereby neutralizing several German offensive successes.[37]

However, the Western Front did witness two terrible years of immobility and useless carnage, and we shall, therefore, turn our attention to that theatre, where the defensive advantage was so pronounced. The undisputable demonstrations of the unbreachable defense climaxed with the German offensive at Verdun and the Allied (British) offensive at the Somme (1916). After these defensive "victories," both sides undertook most seriously to create offensive advantages. Attempts by the Germans and especially by the British to do so demonstrate the extent to which offense was not a total impossibility in World War I.

In 1917 the German Army High Command (OHL) began the purposeful development of an offensive capability for the great strategic offensive planned for 1918. German preparation has been well documented elsewhere,[38] so I will simply recapitulate the central principles. The Germans consciously chose not to pursue a technological solution, but rather to innovate in doctrine and war plans. Previously applied doctrines of envelopment and broad frontal attrition attack were obviously, by then, not promising, and so the OHL developed "infiltration tactics," intended to break through the Allied defensive crust and enable strategic exploitation. The driving principles of this doctrine were: (1) create a narrow gap by incision instead of causing a general collapse by attrition or envelopment; (2) purchase surprise by forgoing preparatory bombardments; (3) pursue enemy weak points instead of strong ones; (4) exploit success instead of reinforcing failure; (5) bypass resistance where possible. Implementation of this doctrinal innovation required organizational changes. Infiltration was effected by small independent units: "detachments" and "groups" within special "storm battalions." The storm battalions spearheaded operations, and were heavily armed with existing light machine guns and flamethrowers. The role and hence methods of fire support were changed in order to bolster the new doctrine. As a general departure from the past, planning and doctrine focused on ensuring successful infantry operations; even artillery doctrine was

---

37. Kenneth Macksey, *Tank Warfare: A History of Tanks in Battle* (London: Rupert Hart-Davis, 1971), pp. 55–58; Lupfer, *Dynamics of Doctrine*, p. 53.
38. The following discussion is based on Lupfer, *Dynamics of Doctrine*, pp. 37–54; and Liddell Hart, *The Real War 1914–1918*, pp. 387–410.

forced to change to provide better support for infantry maneuver. Light artillery was made integral ordnance at the battalion level, in order to improve its independence and coordination. German artillery was organized and trained to provide effective neutralization fire instead of the traditional expensive and ineffective attempts to destroy, to fire for effect without prior registration (to improve surprise), to fire at enemy assets that directly infringed on friendly infantry, and to move forward rapidly so as to assist in the exploitation phase and in defense against counterattacks.

Initial German success in the 1918 offensive was much enhanced by practiced deception which resulted in complete surprise of the Allies in time and place. Such operational surprise against a defender who was also not appropriately prepared in doctrine or organization enabled the Germans to make unprecedented penetrations of forty miles at Amiens and fifteen at Ypres. Ultimately, however, the German offensive petered out. At the grand-strategic level, the Germans were exhausted and could not replace their losses. At the strategic level the Germans failed to pursue their major operational successes. At the operational level they had not worked out a satisfactory doctrinal or technological solution to the problem of exploitation of the penetration, and their enemies learned to use mechanized and motorized forces to attack the German flanks and to array themselves in depth.

Changes in British doctrine between 1916 and 1918 also had a remarkable effect on the battlefield, often unnoticed by offense/defense theorists.

The Somme epitomized traditional offense by attrition and when that came up against the as-yet static German defense, the resultant failure was attended by such a holocaust of death and destruction that the British were compelled to seek an alternative doctrine.[39] The British responded to the challenge, step by step. First they undertook to frustrate the evolving German elastic defense-in-depth by playing on its weaknesses. In the fall of 1917 the British mounted a number of limited-aims attacks. Since the new German doctrine purposely left front lines weak, the shallow British attacks were successful.[40] Then, beginning at Cambrai (November 1917), the British began

---

39. At the Somme about 600,000 Allied troops and 500,000 Germans lost their lives. British doctrine and planning for the Somme are described by Travers, *Killing Ground*, chaps. 6 and 7; and Shelford Bidwell and Dominick Graham, *Fire Power: British Army Weapons and Theories of War, 1904–1945* (London: Allen and Unwin, 1982), pp. 80–83, 112–114. For a vivid description of doctrine and of the actual fighting, see John Keegan, *The Face of Battle: A Study of Agincourt, Waterloo and the Somme* (Harmondsworth, U.K.: Penguin, 1978), chap. 4. See also Lupfer, *Dynamics of Doctrine*, pp. 4–8; Macksey, *Tank Warfare*, pp. 33–38; and works cited in n. 34, above.
40. Lupfer, *Dynamics of Doctrine*, p. 35; Edmonds, *A Short History of World War I*, pp. 250–252.

to employ a revolutionary departure in offensive doctrine and organization, so that in 1918, Allied and especially British offensives bore no resemblance to the earlier debacles. In contrast to the Germans' approach, an important component of developing British offensive capability was technological: the tank.

The evolving British doctrine was predicated on surprise and deep penetration.[41] Surprise was achieved by careful force concentration and by forgoing the traditional lengthy preparatory bombardments. Penetration was effected by the deployment of armor in large concentrations and in full coordination with infantry forces. Also, as with German "infiltration tactics," the infantry was organized to fight in platoons, not lines, and instructed to seek out and exploit the enemy's weak points. Machine guns were given to the attacking infantry units, and artillery-infantry coordination was much improved. The artillery also concentrated on battery suppression, important for sustained attacks. Air support was expanded to provide pre-battle and real-time intelligence, and more efficient spotting for artillery fire direction. In rudimentary form at Cambrai these developments proved effective, and were most impressive in the offensives of the Last Hundred Days, August–November 1918.

The Germans tried to defend with anti-tank ditches and anti-tank guns; the British countered these with thicker armor and by carrying rolls of bracken on the tanks to drop into the ditches as causeways. The British also overcame improved German front-line defenses with "small" tactical innovations, such as night attack, opting for extremely narrow frontal penetration, and repeatedly surprising in time and place of attack.

PREPARING FOR WAR

The fact that operational offensive advantage was constructed and innovated successfully on the Western Front, but only as the war progressed and after years of defensive stalemate, tells us that: (1) there was room for offensive advantage in 1914; and (2) therefore, the protagonists must have prepared

---

41. Actually, the British introduced the tank at the Somme. A small number of tanks were employed in that series of battles, though without an identifiable doctrine, and were dispersed among the infantry in small clusters with no standard techniques for coordination or concerted action. Naturally, they had no operational effect at the Somme. Evolving British concepts and doctrine are described by Bidwell and Graham, *Fire Power*, pp. 125–144. See Macksey, *Tank Warfare*, chaps. 3–5, for evolving British concepts, descriptions of encounters, and German responses in 1917–1918. See also, Edmonds, *A Short History of World War I*, chap. 28; and Liddell Hart, *The Real War 1914–1918*, pp. 118, 249–260, 344–356, 432.

poorly for the war. There must have been a dearth of entrepreneurship in the manner in which the major combatants prepared for conflict.

For grand strategic reasons the major European actors opted for offensive military doctrines in the early years of the century.[42] However, they failed to proceed, as entrepreneurs would have, to create viable offensive capacities and advantages. Indeed, with the possible and only partial exception of Germany, the decision makers of 1914 were not truly competitive; they were non-innovative, failed to consider the implications of new fire technologies, and misused, even abused, historical evidence in devising their approaches to the coming war.

Ironically, the most damning descriptions of this early decision making as non-entrepreneurial are made by the offense/defense balance theorists. Jack Snyder, Stephen Van Evera, and others characterize the prevailing doctrines as inappropriate and one-sided. These writers fault the French and Belgians for "*offensive à outrance*," describe the French Plan Seventeen as mindless, ridicule the British for relying on a "psychological battlefield" theory of victory, scold the Russians for strategic overextension, and criticize the Schlieffen Plan as strategically overextended and a catalyst of early British intervention. Those responsible are faulted for failing to analyze historical data and the implications of emerging technology, and for acting on cults and mystiques.[43] I agree. But these criticisms, therefore, indicate *not* that there was an inherent defensive advantage, but rather that there was much room for creative and analytical preparation for any kind of war, offensive or defensive.

The French approached 1914 in an almost purely non-competitive mode, for at any meaningful level they essentially ignored their expected enemy. Plan Seventeen was an offensive operational plan that was not conceived or designed to overcome a particular set of supposed German contingencies. It was really more of a plan of deployment than one of operations; it did not emerge from a detailed study of the problem at hand and did not, therefore, provide a detailed solution.[44] This is perhaps best revealed by the religiously

42. For an argument that the offensive plans of 1914 reflected and correctly served prevailing balance-of-power considerations, see Scott D. Sagan, "1914 Revisited: Allies, Offense, and Instability," *International Security*, Vol. 11, No. 2 (Fall 1986), pp. 151–175.

43. For these "faults" see Snyder, *Ideology of the Offensive;* Van Evera, "The Cult of the Offensive"; Travers, *Killing Ground*, chaps. 2, 3; and Michael Howard, "Men Against Fire: Expectations of War 1914," in Miller, *Military Strategy;* Van Creveld, *Supplying War*, chap. 4.

44. For critiques of Plan Seventeen and French preparation for war, see S.R. Williamson, "Joffre Reshapes French Strategy, 1911–1913," in Paul M. Kennedy, ed., *The War Plans of the Great*

and singularly *offensive* nature of the plan and of French doctrine. One cannot take war and one's enemy seriously and at the same time believe that offense can exist without defense, or vice versa. In fact, the French ignored concrete evidence about the likely German plans—notably the "wheel" through Belgium and the massive use of the reserves—and did little to counter these. The technological dimensions of the approaching war were also largely ignored. French plans and doctrine ignored the fact that the Germans had relatively large numbers of machine guns and heavy artillery, as well as the potential of such assets for integration into the French offensive doctrine and organization. And, although France had the largest civilian motor-car industry at the time, the potential benefits of motorization for a large offensive campaign were neglected.

France entered the war without having performed either of the two mental leaps required in entrepreneurial thought. First, the French failed to foresee the probable face of a future war. Perhaps this fact is best reflected in their 1914 dress: the traditional *pantalons rouges*. Second, they made no attempt to "engineer" the future battlefield to their advantage on any of the three dimensions: technologically, doctrinally, or strategically. In sum, in 1914 the French did not have a creative theory of victory, but rather a blind faith in one, which led them, in the event, to have a cult not merely of the offensive, but of the "reckless offensive."[45]

The British, too, failed to foresee completely the face of the coming war, although they do seem to have understood that the new fire technologies would be difficult to overcome. But instead of attempting to devise or create advantage through the manipulation of technology and doctrine, they resorted to a psychological battlefield notion, in which victory was to be the fruit of superior morale and will-power.[46] Failure to integrate the machine gun and understand its operational and tactical implications is exemplary: although well acquainted and experienced with these weapons, the British failed until well into the war to adapt both doctrine and organization in order to maximize the effect of machine guns or to acquire them in sufficient quantities, and the British were slow in reacting to their use by the Germans. In confronting the German submarines, again the British failed to foresee

---

Powers, 1880–1914 (Boston: Allen and Unwin, 1985); Snyder, *Ideology of the Offensive*, chap. 3; Tuchman, *Guns of August*, pp. 208–210, chap. 13, pp. 266, 293, 295; Howard, "Men against Fire"; and Theodore Ropp, rev'd. ed., *War in the Modern World* (New York: Collier, 1962), pp. 227–229.
45. Ropp, *War in the Modern World*, p. 263.
46. Travers, *Killing Ground*, chaps. 2,3.

their potential application and strategic menace, and not till well into the war were effective countermeasures developed.

German preparation for the war was the most entrepreneurial of the three. The Germans came closest to completing the required leaps of the imagination, and they were, in fact, the only combatants to achieve offensive success of any kind in the early phases of the war. Given a grand-strategically derived offensive mission, the German army devised the Schlieffen Plan: an attempt to create a viable theory of victory given the expected difficulties on the battlefield and the prevailing technologies. At the highest level, in order to create the required physical balance, the Germans innovated by using reserves in large numbers in combat missions. Also at that level, and for the same reason, the Germans planned to create simultaneously an offensive advantage in the West and a defensive one in the East. At the operational level in the West, the plan's envelopment of the French left wing was meant to obviate the need for frontal attack; meanwhile, by tying down the French right, the plan intended to overcome the danger of lateral rail movement in defense. At the operational and tactical levels, the Germans integrated heavy artillery and machine guns into their offensive doctrine to an extent unmatched by their opponents.

However, the Germans did not push their entrepreneurial thought to its logical conclusions, and here they failed. They foresaw three critical problems: the tactical one of frontal attack; the potential for French lateral movement by rail; and the logistical strains of the German right wing. But their solution came up short.[47] An attacker's envelopment aimed to neutralize his enemy's frontal defense must be of such size and speed that it can unbalance the defender. The Schlieffen Plan was too big an envelopment given its slow speed. Thus, as an operational solution it could not overcome tactical problems: the French could move operationally to meet the operational "trick" in time to *re*-present the Germans with the tactical problems of frontal attack. In the event, the Germans did not stick to their plan of "sucking in" the French right wing, and could not withstand the temptation of attacking on

47. Criticism of the Schlieffen Plan as an unsuccessful operational solution to these problems, which only created more problems, may be found in: L.C.F. Turner, "The Significance of the Schlieffen Plan," in Kennedy, *The War Plans of the Great Powers*, pp. 204, 212; Gerhard Ritter, *The Schlieffen Plan: Critique of a Myth*, trans. Andrew and Eva Wilson (New York; Praeger, 1958), esp. "Foreword" by B.H. Liddell Hart; Van Creveld, *Supplying War*, chap. 4; Addington, *Blitzkrieg Era*, pp. 15–22; Van Evera, "Causes of War," pp. 301–302; and Gunther R. Rothenberg, "Moltke, Schlieffen, and the Doctrine of Strategic Envelopment," in Paret, *Makers of Modern Strategy*, pp. 316–325.

their own left. Their unsuccessful attacks left French forces intact, available, and close enough to be transported to the Marne in time for the "miracle" that defended Paris. I have found no evidence that the Germans actively attempted to obstruct such rail transport.

The Germans also failed to address practically the logistic fragility of their right-wing envelopment. It is here that their thinking was most non-entrepreneurial, reverting to faith that "the necessary is possible";[48] in a sense wishing away, in Anglo-French style, instead of solving a problem they well understood. It is here, also, that the German failure to mobilize new technologies is most egregious: the First Army had only some 162 trucks for its transport missions. This is simply poor preparation to execute in 1914 a plan that had its origins in 1897!

One prevalent complaint about the actors of 1914 is that they ignored or misused the lessons of history—of the American Civil War, the Boer War, and the Russo-Japanese War. These charges are apposite but not, as one might suspect, always as intended by those who make them. The military leaders are often faulted for not diagnosing these wars as symptomatic of an overall defensive advantage. But this is not their central failing. Rather, it is that they did not treat these wars analytically. Scant was the detailed study aimed to uncover particular problems or ideas and opportunities to engineer a future advantage. For the most part their study of recent conflict was motivated—by political, social, or organizational imperatives—to find proof of, and support for, their preferred doctrines. Proponents of defense found in history proof that defense was best; proponents of offense found in it evidence for a general offensive advantage.[49] Both sides were wrong.

Of the historical lessons, the ones most missed by the leaders of 1914 were those regarding the impact of evolving technologies. It is really quite remarkable just how poorly these decision makers understood the implications of new (and old) weapons. The Germans have a mixed record on this count, somewhat better than that of their adversaries. To their credit, they did understand the potential power of machine guns and heavy artillery for offense and defense. In 1914 the German battalion had six machine guns,

48. Snyder, *Ideology of the Offensive*, chap. 5.
49. On the misuse of historical evidence before 1914, see Snyder, *Ideology of the Offensive*, pp. 77–81; Howard, "Men against Fire"; Brodie, *Strategy in the Missile Age*, pp. 42–52; T.H.E. Travers, "Technology, Tactics, and Morale: Jean de Bloch, the Boer War, and British Military Theory, 1900–1919," *Journal of Modern History*, Vol. 51, No. 2 (June 1979), pp. 264–286; and Brodie, "Technological Change," pp. 283–292.

whereas its British counterpart had two. (But even the German six are negligible when the potential benefits are considered; as of 1914 neither side—least of all the British—had really figured out how to utilize this technology within infantry doctrine.) The Germans armed their first-line divisions with twice as many field guns as did the French and Russians, all of higher caliber. At corps level the Germans made available to their divisions heavy artillery (150 mm), while the French were armed with the famous 75s. The Russians and the British also went to war with very few pieces of heavy field artillery. Analysis of the obstacles to offensive operations led the Germans, quite appropriately, to develop and build a small number of heavy siege guns for assaults on major fortresses. Finally, German artillery relied substantially on indirect fire, while the French (and the British to an extent) relied on direct fire from close range. Indeed, in the early stages of the war, the Germans capitalized well on the advantages provided by these differences on both fronts.[50] The Germans also foresaw the potential strategic use of submarines, and being alone in this insight nearly knocked the British out of the war before the Allies found the appropriate counter-measures.[51]

However, all the major actors failed to foresee or apply the opportunities for massive capitalization of the intended land offensives. The knowledge and basic technology to produce tanks or armored cars was surely available to all by 1912. But the British only introduced them in 1916, and only after the original development was pushed, oddly enough, by the Admiralty, while the Germans refused to introduce tanks until the bitter end. Similarly, all failed to foresee the potential of motorization for logistics and troop transport in the coming war, despite the well-developed European motorcar industries at the time.[52]

---

50. For details of artillery development, armament and operations during the war, see Bidwell and Graham, *Fire Power*, Books I and II, and pp. 296–297; Lt.-General Nikolai N. Golovin, *The Russian Army in the World War* (New Haven: Yale University Press, 1931), pp. 33–34, 133–142; and Tuchman, *The Guns of August*, pp. 190–195, 218–220, 234–235, 262–263.

51. Brodie, "Technological Change," pp. 280–282. On the other hand, the Germans invested in a large surface fleet whose only effect was to cause a strategic "spiral" with England, and which may have catalyzed Britain's entrance into the war, all at the expense of capitalization of the land army. On the strategic implications of the German naval build-up, see Paul M. Kennedy, "Tirpitz, England and the Second Navy Law of 1900: A Strategical Critique," *Militärgeschichtliche Mitteilungen*, Vol. 2 (1970).

52. In the decade before the war, a number of British, Russian, and German officers and strategists lobbied for motorization to solve the problems of mobility they foresaw, especially for logistics. The French at the time were the most advanced and capable in automobile production and could have motorized their forces in 1914 had they decided to do so. See Travers, "Technology, Tactics, and Morale," p. 271; Snyder, *Ideology of the Offensive*, pp. 191–192; Van

Whether the explanations lie at the level of organizational-bureaucratic conservative behavior (for example, the difficulty of assimilating the machine gun into doctrine and tactics), organizational politics (for example, the exalted role of horse cavalry),[53] or domestic politics (for example, the German insistence on a large surface fleet, or the French army's insistence on an offensive doctrine),[54] there was nothing exogeneously predetermined about the impact of these technologies. Rather, their influence resulted from biased historical analysis and a reluctance or inability to figure out how best to counter the central and emerging technologies of the day, and how most effectively to exploit their promise. Military leaders failed as entrepreneurs; they stumbled instead of making the necessary leaps of the imagination. The first leap— "what would a war look like today?"—was made by some,[55] if incompletely; but the second—"how, therefore, do I *engineer* my way to offensive victory?"—was performed poorly, and in most cases not at all.

Conclusion: Cults and Revolution

An entrepreneurial military organization must be in a state of permanent revolution; change must be its constant condition. Successful innovation demands leaps of the imagination, the adoption and integration of untried doctrines, organizational changes, and technological application, all in response to each other and to guesses about similar developments by one's opponents. Entrepreneurship involves the intellectual honesty, imagination, and courage to exploit historical failure and success as indications of how to innovate, and to treat history analytically and not in a biased manner. Most importantly, military leaders must force themselves to remain impartial towards offense or defense, and must be prepared to create superior capability in either or both, as grand strategy demands.

These are steep demands. Like business entrepreneurship, the military variety does not come naturally to either individuals or organizations, for it

---

Creveld, *Supplying War*, pp. 110–119; and Paul Kennedy, *The Rise and Fall of the Great Powers: Economic Change and Military Conflict from 1500 to 2000* (New York: Random House, 1987), p. 221.
53. Edward L. Katzenbach, Jr., "The Horse Cavalry in the Twentieth Century," in Robert J. Art and Kenneth N. Waltz, eds., *The Use of Force: Military Power and International Politics*, 3d ed. (Lanham, Md.: University Press of America, 1988).
54. McNeill, *The Pursuit of Power*, pp. 303–305; Snyder, "Civil-Military Relations," pp. 129–133; Alfred Vagts, *A History of Militarism, Civilian and Military*, rev. ed. (New York: Free Press, 1959), chap. 10.
55. Most notably, of course, by Jean de Bloch. See Howard, "Men Against Fire."

requires "unnatural" behavior. Large bureaucratic organizations are normally conservative; they reduce uncertainty by adhering to standard operating procedures, sticking to the tried and true, and learning in a process that is linear, sequential, and cybernetic.[56] Even more than other organizations, militaries are likely to display these traits. The simultaneous orientation towards promotion and discipline make the socialization to the "particular way of doing business"[57] natural to army officers. Changing the way of doing business is not likely in a hierarchical organization whose leaders reached the top by virtue of success in the past. The way of the past is the way in which they are experts, and the source of their authority.

This conservatism is further encouraged by the fact that— especially in peace time—armies are "input organizations"; in the business world a chief executive officer is tested by the profits he produces, or "outputs," while a military leader is tested by how well he trains, by the morale and discipline of his troops, and by the quality of maintenance of his weapons. These are all "inputs," and the comparison of commanders for promotion requires that these all be performed against given and accepted standards or procedures.

Further inertia and obstruction of innovation have their roots in the role of armies in the modern world. These organizations have been important to the economic, social, and political activity of states and their regimes, and therefore have been deeply influenced by national politics in which they participate.[58] The central role of modern armies, of course, is to guarantee the longevity of the state against external threats; risk aversion is extreme in an organization whose profession is about the life and death of the nation. Armies are not perceived, by themselves and others, as just "another business" that might succeed or fail with impunity. This may have a number of related consequences. Armies are unlikely to part with whatever worked in the past. This attitude is further encouraged by the objective difficulty of performing decisive peacetime tests of new doctrine and technology.[59] A similar difficulty in assessing potential adversaries' developments turns military organizations inward, rendering their behavior less competitive and

---

56. John D. Steinbruner, *The Cybernetic Theory of Decision: New Dimensions of Political Analysis* (Princeton: Princeton University Press, 1974). On the barriers to innovation in public service organizations, see Drucker, *Innovation and Entrepreneurship*, chap. 14.
57. Posen, *Sources of Military Doctrine*, p. 44.
58. See note 50 above and accompanying text, on the politically-motivated reluctance in Germany to equip the ground forces with capital (heavy equipment, trucks, tanks), and the German insistence on building a large surface fleet.
59. Katzenbach, "The Horse Cavalry in the Twentieth Century," pp. 162–163.

innovative. The desire to reduce risk and uncertainty also amplifies the desire to impose standard procedures and scenarios and to "control" events. This leads soldiers to prefer and adopt either an offensive or defensive doctrine; usually the former because it appears to allow them to fight and to terminate wars according to plan.[60]

It should not be surprising, therefore, that realization of an entrepreneurial approach has often required immense external pressure, whether from an undeniable previous failure, or from above by a strong, authoritarian, and imaginative personality like Napoleon or Hitler. At times the change in paradigm required of the organization may be too great or sudden for the prevailing cadre of military leaders. This phenomenon has induced some armies (like the IDF) to insist on short careers for its officers, and has forced other leaders to purge the military elite, as Sadat did in preparation for the 1973 War.[61] But a military organization does not have the option of retaining the prevailing paradigm until the anomalies attending it create an evident crisis *and* a better alternative is presented and tested, as in the scientific revolutions described by Thomas Kuhn.[62] A military organization can wait for neither. It may be too late.

The antithesis of such permanent revolutionary thought is the cult—a theological belief that a particular approach, paradigm, or doctrine is correct. Such orthodoxy may be comforting, but it neglects competition, and true believers may fall easy prey to hungry entrepreneurs. Indeed falling into any cult—of the *offensive* in 1914, the *defensive* in 1939, or the *status quo* in the 1990s—may be the greatest gift one could bestow on his enemies.

---

60. Snyder, *Ideology of the Offensive*, chap. 1; Posen, *Sources of Military Doctrine*, pp. 41–50; Major Robert L. Maginnis, "Harnessing Creativity," *Military Review*, Vol. 66, No. 3 (March 1986).
61. Muhammad Hasanayn Haykal, *The Road to Ramadan* (New York: Quadrangle/New York Times Books, 1975), pp. 180–182.
62. Thomas S. Kuhn, *The Structure of Scientific Revolutions*, 2nd ed. (Chicago: University of Chicago Press, 1970), chaps. 5–8.

Crime or Blunder?
Inadvertence, Guilt,
and Historical Responsibility

Détente and Deterrence

Anglo–German Relations, 1911–1914

Sean M. Lynn–Jones

$\mathbf{P}$olitical scientists often have cited the First World War as an example of inadvertent conflict caused by unduly bellicose foreign and military policies. At least four variations on this theme have been prominent. First, some authors argue that the war was the result of mutual incentives for preemptive attacks or rapid mobilizations.[1] A second school of thought suggests that the war arose from rigid organizational routines, especially in Germany and Russia, that restricted the freedom of political decision-makers by requiring wide mobilizations and, in the German case, early attack once mobilization had taken place.[2] A third interpretation, related to the first two, attributes the war to a

---

An earlier version of this article was presented at the Annual Meeting of the Northeastern Political Science Association, Philadelphia, Pennsylvania, November 14–16, 1985. The author wishes to thank Robert Beschel, Karl Lautenschläger, Joseph Nye, and Scott Sagan for their helpful comments and suggestions. He is grateful to Harvard University's Project on Avoiding Nuclear War for support during the research and writing of this article. The author remains responsible for the views expressed here.

Sean M. Lynn–Jones is a Harvard MacArthur Fellow in International Security at the Center for Science and International Affairs, Kennedy School of Government, Harvard University, and a doctoral candidate in Harvard's Department of Government.

---

1. For prominent examples of this interpretation, see Herman Kahn, *On Thermonuclear War* (Princeton: Princeton University Press, 1960), p. 362; Thomas C. Schelling, *Arms and Influence* (New Haven: Yale University Press, 1966), p. 224; George H. Quester, *Offense and Defense in the International System* (New York: Wiley, 1977), pp. 110–111; Richard Ned Lebow, *Between Peace and War: The Nature of International Crisis* (Baltimore: Johns Hopkins University Press, 1981), pp. 238–242; Robert Jervis, *Perception and Misperception in International Politics* (Princeton: Princeton University Press, 1976), p. 94; and Jervis, "Cooperation Under the Security Dilemma," *World Politics*, Vol. 30, No. 2 (January 1978), p. 192. Kahn sees "pressures toward pre-emptive action" influencing statesmen in the July crisis. Schelling claims that "being fast on the draw appeared decisive," and Jervis agrees that "the continental powers believed that the side that struck first would gain a major military advantage." Quester writes that: "Everyone in 1914 could still have preferred peace to war, but everyone surely now preferred war on the offensive, to any war of defense in which the other side had been allowed the first blow."
2. There is a voluminous literature on this question. Barbara W. Tuchman, *The Guns of August* (New York: Bantam, 1980) offers one of the best-known accounts of the development and role of European mobilization plans before 1914. See also A.J.P. Taylor, *War by Time-table* (London: MacDonald, 1969); Paul M. Kennedy, ed., *The War Plans of the Great Powers, 1880–1914* (London: Allen & Unwin, 1979); Kahn, *On Thermonuclear War*, pp. 357–375; and Graham T. Allison, Albert Carnesale, and Joseph S. Nye, Jr., eds., *Hawks, Doves, and Owls: An Agenda for Avoiding Nuclear War* (New York: Norton, 1985), pp. 210–211. For a recent example that offers a sophisticated analysis of the ways in which mobilization plans may have influenced the origins of the war,

---

International Security, Fall 1986 (Vol. 11, No. 2)
© 1986 by the President and Fellows of Harvard College and of the Massachusetts Institute of Technology.

widespread belief in the dominance of the offense in warfare and the con-
comitant adoption of offensive military doctrines by the continental military
powers.[3] The fourth view sees the war as the product of a spiral of hostility
that pervaded relations between Germany and the other European powers
in the years before the war. Proponents of this view claim that the British,
French, and Russian responses to the rise of German power were seen as
manifestations of hostility and that Germany's essentially defensive reactions
were perceived as further manifestations of aggressive intent, thereby creating the climate for the crisis and confrontation of July 1914.[4]

---

see Jack S. Levy, "Organizational Routines and the Causes of War," *International Studies Quarterly*,
in press.

3. See Stephen Van Evera, "The Cult of the Offensive and the Origins of the First World War,"
and Jack Snyder, "Civil–Military Relations and the Cult of the Offensive, 1914 and 1984," in
International Security, Vol. 9, No. 1 (Summer 1984), pp. 58–107, 108–146. For a more general
theoretical treatment of the destabilizing consequences of offense-dominance, see Jervis, "Cooperation Under the Security Dilemma."

4. The First World War is generally regarded as exemplifying how wars can arise from such
spirals. The spiral model is characterized by an action-reaction process in which each country
sees its own actions as defensive, but its opponents regard the same steps as provocative.
Escalating hostility results even when no country desires war. For a comprehensive discussion
of the spiral model, see Jervis, *Perception and Misperception*, pp. 58–113. Jervis concludes that
World War I "has provided much of the inspiration for the [spiral] model" (pp. 94–95). Aaron
Wildavsky argues that World War I is the "one historical case which the spiral model appears
to fit." See his "Practical Consequences of the Theoretical Study of Defense Policy," in Wildavsky,
The Revolt Against the Masses: And Other Essays on Politics and Public Policy (New York: Basic
Books, 1971), p. 165. Jervis also discusses the deterrence model, which suggests that wars occur
because countries fail to convince their adversaries that aggression will be resisted. It is exem-
plified by the failure to deter Hitler prior to the Second World War. A similar distinction is made
in Evan Luard, "Conciliation and Deterrence: A Comparison of Political Strategies in the Interwar
and Postwar Periods," *World Politics*, Vol. 19, No. 2 (January 1967), pp. 167–189. Allison,
Carnesale, and Nye, *Hawks, Doves, and Owls*, divide the causes of wars into three basic categories.
Hawks essentially favor deterrence, Doves prefer conciliation, and Owls fear war by miscalculation or a "loss of control." World War I exemplifies the Owlish concerns. This classification is
superior to the division into "spiral" and "deterrence" models, as it recognizes that war by
miscalculation may be distinct from spurious appeasement.

When applied to World War I, the spiral model is often accompanied by the suggestion that
Germany had no aggressive designs but was forced to go to war by the inability of Britain and
the European powers to pursue more conciliatory policies. Miles Kahler makes this argument:
"Tentative rapprochements were dismissed out of hand by the [British] Foreign Office, and the
worst light was placed on every German deed." See his "Rumors of War: The 1914 Analogy,"
Foreign Affairs, Vol. 58, No. 2 (Winter 1979/80), p. 378. Kahler goes on to suggest that the 1914
analogy indicates that there are flaws in deterrence theory. David Calleo claims that "the proper
lesson is not so much the need for vigilance against aggressors, but the ruinous consequences
of refusing reasonable accommodations to upstarts." See his *The German Problem Reconsidered:
Germany and the World Order, 1870 to the Present* (Cambridge: Cambridge University Press, 1978),
p. 6. See also Joachim Remak, *The Origins of World War I, 1871–1914* (New York: Holt, Rinehart
and Winston, 1967). For a rebuttal of Kahler's argument, see Christopher Layne, "1914 Revisited:
A Reply to Miles Kahler," *Orbis*, Vol. 24, No. 4 (Winter 1981), pp. 719–750.

These images of the origins of World War I overlap to some extent. Taken together, they suggest that the war was inadvertent in two senses.[5] In the first, Europe blundered into war during July 1914 because statesmen lost control over a minor crisis; dangerous military doctrines and plans created irresistible pressures for a conflict that was unwanted and unexpected. In a second sense, the July crisis can be seen as inadvertent or at least avoidable, since it arose from a conflict between Germany and the Triple Entente that was based on mutual misperceptions of hostile intent—misperceptions that could have been avoided if either side had broken the spiral of hostility by pursuing a more conciliatory policy.[6]

The analysts who adopt these interpretations of the outbreak of World War I often present policy recommendations that rest on the premise that unduly bellicose policies provoked the war and that the present international situation is, at least in some respects, analogous to that of Europe in 1914. American policymakers are counselled to adopt a more conciliatory approach to the Soviet Union, to subordinate military plans to political considerations, and to avoid acquiring military forces or doctrines that increase preemptive incentives.[7]

---

5. There is a widespread belief that the First World War was inadvertent. German Chancellor Bethmann–Hollweg seemed to subscribe to this view when he complained on July 30, 1914 that: "We have lost control and the landslide has begun." After the war, former British Prime Minister David Lloyd George claimed "we all stumbled into the war." Sidney B. Fay lent academic respectability to this notion when he concluded that "none of the Powers wanted a European War." More recently George Kennan has argued that World War I was the result of some "monstrous miscalculation." See Konrad H. Jarausch, "The Illusion of Limited War: Chancellor Bethmann Hollweg's Calculated Risk, July 1914," *Central European History*, Vol. 2, No. 1 (March 1969), p. 69; Fritz Fischer, *Germany's Aims in the First World War* (New York: Norton, 1967), p. 88; Sidney B. Fay, *The Origins of the World War* (New York: Macmillan, 1928), Vol. 2, p. 547; and Steven E. Miller, "The Great War and the Nuclear Age: Sarajevo After Seventy Years," *International Security*, Vol. 9, No. 1 (Summer 1984), p. 3.

6. One of the most striking features of the general image of World War I as an inadvertent conflict is the extent to which it ignores the arguments of Fritz Fischer and other historians who contend that Germany adopted an aggressive policy and deliberately provoked World War I. The initially controversial findings of Fischer and his followers have been accepted in varying degrees by many historians. Political scientists, however, seem reluctant to grasp the implications of Fischer's thesis. If Fischer is correct, the assumption that no power wanted a major war in 1914 becomes dubious, and much of the conventional wisdom about the war held by political scientists needs revision. This question, however, is beyond the scope of this article. Important works by Fischer and his followers include Fischer, *Germany's Aims in the First World War*, and *War of Illusions: German Policies from 1911 to 1914*, trans. Marian Jackson (London: Chatto and Windus, 1975); and Imanuel Geiss, ed., *July 1914: The Outbreak of the First World War: Selected Documents* (New York: Charles Scribner's Sons, 1967). For a more recent contribution to the historical debate, see David E. Kaiser, "Germany and the Origins of the First World War," *Journal of Modern History*, Vol. 55, No. 3 (September 1983), pp. 442–474.

7. Kahler, "Rumors of War," argues for a more conciliatory U.S. posture toward the Soviets.

This article proposes an additional interpretation, suggesting that the war arose in part from the Anglo–German détente of 1911–1914. I will argue that relations between Great Britain and Germany improved between 1911 and 1914 and that this improvement contributed to the outbreak of the war. In Britain, the détente produced the false belief that the July 1914 crisis could be resolved through Anglo–German cooperation. British leaders did not want to appear to provoke Germany and thus failed to take early steps to deter German moves that led to war. The détente also fostered false German hopes that Britain would remain neutral in a continental war, thereby encouraging Germany to adopt policies fraught with the risk of such a conflict.

If these arguments are accepted, they may provide the basis for theoretical and practical conclusions that are not included in the more traditional uses of the 1914 analogy. Preemptive incentives and offensive military doctrines coupled with rigid mobilization schedules may have contributed to the onset of war. These factors appear to have been important among the continental powers—France, Russia, and Germany in particular—and the lessons of the continental conflict, which warn of the dangers of preemption, offense, and inflexible organizational routines, may retain their validity regardless of one's interpretation of the Anglo–German conflict. Nevertheless, the continental lessons should be supplemented by those drawn from the improvement in Anglo–German relations in the years immediately before the war.

My arguments also leave room for the view that an Anglo–German spiral of hostility, fueled by naval competition, developed before 1911. This article will suggest, however, that British policy after 1911 displayed a willingness to accommodate Germany so that mutual relations could be improved. There is no question that an Anglo–German antagonism arose in the first decade of the twentieth century, but the years 1911–1914 saw more attempts to improve Anglo–German relations than further exacerbations of the rivalry.[8]

Van Evera, "The Cult of the Offensive," pp. 106–107, concludes that the United States should avoid offensive doctrines and weapons and includes ballistic missile defenses in the latter category. For a discussion of the problem of the command and control of nuclear forces that draws on the apparent lessons of the pre-World War I mobilization plans, see Paul Bracken, "Accidental Nuclear War," in Allison, Carnesale, and Nye, *Hawks, Doves, and Owls*, pp. 25–53. See also Levy, "Organizational Routines and the Causes of War."

8. The emergence of the Anglo–German naval arms race in the early 1900s is cited as the most prominent example of behavior consistent with the spiral model. See Jervis, *Perception and Misperception*, p. 66. This case has become so important in the literature that Bernard Brodie describes it as "the 'classic' arms race of modern times." *War and Politics* (New York: Macmillan, 1973), p. 319. For the most comprehensive account of the development of tension between Great Britain and Germany, see Paul M. Kennedy, *The Rise of the Anglo–German Antagonism, 1860–1914* (London: Allen & Unwin, 1980).

The following section will outline the evolution of the Anglo–German détente and explain its principal components: cooperation during the Balkan crises of 1912–1913, the agreement over the Portuguese colonies, the accord on the Baghdad railway, and the reduced concern over the naval arms race. The second section then explores the manner in which the détente contributed to the outbreak of the war in 1914. The third section then explores two broader questions: (1) How does détente affect the probability of war? and (2) What is the proper way to pursue a policy of détente?

The Anglo–German Détente, 1911–1914

Many historians have suggested that Britain and Germany improved their mutual relations between 1911 and 1914. Although there have been few detailed historical analyses of the apparent détente, its existence has often been noted in discussions of pre-1914 Anglo–German relations. Bernadotte Schmitt argues that "a *détente*, or relaxing of tension, had been effected."[9] Zara Steiner points to "a noticeable improvement in the quality of Anglo–German relations" and concludes that in July 1914: "Relations with Berlin were better than they had been in over a decade."[10] Michael Ekstein refers to "the Anglo–German détente" and suggests that Britain in 1914 was more worried about restraining France and Russia than containing Germany.[11] R.J. Crampton also regards the 1911–1914 Anglo–German détente as important and believes that it "deserves the specialized treatment which historians have already given to other features of international relations in that period."[12]

---

9. Bernadotte E. Schmitt, *The Coming of the War, 1914* (New York: Charles Scribner's Sons, 1930), Vol. 1, p. 74.
10. Zara S. Steiner, *Britain and the Origins of the First World War* (New York: St. Martin's Press, 1977), p. 145; and *The Foreign Office and Foreign Policy, 1898–1914* (Cambridge: Cambridge University Press), p. 153.
11. Michael G. Ekstein, "Great Britain and the Triple Entente on the eve of the Sarajevo crisis," in F.H. Hinsley, ed., *British Foreign Policy Under Sir Edward Grey* (Cambridge: Cambridge University Press, 1977), p. 343.
12. R.J. Crampton, *The Hollow Detente: Anglo–German Relations in the Balkans, 1911–1914* (London: George Prior, 1977), p. vi. Other historians, however, dispute the existence of a détente. Paul Kennedy concedes that "a certain optimism had returned to Anglo–German relations" by 1914, but also sees the improvement as limited and less significant in the absence of any naval agreement. R.T.B. Langhorne argues that "there is evidence to refute the assertion sometimes made that between 1911 and 1914 Anglo–German relations improved." K.G. Robbins sees better relations between Berlin and London but wonders whether this improvement remained on a "false basis." See Kennedy, *The Rise of the Anglo–German Antagonism*, pp. 450–453; R.T.B. Langhorne, "Great Britain and Germany, 1911–1914," in Hinsley, *British Foreign Policy Under Sir*

THE EVOLUTION OF THE DÉTENTE

After the 1911 Agadir crisis, both Britain and Germany showed signs of wanting to improve their tense relations.[13] Between 1911 and 1914, statesmen in the two countries pointed to the need to improve the atmosphere of diplomatic intercourse. Baron Marschall von Bieberstein, the German ambassador to London in 1912, expressed a desire "to create a thoroughly good and healthy atmosphere between the two countries."[14] In Britain, Foreign Secretary Sir Edward Grey is reported to have said, "so long as Bethmann Hollweg is Chancellor we will cooperate with Germany for the peace of Europe."[15]

Britain's desire for a détente reflected domestic political necessities and foreign policy requirements. Grey had been attacked by radical members of the Liberal Party for his diplomacy during the Agadir crisis. His critics charged him with having brought Britain to the brink of war and called for his resignation. This "Grey must go" campaign included the formation of a Liberal foreign affairs committee in Parliament. Over 70 members joined,

---

Edward Grey, p. 313; and K.G. Robbins, "The Foreign Secretary, the Cabinet, Parliament and the parties," in Hinsley, *British Foreign Policy Under Sir Edward Grey*, p. 19.

Most of these arguments do not deny the existence of an improvement in relations, but contend that it was illusory because some critical issues—especially the Anglo–German naval rivalry—remained unresolved. The real question at stake may be the definition of détente. If, as Richard Stevenson has suggested, détente is defined as "the *process of easing of tension between states whose interests are so radically divergent that reconciliation is inherently limited*," then there appears to have been an Anglo–German détente (emphasis in original). If, on the other hand, one insists on viewing détente as a more fundamental improvement in relations, there is a risk of confusing détente with entente or even alliance. For discussions of definition, see Richard W. Stevenson, *The Rise and Fall of Detente: Relaxations of Tension in U.S.–Soviet Relations, 1953–84* (Urbana and Chicago: University of Illinois Press, 1985), p. 11; and Gordon A. Craig and Alexander L. George, *Force and Statecraft: Diplomatic Problems of Our Times* (Oxford and New York: Oxford University Press, 1983), pp. 238–242.

Détente should be considered an inherently limited easing of tension, which does not necessarily lead to further improvements in relations. It may lead to an eventual settlement of political differences between two rivals, but it may remain more limited. Definitions of détente that require significant political differences to be resolved before a détente can be said to exist essentially define the term out of existence by requiring it to be an entente. Britain was able to go beyond a détente in its relations with the United States, France, and Russia during the early twentieth century, but Anglo–German relations did not go beyond this stage between 1911 and 1914. For a study of how U.S.–British and Anglo–French relations went beyond détente to a lasting rapprochement, see Stephen R. Rock, "Why Peace Breaks Out: Power, Economics, and Socio–Culture in Great Power Rapprochement" (Ph.D. dissertation, Cornell University, August 1985).

13. The crisis arose when the German gunboat *Panther* arrived in Agadir to assert German claims in Morocco. For a more complete discussion, see M.L. Dockrill, "British policy during the Agadir Crisis of 1911," in Hinsley, *British Foreign Policy Under Sir Edward Grey*, pp. 271–287.

14. Quoted in Crampton, *The Hollow Detente*, p. 8.

15. P.H.S. Hatton, "Harcourt and Solf: the Search for an Anglo–German Understanding through Africa, 1912–1914," *European Studies Review*, Vol. 1, No. 2 (April 1971), p. 130.

demonstrating the strength of opposition to Grey within his own party.[16] Many members of the British Cabinet also supported an understanding with Berlin at one time or another between 1911 and 1914.[17]

Grey's interest in improving relations with Germany may have reflected a desire to placate his domestic opponents. Although Grey and his Foreign Office were always skeptical about public and parliamentary involvement in foreign policy, he seems to have become more sympathetic to the idea of an Anglo–German détente after his opponents became vocal.[18] He had previously felt that resolving the naval question was the key to improving relations,[19] but after 1912 he was willing to attempt to improve the atmosphere between Berlin and London to achieve "cordial relations *without* any definite political understanding."[20] In short, Grey was converted to a policy of détente.

British foreign policy thus attempted to ease Anglo–German tensions by improving the atmosphere of relations between the two countries. Grey sought relatively minor agreements to demonstrate that relations were improving. This improvement may have been pursued to satisfy Grey's domestic critics, but it was also seen as a means of reducing the likelihood of an Anglo–German conflict.

Germany also sought an Anglo–German détente based on improvements in the atmosphere of the two countries' mutual relations, but Germany's motivations were considerably different. Chancellor Bethmann Hollweg had made détente with Britain one of the cornerstones of his foreign policy. He felt "our most urgent task is a *modus vivendi* with England," hoping that better relations would eventually induce Britain to remain neutral in any continental conflict involving Germany.[21] His interest in a détente led him to

---

16. For an account of the opposition to Grey's foreign policy, see John A. Murray, "Foreign Policy Debated: Sir Edward Grey and His Critics, 1911–1912," in Lillian Parker Wallace and William C. Askew, eds., *Power, Public Opinion, and Diplomacy* (Durham, N.C.: Duke University Press, 1959), pp. 140–171; A.J.P. Taylor, *The Trouble Makers: Dissent Over Foreign Policy, 1792–1939* (London: Hamish Hamilton, 1957), pp. 117–127; and Kennedy, *The Rise of the Anglo–German Antagonism*, chapter 17.

17. Hatton, "Harcourt and Solf," p. 142.

18. K.G. Robbins, "Public opinion, the press and pressure groups," in Hinsley, *British Foreign Policy Under Sir Edward Grey*, p. 85; and Dockrill, "British policy during the Agadir Crisis of 1911," p. 286.

19. Robbins, "The Foreign Secretary, the Cabinet, Parliament and the parties," p. 12.

20. Quoted in Crampton, *The Hollow Detente*, pp. 177–178.

21. Quoted in Jarausch, "The Illusion of Limited War," p. 53. Bethmann–Hollweg's policy may have changed after the December 8, 1912 "war council" at which the Kaiser and his military leaders discussed plans for war. Prior to the meeting, Bethmann–Hollweg may have seen détente with Britain as a means of avoiding war. After it, he seems to have regarded war as likely, but

reciprocate many of Grey's efforts to improve relations. The result was détente in which the two countries eased tensions and cooperated, but did not
attempt to reconcile all of their divergent interests. Such differences, in fact,
were played down so as not to impede efforts at cooperation.

The general tendency of Britain and Germany to attempt to build a détente
by negotiating on issues where agreement seemed possible emerged after
the February 1912 mission to Berlin of the British war minister, Lord Haldane.
The Haldane Mission was the most ambitious attempt to resolve the Anglo–
German antagonism after the Agadir crisis.[22] In the negotiations, Britain
attempted to limit naval armaments and preserve its supremacy on the high
seas, while Germany sought a political understanding that would guarantee
British neutrality in the event of a continental war. Before his departure,
Haldane tried to reassure the French ambassador in London, Paul Cambon,
who was concerned that an Anglo–German understanding might undermine
British ties with France.[23] He claimed that the negotiations "had no other
end than to create a *détente*" but he "hoped more than a détente would follow
later on."[24]

Although the very fact that the mission was undertaken indicates that
Britain and Germany hoped that at least a détente would be possible, the
mission failed to achieve any of its objectives and temporarily embittered
Anglo–German relations. Both countries were willing to make substantial
concessions, but these concessions were not sufficient to bridge the gap
between their divergent positions. Britain was unwilling to offer any pledge
that might oblige it to remain neutral if Germany attacked France. Germany,
for its part, would not accept negotiated limits on its navy in return for
anything less than a guarantee of British neutrality.[25]

he still sought improved Anglo–German relations to reduce the likelihood of an Anglo–French
alliance. For a discussion of the "war council" and Bethmann–Hollweg's response, see Fischer,
War of Illusions, pp. 160–169. See also Fischer, *Germany's Aims in the First World War*; Geiss, *July
1914*; and Kaiser, "Germany and the Origins of the First World War," pp. 463–464, 468. See
Crampton, *The Hollow Detente*, pp. 153, 179, for the argument that German policy did not
consistently aim to persuade Britain to remain neutral.
22. See Langhorne, "Great Britain and Germany, 1911–1914," pp. 288–301; and E.L. Woodward,
Great Britain and the German Navy (London: Oxford University Press, 1935), pp. 323–366, for
detailed accounts of the Haldane Mission.
23. Although the Anglo–French entente was not an alliance, military conversations between
the British and French general staffs had given rise to expectations that Britain would assist
France in a European war. France repeatedly expressed concern that Anglo–German talks might
disrupt Anglo–French relations.
24. Quoted in Craig and George, *Force and Statecraft*, p. 240.
25. The prospects for an agreement in 1912 were reduced by the publication of a new German
Navy Law on the eve of the Haldane Mission, but the two countries repeatedly found it
impossible to reconcile their differences on this point.

Despite the failure of the Haldane Mission to resolve the deeper issues dividing Britain and Germany, Grey continued to hope that the atmosphere created by the visit would provide a basis for resolving less fundamental issues.[26] Haldane had raised several colonial questions with the Germans and there appeared to be some potential for progress on these questions. In Germany, the Kaiser apparently continued to hope for a political understanding. The Austro–Hungarian Foreign Minister, Leopold von Berchtold, noted on March 24, 1912, that: "His Imperial Majesty envisages an understanding in the political sphere instead of one on armaments at sea and on land."[27] Neither the naval question nor a general political agreement was ever again the subject of serious Anglo–German negotiations. In an attempt to find a basis for cooperation, London and Berlin turned their attention to more peripheral issues, including the Balkan crises of 1912–1913, the Portuguese colonies in Africa, and the Baghdad Railway.

COOPERATION IN THE BALKAN CRISES. After the failure of the Haldane Mission, Britain and Germany searched for an area in which they might be able to cooperate to improve relations. The German foreign minister Kiderlen–Wächter wrote that he believed that "practical cooperation with Britain on an important issue of general policy would have a more salutary effect on relations with our cousins on the other side of the Channel than all feasts of brotherhood and paper treaties."[28] The Balkans appeared to be a logical place for Anglo–German cooperation, as neither power had vital interests in the area.[29] On May 2, 1912, Grey informed Berlin that he "put the greatest value on remaining in touch with Germany in eastern matters which could again become somewhat bothersome."[30]

The aftermath of the First Balkan War, in which Greece, Montenegro, Bulgaria, and Serbia virtually eliminated the Turkish presence in Europe, provided an opportunity for Anglo–German cooperation in the Balkans.[31] Grey convened a conference of the London ambassadors of Austria–Hungary, Germany, France, Italy, and Russia to negotiate the division of territory in the wake of the victory of the Balkan allies.

The London Conference convened in December 1912. The representatives of the powers spent much of their time attempting to decide the frontiers of

---

26. See Langhorne, "Great Britain and Germany, 1911–1914," pp. 297–299.
27. Quoted in Fischer, *War of Illusions*, p. 131.
28. Quoted in ibid., p. 156.
29. See Crampton, *The Hollow Detente*, p. 11.
30. Quoted in ibid., p. 10.
31. See Crampton, *The Hollow Detente*, for a detailed account of the Balkan crises.

the newly created state of Albania and the fate of the town of Scutari. These issues involved Austria–Hungary and Russia, as the former wanted to limit Serbian power and to deny the Serbs access to the Adriatic, while the latter supported Serbia's efforts to secure the fruits of the recent victory over the Turks. The conference was eventually able to reach an agreement on these issues and a general settlement of the Balkan boundaries. The Treaty of London incorporating these agreements was signed on May 30, 1913.[32]

Anglo–German cooperation during the Balkan Crisis appears to have averted a major conflict. The crisis included an Austrian mobilization against Serbia in which military units were sent to the Russian border in Galicia.[33] R.W. Seton–Watson concluded: "There can be little doubt that the situation was saved by the friendly co-operation of Berlin and London."[34] Britain and Germany both saw Anglo–German cooperation as one of the most significant features of the crisis. In November 1912, Grey wrote that "the Germans seem to me to desire peace and not to be making mischief."[35] Grey concluded: "Our relations with Germany have improved because Kiderlen worked for peace in the Balkan crisis and Jagow has done the same."[36] Karl Eisendecher, an aide to Bethmann–Hollweg, wrote to Kaiser Wilhelm on December 23, 1912, of the collaboration between Britain and Germany at the London Conference: "Now above all we may have an opportunity of entering into normal and even friendly relations with our English cousins; in fact we seem to be well on the way towards this and this is what we should continue to develop."[37] In April 1913, Bethmann–Hollweg stated that Anglo–German cooperation was *"the* redeeming point in the present circumstances."[38]

The Balkan crisis provided an opportunity for London and Berlin to cooperate in resolving an important issue. This cooperation both demonstrated and contributed to the improving climate of Anglo–German relations. Colonial issues simultaneously provided an opportunity for agreements between the two countries.

THE PORTUGUESE COLONIES. Britain and Germany in late 1911 began negotiations on an agreement that would divide the Portuguese colonies in Africa

---

32. The settlement did not last very long, however. Bulgaria's attempts to gain more territory led to its defeat at the hands of its former allies, as well as Turkey and Romania. The Treaty of Bucharest restored some of Turkey's losses, including the city of Adrianople.
33. Fischer, *Germany's Aims in the First World War*, p. 33.
34. R.W. Seton–Watson, "William II's Balkan Policy," *The Slavonic and East European Review*, Vol. 7, No. 19 (June 1928), p. 9.
35. Quoted in Crampton, *The Hollow Detente*, p. 72.
36. Quoted in Steiner, *Britain and the Origins of the First World War*, p. 115.
37. Quoted in Fischer, *War of Illusions*, p. 166.
38. Quoted in Crampton, *The Hollow Detente*, p. 95.

in the event that Portugal suffered a financial collapse. Britain, which had extended loans to Portugal upon the security of colonial customs receipts, hoped that these negotiations could resolve the contradiction between Britain's 1898 agreement with Germany and the 1899 secret treaty with Portugal. Both agreements had been signed to win the support of Portugal and Germany during the Boer War. The 1898 Anglo–German agreement promised Germany territory in the Portuguese African colonies in return for German neutrality in Britain's conflict with the Boers. The treaty with Portugal pledged London to uphold the territorial integrity of the Portuguese Empire; in return, Portugal allowed Britain to use territory in its colonies during the war.[39] Britain also hoped that the negotiations could reduce Anglo–German tensions and demonstrate to Grey's radical critics that a détente was under way. After the negotiations had taken place, Grey wrote to Goschen: "The most important motive had been the improvement of relations with Germany."[40] Germany also appears to have sought the talks primarily as a means for improving relations. In April 1912, Kiderlen–Wächter wrote to King Carol of Rumania, noting the slow progress of Anglo–German relations, but pointing out that "we intend, to begin with, to start with agreements in the colonial sphere."[41]

Grey entrusted responsibility for the actual negotiations to Harcourt, the colonial secretary, who was regarded as a Germanophile.[42] The German colonial secretary, Solf, assumed responsibility on the German side. Harcourt hoped "that Anglo–German relations could be permanently improved if we had 'conversations' leading to an exchange of territory which might give Germany 'a place in the sun' without injury to our colonial or Imperial interests."[43] His policy was thus based on the assumption that minor concessions might persuade Germany to reduce its hostility toward Britain. The negotiations were concluded by August 13, 1913, and the new agreement gave Germany a larger share of the Portuguese colonies.[44] But the formal

---

39. See Langhorne, "Great Britain and Germany, 1911–1914," pp. 309–310.
40. Quoted in Steiner, *The Foreign Office and Foreign Policy, 1898–1914*, p. 144. Fritz Fischer argues that the British government had no interest in the question itself and merely negotiated to placate the opposition. See *Germany's Aims in the First World War*, p. 39.
41. Quoted in Fischer, *War of Illusions*, p. 131.
42. See Hatton, "Harcourt and Solf," for a detailed account of the negotiations on the Portuguese colonies.
43. Quoted in ibid., p. 131.
44. Steiner, *Britain and the Origins of the First World War*, p. 106. See also A.J.P. Taylor, *The Struggle for Mastery in Europe, 1848–1918* (London: Oxford University Press, 1954), pp. 502–504.

signing of the agreement was delayed because Britain and Germany disagreed over whether it should be published.

Britain, according to senior Foreign Office official Eyre Crowe, hoped that publication would show "her goodwill towards Germany."[45] Germany, however, feared that publication would stiffen Portugal's resolve to stave off a financial collapse and make Germany look gullible by implying that Britain never intended to partition the colonies.[46] Despite the disagreement over publication, P.H.S. Hatton argues that the negotiations "can be seen as the most significant contribution to the improved Anglo–German relations of the period from late 1911 to mid-1914."[47] Even in the midst of the July crisis, Berlin instructed Ambassador Lichnowsky to seek a formula that would guarantee the signing of the treaty.

THE BAGHDAD RAILWAY. The 1911–1914 improvement in Anglo–German relations was also reflected in the ability of the two countries to reach an agreement on the construction of the Baghdad railway. Britain had long feared that a German-controlled railway to the Persian Gulf would pose a strategic threat to Britain's interests in that region. Haldane had returned from Berlin in 1912 with a memorandum on the issue from Bethmann–Hollweg, but negotiations did not begin until Britain reached a preliminary agreement with Turkey in 1913.[48] After Britain had abandoned its outright opposition to the railway and allowed Turkey to increase its customs duties, an Anglo–German agreement was reached that prevented railway construction beyond Basra, which was 100 miles from the Gulf. Britain would retain a veto over any extension of the railway to the Gulf, but Germany would be able to use the Shatt-al-Arab to transport goods by water to and from Basra. The convention, which was initialled on June 15, 1914, also gave Britain a monopoly on river transportation in Mesopotamia in return for promises of nondiscrimination against German goods. Germany gave a similar pledge of nondiscrimination against British goods on the railway. The convention also included provisions regarding the British and German interests in the Smyrna–Aidin Railway in Asia Minor and irrigation projects in the region.[49]

45. Quoted in Langhorne, "Great Britain and Germany, 1911–1914," p. 311.
46. Hatton, "Harcourt and Solf," p. 137.
47. Ibid., p. 124.
48. Maybelle Kennedy Chapman, "Great Britain and the Bagdad Railway, 1888–1914," *Smith College Studies in History*, Vol. 31 (Northampton, Mass.: Smith College, 1948), p. 171.
49. For a summary of the provisions of the agreement, see Edward Mead Earle, *Turkey, The*

Although some interwar historians viewed the torturous negotiations on the Baghdad railway as a manifestation of the imperialistic "old diplomacy," the 1914 agreement removed a long-standing source of Anglo–German tension.[50] The ability of Berlin and London to reach an agreement showed that both sides were willing to adopt "a businesslike approach" to resolving their differences.[51]

THE NAVAL ARMS RACE. The improvement in Anglo–German relations connected with the Balkan crises, the Portuguese colonies, and the Baghdad railway was accompanied by the virtual disappearance of the naval issue as a point of contention between Britain and Germany, although there was no formal agreement on naval armaments. The subject was barely discussed after the failure of the Haldane Mission in 1912. British officials recognized that any discussion of the naval question would undermine other efforts to achieve a détente. In 1913, Eyre Crowe wrote "that one of the main reasons why Anglo–German relations are now much more cordial (—I do not overlook the obvious other reasons—) is that we have entirely ceased to discuss the question of a limitation of armaments. I feel equally certain that any resumption of that discussion will have the inevitable effect of making relations worse again."[52] This impression was confirmed by the hostile German response to Winston Churchill's repeated overtures for a "naval holiday."[53] Grey also concluded that any effort to revive naval conversations would only exacerbate Anglo–German relations.[54]

Great Powers, and the Bagdad Railway: A Study in Imperialism (New York: Macmillan, 1924), pp. 255–256; and Chapman, "Great Britain and the Bagdad Railway," pp. 201–202.

50. See John B. Wolf, "The Diplomatic History of the Bagdad Railroad," *The University of Missouri Studies*, Vol. 11, No. 2 (April 1, 1936); and Paul K. Butterfield, *The Diplomacy of the Bagdad Railway, 1890–1914* (Göttingen, 1932). Morris Jastrow, *The War and the Bagdad Railroad* (Philadelphia: Lippincott, 1917), attempts to blame the First World War on the railway.

51. Kennedy, *The Rise of the Anglo–German Antagonism*, p. 415.

52. Quoted in Langhorne, "Great Britain and Germany, 1911–1914," p. 306. The Germans privately made it clear that they would not welcome further proposals, arguing that they "can only harm the tender plant of a German–English détente." See R.T.B. Langhorne, "The Naval Question in Anglo–German Relations, 1912–1914," *Historical Journal*, Vol. 14, No. 2 (June 1971), p. 364.

53. See Langhorne, "Great Britain and Germany, 1911–1914," pp. 306–307; and Winston S. Churchill, *The World Crisis* (New York: Charles Scribner's Sons, 1923), Vol. 1, pp. 111–112. Churchill at that time was First Lord of the Admiralty.

54. See Robbins, "The Foreign Secretary, the Cabinet, Parliament and the parties," p. 20. Bethmann–Hollweg apparently agreed, and told Goschen in January 1913 that Anglo–German cooperation on the Near Eastern question was "worth more than any naval agreement or political understanding as a starting point for future good relations." Quoted in Woodward, *Great Britain and the German Navy*, p. 398.

Despite the absence of negotiations, "The Anglo–German naval race slackened after 1912."[55] There was no formal agreement, but Germany seems to have resigned itself to accepting the 16:10 ratio in capital ships, which Winston Churchill had promised to maintain, even if it required laying two new British keels for every additional one the Germans laid.[56] The Germans made no formal statement to this effect, but Admiral Tirpitz made a conciliatory speech in the Reichstag in February 1913 suggesting a 16:10 ratio in dreadnoughts.[57] Joachim Remak even calls this outcome an "informal understanding."[58] German acquiescence to British naval supremacy reflected financial necessities, the realization that Britain was determined to maintain its lead, and Bethmann–Hollweg's desire to expand the German army.[59] But he also believed that slowing the pace of German naval construction and not calling attention to Germany's naval program could improve Anglo–German relations and ultimately increase the prospects for British neutrality in a conti-

55. Samuel P. Huntington, "Arms Races: Prerequisites and Results," *Public Policy*, Vol. 8 (1958), p. 64. Paul Kennedy appears to agree with this conclusion. See his "The First World War and the International Power System," *International Security*, Vol. 9, No. 1 (Summer 1984), p. 27.
56. See Huntington, "Arms Races," p. 64; Robbins, "The Foreign Secretary, the Cabinet, Parliament and the parties," p. 19. Germany did not alter the building rates of the 1912 *Novelle*, which called for three additional dreadnoughts between 1912 and 1917. The tempo of construction thus would be 3–2–3–2–3–2 instead of the previous two per year, although construction of the third ship was never scheduled, thus making the tempo 2–3–2–2–3–2. Admiral Tirpitz attempted to increase this rate to a steady three per annum in 1913, but his request was rejected. Admiral von Müller, Chief of the Kaiser's naval cabinet, suggested that the Kaiser resisted pressure for a new Navy Bill because of "the growing intimacy of relations with England." See J.C.G. Röhl, "Admiral von Müller and the Approach of War, 1911–1914," *Historical Journal*, Vol. 12, No. 4 (December 1969), p. 666. For general discussions of German naval programs between 1912 and 1914, see Holger H. Herwig, *"Luxury Fleet": The Imperial German Navy, 1888–1918* (London: Allen & Unwin, 1980), pp. 73–92; and Arthur J. Marder, *From the Dreadnought to Scapa Flow: The Royal Navy in the Fisher Era, 1904–1919* (Oxford: Oxford University Press, 1961), Vol. 1, pp. 279–284. On Churchill's 16:10 ratio, see his *The World Crisis*, pp. 97–98.
57. The speech, delivered on February 6–7, 1913, made an impression on the Liberal press in Britain, but it was apparently not seen as an important concession by the government. E.L. Woodward points out that Churchill's 16:10 ratio was meant to apply before the passage of the 1912 German Naval Bill and only operated during the life of Britain's pre-dreadnought battleships. Churchill later said the ratio only applied in British home waters and could be changed if necessary. See Woodward, *Great Britain and the German Navy*, pp. 405–406, 429; and Marder, *From the Dreadnought to Scapa Flow*, pp. 311–312.
58. Remak, *The Origins of World War I, 1870–1914*, p. 92.
59. Kurt Riezler, Bethmann–Hollweg's aide, in 1914 concluded that "the English can, and always will be able to build twice what we can." In 1911, the German navy's budget was 54.8 percent of the army's, but this figure had fallen to 32.7 percent by 1913. See Herwig, *"Luxury Fleet,"* pp. 91, 78. By 1914, even Admiral Tirpitz opposed increasing the German tempo of construction or setting a date for laying the keel of the third dreadnought of the 1912 Naval Law, calling such steps a "great political blunder" because "the bow is overstrung here as much as in England." The British government, however, probably did not become aware of this new attitude. See Marder, *From the Dreadnought to Scapa Flow*, p. 430.

nental war.[60] In the spring and summer of 1914, Anglo–German naval relations were generally quiet. The naval competition thus stabilized, and there was no repetition of the 1909 British fears of a "Dreadnought gap."[61] The end of repeated public disagreements over the Anglo–German naval arms race contributed to the overall warming climate of relations and set the stage for the British fleet to pay a ceremonial visit to Kiel in June 1914.

CONTEMPORARY VIEWS OF THE DÉTENTE ON THE EVE OF WAR

The combination of these developments created an overall impression that an Anglo–German détente had emerged by 1914. In retrospect, it is possible to argue that the improvement in relations was illusory. Several historians have pointed out that Britain and Germany could cooperate only on peripheral issues; the two countries failed to reach a formal agreement on naval armaments or a comprehensive political understanding.[62] Contemporary observers also may have exaggerated the extent of Anglo–German cooperation in resolving the 1912–1913 Balkan crises.[63] But these retrospective judgments cannot alter the fact that British and German leaders on the eve of war in 1914 believed that their countries' relations had improved considerably. Historians have had the benefit of time to discern flaws in the détente of 1911–1914, but the actions of contemporary decision-makers were shaped by their perceptions of an emergent détente.

In London, the belief that Anglo–German relations had improved was held by members of the Cabinet, the professional diplomats of the Foreign Office, and even by radical and pacifist proponents of an Anglo–German rapprochement. On July 7, 1914, Sir Edward Grey could write: "We are on good terms with Germany and we wish to avoid a revival of friction with her."[64] Lloyd George had previously claimed, in an interview published in the *Daily Chronicle* of January 1, 1914, that relations had improved to such a degree that

---

60. See Fischer, *War of Illusions*, p. 114; and Herwig, "*Luxury Fleet*," p. 73.
61. See Marder, *From the Dreadnought to Scapa Flow*, p. 429. On the 1909 naval scare in Britain, see Kenneth L. Moll, "Politics, Power, and Panic: Britain's 1909 Dreadnought 'Gap,'" in Robert J. Art and Kenneth N. Waltz, eds., *The Use of Force: International Politics and Foreign Policy* (Boston: Little, Brown, 1971), pp. 431–447.
62. See Langhorne, "Great Britain and Germany, 1911–1914"; and Kennedy, *The Rise of the Anglo–German Antagonism*. George Liska has argued that the improvement in Anglo–German relations before August 1914, like the U.S.–Soviet détente of the 1970s, constituted a "limited accommodation." He implies that such "partial measures" are likely to fail. See his "From Containment to Concert," *Foreign Policy*, No. 62 (Spring 1986), p. 4.
63. See Crampton, *The Hollow Détente*, pp. 171–180, for this argument.
64. Quoted in Steiner, *Britain and the Origins of the First World War*, p. 123.

further British naval increases might not be required.[65] In the House of Commons on July 23, 1914, he declared: "The two great Empires begin to realize that the points of co-operation are greater and more numerous than the points of possible controversy."[66]

The British ambassador in Berlin, Sir W. Edward Goschen, spoke of Anglo–German tension as a thing of the past, referring to "our former cold terms with Germany" in a dispatch of April 24, 1914.[67] Ambassador to France Sir Francis Bertie reported as late as June 25, 1914 that "Grey thinks the German government are in a peaceful mood and that they are very anxious to be on good terms with England, a mood he wishes to encourage."[68] Even Foreign Office permanent undersecretary Arthur Nicolson, who took a highly skeptical view of German intentions, wrote in May 1914 that "since I have been at the Foreign Office, I have not seen such calm waters."[69] On July 6, he saw "no very urgent and pressing question to preoccupy us in the rest of Europe."[70] The Foreign Office, which earlier had objected to a visit of the band of the Coldstream guards to Germany, now made no protest as the British fleet docked in Kiel for an official visit.[71] Grey was making plans to go to Germany himself to see a famous oculist when the July crisis erupted.

The groups that had previously opposed Grey's foreign policy on the grounds that it was anti-German also joined in seeing the signs of a détente. One of their journals in June 1914 found it "almost difficult to realize that there were still unresolved problems affecting the relations of the two countries."[72] Another, *The Nation*, had written on December 15, 1913 that: "Nothing more than a memory remained of the old Anglo–German antagonism."[73] Grey had defused the radical opposition to his foreign policy by pursuing a policy of easing tensions with Germany. The Germans had reciprocated this

65. Robbins, "The Foreign Secretary, the Cabinet, Parliament and the parties," p. 21.
66. Quoted in Taylor, *The Trouble Makers*, p. 126.
67. Quoted in Ekstein, "Great Britain and the Triple Entente on the eve of the Sarajevo Crisis," p. 344.
68. Quoted in Robbins, "The Foreign Secretary, the Cabinet, Parliament and the parties," p. 21. See also Michael Ekstein, "Some Notes on Sir Edward Grey's Policy in July 1914," *Historical Journal*, Vol. 15, No. 2 (June 1972), p. 323.
69. Quoted in Steiner, *The Foreign Office and Foreign Policy, 1898–1914*, p. 153.
70. Quoted in ibid., p. 155.
71. The Foreign Office had objected to the band's proposed visit on the grounds that a similar visit was not planned for France. British diplomats feared that the Anglo–French entente was very fragile, but these fears were apparently less significant in 1914.
72. *The Peacemaker*, June 1914. Quoted in Robbins, "Public opinion, the press and pressure groups," p. 83.
73. Quoted in Taylor, *The Trouble Makers*, p. 126.

policy, although they had different motives and were definitely not trying to placate domestic advocates of détente.

German observers shared the impression that relations were improving. In June 1913, Jagow wrote to the British ambassador in Rome: "Many clouds in the Anglo–German sky have dispersed . . . much mutual distrust has vanished."[74] Much evidence also indicates that Bethmann–Hollweg had concluded that his policy of improving relations with Britain had produced a rapprochement.[75] In April 1914, he wrote that "progress continues with England"[76] and two months later he declared that "whether a European conflagration comes depends solely on the attitude of Germany and England."[77] Winston Churchill later summed up the mood in the months before the war: "The Spring and Summer of 1914 were marked in Europe by an exceptional tranquility."[78]

The precise reasons why these views were so widespread remain unclear, as do the implications that various statesmen saw in the apparent détente. To some British observers, the actual behavior of Germany during the Balkan crises might have suggested that German policy had changed. To others, the more friendly tone of Anglo–German discourse might have seemed reassuring. On the German side, it is possible that friendly overtures from Britain were interpreted as signals of British willingness to allow Germany to dominate the European continent. German observers also may have concluded that the British government would not be able to garner parliamentary support for war with Germany if relations appeared to have improved. Decision-makers in both countries may have seen concessions where none were intended. Regardless of the basis for beliefs in détente or the reasoning used to draw conclusions from such beliefs, the general impression that there was a détente influenced the origins of the war in July 1914.

Détente and the Outbreak of War

The Anglo–German détente is significant among the factors that contributed to the outbreak of World War I because it helps to explain British and German policies in the July crisis. On the British side, the apparent improvement in

---

74. Quoted in Crampton, *The Hollow Detente,* p. 136.
75. See Jarausch, "The Illusion of Limited War."
76. Quoted in ibid., p. 54.
77. Quoted in Hatton, "Harcourt and Solf," p. 84.
78. Quoted in Steiner, *Britain and the Origins of the First World War,* p. 215.

relations with Germany contributed to Grey's hopes that the crisis could be managed not by threatening Germany, but by attempting to cooperate with Berlin. In Germany, the détente contributed to the ultimately false expectations that Britain would remain neutral. The combination of these two effects may have played an important role in the outbreak of the war, as many historians have argued that German policy in July 1914 was based on the assumption of British neutrality and that Germany would not have risked war if it had known Britain would intervene.[79]

BRITAIN'S AMBIGUOUS STANCE IN THE JULY CRISIS

Sir Edward Grey has often been castigated for his failure to make it clear to Germany that Britain would fight with France if war came in July 1914. Zara Steiner, sympathetic to Grey's predicament, concludes that Grey "followed the wrong course during July" and that he "may have encouraged Bethmann to gamble on his ultimate neutrality."[80] David Calleo offers more scathing criticism, finding Grey "to have been remarkably slow-witted and diffident" throughout the July crisis.[81]

These criticisms of Grey are justified to some extent. Although a detailed reconstruction of his diplomacy at that time lies beyond the scope of this article, it is clear that Grey did not give Germany unambiguous warning that Britain would side with France until very late in the crisis.[82] Grey initially attempted to reassure Berlin that Britain wanted a diplomatic solution and refrained from giving France or Russia any guarantees of support that might have encouraged them to adopt a more aggressive posture.[83]

Grey's ambiguity can be explained partly by the domestic constraints under which he operated. The foreign secretary could not have adopted a firm position against Germany because much of the Liberal Cabinet opposed a

---

79. See, for example, Schmitt, *The Coming of the War, 1914*, Vol. 2, p. 409; and Luigi Albertini, *The Origins of the War of 1914*, ed. and trans. Isabella M. Massey (London: Oxford University Press, 1953), Vol. 2, pp. 514–515.
80. Steiner, *Britain and the Origins of the First World War*, p. 227.
81. Calleo, *The German Problem Reconsidered*, p. 34. Albertini offers a similar set of criticisms of Grey. See his *The Origins of the War of 1914*, Vol. 2, pp. 514–516 and Vol. 3, pp. 523–524.
82. On July 29, Grey strongly hinted to Lichnowsky that Britain could not remain neutral in the event of an attack on France. See Schmitt, *The Coming of the War, 1914*, Vol. 2, pp. 160–161. On July 31 he wrote to Sir Edward Goschen, the British ambassador in Berlin: "I told [the] German Ambassador that if France became involved we should be drawn in." Quoted in Albertini, *The Origins of the War of 1914*, Vol. 2, p. 643. Both of these warnings were issued without Cabinet authorization.
83. See Michael G. Ekstein and Zara Steiner, "The Sarajevo Crisis," in Hinsley, *British Foreign Policy under Sir Edward Grey*, pp. 397–410.

commitment to France. Others preferred to avoid making the choice and hoped that war could be avoided altogether. As late as August 2, a majority of the Cabinet remained opposed to giving France assurances of support.[84]

But domestic constraints alone cannot explain Grey's inability to take a firm stand against Germany in the July crisis. The division within the Cabinet did not become a factor until July 27. Although the reluctance of the Cabinet did restrict Grey's freedom of action in the final, agonizing days before the war, Grey had pursued his policy of seeking a diplomatic solution with "singular independence."[85] As Zara Steiner has suggested: "It was only during the very last phase of the crisis that Grey was constrained by the divisions in the Cabinet and his apprehension over public reaction."[86] Even while the Cabinet remained divided, Grey was able to inform Lichnowsky that Britain would not remain neutral in the event of a German attack on France. He could have issued such a warning earlier, when it might have been more effective.[87]

Before the final stages of the crisis, Grey had attempted to conciliate Germany not because of domestic constraints, but because he believed a conciliatory policy offered the best hope for preserving the peace. There is evidence to suggest that Grey still thought an uncommitted position could avoid war even when the conflict seemed likely or even imminent. As late as July 30, in his reply to the German attempt to win British neutrality by promising not to dismember France, Grey could still claim that "the one way of maintaining good relations between England and Germany is to continue to work together for the peace of Europe."[88]

Grey's hopes for a diplomatic solution and his belief in the need for a conciliatory policy toward Germany reflected his understanding of Anglo–German cooperation in the previous Balkan crises. Believing that a détente

---

84. See Zara Steiner, "The Foreign Office under Sir Edward Grey, 1905–1914," in Hinsley, *British Foreign Policy under Sir Edward Grey*, p. 401; and Tuchman, *The Guns of August*, p. 113. This argument is used by Schmitt to at least partly exonerate Grey. See *The Coming of the War, 1914*, Vol. 2, p. 409.
85. Steiner, *Britain and the Origins of the First World War*, p. 227.
86. Ibid., p. 241; and Steiner, *The Foreign Office and Foreign Policy*, p. 156.
87. See Albertini, *The Origins of the War of 1914*, Vol. 3, p. 643.
88. Grey went on to argue that if the crisis were resolved, "my own endeavour would be to promote some arrangement to which Germany could be a party, by which she could be assured that no hostile or aggressive policy would be pursued against her or her allies by France, Russia, and ourselves, jointly or separately. I have desired this and worked for it, as far as I could, through the last Balkan crisis, and Germany having a corresponding object, our relations sensibly improved." Quoted in Schmitt, *The Coming of the War, 1914*, Vol. 2, pp. 259–260. See also Steiner, *The Foreign Office and Foreign Policy*, p. 158.

had emerged between the powers, he placed his faith in cooperation with Bethmann–Hollweg to resolve the crisis.[89] Grey's belief in the efficacy of Anglo–German cooperation was reinforced by the emergence of a détente during the 1912–1913 Balkan crises. Grey believed that the Anglo–German détente in the Balkans had averted an Austro–Russian clash. He concluded that Germany had worked with Britain and promised that "I shall do my part to keep our relations cordial as long as the German Government will do their part in good faith."[90] He may have exaggerated the impact of his earlier diplomatic successes, but he clearly believed that they could be repeated by following the same approach in July 1914.[91]

The foreign secretary's beliefs were reflected in comments he made on the eve of the July crisis. In May 1914, he wrote to George Buchanan, the British ambassador to Russia, that "it seemed to me that in essential matters of policy that were really important Germany sometimes restrained Austria and Italy, particularly the former, and allowed them only to go to a certain point."[92] On July 9, after Germany had already given Austria its "blank check," he told the German ambassador, Lichnowsky, that "I would continue the same policy I had pursued through the Balkan crisis. . . . the greater the risk of war the more I would adhere to this policy."[93] Years later, in 1936, former Cabinet member Lord Crewe wrote to the historian G.M. Trevelyan: "All through the month, we attempted to exercise a mediating influence; probably the whole government, including Grey, were a little overflattered by the success of the Balkan Conference the year before.[94]

Grey's confidence in German cooperation in July 1914 turned out to be fatally misplaced. Instead of restraining Austria–Hungary, as it had in 1912, Germany encouraged Austria–Hungary to take decisive action against Serbia.[95] British proposals for a diplomatic solution to the crisis were passed on to Austria–Hungary without comment, delayed, and ignored.[96] Many historians now agree that Germany was willing to risk war in 1914 because

89. See above, pp. 126–128 for a discussion of the motivations for the British and German attempts to achieve a détente.
90. Quoted in Steiner, *Britain and the Origins of the First World War*, p. 115.
91. Kennedy, *The Rise of the Anglo–German Antagonism*, p. 456.
92. Quoted in Ekstein and Steiner, "The Sarajevo Crisis," p. 397.
93. Quoted in ibid., p. 399.
94. Quoted in ibid., p. 402.
95. The argument that Germany was not dragged into the war by Austria is made in Fischer, *Germany's Aims in the First World War*; Jarausch, "The Illusion of Limited War"; Kaiser, "Germany and the Origins of the First World War"; and Geiss, *July 1914*, p. 364.
96. Fischer, *Germany's Aims in the First World War*, pp. 65–66.

elements of the German elite, especially the army, feared that German power was declining vis-à-vis Russia and the opportunity for expansion was slipping away.[97] The Anglo–German détente led Grey to adopt the wrong course. He was not "lulled by crisis management," as Miles Kahler suggests, but instead was lulled into believing that the Anglo–German détente meant that Germany would seek to avoid war by restraining Austria and cooperating with Britain.[98] The Germans, unfortunately, had a very different understanding of the improvement in relations.

THE DÉTENTE AND GERMAN EXPECTATIONS OF NEUTRALITY

Grey's failure to warn Germany that Britain would support France in 1914 may have contributed to German hopes that Britain would remain neutral. German expectations were based not only on Grey's behavior during the crisis, but also on the pattern of amicable Anglo–German relations that had emerged between 1911 and 1914.[99] Although Germany's hopes for neutrality may have led it to ignore or discount any evidence that Britain would not remain neutral, the conciliatory policy of Grey in 1914 may have appeared as a logical continuation of the détente that had emerged in the preceding years. The unwillingness of the Germans to acknowledge any of the evidence that Britain might side with France in 1914 may not have reflected "cognitive closure" but a rational expectation based on the German view of the 1911–1914 détente.[100]

---

97. See, for example, Kaiser, "Germany and the Origins of the First World War"; and Jarausch, "The Illusion of Limited War."

98. Kahler, "Rumors of War," p. 395.

99. See Geiss, *July 1914*, p. 38, for the argument that British neutrality was the goal of Germany's policy of détente.

100. For an example of the argument that German leaders suffered from "cognitive closure" and refused to believe that Britain would enter the war, see Lebow, *Between Peace and War*, pp. 119–147. Lebow basically argues that the German leadership had invested such hopes in their efforts to secure British neutrality that they discounted any signs that Britain would intervene. In particular, he claims that Lichnowsky's warnings were ignored before July 29. This argument overlooks the fact that other information gave Berlin the impression that British neutrality was likely. After a July 24 dinner with Haldane and Churchill and a subsequent talk with Grey and Haldane, Albert Ballin mistakenly concluded that Britain might remain neutral if Germany did "not swallow up" France. Prince Henry, the Kaiser's brother, had breakfast with King George V on July 26 and reported, probably erroneously, that the King had said Britain would remain neutral in any continental war. See Schmitt, *The Coming of the War, 1914*, pp. 38–39, 52–53. Moreover, the belief that improved Anglo–German relations had reduced the likelihood that Britain would side with France was not confined to Germany. The Belgian ambassador to Berlin, Baron Beyens, who certainly had no vested interest in British neutrality, reported in late 1913: "It is by no means certain that Britain will take France's side in a war with Germany. . . . it is less likely as relations between Germany and Britain have visibly improved." Quoted in Fischer,

In December 1912, Bethmann–Hollweg had written: "The British attitude [in the Balkan crisis] is only one of several symptoms which suggest that the Entente has passed its climax and that we may look forward to a re-orientation of British policy."[101] Noting Grey's willingness to restrain Russia and France in the Balkan crisis, Bethmann–Hollweg wrote on December 18, 1912 that it was "at least doubtful whether England would intervene actively if the *provocation* appeared to come directly from Russia and France."[102] He therefore waited until July 1914, when "a new phase of Anglo–German cooperation" seemed to have begun.[103]

In the July crisis, Bethmann–Hollweg thus deliberately attempted to avoid actions that would provoke Britain. He assumed that his goal of British neutrality would be attainable if the blame for any war could be pinned on Russia or France. This confidence reflected the German belief that a détente had emerged between Berlin and London. Szögyény, Austria–Hungary's ambassador to Germany, informed his capital that "Anglo–German relations [have] so improved that Germany feels that she need no longer fear a directly hostile attitude by Britain."[104] The German publicist Victor Naumann, a confidant of the German Foreign Ministry, reported in July that the Anglo–German African settlement had "made it certain that Britain would not intervene in a European war."[105] Thus the détente contributed to repeated statements, like that of Foreign Minister Jagow on July 26, 1914, that Germany was "sure of England's neutrality."[106]

THE SIGNIFICANCE OF GERMAN HOPES FOR NEUTRALITY

The argument that Grey was mistaken in his attempts to avoid threatening Germany is only significant if Germany would have adopted a different policy if he had made it clear that Britain would not remain neutral. Grey's critics

---

War of Illusions, p. 228. The Germans may have been somewhat obtuse, but they were not totally unjustified to conclude that the Anglo–German détente might have reduced the probability of British intervention. For a rebuttal of Lebow's argument, see Scott D. Sagan, "1914 Revisited: Allies, Offense, and Instability," *International Security*, Vol. 11, No. 2 (Fall 1986), pp. 169–170.
101. Quoted in Geiss, *July 1914*, p. 44. Fischer concurs in *Germany's Aims in the First World War*, p. 31.
102. Quoted in Fischer, *Germany's Aims in the First World War*, p. 31.
103. Geiss, *July 1914*, p. 44.
104. Quoted in Fischer, *Germany's Aims in the First World War*, p. 58.
105. Quoted in ibid., p. 53.
106. Quoted in Van Evera, "The Cult of the Offensive and the Origins of the First World War," p. 101.

assume that Germany would not have taken the steps that led to World War I if London had warned Berlin that it could intervene.[107] It is always difficult to speculate on alternative courses of history, but there is much evidence to suggest that Germany would have tried to avoid war if it had not assumed British neutrality. Bethmann–Hollweg had sought a détente with Britain since he became Chancellor in 1909. In July 1914, he was willing to risk an Austro–Serbian conflict or even a continental war involving France and Russia.[108] Bethmann–Hollweg encouraged Austria–Hungary to take decisive action against Serbia, believing that this policy would produce either a major diplomatic triumph or a war that would ensure German hegemony in Europe.[109]

Bethmann–Hollweg was not eager to fight a world war involving Britain, however, and he hoped that London would remain neutral if the war appeared to have been provoked by Russia or France. Although he realized that an "attack on Serbia can lead to world war,"[110] he believed that he could avoid such an outcome by placing the onus for starting the conflict on Russia and France, thereby guaranteeing British neutrality. On July 27, Jagow emphasized the need to keep Britain out of the war: "The German government's point of view was that it was at the moment of the highest priority to prevent Britain from making common cause with Russia and France."[111] As Fritz Fischer argues, "so long as England remained out . . . the Chancellor was not in the least afraid of putting the Triple Alliance to the test of a European war."[112]

The importance that Germany placed on securing British neutrality was revealed by Berlin's reaction to the news that Britain might side with France. When this outcome first appeared possible, on July 29 and 30, Bethmann–Hollweg reversed his policy and attempted to restrain Austria–Hungary. He recommended that Vienna accept Grey's proposal for mediation and a "halt

---

107. See, for example, Calleo, *The German Problem Reconsidered*, p. 34.

108. See Jarausch, "The Illusion of Limited War"; Snyder, "Civil–Military Relations and the Cult of the Offensive," p. 128; Fritz Stern, "Bethmann Hollweg and the War: The Limits of Responsibility," in Leonard Krieger and Fritz Stern, eds., *The Responsibility of Power; Historical Essays in Honor of Hajo Holburn* (Garden City, N.Y.: Doubleday, 1967), pp. 252–285; Van Evera, "The Cult of the Offensive and the Origins of the First World War," p. 83; and Schmitt, *The Coming of the War, 1914*, Vol. 2, pp. 68, 129.

109. Austria–Hungary may have had its own reasons for attacking Serbia, but Germany encouraged Austria to take decisive action and would have urged this course even if Austria had been more reluctant. Germany was not forced into the war by its weaker ally. See Kaiser, "Germany and the Origins of the First World War," p. 466.

110. Quoted in Jarausch, "The Illusion of Limited War," p. 58.

111. Quoted in Fischer, *Germany's Aims in the First World War*, p. 70.

112. Ibid., p. 75.

in Belgrade." The German foreign ministry was thrown into an "immense commotion," as Bethmann–Hollweg sent six telegrams to Vienna during the night of July 29–30.[113] If Britain had made its intentions clear earlier, Germany might have restrained Austria sooner, and the crisis would have evolved very differently.

It can be argued that the German military did not care if Britain intervened and therefore would not have been deterred by a clearer threat in July 1914. Moltke had discounted the military significance of the British Expeditionary Force, even suggesting "the more English the better."[114] But the German decisions of July 1914 were made by Bethmann–Hollweg. David Kaiser argues that Moltke was out of Berlin, and "the military seems to have played no role whatever in the July decisions that actually led to the conflict."[115] On August 2, after his return to the capital, Moltke even said that "England's neutrality is of such importance to us," implying that he did not entirely discount the British army.[116]

The importance of British neutrality to Germany is also indicated by the reaction of German leaders to Britain's entry into the war. Kaiser Wilhelm reacted emotionally, complaining about "perfidious Albion" and "that filthy nation of grocers."[117] He later lamented, "If only someone had told me beforehand that England would take up arms against us."[118] Bethmann–Hollweg bitterly blamed Britain for the world war: "The war turns into an unlimited world catastrophe only through England's participation."[119] Germany clearly had seen a need for Britain's neutrality, and German disappointment reflected the importance it had placed on Britain remaining out of the war. Ironically, the dashing of the expectations raised by the Anglo–German détente actually deepened Germany's hostility toward Britain.

It is highly likely that a clearer statement of Britain's intention to intervene on behalf of France would have deterred Germany, thereby preventing or at least limiting World War I. This understanding of the outbreak of the war at

---

113. See Ekstein and Steiner, "The Sarajevo Crisis," p. 402; Fischer, *Germany's Aims in the First World War*, pp. 78–81; Jarausch, "The Illusion of Limited War," pp. 65–68; and Schmitt, *The Coming of the War, 1914*, Vol. 2, pp. 160–167.
114. Quoted in Tuchman, *The Guns of August*, p. 144.
115. Kaiser, "Germany and the Origins of the First World War," p. 469. See also Schmitt, *The Coming of the War, 1914*, Vol. 2, p. 58.
116. Quoted in Geiss, *July 1914*, p. 351.
117. Quoted in Fischer, *Germany's Aims in the First World War*, p. 85.
118. Quoted in Tuchman, *The Guns of August*, p. 143.
119. Quoted in Jarausch, "The Illusion of Limited War," p. 72.

the very least must supplement and modify the images of preemptive war or the spiral model prevalent in the political science literature. If Germany could have been deterred by a more decisive British stand, then the start of the war resembles the deterrence model more closely associated with World War II. Russian and German fears that the other would mobilize first would not have exercised any influence if Germany had been deterred by an earlier British commitment to support France. Germany may have lost control over events shortly before the conflict became a world war, and the conventional wisdom about the impact of mobilization schedules and offensive doctrines may still apply here; but the existence of the Anglo–German détente created the conditions in which Germany felt confident enough to run the risk of continental or global war.

The 1914 Analogy and the Management of Détente

Anglo–German relations between 1911 and 1914 provide insights into the nature of détente that may be applicable to current problems of U.S.–Soviet relations. Some caveats are in order, however. American and Soviet leaders do not have to contend with the complexities of a multipolar world, and they have the added impetus for caution that comes from the existence of nuclear weapons. In addition, it is always dangerous to draw conclusions from one historical case, demonstrated by the history of attempts to apply the "lessons" of the origins of World War I and World War II. Nevertheless, pre-1914 Anglo–German relations provide an additional case of great power détente that may supplement conclusions that are based solely on U.S.–Soviet relations.

DÉTENTE AND THE RISK OF WAR

The pre-World War I Anglo–German détente suggests that détente may, under some conditions, actually contribute to the outbreak of conflict. Although most analysts probably intuitively associate détente with a reduced risk of war, it may have had the opposite effect in 1914.[120] In the absence of an Anglo–German détente, both countries might have adopted different

---

120. For two exceptions, see Philip Windsor, "The Savior From The Sea," *Foreign Policy*, No. 22 (Spring 1976), pp. 171–172; and Kalevi J. Holsti, "Detente as a Source of International Conflict," in Nissan Oren, ed., *Images and Reality in International Politics* (New York: St. Martin's, 1984), pp. 125–142. See also John Lewis Gaddis, "The Long Peace: Elements of Stability in the Postwar International System," *International Security*, Vol. 10, No. 4 (Spring 1986), pp. 139–140.

policies in the July crisis. The British might have had no reservations about making clear their intention to fight on the side of the French and Russians, while the Germans might have recognized that there was little possibility that Britain would allow them to attack France or even to dominate the continent.

The Anglo–German détente contributed to the mistaken British and German policies during July 1914 by fostering a set of misperceptions. Leaders in both countries underestimated the hostility of their adversary. The policies of détente that Grey and Bethmann–Hollweg pursued led both countries to neglect their differences while they focused on areas in which practical cooperation or negotiated agreements could improve the tense atmosphere of post-Agadir Anglo–German relations.

In July 1914, these mutual misperceptions took the form of Grey and Bethmann–Hollweg drawing the wrong conclusions from their experience in the 1912–1913 Balkan crises. Grey concluded that crisis management required Anglo–German cooperation and the avoidance of threats that might provoke German hostility. Under such conditions, he felt that Germany would restrain Austria–Hungary and work to prevent any conflict from escalating. This policy had succeeded in the earlier crises, and the improving climate of Anglo–German relations led Grey to believe it would be appropriate again. Bethmann–Hollweg, on the other hand, concluded that Britain would not support an apparently aggressive Russian policy and might remain neutral if Germany could avoid appearing responsible for any war. These two sets of mistaken lessons indicate that détente can create conditions under which leaders can incorrectly base their behavior on their understanding of past events. The problem of leaders drawing inappropriate conclusions from historical analogies does not occur only in cases of great power détente,[121] but the likelihood and risks of drawing inappropriate conclusions may be magnified under conditions of détente. Because détente is a policy of improving relations conducted by two states with many incompatible interests,[122] the lessons drawn from cooperative experiences may be fundamentally inapplicable to events in which the conflictual aspects of a relationship are para-

---

121. See Jervis, *Perception and Misperception*, pp. 217–315, for an excellent discussion of the way in which decision-makers read or misread lessons of history or of previous experiences. For a more recent examination of how decision-makers use history, see Richard E. Neustadt and Ernest R. May, *Thinking in Time: The Uses of History for Decision-Makers* (New York: The Free Press, 1986).
122. See above, fn. 12, pp. 125–126.

mount. The complexity of pursuing a mixed relationship of cooperation and competition may foster misperceptions and the inappropriate use of conclusions based on past experiences. Neither Grey nor Bethmann–Hollweg, for example, was able to understand how the situation of July 1914 differed from earlier crises.

Détente may also contribute to misperceptions about one's adversary. These misperceptions may then lead to inappropriate policies. Critics of the U.S.–Soviet détente of the 1970s often argue that the climate of improved relations merely "lulled" the United States into believing that the Soviet threat had diminished and that it could reduce its vigilance and military preparedness.[123] Applied to pre-1914 Anglo–German relations, this argument would suggest that the détente between the two countries lulled the British into a less vigilant posture by leading them to believe that Germany was not likely to pursue an aggressive policy. Apparent German concessions, such as the slowing of the naval arms race and willingness to restrain Austria–Hungary in 1912–1913, may have contributed to British misunderstandings of German foreign policy.[124] Although Grey may have held some misconceptions about Germany when he embarked on his policy of détente, the apparent success of his policy may have increased his misconceptions about German aims and encouraged him to believe that there was a substantial "peace party" in Berlin which would be strengthened by a conciliatory British policy.[125] Despite the warnings of his Foreign Office advisers, particularly Eyre Crowe, Grey may have exaggerated the degree to which German intentions were peaceful and non-threatening. The Anglo–German détente may have ob-

---

123. See, for example, Norman Podhoretz, "The Future Danger," *Commentary*, April 1981, pp. 29–47; and Eugene V. Rostow, "The Case Against SALT II," *Commentary*, February 1979, pp. 23–32. Whether the United States actually was lulled by détente is highly debatable. American unwillingness to confront Soviet challenges in the Third World can be traced to the impact of the Vietnam War on public attitudes toward the use of force overseas. The same factor explains much of the decline in U.S. military spending in the early 1970s. In any case, the U.S.–Soviet détente is not analogous to the Anglo–German détente in many important respects. While the former took place in an essentially bipolar world in which the actions of the two leading powers toward each other were of central importance, German policy toward Britain aimed to loosen the Anglo–French entente, not to prepare for an Anglo–German conflict.
124. The improvement in Anglo–German relations did encourage British domestic critics of spending on naval armaments to believe that increased expenditures were no longer necessary, but these arguments did not lead to a retrenchment in naval programs. See Howard Weinroth, "Left-Wing Opposition to Naval Armaments in Britain Before 1914," *Journal of Contemporary History*, Vol. 6, No. 4 (1971).
125. Germany may have deliberately fostered this impression. See Michael Ekstein, "Sir Edward Grey and Imperial Germany in 1914," *Journal of Contemporary History*, Vol. 6, No. 3 (1971), pp. 121–131.

scured evidence of German ambitions and willingness to risk war under certain conditions. Without such misconceptions about Germany, Grey may have given earlier and clearer warnings during the July crisis.

The risks that may accompany a policy of détente do not necessarily imply that a policy of confrontation would be more effective. Instead, they suggest that détente must be pursued without illusions and that decision-makers need to be careful about applying any conclusions drawn from instances of cooperation with their adversary. Such conclusions may not apply in future crises, and they may not resemble the conclusions drawn by the other party to the détente.

VARIETIES OF DÉTENTE

The Anglo–German détente emerged because both countries sought to improve the atmosphere of their mutual relations. They negotiated on minor issues and attempted to cooperate so that overt hostility was no longer emphasized in the relationship. By deliberately seeking areas in which cooperation seemed feasible, Grey and Bethmann–Hollweg apparently hoped to reduce Anglo–German tension.[126]

This approach to détente is by no means the only one possible. Several other types of détente can be imagined or recognized in other great power relationships. First, two countries could systematically attempt to resolve all the important issues that divided them. R.J. Crampton, one of the few historians to engage in a detailed examination of the Anglo–German détente, suggests that it failed because neither country was interested in explicitly addressing the issues of naval armaments and the British commitment to France.[127] These issues were discussed during the Haldane mission, but the two countries thereafter regarded them as intractable and did not attempt further negotiations on either issue. Such a policy could have led beyond the limited détente that emerged, but it might also have undermined the desire for improved relations by making it clear how wide Anglo–German differences were.

---

126. Henry Kissinger describes and criticizes this type of approach in *White House Years* (Boston: Little, Brown, 1979), p. 120.
127. Crampton, *The Hollow Detente*, p. vi. Crampton suggests that the United States and the Soviet Union appear to be attacking the "fundamental issues" that divide them in the SALT talks. Regardless of whether these issues are truly fundamental, his optimism (expressed in 1977) now seems misplaced.

Second, one country could attempt to systematically make concessions that would remove any basis for conflict. This policy, which deserves the name of "appeasement" despite the disrepute into which that word has fallen, was not pursued by Britain before World War I, although some elements of it were present in the British attempt to placate the Germans by awarding them a larger share of the Portuguese colonies.[128]

Third, two countries might achieve a détente by agreeing upon rules and procedures for regulating conflict. In U.S.–Soviet relations, such rules have included tacit recognition of spheres of influence, agreements on specific procedures for dealing with dangerous situations, such as the Hot Line Agreement and the 1971 Accident Measures Agreement, and broader agreements on general principles, such as the Basic Principles Agreement.[129] Grey's attempt to revive the Concert of Europe by convening the London Conference during the 1912–1913 Balkan crises may represent an attempt to apply this approach, although Grey only used it during this particular episode.

Historical cases of attempts to achieve a détente generally will combine aspects of each of these basic approaches. The Anglo–German case, however, seems to fit mainly into the "improve the atmosphere" category. The statements of Grey and Bethmann–Hollweg indicate a strong desire to improve relations without resolving major issues. This approach may have been a particularly effective way for Grey to satisfy his domestic critics by providing evidence of an improved relationship without requiring fundamental concessions. But it may also be the type of détente most likely to generate misperceptions about the nature of one's adversary and the utility of improved relations. The "improve the atmosphere" approach may be desirable when the alternative is a continuing spiral of hostility, but it tends to emphasize

---

128. See above, pp. 13–14. On the concept of appeasement, see Craig and George, *Force and Statecraft*, pp. 241, 245–248. It is important to distinguish British policy before World War I from the attempted appeasement of Hitler in the 1930s. The German leadership before World War I may have been willing to avoid war under certain conditions, whereas Hitler seemed to be determined to launch a war. The British response to Hitler also assumed that by satisfying legitimate German grievances, such as the question of restrictions on German rearmament and the status of Sudeten Germans, Hitler's motives for war might be removed. Before World War I, however, British policy aimed to change the climate of relations without making important concessions. Germany's potential reasons for war were less clear to British policymakers, although Grey apparently saw a need to allay German fears of encirclement.
129. For a discussion of various attempts to introduce "rules" into the U.S.–Soviet relationship, see Alexander L. George, ed., *Managing U.S.–Soviet Rivalry: Problems of Crisis Prevention* (Boulder, Colo.: Westview Press, 1983).

the appearance of good relations over the reality of continued disagreement. It may foster misperceptions and, eventually, disillusionment when the actual state of relations does not appear to match the apparent overall climate.

Conclusions

Reconsidering the origins of World War I and the 1911–1914 Anglo–German détente indicates that many of the conclusions that political scientists have drawn from the 1914 analogy deserve qualification. The First World War was partly the result of a miscalculation, but, at least between Britain and Germany, it was a miscalculation that resulted from excessive conciliation, not deterrence that turned into provocation. European statesmen may have made many mistakes and miscalculations in late July, when the crisis was at its peak, but the crisis developed to this stage only because Germany assumed that Anglo–German relations had improved to such an extent that Britain would remain neutral in a European war. The argument that Britain made no effort to accommodate Germany is not supported by the evidence of the Anglo–German détente. Many efforts were made to achieve a détente, but this policy ultimately encouraged Germany's false hopes for British neutrality.

Simple models may not capture the complexity of the causes of World War I. As Paul Kennedy has written, "the First World War offers so much data that conclusions can be drawn from it to suit any *a priori* hypothesis which contemporary strategists and politicians wish to advance."[130] The complex, multipolar diplomatic maneuverings that preceded the First World War offer such a rich basis for lessons that political scientists should be careful about drawing simple analogies from the outbreak of the war. The outbreak of the war among the European powers probably should be interpreted as evidence of the dangers of offensive doctrines and rigid mobilization schedules, but the history of Anglo–German relations between 1911 and 1914 should be used to supplement these lessons with an awareness of how the détente may have contributed to the policies Great Britain and Germany pursued during the July crisis. The origins of World War I can offer an ample number of lessons and analogies, but no single analogy can capture all the lessons offered by the outbreak of the conflict.

---

130. Kennedy, "The First World War and the International Power System," p. 37.

The Meaning of Mobilization in 1914

Marc Trachtenberg

$\mathbf{T}$he idea that a great war need not be the product of deliberate decision—that it can come because statesmen "lose control" of events—is one of the most basic and most common notions in contemporary American strategic thought. A crisis, it is widely assumed, might unleash forces of an essentially military nature that overwhelm the political process and bring on a war that nobody wants. Many important conclusions about the risk of nuclear war, and thus about the political meaning of nuclear forces, rest on this fundamental idea.

This theory of "inadvertent war" is in turn rooted, to a quite extraordinary degree, in a specific interpretation of a single historical episode: the coming of the First World War during the July Crisis in 1914.[1] It is often taken for granted that the sort of military system that existed in Europe at the time— a system of interlocking mobilizations and of war plans that placed a great emphasis on rapid offensive action—directly led to a conflict that might otherwise have been avoided. George Quester's view is typical of the way the issue is treated in much of the political science literature. "World War I," he writes, "broke out as a spasm of pre-emptive mobilization schedules."[2]

A longer version of the present article is being published as a chapter in my forthcoming book, *History and Strategy* (Princeton: Princeton University Press, 1991). That chapter will go into a number of issues which, for reasons of space, could not be dealt with here.

Marc Trachtenberg is Associate Professor of History at the University of Pennsylvania.

---

1. The term "inadvertent war" is used here in the specific sense of a war brought on by forces of a military nature; it is not to be taken as referring to the much more general idea that war may break out even though it may not have been intended or anticipated by any of the major actors at the beginning of a crisis. For interpretations of the coming of the First World War which emphasize the role played by the mobilization system in bringing on the conflict, see, for example: Thomas Schelling, *Arms and Influence* (New Haven: Yale University Press, 1966), pp. 221–225; Graham T. Allison, Albert Carnesale, and Joseph S. Nye, Jr., eds., *Hawks, Doves, and Owls: An Agenda for Avoiding Nuclear War* (New York: Norton, 1985), pp. 17–18, 30, 43, 210, 217; Richard Ned Lebow, *Nuclear Crisis Management: A Dangerous Illusion* (Ithaca: Cornell University Press, 1987), pp. 24–26, 32–35, 59–60, 109–113, 122–123. Note also the rather extreme argument in Paul Bracken's *The Command and Control of Nuclear Forces* (New Haven: Yale University Press, 1983). This book is laced with references to the July Crisis; see esp. p. 65 where Bracken admits that his argument about how a nuclear war could begin might sound a bit extreme "were it not for the history of the outbreak of World War I."
2. George Quester, *Deterrence Before Hiroshima* (New York: Wiley, 1966), p. 17.

International Security, Winter 1990/91 (Vol. 15, No. 3)
© 1990 by the President and Fellows of Harvard College and of the Massachusetts Institute of Technology.

And many well-known historians make the same sort of argument. According to Barbara Tuchman, for example, statesmen tried to draw back on the eve of the war, "but the pull of military schedules dragged them forward."[3] A.J.P. Taylor agrees. The German war plan, the famous Schlieffen Plan, was, he argues, instrumental in precipitating the war: in 1914, Schlieffen's "dead hand automatically pulled the trigger."[4] My aim here is to examine the claim that the mobilization system played an important role in bringing on the conflict; this examination will show, I think, just how weak this argument is.

It is not that the conventional wisdom is wrong in assuming that there was a system of interlocking mobilization plans in 1914. A system of this sort certainly did exist, with the Schlieffen Plan as its linchpin. That strategy proposed to take advantage of the relative slowness of Russian mobilization: Germany, by mobilizing rapidly and then attacking in the west with the great mass of her army, would be able to defeat France before having to face Russia. The Germans could not, therefore, allow a Russian general mobilization to run its course without ordering their own mobilization and in fact attacking France. Russian mobilization would lead to German mobilization, and under the German war plan, mobilization meant war.

A mechanism of this sort clearly existed, but was it actually a *cause* of the war? It is important to think through what is implied by the claim that this mechanism of interlocking mobilization plans helped bring on the cataclysm. A simple analogy may be helpful. Suppose it takes me thirty minutes to get home when the traffic is light, but a full hour during the rush hour. I promise to be home by 6:00, but I choose to leave at 5:30 and arrive a half-hour late, blaming the bad traffic for the delay. The rush hour traffic, however, could hardly be held responsible for my lateness, since I had chosen to leave at 5:30, knowing full well what the situation was: knowledge of the situation had been factored into the original decision. On the other hand, if the heavy traffic had been caused by an accident, or indeed by anything that had not been anticipated, then it would make more sense to blame it for the delay.

Similarly, if in 1914 everyone understood the system and knew, for example, that a Russian or a German general mobilization would lead to war, and if, in addition, the political authorities were free agents—that is, if their hands were not being forced by military imperatives, or by pressure from

---

3. Barbara Tuchman, *The Guns of August* (New York: Macmillan, 1962), p. 72.
4. A.J.P. Taylor, *Illustrated History of the First World War* (New York: Putnam, 1964), p. 15.

the generals—then the existence of the system of interlocking mobilization plans could hardly be said in itself to have been a cause of war. Some people argue that the mobilization system was a "cause" of war because, once it was set off, the time for negotiation was cut short. But if the working of the system was understood in advance, a decision for general mobilization was a decision for war; statesmen would be opting for war with their eyes open. To argue that the system was, in such a case, a "cause" of the war makes about as much sense as saying that any military operation which marked the effective beginning of hostilities—the crossing of borders, for example, or an initial attack on enemy forces—was a real "cause" of an armed conflict, simply because it foreclosed the possibility of a negotiated settlement. Such operations are in no real sense a "cause" of war, if in fact their implications are universally understood in advance. Similarly, if it was generally understood how the system worked, and if the statesmen were free agents when they made their mobilization decisions, then in that case the mobilization process should not be viewed as a cause of the war, but should instead be seen simply as its opening phase.

It follows, therefore, that for the inadvertent war theory to hold for the July 1914 case, it must be shown *either* that the implications of mobilization were not understood, *or* that the political leadership was under such great pressure to act that it was not really free to hold back. The arguments that the mobilization system played a crucial role in bringing on the war fall into these two categories.

The first set of arguments focuses on the alleged failure of the political leaders to understand what the military plans actually meant. As a result, it is said, they made their moves and ordered their mobilizations "light-heartedly," thinking that they were engaged in simple political maneuvering, seeking only to deter their adversaries. But once set loose, the forces they had unleashed could scarcely be controlled.[5] "The absence of all understanding of military matters on the part of the responsible statesmen" is for Luigi Albertini, author of what is still by far the most important study of the immediate origins of the conflict, a major cause of the war. "It was," he says, "the political leaders' ignorance of what mobilization implied and the dangers it involved which led them light-heartedly to take the step of mobilizing and

---

5. Taylor, *Illustrated History*, pp. 14–15; Michael Howard, "Lest We Forget," *Encounter*, January 1964, p. 65; Lebow, *Nuclear Crisis Management*, pp. 26, 109–112.

thus unleash a European war."[6] The basic contention, that the statesmen did not understand that general mobilization meant war, will be examined in the next section.

But it is also argued that the political leadership failed to understand that even a *partial* Russian mobilization, directed only against Austria, would have led to war "no less surely than general mobilization," and that this was also a major cause of the disaster.[7] So to test the claim that ignorance of crucial military realities played an important role in bringing on the conflict, a second section will examine the argument that even a partial mobilization would have inevitably led to war.

The second set of arguments focuses on the claim that the statesmen were not really free agents when the mobilization decisions were made. The basic argument is that military considerations, and especially the pressure to move preemptively, came at the crucial moment to dominate policy. It is sometimes taken for granted that the very existence of a military regime based on mass armies and mobilizations automatically generated pressure for preemption. Writing of World War I, for example, Herman Kahn remarked: "This ability to increase one's force by a large factor and in a very short period of time gave a disastrous instability to the situation, because it promised to give the nation that mobilized first a crucial advantage."[8] The point is hardly self-evident, since mobilizations are difficult to conceal, and if detected quickly might lead to such rapid counter-mobilizations that there might be scarcely any advantage to going first.[9] Was it in fact the case, however, that the incentive to go first, to the extent that it really did exist, played a significant role in shaping at least some of the key decisions that were made on the eve of the war? Was it true that "general staffs, goaded by their relentless time-tables, were pounding the table for the signal to move lest their opponents gain an hour's head start"?[10]

Closely related is the issue of whether the military effectively took control of policy—at least in Germany and perhaps in Russia as well. According to

6. Luigi Albertini, *The Origins of the War of 1914*, 3 vols., trans. and ed. Isabella M. Massey (London: Oxford University Press, 1952–57), Vol. 2, pp. 479–483, 579. L.C.F. Turner, *Origins of the First World War* (New York: Norton, 1970), p. 99, follows Albertini on this point.
7. Turner, *Origins of the First World War*, pp. 92, 108; Albertini, *Origins*, Vol. 2, pp. 392, 485n (for the quote), 529–530, 541.
8. Herman Kahn, *On Thermonuclear War* (Princeton: Princeton University Press, 1960), p. 359.
9. As far as I can tell, Stephen Van Evera is the only one to make this point. Stephen Van Evera, "The Cult of the Offensive and the Origins of the First World War," *International Security*, Vol. 9, No. 1 (Summer 1984), p. 75.
10. Tuchman, *Guns of August*, p. 72.

Gordon Craig, for example, by the end of the crisis General von Moltke, the head of the general staff, "had superseded the Chancellor in all but name"; the military technicians "had overborne the civilian authorities and brought war on in their own way"; in the end, "the great decision of 1914 was made by the soldiers."[11] Albertini also has the chancellor, Bethmann Hollweg, "surrendering" to Moltke, "capitulating" to his "will to war," and says: "At the decisive moment the military took over the direction of affairs and imposed their law."[12] With regard to Russia, Albertini remarks that after the Austrian declaration of war on Serbia, the Russian foreign minister, S.D. Sazonov, lost "control of the situation" which "passed into the hands of the military."[13] If these claims are valid, it would make sense to hold the military system in some measure responsible for the coming of the war.

The claim that policy makers were "stampeded" into war in 1914 thus needs to be tested.[14] This set of issues will therefore be examined in a third section focusing on the most important phase of the crisis: the final hours before Russia ordered general mobilization on July 30.

The Meaning of Mobilization

The July Crisis began on June 28, 1914, with the assassination of the heir to the Austrian throne. Serbia was the base of the nationalist movement that had been responsible for that terrorist act, and Austria, having secured German support, was determined to use force against Serbia in order to put an end to what was, for Austria, an intolerably subversive movement. On July 23 the Austrians issued a series of demands; the Austrian terms were designed to be unacceptable. The Serbs were given 48 hours to reply to this ultimatum. On July 24 the Russian government, which saw itself as the protector of Serbia, considered, and on July 25 decided to prepare, a partial mobilization against Austria. The Russians also decided on the 25th to enforce "throughout the entire Empire the order for the period preparatory to war." Important pre-mobilization measures were to be put into effect secretly the

11. Gordon Craig, *The Politics of the Prussian Army* (New York: Oxford University Press, 1964), pp. 291, 294, 295.
12. Albertini, *Origins*, Vol. 3, pp. 13, 27, 31, 190, 232, 248.
13. Ibid., Vol. 2, p. 540.
14. See, for example, Lebow, *Nuclear Crisis Management*, pp. 34, 60.

next day.[15] Reservists, for example, were called up to bring the army divisions on Russia's frontiers, including her frontiers with Germany, up to strength.

With the decisions of July 25, Russia was moving closer to general mobilization. Did the Russian leaders understand what they were doing—that their full mobilization would lead to a German mobilization, and that for Germany mobilization meant war? It is an important element of the "inadvertent war" thesis that they did not, and Albertini returns to this point repeatedly. "Russia," he says, "had no knowledge of the fact that for Germany mobilization meant going to war," and Sazonov, in particular did not understand that Germany could not afford delay, but would begin military operations almost immediately.[16] Many political scientists seem to have accepted these arguments, and have perhaps even taken them a step or two further. According to Ned Lebow, for example, "Russian political leaders mobilized in 1914 in the belief that mobilization would be a deterrent to war." "Neither the czar nor Sazonov," he says, "believed that their action would directly trigger war."[17]

It is quite clear, however, from the evidence that Albertini himself presents, that the Russian government understood very well what mobilization meant when it made its mobilization decisions at the end of July. The Russian documents show, first of all, that support for general mobilization was rooted in a belief in the virtual inevitability of war. On July 30, the day the fateful decision was made, A.V. Krivoshein, the dominant figure in the government, met with Sazonov before the latter was scheduled to see the Tsar. According to the official diary of Baron M.F. Schilling, the chief of the chancellery at the Russian foreign ministry, their conversation "was almost exclusively concerned with the necessity for insisting upon a general mobilization at the earliest possible moment, in view of the inevitability of war with Germany, which every moment became clearer." When Sazonov saw Tsar Nicholas II, he argued along similar lines. "During the course of nearly an hour," Schilling reported, "the Minister proceeded to show that war was becoming inevitable, as it was clear to everybody that Germany had decided to bring about a collision, as otherwise she would not have rejected all the pacificatory pro-

---

15. Albertini, *Origins*, Vol. 2, pp. 290–294, 304–308.
16. Albertini, *Origins*, Vol. 3, p. 245, Vol. 2, pp. 579–581. See also Paul Kennedy's comments in Paul M. Kennedy, ed., *The War Plans of the Great Powers, 1880–1914* (London: Allen and Unwin, 1979), p. 16; and Stephen Van Evera, "Why Cooperation Failed in 1914," *World Politics*, Vol. 38, No. 1 (October 1985), p. 104.
17. Lebow, *Nuclear Crisis Management*, pp. 26, 111.

posals that had been made and could easily have brought her ally to reason. . . . Therefore it was necessary to put away any fears that our warlike preparations would bring about a war and to continue these preparations carefully, rather than by reason of such fears to be taken unawares by war."

Sazonov here was virtually conceding that mobilization ("our warlike preparations") would in all probability bring on war; his argument was that since war was now unavoidable, this point could no longer carry weight. The Tsar, however, resisted Sazonov's arguments, because he also knew what mobilization meant: "The firm desire of the Tsar to avoid war at all costs, the horrors of which filled him with repulsion, led His Majesty, in his full realization of the heavy responsibility which he took upon himself in this fateful hour, to explore every means for averting the approaching danger." As a result, the Tsar "refused during a long time to agree to the adoption of measures which, however indispensable from a military point of view [again, an allusion to general mobilization], were calculated, as he clearly saw, to hasten a decision in an undesirable sense," that is, to precipitate the war. But finally Nicholas agreed that "it would be very dangerous not to make timely preparations for what was apparently an inevitable war, and therefore gave his decision in favour of an immediate general mobilization."[18]

The argument for holding back had thus been based on the idea that it might still be possible to save the peace. This in turn reflected an assumption that a decision for mobilization would in itself for all practical purposes make war unavoidable. It was taken for granted that there was a trade-off between seizing the military advantages of the first mobilization and paying the price of precipitating the war; the argument for making the move thus turned on the point that the price now was really low, because war was virtually inevitable anyway. The notion that the Russians ordered general mobilization in the belief that "mobilization would be a deterrent to war" is without foundation. They clearly understood that to order mobilization was to cross the Rubicon: there could be no turning back.

Sazonov had certainly been told many times what the situation was. As early as July 25, for example—that is, before any irrevocable decision had been taken—the British ambassador had warned him that "if Russia mobi-

18. Baron M.F. Schilling, *How the War Began in 1914: The Diary of the Russian Foreign Office* (London: Allen and Unwin, 1925), pp. 62–66; Albertini, *Origins*, Vol. 2, pp. 565, 571–572. Note also the account of the meeting held the previous day that had led to Russia's first decision for general mobilization, a decision later revoked by the Tsar: Schilling, *How the War Began*, pp. 49–50; Albertini, *Origins*, Vol. 2, p. 555.

lized, Germany would not be content with mere mobilization or give Russia time to carry out hers, but would probably declare war at once." Sazonov did not dispute the point. He simply stated that because the political stakes were so great, Russia, sure of French support, would "face all the risks of war."[19] The following day, Bethmann instructed Count Pourtalès, the German ambassador in Russia, to issue a warning: "Preparatory military measures on the part of Russia aimed in any way at us would compel us to take measures for our own protection which would have to consist in the mobilization of the army. Mobilization, however, would mean war."[20] The warning was issued the next day, but Sazonov did not show alarm, and Albertini infers from this that it failed to register on the foreign minister.[21]

The evidence that Albertini gives to support his argument that Sazonov did not understand what mobilization meant is extremely weak. Sazonov had admitted in his memoirs that Pourtalès had warned him that German mobilization would immediately lead to war. But according to Albertini, the foreign minister was mistaken about having been warned, and the proof, he says, comes from Pourtalès himself: "Sazonov put the question: 'Surely mobilization is not equivalent to war with you, either, is it?' I replied: 'Perhaps not in theory. But . . . once the button is pressed and the machinery of mobilization set in motion, there is no stopping it'."[22] Pourtalès was thus clearly saying that, for all practical purposes, mobilization meant war, but Albertini insists on interpreting the remark in exactly the opposite sense: the ambassador's remark "seemed to imply that mobilization was not yet war."[23] Similarly, referring to Bethmann's important warning to the Russians of July 29 that "further progress of Russian mobilization measures would compel us to mobilize and that then a European war could scarcely be prevented," Albertini emphasizes that Bethmann said "'scarcely,' but not 'not at all',"— as though this had the slightest practical importance.[24]

19. Buchanan to Grey, July 25, 1914, Great Britain, Foreign Office, *British Documents on the Origins of the War*, Vol. 11 (London: H.M. Stationery Office, 1926), No. 125; Albertini, *Origins*, Vol. 2, p. 307.
20. Bethmann to Pourtalès, July 26, 1914, *German Documents Relating to the Outbreak of the World War*, collected by Karl Kautsky (New York: Oxford University Press, 1924), No. 219; Albertini, *Origins*, Vol. 2, p. 428.
21. Albertini, *Origins*, Vol. 3, p. 43.
22. Albertini, *Origins*, Vol. 3, p. 42.
23. Ibid., p. 43.
24. Ibid., p. 43. Note, similarly, the discussion in Lebow, *Nuclear Crisis Management*, pp. 112–113.

Indeed, earlier that day Pourtalès and Sazonov had had another meeting, the record of which shows that the Russian foreign minister understood that for Germany mobilization meant war. Sazonov pointed out that "in Russia, *unlike western European states*, mobilization is far from being the same as war. The Russian army could, at need, stand at ease for weeks without crossing the border."[25] There is no question that by "western European states," Sazonov had Germany in mind, and Albertini acknowledges this point later in the book.[26] The Russians, of course, had an interest in arguing that their mobilization did not necessarily mean war, since if they could get Germany to tolerate a Russian mobilization, the military position of the Entente in the event of war would improve dramatically. This point was very widely understood in Europe; even the British foreign secretary realized that asking Germany to acquiesce in a Russian mobilization of any sort, even one directed only against Austria, would be tantamount to asking her to "throw away the advantage of time."[27] For the same reason, however, the Germans had a great interest in explaining why they could not do this.[28] Thus, for example, Pourtalès pointed out to Sazonov on the 29th that "the danger of all military measures lies in the counter-measures of the other side. It is to be expected that the General Staffs of eventual enemies of Russia would not want to sacrifice the trump card of their great lead over Russia in mobilization and would press for counter-measures."[29] If Sazonov had not already understood this, one would again expect some expression of surprise or dismay. But in Pourtalès's account, there is no record of any such reaction. Sazonov once again took the point in stride.

In short, the Russian leadership certainly understood what mobilization meant. The evidence is quite overwhelming. Albertini himself admits in the end that Sazonov advised the Tsar to order general mobilization, although he was "well aware that this would bring Germany on the scene, and render

---

25. Pourtalès to Foreign Office, July 29, 1914, quoted in Albertini, *Origins*, Vol. 2, p. 549. Emphasis added.
26. Ibid., Vol. 2, p. 658.
27. Quoted in ibid., Vol. 2, p. 339. See also the extract from Grey's memoirs quoted in ibid., p. 392.
28. This assumes that the German goal was to avoid war by getting the Russians to back down. If, as Fritz Fischer and his followers argue, their aim was to provoke a war for which Russia would be blamed, a Russian mobilization would have been welcome, and the German government would not have attempted to deter Russia from ordering it by issuing this series of warnings. See especially Fritz Fischer, *War of Illusions: German Policies from 1911 to 1914*, trans. Marian Jackson (New York: Norton, 1975), chap. 22.
29. Albertini, *Origins*, Vol. 2, p. 549.

war practically inevitable."[30] Even the Tsar, more removed from the situation than Sazonov, spoke about being "forced to take extreme measures which will lead to war," an obvious reference to general mobilization.[31] At the crucial moment, moreover, when he was asked to sign the general mobilization decree, Nicholas clearly realized what was at stake. "Think of the responsibility you are advising me to assume," he said to Sazonov. "Consider that it means sending thousands and thousands of men to their deaths."[32]

It follows that a failure to understand what general mobilization meant was not the problem. For tactical reasons, certain statesmen might have pretended to believe that a Russian general mobilization need not lead to war, but such assertions can scarcely be taken at face value. The Russian political leadership certainly understood how risky this movement toward mobilization was, and, as Bethmann's warnings show, German statesmen were also fully aware of the situation.

The Russian Partial Mobilization

On July 28, Austria, finding the Serbian reply to her ultimatum unsatisfactory even though most of her demands had been accepted, declared war on Serbia. As a result, the Russian government decided later that day to order a partial mobilization against Austria. Neither of these moves was made for essentially military reasons. From the military point of view, the Austrian declaration of war came two weeks too early. Baron Conrad von Hötzendorff, the chief of the Austrian general staff, had told the foreign minister, Count Berchtold, that he wanted war declared only when he was capable of beginning military operations, "say on August 12." But the foreign minister wanted to act quickly in order to put an end to what he vaguely referred to as "various influences." "The diplomatic situation," he told Conrad, "will not hold so long."[33]

---

30. Albertini, *Origins*, Vol. 2, p. 581. As for the French mobilization, note the analysis in ibid., Vol. 3, pp. 105–108. Albertini argues, quite persuasively in this case, that President Poincaré and Prime Minister Viviani were disingenuous in declaring that "mobilization is not war," and that it was "the best means of assuring peace with honor."

31. This is from a telegram the Tsar sent to the Kaiser, dispatched at 1 a.m. on July 30, quoted in Albertini, *Origins*, Vol. 2, p. 542.

32. Bernadotte Schmitt, *The Coming of War 1914*, 2 vols. (New York: Scribner's, 1930), Vol. 2, p. 243. See also Albertini, *Origins*, Vol. 2, p. 558.

33. Baron Franz Conrad von Hötzendorf, *Aus meiner Dienstzeit 1906–1918*, 5 vols. (Vienna, 1921–25), Vol. 4, pp. 131–132, quoted in Turner, *Origins of the First World War*, p. 98.

As for the Russian decision to mobilize against Austria, this too was taken for political and not military reasons.[34] "Its object," Bernadotte Schmitt writes, "was to indicate Russia's earnestness of purpose and to compel Austria-Hungary, under pressure of a 'military demonstration,' to consent to negotiate a pacific settlement of her quarrel with Serbia."[35] Moreover, Albertini and L.C.F. Turner go even further and argue that it did not make much sense militarily to mobilize against Austria alone at that point; Russia, they say, would have been better off waiting until Austria had concentrated her forces in the south and perhaps had even become involved in military operations against Serbia. Then Austria would be more vulnerable in the north, and thus more susceptible to the pressure of a Russian partial mobilization.[36] Conrad himself thought that this was the most dangerous, and therefore the most likely, Russian strategy.[37] The original Russian plan had in fact been to wait until Austria actually invaded Serbia before ordering partial mobilization, but Sazonov impulsively jumped the gun and opted for this measure right after hearing about the Austrian declaration of war.[38]

The "inadvertent war" argument turns in this case not on causes but on consequences. The decisions had been made freely, not as the result of undue pressure from the military. But the statesmen, it is argued, had set off a process they simply could not control. "For the Austrian government," Michael Howard writes, "a declaration of war was a political manoeuvre, for the Russian government a mobilisation order was a counter-manoeuvre; but such orders set in motion administrative processes which could be neither halted nor reversed, without causing a chaos which would place the nation at the mercy of its adversaries."[39]

34. See Albertini, *Origins*, Vol. 2, pp. 291–292, 529.

35. Schmitt, *Coming of the War*, Vol. 2, p. 94. Note also the discussion in D.C.B. Lieven, *Russia and the Origins of the First World War* (New York: St. Martin's, 1983), pp. 142–144. The goal was to deter Germany, but the Russian leaders were acutely conscious of the fact that this might not work; in such a case, they were prepared to go to war.

36. See Turner, *Origins of the First World War*, pp. 92–93; Albertini, *Origins*, Vol. 2, p. 482.

37. Norman Stone, "Moltke and Conrad: Relations between the Austro-Hungarian and German General Staffs, 1909–1914," in Kennedy, *War Plans of the Great Powers*, p. 228.

38. Albertini, *Origins*, Vol. 2, pp. 532, 538, 305, 484. Albertini says that Sazonov acted precipitately "possibly in the belief that the invasion of Serbia would follow immediately" (p. 538). But the Austrians had told the British that if the Serbs did not accept their demands, they would not begin military operations immediately, and the British had passed this information on to the Russians. See *British Documents on the Origins of the War*, Vol. 11, Nos. 104 and 105; and Schilling, *How the War Began*, pp. 35–36.

39. Howard, "Lest We Forget," p. 65. The importance of Howard's article derives from the fact that it was one of only two sources cited by Thomas Schelling to support his account of the

The political leaders—not just Sazonov, but British Foreign Secretary Sir Edward Grey and his German counterpart Gottlieb von Jagow, who each in his own way had consented to the Russian partial mobilization—certainly did not believe that it would lead inevitably to war. If they were wrong in this regard—if, in fact, irreversible "administrative processes" had been set off—then this would be an important point in support of the argument that the political leaders' ignorance of military matters helped bring about the war.

Albertini and various other scholars in fact argue along these lines. The claim is that a Russian partial mobilization against Austria would have led to an Austrian general mobilization, which "in turn would require Germany to mobilize." It was "ridiculous," Albertini says, to think that Germany could stand idly by and allow Russia, through even a partial mobilization, to deploy her forces more quickly in the event of a European war and thus make the success of the Schlieffen Plan more problematic. "It is quite clear," he argues, "that even if Russia had confined herself to ordering partial mobilization, the logic of the case as presented by Conrad and Moltke would have forced Germany to demand that it be cancelled, or, in case of a refusal, mobilize in her turn in order to go to the help of Austria. In short partial mobilization would have led to war no less surely than general mobilization."[40]

Germany's alliance arrangements with Austria were, however, a good deal more ambiguous than Albertini and his followers imply. The important exchange of letters between Moltke and Conrad that had taken place in 1909 during the Bosnian crisis was, as Schmitt says, the equivalent of a military convention. With the emperor's and the chancellor's approval, Moltke had promised that "at the moment that Russia mobilizes, Germany will also mobilize and will mobilize her entire army."[41] But it is by no means clear

---

coming of World War I—an account which plays an important role in his analysis of the "dynamics of mutual alarm" in *Arms and Influence*. (The other was Ludwig Reiners' popular account, *The Lamps Went Out in Europe* [New York: Pantheon Books, 1955].)

40. Albertini, *Origins*, Vol. 2, pp. 340, 344, 392, 529–530, 541 and (for the final quotation) 485n; Turner, *Origins of the First World War*, pp. 92, 104. Fischer also accepts this conclusion; see *War of Illusions*, p. 491. Albertini makes this argument even though he accepts the view of the Russian military leaders that a partial mobilization would have made a general mobilization more difficult, and thus would have placed Russia in a weaker position in the event that war broke out with Germany. Albertini, *Origins*, Vol. 2, pp. 292–294, 541–543. Given that view, the Germans therefore should have had no military basis for objecting to partial mobilization, since it would have placed them in a stronger position if war came, all the more so since it would have put pressure on the Austrians to deploy their forces along their border with Russia instead of against Serbia, which would have facilitated the implementation of the Schlieffen Plan.

41. Quoted in Schmitt, *Coming of the War*, Vol. 1, pp. 15, 17.

that this arrangement applied to the case of a partial Russian mobilization against Austria. In view of Austria's well-known alliance with Germany, Moltke may have calculated that mobilization against Austria alone made little military sense, that this contingency was thus unlikely to arise, and that it was therefore not worth worrying about.[42]

It is striking that neither Conrad nor Moltke nor the Russians took it for granted that mobilization by Austria and Russia against each other would in itself lead to war. Berchtold, on July 30, did say that such a joint mobilization would lead to war, but Conrad replied that "if the Russians do not touch us, we need not touch them either."[43] The Russians, who of course had an interest in allowing their mobilization to proceed for as long as possible before hostilities broke out, and who in any event had an interest in avoiding blame for the war, naturally made the same sort of argument, even about a general mobilization. "There was no fear," said Sazonov, "that the guns would go off by themselves."[44] It is much more significant that Moltke himself, after learning of the partial mobilization, told the Austrians in very direct language on the morning of the 30th that the Russian move gave the Germans "no reason" to mobilize. German mobilization, he said, would only begin after war broke out between Austria and Russia, and he advised the Austrians not to "declare war on Russia but wait for Russia to attack."[45] It is true that his attitude was to change that afternoon, but this apparently had more to do with early indications that the Russians were moving toward *general* mobilization than with his changing his mind about *partial* mobilization.[46]

---

42. The Entente, on the other hand, was more careful in this regard, and its members in their military understandings with one another took such contingencies explicitly into account. Under the 1913 arrangement, any German mobilization or attack would automatically lead to French and Russian mobilization, but even a general Austrian mobilization would not have such an automatic effect; specific arrangements would have to be worked out at the time. "Procès-verbal des Entretiens du mois d'août 1913 entre les chefs d'état-major des armées française et russe," *Documents diplomatiques français*, Series 3, Vol. 8, Doc. 79.

43. Conrad, *Dienstzeit*, Vol. 4, pp. 150–151; quoted in Albertini, *Origins*, Vol. 2, p. 670.

44. Quoted in Albertini, *Origins*, Vol. 2, p. 682.

45. Ibid., pp. 671–672, quoting a telegram and a letter from the Austrian liaison officer in Berlin, Captain Fleischmann, to Conrad, both of July 30, 1914. It is important to note that Moltke was now drawing back from the position he had taken earlier. On July 28, Moltke had drafted his well-known memorandum for Bethmann analyzing the situation. In it, he had argued that a Russian partial mobilization would lead Austria to order general mobilization, and that then "the collision between herself and Russia will become inevitable." Imanuel Geiss, ed., *July 1914: The Outbreak of the First World War: Selected Documents* (New York: Scribner's, 1967), p. 283.

46. See Ulrich Trumpener, "War Premeditated? German Intelligence Operations in July 1914," *Central European History*, Vol. 9, No. 1 (March 1976), p. 79.

Finally, there is the argument that Germany could not tolerate even a partial Russian mobilization directed only against Austria: after having encouraged the Austrians to move against Serbia, the Germans would find it impossible to stand by while Austria was subjected to this form of extreme Russian military pressure. The Germans therefore had to try to prevent the Russians from implementing the partial mobilization order. Albertini argues that Bethmann, therefore, on July 29 "sent Pourtalès a telegram containing such threats that they powerfully contributed to persuading Sazonov that he must mobilize not only against Austria but also against Germany."[47] In this way the partial mobilization, Albertini says, helped bring on the war.

It is wrong, however, to say that Russia's partial mobilization led to Bethmann's warning on the 29th, which in turn led to general mobilization and thus to war. This could not possibly have been the case, because, as Albertini's own evidence shows, the warning had been issued *before* the Germans even knew about the partial mobilization. Bethmann's telegram—"Kindly impress on M. Sazonov very seriously that further progress of Russian mobilization measures would compel us to mobilize and that then European war could scarcely be prevented"[48]—left Berlin a little before 1 p.m. on the 29th. The Germans only learned of the partial mobilization later that afternoon.[49] What the Germans seem to have been reacting to when they issued their warning were the far-reaching Russian pre-mobilization measures, many of which were directed against them.[50] In any case, the Germans seemed to be demanding a standstill, and not a revocation of measures already put into effect.

Instead of leading to war, the partial mobilization played a key role in bringing about an important softening of German policy on the night of July 29–30. Up to the 29th, Germany had been hoping for a localization of the conflict. But now the partial mobilization order was demonstrating quite dramatically that this probably would not be possible. It was one thing to

---

47. Albertini, *Origins*, Vol. 2, p. 485.
48. Ibid., p. 553.
49. Ibid., pp. 553, 498. Jagow, however, did threaten war as a response, which was quite extraordinary, given that he himself (as his interlocutor, the Russian ambassador Sverbeev, was quick to point out) was the one who had just given assurances that Germany would tolerate such a move. Jagow added, however, that the views he expressed were purely personal, and that he would have to talk with Bethmann before giving a definite reply. Ibid., p. 499. Sazonov used the warning to defend his policy of moving toward general mobilization; but this was evidently a debater's argument, since he had begun to push energetically for general mobilization the previous day. Ibid., pp. 556, 540.
50. See ibid., pp. 489, 592.

talk about backing Austria even at the risk of a European war at the beginning of the crisis when that risk was judged to be low. But it was an entirely different matter to take such a line at a time when the risk appeared much greater. Bethmann's attitude, in fact, began to shift almost as soon as he learned of the Russian move. The reply he sent off at 11 p.m. on July 29 to the telegram from Pourtalès reporting the partial mobilization "struck a different note," as Albertini says, "from his earlier one of intimidation." "Russian mobilization on the Austrian frontier," Bethmann pointed out, "will, I assume, lead to corresponding Austrian measures. How far it will still be possible to stop the avalanche then it is hard to say."[51] The reference here to Austrian, rather than German, countermeasures was particularly significant.

Indeed, Bethmann's general attitude on the night of July 29–30 underwent a stunning shift. He comes across as a man desperately anxious to avoid war. Up to then, he was scarcely interested in working out any kind of peaceful settlement. He had effectively sabotaged all proposals that might have prevented an Austrian attack on Serbia, including an important one that had come on July 28 from the Kaiser himself.[52] But on the night of July 29–30, the chancellor sent off a series of increasingly tough telegrams demanding that the Austrians do what was necessary to head off a war. This effort culminated in a dispatch sent out at 3 a.m.: we "must decline to let ourselves to be dragged by Vienna, wantonly and without regard to our advice, into a world conflagration."[53]

Why this shift? Albertini contends that it was a threat from Grey, warning that Britain would intervene in a continental war, that had led Bethmann to alter his position so radically. The chancellor, he says, had "based his whole policy on the assumption that, in case of war, England would remain neutral."[54] Fritz Fischer and his followers also argue that Grey's warning explains the series of telegrams Bethmann sent to Vienna in the early hours of July 30. The German leaders, Fischer says, had been willing to face war "with equanimity" because they believed that Britain would probably stay out. When they received the telegram from Prince Lichnowsky, the German am-

---

51. Ibid., p. 562.
52. The Kaiser had suggested that a settlement be based on the Serbian reply to the ultimatum; compliance would be guaranteed by the temporary occupation of Belgrade. Bethmann, in passing on a somewhat distorted version of the idea to Vienna, told the German ambassador there that in presenting it, he was "to avoid very carefully giving rise to the impression that we wish to hold Austria back." Geiss, *July 1914*, pp. 256–257, 259–260.
53. Albertini, *Origins*, Vol. 2, pp. 504, 522–525.
54. Ibid., Vol. 2, p. 520, Vol. 3, pp. 3, 4.

bassador in London, containing Grey's warning, they were "shattered" and "grew unsure of themselves." "The foundation of their policy during the crisis"—the belief that Britain would remain neutral if Germany handled events the right way—"had collapsed." Imanuel Geiss thinks that Bethmann really shifted course and was now trying to avert the catastrophe; Fischer himself sees only momentary shock, followed by a return the next morning to the earlier policy.[55]

The problem with this interpretation, in any of these variants, is that it vastly overestimates the degree to which the Germans had been counting on British neutrality, ignores the degree to which the Germans had already been warned that Britain would intervene in a European war, and—most important of all in this context—plays down the significance of the one really great event, the announcement of Russian partial mobilization, that immediately preceded the change in Bethmann's policy.

There is little evidence to support the claim that Bethmann had been confidently counting on British neutrality. On the eve of the crisis (which according to Fischer the Germans had provoked with this calculation about Britain in mind), Bethmann was quite pessimistic about the chances that Britain would stay neutral in a continental war.[56] During the crisis itself, moreover, he was repeatedly warned by Lichnowsky that Britain would not stay out of any war in which France was involved.[57]

---

55. Fritz Fischer, *Germany's Aims in the First World War* (New York: Norton, 1967) pp. 78–80, Fischer, *War of Illusions*, pp. 495–496; Geiss, *July 1914*, p. 269.

56. See, for example, the evidence in Wolfgang J. Mommsen, "Domestic Factors in German Foreign Policy before 1914," *Central European History*, Vol. 6, No. 1 (March 1973), p. 38n. Fischer's contrary argument on this point is laid out most extensively in Fischer, "The Miscalculation of English Neutrality: An Aspect of German Foreign Policy on the Eve of World War I," in Solomon Wank, et al., eds., *The Mirror of History: Essays in Honor of Fritz Fellner* (Santa Barbara, Calif.: ABC-Clio, 1988). But the evidence he presents here shows only that the Germans hoped for British neutrality in a European war, not that they were counting on it. At one point, Fischer even quotes Bethmann (evidently without realizing how this contradicts his basic argument) as writing to a friend in December 1912 that "Britain continues to uphold the policy of the balance of power and that it will therefore stand up for France if in a war the latter runs the risk of being destroyed by us" (p. 374). Bethmann did at this point understand that the main goal of the Schlieffen Plan was indeed to crush France.

57. Albertini, *Origins*, Vol. 2, pp. 432, 442, 501. During the crisis, Bethmann and Jagow did occasionally predict—to the French ambassador, for example, and to the emperor—that Britain would remain neutral, at least at the start of the war, but the aim here was probably tactical in nature: to convince the French of German resolve, or to dissuade the emperor from calling a halt to the tough policy the government was pursuing. The Berlin authorities, moreover, may have viewed Lichnowsky as "soft," and thus might have discounted his opinions; but his reports of British thinking could not be dismissed out of hand, and Bethmann and Jagow were too experienced to think they could be confident of British neutrality without hard evidence—and

While the German government certainly would have been delighted if Britain remained neutral, and did what it could to maximize the probability that Britain would stay out of the war, it is going much too far to say that the hope of British neutrality was the basis of German political or military calculations. Grey's warning was of course a blow to Bethmann, but not quite as severe a blow as is often argued, since there had been many earlier indications that Britain would probably not stand by and allow France to be crushed.

It seems rather that it was the news from Russia about partial mobilization that played the key role in bringing about the shift in Bethmann's attitude. The evidence strongly suggests that the decisive change took place *before* the chancellor learned of Grey's warning, but *after* he had found out about Russia's partial mobilization. The authorities in Berlin became aware of Russia's move at about 5 p.m. on July 29; the telegram containing Grey's warning was received at the Foreign Office at 9:12 p.m. The first of the telegrams reflecting Bethmann's newly-found eagerness for a negotiated settlement was dispatched from Berlin at 10:18 p.m.[58] Given how long it generally took for a dispatch to be deciphered, delivered and read, and for a new dispatch to be thought out, composed, sent over for coding, and then encoded and transmitted, it is very hard to believe that all this could have been done in barely more than an hour.[59] And yet this would have had to be the case for the telegram received at 9:12 to have led directly to the telegram sent out at 10:18—that is, for the news from London to have brought about the dramatic shift in Bethmann's position. It is much more likely that it was the information about Russia's partial mobilization that led to this change in policy. Albertini himself recognizes the importance of the news from Russia in bringing about this shift on Bethmann's part, and he says explicitly that even before receiving the message containing Grey's warning, "the Chancellor was clutching at the idea"—the Kaiser's proposal for a peaceful settlement, which Bethmann had tried to sabotage the previous day—"like a shipwrecked man at a lifebuoy."[60]

---

no really satisfactory indicators were forthcoming during the crisis. Indeed, the amount of attention the Germans gave to Britain and the important efforts they made to influence British policy show in themselves that British neutrality was not simply taken for granted.
58. Ibid., pp. 498, 520, 504.
59. For a brief discussion of these sorts of delays, see ibid., p. 525 n. 6.
60. Ibid., pp. 500–502, 522.

Thus, far from leading inevitably to German counter-measures which would have brought on a war, the Russian decision to order partial mobilization appears actually to have led to a *softening* of German policy, breaking the deadlock and at least in theory opening the way to a political settlement.

The Final Hours

Thus Bethmann now wanted to head off a European war. So did the Entente powers. Austria by herself could not have stood in their way. How then was war possible? Many assume there is only one answer to the riddle: the political process that should normally have brought about a negotiated settlement was overwhelmed in those momentous final hours of the crisis by forces welling up from within the military sphere, by generals "pounding the table for the signal to move lest their opponents gain an hour's head start."[61] The validity of the whole "inadvertent war" thesis, therefore, turns on a close analysis of the events of those fourteen fateful hours, the period from Bethmann's dramatic dispatch to Austria sent out at 3 a.m. on July 30, to the Russian order for general mobilization, issued at 5 p.m. that afternoon.

One can begin with the case of Germany, the most militaristic of the European powers, the state whose whole strategy was most strongly based on the idea of swift offensive action. If there is anything to the argument about the importance of preemption in 1914, surely here is where the evidence will be found. Yet as one studies the German case, one is struck by the unwillingness of the German government to force the pace of the crisis in those final days, and by its preference for leaving the initiative in the hands of others. A basic goal, shared by the political and the military leadership, was that Germany not appear the aggressor. Germany would, of course, have to *react* quickly if Russia or France mobilized first; but the more rapidly Germany could respond, the less incentive there would be for her adversaries to make the first move.

The Germans, in fact, were reluctant to take even the sort of pre-mobilization measures that they knew that the Russians (and eventually even the French and the British) were taking. On the 29th, but before the news of Russia's partial mobilization had reached them, the top German leaders met

---

61. Tuchman, *Guns of August*, p. 72.

at Potsdam. General Erich von Falkenhayn, the war minister, called for the pre-mobilization regime to be put into effect—for the proclamation of the *Kriegsgefahrzustand*, the declaration of "threatening danger of war"—but Moltke was opposed even to that and Falkenhayn deferred to the chief of staff.[62] Later that evening, the new situation resulting from the Russian partial mobilization was discussed. "Against slight, very, very slight opposition from Moltke," Bethmann ruled out German mobilization as a response; this would have to wait until Russia actually unleashed a war, "because otherwise we should not have public opinion with us either at home or in England." As for Falkenhayn, he was by no means pressing for preemptive action. There was no need, he thought, to be the first to move, because "our mobilization, even if two or three days later than that of Russia and Austria, would be more rapid than theirs."[63]

The following afternoon, Moltke began to call for a tougher policy, probably because new information had been received about the seriousness of Russian military preparations.[64] He and Falkenhayn now asked for the proclamation of the *Kriegsgefahrzustand*. Bethmann refused to agree to it then and there (even though this would by no means have made mobilization, and therefore war, automatic), and simply promised that the generals would get an answer by noon the next day.[65] By that point, the news of Russia's general mobilization had reached Berlin, so the issue had been overtaken by events. But some new evidence on Moltke's reaction to this information hardly supports the image of a general "pounding the table for the signal to move." Moltke reacted to the first report of general mobilization "with some skepticism" and wondered whether the evidence had been misinterpreted. When he was told that the report had been "very specific" and that "similar information had just arrived" from two other intelligence posts, he "turned toward the

---

62. Albertini, *Origins*, Vol. 2, pp. 495–497, 499–500 (for the chronology).
63. Ibid., p. 502.
64. Trumpener, "War Premeditated?" p. 79.
65. Albertini, *Origins*, Vol. 3, pp. 10, 18; on the issue of the *Kriegsgefahrzustand*, see ibid., Vol. 2, pp. 491, 599. When defending his decision not to proclaim the *Kriegsgefahrzustand*, Bethmann did claim that it meant mobilization and therefore war, but this can scarcely be taken at face value. See ibid., Vol. 3, p. 15. An Army document also strongly suggests that war was not viewed as following automatically from the proclamation of the *Kriegsgefahrzustand*. See the extract from the "Protokoll der Chefkonferenz in Frankfurt a. M. am 21. Januar 1914," in W. Knoll and H. Rahne, "Bedeutung und Aufgaben der Konferenz der Generalstabschefs der Armeekorps in Frankfurt a. M. am 21. Januar 1914," *Militärgeschichte*, Vol. 25, No. 1 (1986), p. 58: "The Corps should not allow their hands to be tied" by a proclamation of threatening danger of war, "for example, by buying horses."

window, took a deep breath, and said: 'It can't be helped then; we'll have to mobilize too'."[66]

Nor did Bethmann, contrary to what both Craig and Albertini argue, "capitulate" to the generals during the crisis. It is amazing how common this notion is, given how little evidence there is to back it up. Moltke was not able to get Bethmann to agree even to the *Kriegsgefahrzustand* until after news of the Russian general mobilization reached Berlin. The chief of staff did go behind Bethmann's back on the afternoon of the 30th, urging Austria to mobilize against Russia and reject mediation.[67] But this is hardly proof that Bethmann was capitulating to the military, or even that Moltke was overstepping his own authority, since the Kaiser may have authorized his messages to the Austrians.[68] In any case, the move could hardly be viewed as a cause of the war, because, as Gerhard Ritter, for example, has pointed out, Moltke's messages were received by the Austrian ministers after they had decided on general mobilization, and thus had no "practical effect."[69]

Two other stories are commonly used to support the argument that the military had, by the end of the crisis, effectively taken control of German policy. First, there is the episode of Telegram 200, which Albertini treats as decisive. In this dispatch, sent out on the evening of July 30, Bethmann told his ambassador in Vienna to press Austria once again to accept mediation. His language was not as strong as it had been the previous night, but even so the instruction contained in the telegram was suspended soon after it was dispatched. The telegram ordering the suspension referred to information from the General Staff about "the military preparations of our neighbors, especially in the east." Albertini interprets this suspension as a "capitulation" and says that the "Chief of Staff was no longer allowing the political leadership to waste time in attempts to save the peace and compose the conflict."[70] But again, this conclusion hardly follows from the evidence. The fact that Bethmann agreed with, or was convinced by, arguments and information coming from the military scarcely proves that he was surrendering to their will. In fact, Albertini himself suggests that information was being received in Berlin that evening indicating that the Russian general mobilization, which

---

66. Trumpener, "War Premeditated?" p. 82.
67. Albertini, *Origins*, Vol. 3, p. 11.
68. Ibid., Vol. 3, pp. 11–13; Schmitt, *Coming of the War*, Vol. 2, p. 198.
69. Gerhard Ritter, *The Sword and the Scepter: The Problem of Militarism in Germany*, 4 vols. (Coral Gables: University of Miami Press, 1969–73), Vol. 2, p. 258.
70. Albertini, *Origins*, Vol. 3, pp. 21–24.

indeed had been decided upon at 5 p.m. that afternoon, might be imminent.[71] If that were the case, and war was about to break out, what was the point of irritating Germany's only ally with a démarche which would almost certainly do no good anyway? If this, as seems likely, was Bethmann's calculation, the cancellation of Telegram 200 can hardly be interpreted as a "capitulation."

The other story supporting the claim about the inability of the civilian leadership to control the military at the peak of the crisis is even more widely known. At the very last minute, on August 1, with the storm in its full fury about to break, the German government was told by its ambassador in London that Britain might remain neutral, and might even guarantee French neutrality, if Germany did not attack France and would conduct the war only in the east. The Kaiser was jubilant and wanted to take the British up on this offer and march only against Russia. But Moltke explained that Germany had only one plan, the Schlieffen Plan, and it was too late now to change that strategy; the plan would have to be carried out. The chancellor and the Kaiser, Craig writes—and this is characteristic of the way this story appears in many accounts—"had no answer for this and gave way."[72] It soon turned out that British views had been misunderstood, but Bernard Brodie's comment on the affair is typical of the way this story is interpreted: "The falsity of the initial report saved that particular episode from being utterly grotesque; but the whole situation of which it formed a part reveals a rigidity and a habit of pleading 'military necessity' that made it impossible after a certain point to prevent a war which no one wanted and which was to prove infinitely disastrous to all the nations concerned."[73]

This is certainly a wonderful story. The only problem with it is that it happens to be wrong on the most important point. On the issue of whether the attack on France had to proceed as planned, it was the Kaiser and not Moltke who won. This should have been clear from the most important source on the incident, Moltke's memoirs, written in November 1914 and published posthumously in 1922; Moltke's account is confirmed by a number of other sources, extracts from which appear in the sections on the episode

---

71. Ibid., pp. 24, 27.
72. Craig, *Politics of the Prussian Army*, p. 294; Fischer, *Germany's Aims*, p. 86; Barry Posen (citing Craig), "Inadvertent Nuclear War? Escalation and NATO's Northern Flank," *International Security*, Vol. 7, No. 2 (Fall 1982), p. 32.
73. Bernard Brodie, "Unlimited Weapons and Limited War," *The Reporter*, November 18, 1954, p. 21.

in Albertini's book.[74] It is true that there was a violent argument on August 1 between Moltke and the political leadership about whether to accept what appeared to be the British proposal. Although Moltke succeeded in convincing the Kaiser that for technical reasons the concentration in the west would have to "be carried out as planned," and that only after it was completed could troops be transferred to the east, a basic decision was made to accept the "offer." "In the course of this scene," Moltke wrote, "I nearly fell into despair." Bethmann then pointed out how important it was, in connection with this British proposal, that the plan for the occupation of neutral Luxembourg be suspended. "As I stood there the Kaiser, without asking me," Moltke went on, "turned to the aide-de-camp on duty and commanded him to telegraph immediate instructions to the 16th Division at Trier not to march into Luxembourg. I thought my heart would break." Moltke again pleaded that the very complicated mobilization plan, "which has to be worked out down to the smallest details," could not be changed without disastrous results. It was essential, he said, for Germany to secure control over the Luxembourg railroads. "I was snubbed with the remark that I should use other railroads instead. The order must stand. Therewith I was dismissed. It is impossible to describe the state of mind in which I returned home. I was absolutely broken and shed tears of despair."[75]

---

74. Helmuth von Moltke, *Erinnerungen—Briefe—Dokumente, 1877–1916* (Stuttgart: Der Kommendetag, 1922); extracts appeared in English translation in *Living Age*, January 20, 1923, pp. 131–134. Albertini, *Origins*, Vol. 3, pp. 171–181, 380–385. See also Harry Young, "The Misunderstanding of August 1, 1914," *Journal of Modern History*, Vol. 48, No. 4 (December 1976), pp. 644–665.

75. Quoted in Albertini, *Origins*, Vol. 3, pp. 172–176. It is sometimes argued that despite the Kaiser's order, the Luxembourg frontier was violated, and that this shows that the plans had a momentum of their own which the political leadership was unable to control. In fact, an infantry company had moved into Luxembourg before the Kaiser's order had been received, but a little later a second detachment arrived and ordered it out (in accordance, one assumes, with the Kaiser's instructions). This episode thus scarcely proves that central control over military operations had been lost. The story has been clear since the publication of the Kautsky documents in 1919, the source Tuchman relies on for her accurate account of this episode in *Guns of August*, p. 82. Note also the story about the revocation of the Russian general mobilization order by the Tsar, after he had agreed to it the first time on July 29: according to one account, when the chief of staff told him "that it was not possible to stop mobilization, Nicholas had replied: 'Stop it all the same'," and this order was respected. Albertini, *Origins*, Vol. 2, p. 560. See also Norman Stone's excellent analysis and refutation of Conrad's claim that technical military requirements prevented him from adjusting his strategy to the new situation created by Russian mobilization, "Moltke and Conrad," in Kennedy, *War Plans*, pp. 235–241; and also Stone's chapter on Austria-Hungary in Ernest May, ed., *Knowing One's Enemies: Intelligence Assessment before the Two World Wars* (Princeton: Princeton University Press, 1984).

Thus the political leadership had hardly "capitulated" to the generals. The real problem was not that the civilians had lost control, but rather that Germany's political strategy and her military strategy were pulling in opposite directions. The demands of the Schlieffen Plan implied that Germany had to act quickly, but this meant that Germany would be the first to cross borders. Germany would have to invade Belgium and attack France, but one of Bethmann's basic goals was for Germany to avoid coming across as the aggressor and to make it appear that Russia was responsible for the war. "The fact is," says Albertini, "that Bethmann, who had made every effort to cast the blame on Russia, failed to see that his endeavours would be defeated by the very demands of the Schlieffen Plan."[76] On the other hand, important military measures had been delayed for political reasons, and given Germany's military strategy, even short delays might have had serious consequences. The two sides of their policy were working at cross purposes, but this particular difficulty did not actually help bring on the war. It should have had the opposite effect of pushing Germany toward a peaceful settlement. If the German leadership had faced up to the problem, which was to some extent rooted in an astonishing lack of coordination between the political and the military authorities,[77] they would have recognized that this was a major source of weakness, and, as Albertini argues, this should have made them move energetically to settle the dispute.[78] But instead events were allowed to take their course.

The most striking thing, in fact, about German policy on the 30th is that Bethmann did seem to resign himself to the situation and gave up trying to prevent war. On the night of July 29–30, he had begun to move energetically to head off a war, but by the following morning—that is, even before Moltke's shift that afternoon—the effort had ended. The pressure on Austria subsided,

---

76. Albertini, *Origins*, Vol. 3, p. 249. See also the discussion of this issue, ibid., pp. 186–187.
77. Ibid., p. 250. Nor was there any serious coordination between the Army and Navy general staffs. Admiral Tirpitz claimed that he "was never even informed of the invasion of Belgium." Alfred von Tirpitz, *My Memoirs* (New York: Dodd Mead, 1919), Vol. 1, p. 346. Similarly, the lack of military coordination with Austria is astounding. Although some loose agreements covering this matter had been reached in 1909, more precise arrangements were not worked out during the crisis, and it was only at the last minute that Moltke asked Austria "to employ her main strength against Russia and not disperse it by a simultaneous offensive against Serbia." But this the Austrians refused to do. Albertini, *Origins*, Vol. 3, pp. 45–46; Stone, "Moltke and Conrad." This hardly fits in with the picture of a German government carefully and systematically plotting a war of aggression. For a similar point based on a study of German intelligence operations during the crisis, see Trumpener, "War Premeditated?" pp. 83–85.
78. Albertini, *Origins*, Vol. 3, p. 249.

and Bethmann certainly did not do the one thing he would have had to do if he had really wanted to prevent war. His first priority, in that case, would have been to keep the Russians from ordering general mobilization, and to do this, he would have had to make it clear to them that war was not inevitable, that a political settlement was within reach, that Austria could be led to moderate her demands on Serbia, but that he needed a little time to bring her around. And to increase the pressure on Russia to hold back, he could have approached the western powers, explained why a political settlement was within sight, and asked them to do what they could to keep Russia from resorting to general mobilization and thus setting off the avalanche. But Bethmann made none of these moves. The Russians ordered general mobilization that afternoon, and the great war could no longer be prevented.

Had the war come because, as Bethmann himself said at the time, "control had been lost"? The "stone had started rolling," he declared; war was being unleashed "by elemental forces."[79] But there had been no "loss of control," only an abdication of control. Bethmann had chosen not to act. He had decided to let events take their course—and thus to take his "leap into the dark."[80] If war had to come—and if the Russians were not going to give way this time when they were relatively weak, a conflict with them was probably unavoidable in the long run—then maybe the generals were right, maybe it was better to have it now rather than later. His hands were clean—more or less. He had not set out to provoke a great war with this calculation in mind. He had even made a certain effort to get the Austrians to pull back. But war was almost bound to come eventually, so he would just stand aside and let it come now. The preventive war argument, which had not been powerful enough to dictate German policy at the beginning of the crisis, now proved decisive. It might have been difficult, if only for moral reasons, for the German leadership to set out deliberately to provoke a great war. It was much easier just to let the war come—not to "hide behind the fence," as Jagow put it.[81] Bethmann probably had something of this sort in mind when he later admitted that "in a certain sense, it was a preventive war."[82]

---

79. Ibid., pp. 15–17.
80. K.D. Erdmann, ed., *Kurt Riezler: Tagebücher, Aufsätze, Dokumente* (Göttingen: Vandenhoeck and Ruprecht, 1972), entry for July 14, 1914, p. 185.
81. Jagow to Lichnowsky, July 18, 1914, in Geiss, *July 1914*, p. 123.
82. Quoted, for example, in Konrad Jarausch, "The Illusion of Limited War: Chancellor Bethmann Hollweg's Calculated Risk, July 1914," *Central European History*, Vol. 2, No. 1 (March 1969), p. 48.

This, however, has nothing to do with preemption: there had been no "loss of control" resulting from the pressure to mobilize first. Indeed, as far as the German side is concerned, the argument about preemption has surprisingly little support. With the Russian mobilization the die had been cast: after that point, any specific incentive to move quickly that the Germans may have felt could do little more than affect the exact timing of the German attack. From that point on, it was extremely unlikely that war itself could be avoided.[83]

It remains to be seen, however, whether preemption was a more compelling factor on the Entente side. To begin with France: the chief of staff and the war minister did urge Russia to move against Germany as soon as possible after war broke out, which of course was exactly what the pre-war military arrangements had called for. L.C.F. Turner, for example, argues that this was pressure "calculated to drive the Russian General Staff into demanding general mobilization."[84] Perhaps so, but the evidence presented is

83. The Germans' need to seize Liège quickly is often cited as a major source of such pressure for preemption. But while the German general staff was certainly concerned with the Liège situation at the end of July, there is little evidence that this factor contributed in any major way to the German decision for war. Ritter, for example, blamed the Liège problem for Germany's "unbelievable haste" in declaring war on Russia on August 1, and Churchill thought that if it were not for Liège, the armies might have mobilized without crossing frontiers while a peace settlement was worked out. Gerhard Ritter, "Der Anteil der Militärs an der Kriegskatastrophe von 1914," *Historische Zeitschrift*, Vol. 193, No. 1 (August 1961), pp. 89–90, Winston Churchill, *The World Crisis: The Eastern Front* (London, 1931), p. 93, quoted in L.C.F. Turner, "The Significance of the Schlieffen Plan," in Kennedy, *War Plans*, p. 213. Jack Snyder, on the other hand, says that "Moltke's attitude was not decisively influenced by this incentive to preempt." Jack Snyder, "Civil-Military Relations and the Cult of the Offensive, 1914 and 1984," *International Security*, Vol. 9, No. 1 (Summer 1984), p. 113. There is much about the Liège issue that remains obscure. It is not clear exactly when German troops would have begun their attack and crossed the Belgian frontier if the earlier plan had not been altered in 1911 to include the Liège operation as one of its vital elements. Given the basic philosophy of the Schlieffen strategy, which even in its original form of a one-front war against France "depended," as Ritter says, "on the speed and surprise of the German advance through Belgium," Germany could not hold off for long after the Russian general mobilization had begun. Gerhard Ritter, *The Schlieffen Plan: Critique of a Myth* (London: Wolff, 1958), p. 90. If it were not for Liège, would Germany have postponed her declaration of war for a brief period after ordering mobilization? The answer is by no means obvious, but even if a certain delay was possible, the argument that the Liège factor played a key role in bringing on the war would turn on the claim that there was a real chance of saving the peace during those extra few days while Germany was still mobilizing, but before war absolutely had to be declared. There is, however, little basis for this assumption. It is not as though serious negotiations had been going on that might have led to a settlement, had they not been cut off by the declarations of war.
84. Turner, *Origins of the First World War*, p. 104. See also Turner's "The Role of the General Staffs in July 1914," *Australian Journal of Politics and History*, Vol. 9 (1965), pp. 320–321. The sort of attitude to which Turner refers was evidently not limited to French military circles: see, for

hardly sufficient in itself to warrant this conclusion, and there is really no indication in the Russian sources that pressure from French military authorities made any important difference.

It is therefore on Russian policy that an analysis of the preemption question in 1914 must focus. In this case it does turn out to have some substance. It clearly mattered a great deal to the Russian authorities whether Germany or Russia was the first to mobilize. This is the only way to make sense of the constant allusions to the great risks of delaying a general mobilization that one finds in the records of the meetings where these mobilization decisions were made. On July 30, for example, the chief of staff "pleaded" with Sazonov to convince the Tsar "to consent to a general mobilization in view of the extreme danger that would result for us if we were not ready for war with Germany." Sazonov did precisely that. Since "war was becoming inevitable," he told the Tsar when he saw him that afternoon, "it was necessary to put away any fears that our warlike preparations would bring about a war and to continue these preparations carefully, rather than by reason of such fears to be taken unawares by war." The Tsar "agreed that in the existing circumstances it would be very dangerous not to make timely preparations for what was apparently an inevitable war, and therefore gave his decision in favour of a general mobilisation."[85] The mobilization decision was thus based on a political assessment: there was a diplomatic deadlock, Austria was beginning to move against Serbia, the issue could no longer be avoided. It is important to note that the Russian mobilization decision was not rooted in the fear that Germany was about to mobilize first. In the key meetings at which the Russian mobilization decisions were made, the argument was that it was war itself, and not a German mobilization as such, that was imminent.

Did "pressure from the Russian generals" cause the political leadership to "lose control" of the situation?[86] The generals' main argument was that "in resorting to partial mobilization, there was a big risk of upsetting plans for general mobilization."[87] Albertini, who blames pressure from these generals for helping push Europe into war, thinks that they were correct in this assessment: a partial mobilization, he says, would "have been a blunder,"

---

example, Doumergue's comments quoted in Maurice Paléologue, *Au Quai d'Orsay à la veille de la tourmente. Journal 1913–1914* (Paris: Plon, 1947), p. 269.
85. Schilling, *How the War Began*, pp. 64–66.
86. Albertini, *Origins*, Vol. 2, 539–545.
87. Quartermaster-General Yuri Danilov, quoted in ibid., p. 542.

since if war came, Russia would have to face both Austria and Germany.[88] But could the Russian generals be blamed for exercising undue influence if they had simply given an accurate assessment of the situation? As long as they limited themselves to a purely military judgment, only one conclusion followed: partial mobilization was out of the question, so the choice had to be between "general mobilization and none at all."[89] Their preference for general mobilization was based on political considerations, and especially on the belief that it would be impossible to abandon Serbia, that the Central Powers were intent on crushing the Serbs, and that war could therefore not be avoided.[90] If the political leadership had held more moderate views, and especially if the generals rationalized their preference for general mobilization with spurious military arguments, there would be some basis for the argument that pressure from the generals was a major cause of the war. But the striking thing here is that Sazonov shared their assessment of the probability of war. It was not as though he tried to resist the generals' views and only reluctantly gave way. On July 28, he was, according to General Dobrorolski, "penetrated by the thought that a general war is unavoidable," and even went so far as to express his astonishment to the chief of staff that full mobilization had not been begun earlier.[91]

Had Sazonov, however, been trapped by his own ignorance and impulsiveness? The argument is that he had blindly ordered a partial mobilization without any real understanding of the problems it would cause; but having ordered it, he had no answer for the technical arguments the generals raised against it. He therefore had to choose between revoking the partial mobilization order or escalating to general mobilization. To cancel the partial mobilization order would be taken as a sign of weakness; Sazonov was therefore led, however reluctantly, to opt for a full mobilization.[92] But again this theory cannot withstand the simple test of chronology. Sazonov had accepted the generals' argument about the dangers of partial mobilization on July 28— that is, before the partial mobilization had actually begun, probably before the decision to order it had even been made, and certainly long before the Germans learned of the order.[93] The real puzzle here is that Sazonov opted

---

88. Ibid., p. 543.
89. Ibid.
90. Ibid.
91. Dobrorolski is commonly viewed as a reliable source; his account is quoted in ibid., p. 540.
92. See, for example, Van Evera, "Why Cooperation Failed in 1914," p. 104.
93. Albertini, *Origins*, Vol. 2, pp. 540–545.

for partial mobilization even though he had already been persuaded by the arguments against it. One possible answer is that once partial mobilization was ordered, the Tsar could more easily be brought to accept a full mobilization against both Germany and Austria, which Sazonov had by then come to view as necessary. Sazonov had not been trapped by his own ignorance, nor had he been overwhelmed by pressure from the generals. He had made his choices with his eyes open; he had not been stampeded into them.

So to sum up: although preemption evidently was a factor in 1914, its importance is greatly exaggerated in much of the literature. It played a role on the Russian side in the final hours of the crisis, and even then only because the political judgment had been made that war was inevitable. Its role was quite marginal in comparison with all those factors that had given rise to this judgment in the first place. On the German side, its role was minimal. The Germans wanted Russia to be the first to order mobilization, and they would have been delighted if, after mobilization, France had been the first to attack.[94] Their strategy was not preemptive but reactive: for political reasons, they were conceding the first move to their adversaries. In contemporary terms, this was more like a "second strike" than a "first strike" strategy, and thus in this respect can hardly be considered "destabilizing."

Conclusion

The aim here was not to offer yet another interpretation of the coming of the First World War. The goal was simply to test a particular set of claims about the role of the mobilization system in bringing on the war in 1914. And the conclusion is quite clear: it was not because statesmen had "lost control" of events that the First World War came about; preemption was not nearly as important in 1914 as is commonly assumed. Instead of generals "pounding the table for the signal to move," one finds Falkenhayn saying on July 29 that it would not matter much if Germany mobilized two or three days after Russia, and Moltke that same day not even supporting the proclamation of the *Kriegsgefahrzustand*. On the afternoon of the 30th, Moltke did begin to press for military measures, but this was very probably in reaction to what the Russians were doing in this area. As long as German

---

94. "For about forty-eight hours after the issue of the respective mobilization orders the [French and German] armies stood face to face, each waiting and hoping that the other would be the first to open hostilities." Ibid., Vol. 3, p. 204.

policy was reactive, it can hardly be considered a source of "instability" in the contemporary sense of the term.

The Russian generals, on the other hand, did press for early mobilization. But this was only because they thought that war was unavoidable for political reasons, a view that the civilian government also shared. A decision for general mobilization was quite consciously a decision for war: it was not the case that Sazonov and the political leadership as a whole, trying desperately to preserve the peace, were drawn into the abyss by the "pull of military schedules." It hardly makes sense, therefore, to see the Russian decision to seize the military advantages of the first mobilization as proof that "control had been lost" or that war had come "inadvertently." In 1941, the Japanese government attacked American forces at Pearl Harbor and in the Philippines after becoming convinced that war with the United States could not be avoided. Even if this judgment had been mistaken—even if one assumes that President Roosevelt could not have taken the country into war if the Japanese had avoided contact with American forces and limited their attack to the Dutch East Indies—no one would say that the fact that the Japanese chose to seize the first-strike advantage by launching a surprise attack against vulnerable American forces means that the War in the Pacific was essentially an "inadvertent" conflict. The same point applies to 1914.

The idea that the First World War came about because statesmen were overwhelmed by military imperatives and thus "lost control" of the situation came to be accepted for essentially political reasons, and not because it was the product of careful and disinterested historical analysis. It was hardly an accident that the first to propagate this idea were the statesmen whose policies in 1914 had led directly to the conflict—that is, the very people who had the greatest interest in avoiding responsibility for the catastrophe. On the very eve of the disaster—on July 31, 1914—Bethmann was already arguing along these lines.[95]

After the war, it became apparent in Western Europe generally, and in America as well, that the Germans would never accept a peace settlement based on the notion that they had been responsible for the conflict. If a true peace of reconciliation were to take shape, it required a new theory of the origins of the war, and the easiest thing was to assume that no one had really been responsible for it. The conflict could be readily blamed on great

---

95. Ibid., pp. 15–17.

impersonal forces—on the alliance system, on the arms race and on the military system that had evolved before 1914. On their uncomplaining shoulders the burden of guilt could be safely placed.

In the 1930s the idea that the military system was to blame for World War I became even more attractive. With the resurgence of German power in the latter part of the decade, the great war itself came to be widely regarded in the West as a terrible mistake which could only be explained if it was assumed that the political leaders had stumbled into it blindly, pulled along by their military advisers, or trapped by military arrangements whose implications they had never really understood.[96]

By the 1950s and 1960s, these ideas had taken on a life of their own. During this period, American stategists developed a way of thinking about issues of war and peace that placed an extraordinary emphasis on military factors, especially on preemption and the "reciprocal fear of surprise attack." In such an environment, the notion that the First World War had come about because of the working of the military system of the day had an obvious appeal. This interpretation seemed to provide an important degree of empirical support for conclusions reached through an essentially abstract process of analysis. Thomas Schelling's work is perhaps the best example.

In the 1970s and 1980s, the environment again shifted, but the theory, which by now had been around long enough to become part of the conventional wisdom, was once more able to find a new niche. In the aftermath of the Vietnam War, and even more with the fading of the Cold War in the 1980s, the "Munich analogy" was discredited as a basic paradigm for foreign policy. The "Sarajevo analogy" was drawn into the vacuum. It might be hard to believe that general war could result from deliberate aggression. But for this very reason, it was important—the argument now ran—to remember what had happened in 1914. Secretary of State Henry Kissinger, for example, pointed out in 1976 that the lesson of the July Crisis was that one could have a war "without any conscious decision to overturn the international structure." War could come about because "a crisis much like any other went out of control. Nation after nation slid into a war whose causes they did not understand but from which they could not extricate themselves."[97]

It was in fact commonly assumed that even in the nuclear age there was a real danger that the world might slip into war in this way. Today, in a

96. Note especially Lloyd George's comments in his exchange with Duff Cooper in March 1936, summarized in ibid., pp. 524–525.
97. Speech of March 11, 1976, *New York Times*, March 12, 1976, p. 4.

world where all of the major powers obviously want very much to avoid a new world war, the only real fear is that the great nations might somehow stumble into one more or less inadvertently. The "inadvertent war" interpretation of the events of 1914 gives focus and substance to this fear and thus appeals particularly to those in the defense and arms control communities who have a professional interest in taking the risk of great-power war seriously.

During this whole process, the inadvertent war interpretation was accepted because it was what people wanted to believe. It is important, however, that our basic thinking about issues of war and peace not be allowed to rest on what are in the final analysis simply myths about the past. The conventional wisdom does not have to be accepted on faith alone; claims about the past can always be translated into historically testable propositions. In this case, when one actually tests these propositions against the empirical evidence, which for the July Crisis is both abundant and accessible, one is struck by how weak most of the arguments turn out to be. The remarkable thing about the claims that events moved "out of control" in 1914 is how little basis in fact they actually have.

Preferences, Constraints, and Choices in July 1914

Jack S. Levy

Did World War I occur primarily because of the conflicting interests of the European great powers in 1914, or was it the result of the misperceptions, miscalculations, overreactions, and loss of control by political leaders? Could statesmen have acted to avoid war while preserving their vital interests? Did political leaders mismanage the crisis, or did they perceive no interest in managing the crisis to avoid war in the first place? These questions are still critical. World War I is the most frequently cited illustration of "inadvertent war," the primary source of many hypotheses on the subject, and a common historical and strategic metaphor in the nuclear age. Thus it is essential that we understand precisely in which respects (if any) World War I was inadvertent.[1] This is especially important in light of the ongoing debate over Fritz Fischer's argument that German elites provoked a great power war in 1914 in order to secure Germany's position on the continent, establish its status as a world power, and to solve its domestic political crisis.[2]

A Social Science Research Council/MacArthur Foundation Fellowship in International Peace and Security provided partial support for this study. I have benefited from helpful comments from Michael Adas, Raymond Duvall, John Freeman, Alexander George, Cliff Morgan, Scott Sagan, Stephen Van Evera, John Vasquez, Phil Williams, and various participants in international relations colloquia at the University of Minnesota, Washington University–St. Louis, and at Rutgers University.

Jack S. Levy is Professor of Political Science at Rutgers University. An earlier version of this study was presented at the 1988 annual meeting of the American Political Science Association, and an expanded version will appear as "The Role of Crisis Management in the Outbreak of World War I," in Alexander L. George, ed., Avoiding War: Problems of Crisis Management (Westview, forthcoming 1991).

1. See Barbara Tuchman, *The Guns of August* (New York: Dell, 1962); Miles Kahler, "Rumors of War: The 1914 Analogy," *Foreign Affairs*, Vol. 58, No. 2 (Winter 1979/1980), pp. 374–396; Richard Ned Lebow, *Nuclear Crisis Management* (Ithaca: Cornell University Press, 1987), chap. 2–4; Paul Bracken, *The Command and Control of Nuclear Forces* (New Haven: Yale University Press, 1983), pp. 2–3, 65, 222–223. For a summary and critique of the inadvertent war hypothesis, see Marc Trachtenberg, "The Meaning of Mobilization in 1914," *International Security*, Vol. 15, No. 3 (Winter 1990/91), pp. 120–150.
2. Fritz Fischer, *Germany's Aims in the First World War* (New York: Norton, 1961/1967); Fischer, *War of Illusions: German Policies from 1911–1914*, trans. Marian Jackson (New York: Norton, 1975); Fischer, *World Power or Decline*, trans. Lancelot L. Farrar, Robert Kimber, and Rita Kimber (New York: Norton, 1974). On the debate see H.W. Koch, ed., *The Origins of the First World War: Great Power Rivalry and German War Aims* (London: Macmillan, 1972); John A. Moses, *The Politics of*

International Security, Winter 1990/91 (Vol. 15, No. 3)
© 1990 by the President and Fellows of Harvard College and of the Massachusetts Institute of Technology.

Previous attempts to answer these questions have failed, in part because of a lack of rigor in their formulations of the problem and the failure to use a theoretical framework adequate to the task. Crisis management frameworks generally do not acknowledge that some crises are structured in such a way— in terms of the preferences of the actors and their military and diplomatic constraints—that induce rational actors to take a series of actions that lead to a war they would prefer to avoid.[3] Hypotheses of inadvertent war are weakened by the ambiguity of that concept. Assertions that actors "did not want war" are meaningless without the precise specification of the full range of policy alternatives and the perceived costs of each; the simple war/non-war dichotomy is not analytically useful. Psychological and other actor-oriented explanations usually neglect structural constraints;[4] analyses of power distributions, alliance patterns, and the structural instability of the international system rarely consider the motivations of individual actors;[5] and neither acknowledges the importance of domestic politics.[6]

On theoretical grounds, neither an actor-based nor a structure-based explanation is complete without the other,[7] and it has become increasingly evident that neither actor preferences nor the constraints on their choices

Illusion: The Fischer Controversy in German Historiography (London: George Prior, 1975); and David E. Kaiser, "Germany and the Origins of the First World War," *Journal of Modern History*, Vol. 55, No. 3 (September 1983), pp. 442–474.

3. On rational models of "wars that nobody wanted and everybody tried to prevent," see Zeev Maoz, *Paradoxes of War: On the Art of National Self-Entrapment* (Boston: Unwin Hyman, 1990), chap. 4. On crisis management and inadvertent war see Alexander L. George, ed., *Avoiding War: Problems of Crisis Management* (Boulder, Colo.: Westview, forthcoming 1991).

4. For psychological explanations of the 1914 case (which also incorporate other variables) see Ole R. Holsti, *Crisis, Escalation, War* (Montreal: McGill–Queens University Press, 1972); Richard Ned Lebow, *Between Peace and War: The Nature of International Crisis* (Baltimore: Johns Hopkins University Press, 1981); Jack Snyder, *The Ideology of the Offensive: Military Decision Making and the Disasters of 1914* (Ithaca: Cornell University Press, 1984).

5. For structural analyses of the pre-1914 international system see Manus I. Midlarsky, *The Onset of World War* (Boston: Unwin Hyman, 1988); Charles F. Doran, "Systemic Disequilibrium, Foreign Policy Role, and the Power Cycle," *Journal of Conflict Resolution*, Vol. 33, No. 3 (September 1989), pp. 371–401; Paul W. Schroeder, "World War I as Galloping Gertie," *Journal of Modern History*, Vol. 44, No. 3 (September 1972), pp. 319–345.

6. For domestic political explanations see Arno J. Mayer, "Domestic Causes of the First World War," in Leonard Krieger and Fritz Stern, eds., *The Responsibility of Power* (New York: Doubleday, 1967), pp. 286–300; Fischer, *War of Illusions;* Jack S. Levy, "Domestic Politics and War," *Journal of Interdisciplinary History*, Vol. 18, No. 4 (Spring 1988), pp. 553–673. Both systemic and internal variables are included by Nazli Choucri and Robert C. North, *Nations in Conflict: National Growth and International Violence* (San Francisco: W.H. Freeman, 1974); Lebow, *Between Peace and War;* and Snyder, *The Ideology of the Offensive.*

7. James D. Morrow, "Social Choice and System Structure in World Politics," *World Politics*, Vol. 41, No. 1 (October 1988), pp. 75–99.

can be fully specified in the absence of domestic variables.[8] With these considerations in mind, I use a rational-choice framework based on preferences, constraints, and choices to organize an analysis of the outbreak of the First World War. I do not assume unitary nation-state actors, however, and I define constraints to include internal bureaucratic, organizational, and domestic variables as well as external military and diplomatic factors.[9] I reformulate my initial question as follows: To what extent was the outbreak of World War I determined by the foreign policy preferences of the great powers and the strategic and domestic constraints on their choices?

I begin by specifying four possible outcomes of the July crisis and the *preferences* of each of the great powers over these outcomes.[10] I then identify a number of *critical decision points* in the processes leading to war; at each, I specify the options available to each of the great powers, the external and internal *constraints* on political leaders, and decision-makers' *expectations* regarding the intentions of their adversaries and the likely consequences of various courses of action. I analyze the extent to which the strategic choices of political leaders were compelled by their perceived interests, expectations, and the constraints under which they operated, and the extent to which those actions can be better explained by theories of flawed information processing, decision-making, and crisis mismanagement. I also examine whether the expectations and probability assessments of political leaders were reasonable in light of the information available at the time, and I utilize counterfactual reasoning to analyze whether more timely or different actions might have had more favorable consequences, and whether more creative statecraft might have generated new options and changed the structure of incentives in a way which could have led to a less costly outcome.[11]

---

8. Jack S. Levy, "The Causes of War: A Review of Theories and Evidence," in Philip E. Tetlock, et al., eds., *Behavior, Society, and Nuclear War* (New York: Oxford University Press, 1989), Vol. 1, pp. 209–333.

9. Most rational actor models in the international relations literature assume unitary national actors. See Graham T. Allison, *Essence of Decision: Explaining the Cuban Missile Crisis* (Boston: Little Brown, 1971), chap. 1. See also Bruce Bueno de Mesquita, *The War Trap* (New Haven: Yale University Press, 1981).

10. The concept of *preferences* refers (in the formal decision-theoretic sense) to preferences over possible *outcomes* of the crisis, not preferences over alternative *strategies* to achieve those outcomes. Preferences are not always uniform among leading political and military decision-makers, and I note important differences among key factions within each state.

11. Because my primary concern is to evaluate whether the combination of interests and constraints precluded political leaders from acting in ways that might have avoided a major war, and to do so within a reasonably parsimonious framework, I will not give much attention to the psychological factors and human limitations that affected the behavior of decision-makers.

I conclude that the image of World War I as inadvertent and the image of World War I as the intended consequence of Germany's drive for world power are both exaggerated. Germany wanted a local war, but neither Germany nor any other great power wanted a general European war with British involvement. Although there were several points at which political leaders could have done more to manage the crisis so as to secure their vital interests without the costs of a general war, their ranges of choices were extremely limited. The primary causes of World War I were the underlying international and domestic forces which shaped the preferences of the great powers and the strategic and political constraints on their actions. The mismanagement of the crisis by political leaders was a secondary factor contributing to the outbreak of the war.

The Interests, Preferences, and Expectations of the Actors

In the aftermath of the assassination of Archduke Franz Ferdinand, political leaders throughout Europe expected that Austria-Hungary would seek some form of compensation from Serbia, and that significant Serbian concessions would be forthcoming and be sufficient to maintain the peace. Few feared war or even a major crisis, but this changed abruptly on July 23–24 with the news of the extreme demands of the Austrian ultimatum to Serbia.[12] Interlocking alliance agreements increased the fear that a Austro-Serbian war might draw in Russia in support of Serbia, Germany in support of Austria-Hungary, and France in support of Russia, along with the Balkan allies of each of the great powers.[13] Such a continental war could expand further into a general European or world war through the intervention of Britain on the side of the Entente.

Thus most leading European decision-makers in July 1914 recognized four possible outcomes of the July crisis:

---

12. Fischer, *Germany's Aims*, pp. 51, 66; Herbert Butterfield, "Sir Edward Grey in July 1914," *Historical Studies*, Vol. 5 (1965), pp. 7–8; James Joll, *The Origins of the First World War* (London: Longman, 1984), p. 9; Sidney B. Fay, *The Origins of the World War* (New York: Free Press, 1966; orig. pub. 1928), Vol. 2, pp. 286–291.
13. Scott D. Sagan, "1914 Revisited," *International Security*, Vol. 11, No. 2 (Fall 1986), pp. 151–175; Thomas J. Christensen and Jack Snyder, "Chain Gangs and Passed Bucks: Predicting Alliance Patterns in Multipolarity," *International Organization*, Vol. 44, No. 2 (Spring 1990), pp. 137–168.

1) a peaceful but one-sided *negotiated settlement* based on extensive but not unconditional Serbian concessions to Austria;
2) a *localized Austro-Serbian war* in the Balkans;
3) the expansion of the Austro-Serbian conflict into a *continental war* involving Russia, Germany, and France as well as Austria-Hungary and Serbia;
4) the expansion of the continental war into a *world war* through the intervention of Britain.[14]

These four possibilities constitute the set of feasible outcomes of the crisis in the decision-theoretic framework that guides this study. Next, I explain how each key state defined its interests and preferences.

AUSTRIA-HUNGARY. Faced with increases in the strength and hostility of Serbia, intractable ethnic problems and internal decay in Austria-Hungary's multinational empire, and the decline of her position among the great powers, Austro-Hungarian leaders believed that they must break Serbia's hold on the loyalties of the Serbian and Croatian minorities of the Dual Monarchy, and that this required war.[15] Austrian leaders preferred a local war over a riskier continental war, but preferred the latter over a negotiated peace that failed to eliminate Serbian influence.[16] Although they were willing to risk a continental war, Austrian decision-makers believed they could minimize the risk of Russian intervention by a *fait accompli* against Serbia backed by firm assurances of German support, particularly since the assassination provided

---

14. Additional outcomes might include an unconditional Serbian acceptance of all terms of the Austrian ultimatum, a limited Austro-Hungarian invasion of Serbia based on the "Halt-in-Belgrade" plan, or an earlier punitive strike, but the inclusion of these considerations would unnecessarily complicate the analysis at this time.

15. Since 1867, Austria and Hungary had shared a common monarch. They also shared a Ministry of Foreign Policy and Ministry of War, which were dominated by Austrian officials, particularly during the July crisis. Austro-Hungarian leaders believed that without the reconstruction of the Balkans under Austrian domination, the Dual Monarchy would collapse. They would have accepted an unconditional capitulation by Serbia, but recognized that would be politically impossible for any Serbian regime, and constructed a humiliating ultimatum that would certainly be rejected but which they hoped would provide a rationale for Austrian military action. When Serbia unexpectedly accepted nearly all of the terms of the ultimatum, Austria-Hungary still proceeded with a declaration of war. See Luigi Albertini, *The Origins of the War of 1914*, trans. Isabella M. Massey (Westport, Conn.: Greenwood, 1980; orig. pub. 1943), Vol. 2, pp. 168–69, 286–289; L.L. Farrar, Jr., "The Limits of Choice: July 1914 Reconsidered," *Journal of Conflict Resolution*, Vol. 16, No. 1 (March 1972), p. 10.

16. The worst case for Vienna involved British intervention, for that would put more pressure on Germany in the West, delay Berlin's ability to divert its armies to the East, and therefore leave Austria-Hungary in a very vulnerable position with respect to Russia. But Austrian leaders dismissed this possibility as being extremely unlikely.

a cover of legitimacy for military action and since Russia and France were not yet ready for war.[17] They also believed that a preventive war against Serbia to arrest both external and internal decline was necessary while the military and diplomatic context were still favorable.[18]

Vienna's preference for a local war over a negotiated settlement based on Serbian concessions was not unconditional, but for both strategic and domestic political reasons was clearly contingent on German support, which was forthcoming in the "blank check" of July 5–6.[19] Luigi Albertini concludes that if Germany had not wanted Austria to move against Serbia, "neither [Emperor] Francis Joseph, nor [Austro-Hungarian Foreign Minister] Berchtold, nor even [Chief of the General Staff] Conrad would have gone ahead with the venture." Thus German support was a necessary condition for an Austro-Hungarian war against Serbia.[20]

SERBIA. Serbia preferred peace to war with Austria, and was willing to make significant concessions in order to preserve it, but only up to a point. Prime Minister Nikola Pašić was determined not to accept any Habsburg demands that infringed on Serbian sovereignty, and while his uncompromising position predated both the ultimatum and Russian pressures for firmness against Austria, his confidence in Russian support undoubtedly strengthened his resolve. Pašić was further constrained by a severe domestic political crisis and by tensions between the army and his civilian government, and in fact he was away campaigning for the general elections when the ultimatum was

---

17. Samuel R. Williamson, Jr., "The Origins of World War I," *Journal of Interdisciplinary History*, Vol. 18, No. 4 (Spring 1988), p. 610; Joll, *First World War*, pp. 10–11.

18. On the decline of Austria-Hungary see Paul Kennedy, *The Rise and Fall of the Great Powers: Economic Change and Military Conflict from 1500 to 2000* (New York: Random House, 1987), pp. 215–219. On preventive war see Gerhard Ritter, *The Sword and the Scepter*, 4 vols., trans. Heinz Norden (Coral Gables, Fl.: University of Miami Press, 1969–73), Vol. 2, pp. 227–239; and Jack S. Levy, "Declining Power and the Preventive Motivation for War," *World Politics*, Vol. 40, No. 1 (October 1987), pp. 82–107.

19. Both Foreign Minister Leopold Berchtold and Chief of Staff Conrad von Hötzendorf feared abandonment by Germany, and preferred a negotiated settlement to fighting a two-front war with Russia and Serbia without German support. They also believed that their decaying monarchy could embark on war only if it was united internally. But Hungarian Prime Minister Stephen Tisza opposed war and Emperor Franz Joseph wanted to wait until the official investigation of the assassination proved Serbian complicity. The "blank check" satisfied Conrad and (after some negotiation) the political opposition within Austria-Hungary. Fischer, *War Aims*, pp. 52, 56; Ritter, *Sword and the Scepter*, Vol. 2, p. 236; A.J.P. Taylor, *The Struggle for Mastery in Europe 1848–1914* (New York: Oxford University Press, 1971), p. 527.

20. Albertini, *Origins*, Vol. 2, p. 162. German support might not have been necessary for a limited Austrian punitive strike against Serbia, or for an Austrian decision for war after Vienna declared war on July 28. (A declaration of war was not equivalent to war.) Williamson, "Origins of World War I," p. 807.

received.[21] Pašic accepted most of the terms of the Austrian ultimatum, and thereby won the sympathies of Europe. But he carefully evaded the demands that representatives of the Austro-Hungarian government be allowed to participate in the Serbian inquiry into the origins of the assassination plot (for Pašic knew where such an inquiry could lead) and in the suppression of subversive activities directed against the Austro-Hungarian state.[22] The conciliatory but brilliantly evasive Serbian reply represented Serbia's maximum concessions, but they still fell short of Austria's minimum demands.[23]

RUSSIA. Russian decision-makers believed that their strategic and economic interests in the Turkish Straits depended on maintaining Serbia and Romania as buffer states, and that Russian influence in the Balkans and indeed its great power status depended on maintaining its influence among the southern Slavs and its patronage of Serbia. But Tsar Nicholas II was appalled by the royal assassination and could not risk alienating Britain by giving unconditional support to Serbia. On balance, he was willing to allow Serbia to be chastised severely as long as Austria removed from the ultimatum "those points which infringe on Serbia's sovereign rights." Although Russian leaders preferred peace based on some Serbian concessions to a Austro-Serbian war, for both diplomatic and domestic political reasons they preferred a continental war, and therefore preferred a world war with British intervention on their side over a local war in the Balkans in which Serbia would undoubtedly be crushed by Austria. Sensitive to Russia's humiliating defeats in the 1904–05 Russo-Japanese War and the 1908–09 Bosnian crisis, Russian leaders feared that another retreat would permanently undermine Russian influence in the Balkans and reduce Russia to "second place among the powers."[24] Many

---

21. See Williamson, "Origins of World War I," pp. 811–813. Albertini (*Origins*, Vol. 3, pp. 352–362) gives more emphasis to Russian pressure. On the domestic political crisis in Serbia, see Albertini, *Origins*, Vol. 2, p. 351; Joll, *First World War*, p. 73.
22. The Austrian ultimatum also demanded that Serbia suppress anti-Austrian propaganda in Serbia in general and in its public schools in particular, remove all army officers and civilian officials who had engaged in such propaganda, arrest two named officials suspected in the assassination, dissolve the Serbian nationalist association *Narodna Obrana* and prevent the formation of similar societies in the future, and eliminate the traffic in arms across the border between Serbia and Austria-Hungary. For the text of the ultimatum, Serbia's reply, and Austria's line-by-line response, see Albertini, *Origins*, Vol. 2, pp. 286–289, 364–371.
23. Serbia preferred a continental war with Russian support (and therefore also a world war with British intervention), to a localized war with Austria-Hungary, but its role in the expansion of the war is negligible.
24. Russian Foreign Minister Sazonov, quoted in D.C.B. Lieven, *Russia and the Origins of the First World War* (New York: St. Martin's, 1983), pp. 141–147; Joll, *First World War*, p. 55.

Russian leaders also believed that domestic stability and their own political interests required an assertive foreign policy.[25]

BRITAIN. Although British Foreign Secretary Edward Grey, like most others in England, preferred a negotiated settlement to any war, he was more concerned to localize the conflict and prevent a great power war than to avoid Austrian action *per se*. Grey strongly preferred a local war to a continental war as long as Austrian actions were limited,[26] but recognized that the best way to avoid a continental war was to prevent a local war, and to that end he undertook several diplomatic initiatives. These included his July 26 proposal for a four-power conference in London, and his July 29 proposal that Austria halt its military advance in Belgrade. But if the war were to escalate to a general continental war, Grey and his political allies recognized that British interests in the integrity of France and the balance of power in Europe required British intervention, and Grey thus preferred a world war to a continental war. But significant factions in the Cabinet, Parliament, the financial community, and elsewhere preferred neutrality, and it took the German violation of Belgian neutrality to sway the idealists on the left.[27]

FRANCE. France had no direct strategic or reputational interests in the Balkans, but the French alliance with Russia was the cornerstone of French security policy. French leaders feared entrapment in a Russo-German dispute involving Austria and the Balkans, but not as much as they feared abandonment in a Franco-German conflict. They had to support Russia in any war with Germany,[28] but could not behave so provocatively as to alienate Britain, whose military support would be essential. President Raymond Poincaré and

---

25. There was a strong pro-Serbian reaction by public opinion and the press in Russia. Albertini, *Origins*, Vol. 2, pp. 403–405; Imanuel Geiss, ed., *July 1914, The Outbreak of the First World War: Selected Documents* (New York: Scribner's, 1967), nos. 90, 100, 141a. The Russian incentive for diversionary action was offset by the fear that war could lead to revolution. Lieven, *Russia and the First World War*, pp. 121, 153. Also Jack S. Levy, "The Diversionary Theory of War: A Critique," in Manus I. Midlarsky, ed., *Handbook of War Studies* (Boston: Unwin Hyman, 1989), pp. 259–288.
26. Butterfield, "Sir Edward Grey," p. 7; Fischer, *Germany's Aims*, p. 66.
27. Thus British preferences between a continental war and a world war were context-dependent and unstable, and were crystalized only by the end of the crisis. Zara S. Steiner, *Britain and the Origins of the First World War* (New York: St. Martin's Press, 1977), chap. 7–10; K.M. Wilson, "The British Cabinet's Decision for War, 2 August 1914," *British Journal of International Studies*, Vol. 1 (1975), pp. 148–159; Paul Kennedy, *The Realities Behind Diplomacy: Background Influences on British External Policy, 1865–1980* (London: Allen and Unwin, 1981), pp. 136–139.
28. For domestic reasons it was highly desirable that French public opinion perceive that the issue over which the war was fought involved a direct threat to France, and that Russia not initiate the war. Joll, *First World War*, p. 99; Taylor, *Struggle for Mastery*, pp. 486–488.

Premier René Viviani hoped that Austria would not push too hard and that Russia could tolerate some Serbian concessions, and their first preference was thus a negotiated peace, their second a local war. They attempted to restrain Russia without alienating her, and to support plans for the localization of any Austro-Serbian war (including the "Halt-in-Belgrade" Plan), but their absence from France during much of the crisis limited their role.[29] Thus France preferred a negotiated peace to a local war, and the latter to a continental war. But if Russia insisted on war, French leaders knew that they had to follow rather than risk the disintegration of the alliance, and in that case preferred a world war with Britain on the French side.[30]

GERMANY. Germany is the critical case, for key Austrian and particularly Hungarian decision-makers were unwilling to move against Serbia without German support. I argue that German officials preferred a local war in the Balkans to even a one-sided negotiated settlement, and that while they preferred a local war to a continental war, they were willing to risk the latter if necessary to achieve these goals. All of this was conditional, however, upon German confidence that they could avoid their worst-case scenario, a world war resulting from British intervention.

There is substantial evidence that the "blank check" granted by Germany went beyond giving Austrian leaders a free hand, and encouraged them to move militarily against Serbia.[31] Many German leaders doubted Vienna's resolve, repeatedly urged Vienna to move as quickly as possible against Serbia, and subsequently did their best to sabotage the crisis management efforts and mediation proposals of Grey and Russian Foreign Minister Sergei Sazonov.[32] While willing to risk a continental war, and acknowledging that

---

29. Poincaré's and Viviani's absence also increased the influence of Maurice Paléologue, the revanchist ambassador to Russia. John F.V. Keiger, *France and the Origins of the First World War* (New York: St. Martin's, 1983), chap. 7.
30. Some early revisionists claimed that France wanted a world war to recover Alsace-Lorraine, and that Russia wanted such a war to seize the Turkish Straits. See, e.g., Harry Elmer Barnes, *The Genesis of the World War: An Introduction to the Problem of War Guilt* (New York: Knopf, 1926).
31. The revisionist view in the 1920s held that Germany did not want war of any kind but needed to maintain Austria-Hungary as Germany's only great power ally, and that in spite of its best efforts to restrain Vienna, Germany was ultimately dragged into a world war by its weaker ally. Fay, *Origins*, Vol. 2. This hypothesis has been discredited by the path-breaking work of Fischer (see fn. 2), but I differ from Fischer's conclusion that Germany preferred a continental war to a local war.
32. Fischer, *Germany's Aims*, pp. 53–64, 69; Konrad H. Jarausch, "The Illusion of Limited War: Chancellor Bethmann Hollweg's Calculated Risk, July 1914," *Central European History*, Vol. 2, No. 1 (March 1969), p. 56; John Röhl, ed., *1914: Delusion or Design* (New York: St. Martin's, 1973).

those risks were real, German decision-makers hoped and expected that an Austrian *fait accompli* against Serbia in the immediate aftermath of the royal assassination, backed by German warnings to Russia, would minimize the likelihood of Russian intervention.[33] Austria would almost certainly defeat Serbia in a local war, increase its relative strength, and reduce the Slavic threat in the Balkans. Moreover, German Chancellor Theobald von Bethmann Hollweg believed that if France were economically and militarily unable or unwilling to come to the aid of Russia, the Entente might very well split apart and give way to a new diplomatic realignment, which was Germany's primary foreign policy objective.[34]

There is little doubt that world war was seen as the worst case by all German leaders. As Konrad Jarausch concludes, "Bethmann clearly preferred local war, was willing to gamble on continental war, but he abhorred world war."[35] Even Fritz Fischer and Imanuel Geiss, the strongest supporters of the German war guilt hypothesis, argue strongly that Bethmann sought the neutrality of Britain.[36] It would be much easier to handle Britain after the defeat of France and Russia, or after Austria smashed Serbia, leaving the Entente in shambles.[37]

---

33. Jagow to Lichnowsky, July 18, in Geiss, *July 1914*, pp. 122–124; Albertini, *Origins*, Vol. 2, pp. 159–164; Fischer, *Germany's Aims*, p. 60; Stephen Van Evera, "The Cult of the Offensive and the Origins of the First World War," *International Security*, Vol. 9, No. 1 (Summer 1984), p. 83.

34. Fischer, *Germany's Aims*, p. 60. On July 8 Bethmann said that the assassination provided the opportunity for a victorious war or for a crisis in which "we still certainly have the prospect of maneuvering the Entente apart." Quoted in Van Evera, "Cult of the Offensive," p. 80n. See also Bethmann to Roedern (Secretary of State for Alsace-Lorraine), July 16, in Geiss, *July 1914*, p. 118. Similarly, Jarausch argues, in "Illusion of Limited War," p. 58, that "a local Balkan war would bring a diplomatic triumph, a realignment of the south-eastern states and the break-up of the Entente." But it is not clear exactly how confident Bethmann was that a local war would split the Entente or why he believed it. He may have assumed that France would support Russia if and only if Russia were directly threatened by Germany (as stipulated by the terms of the Franco-Russian alliance), and that the absence of French support would not only prevent Russia from coming to Serbia's aid, but also lead it to drop France as an unreliable ally. I have argued that, although France preferred to stay out of a local war, and might try to convince Russia that it was in Russia's interests to do the same, France would follow its ally if necessary and give whatever support Russia needed.

35. Jarausch, pp. 58, 61, 75. See also V.R. Berghahn, *Germany and the Approach of War in 1914* (New York: St. Martin's, 1973), pp. 192, 196; Van Evera, "Cult of the Offensive," p. 83; Sagan, "1914 Revisited," p. 168; Sean M. Lynn-Jones, "Détente and Deterrence: Anglo-German Relations, 1911–1914," *International Security*, Vol. 11, No. 2 (Fall 1986), pp. 142–143.

36. Fischer, *Germany's Aims*, chap. 2; Geiss, "Outbreak of the First World War," pp. 84, 88.

37. It is more difficult to establish the *intensity* of the preferences for a continental war or a negotiated peace over a world war among various German decision-makers, and therefore the risk of British intervention they were willing to tolerate. The German military were most willing to take this risk; unlike their civilian counterparts, many expected British intervention. See note 49 below.

The question of German preferences between a continental war and a local war are more difficult to establish. Fischer and his associates argue that German political and military elites preferred a continental war because they wanted a preventive war against Russia before Russia completed its "Great Program" and the modernization of its railroad system, expected by 1917.[38] A military victory would bolster the German elites' domestic political support, and give them added time to deal with internal crises generated by industrialization and the rise of social democracy.[39] I argue that the fear of Germany's decline as a great power and the need for a dramatic foreign policy victory for domestic purposes led German political leaders to prefer a continental war over the status quo, but that their expectations that a localized Austro-Serbian war would split the Entente led them to an even higher preference for such a war, as a less costly and less risky means of achieving Germany's larger security interests.[40] That is, German leaders preferred a local war to a continental war, and the latter to a negotiated settlement, but they were willing to risk a continental war in order to avoid an unfavorable status quo.

SUMMARY OF PREFERENCE ORDERS

Table 1 summarizes the preferences of the five leading great powers plus Serbia over the set of the four most likely outcomes of the crisis. All of the European great powers plus Serbia preferred a negotiated settlement to a world war, yet they found themselves entrapped in a world war that involved enormous human and economic costs, led to the collapse of three empires, settled little, and set the stage for another cataclysmic world war only two decades later. An analysis of the calculus of choice at each of a series of critical decision points demonstrates that this unwanted outcome resulted

---

38. The Russian program called for a 40 percent increase in the size of the army and a 29 percent increase in officer corps over the next four years. Lieven, *Russia and the First World War*, p. 111; Van Evera, "Cult of the Offensive," pp. 79–85; Fischer, *War of Illusions*, pp. 480, 515; Geiss, "Outbreak of the First World War," pp. 79, 86; Bernadotte E. Schmitt, *The Coming of the War, 1914* (New York: Howard Fertig, 1966), Vol. 1, pp. 321–325.

39. Fischer, *War of Illusions*; Berghahn, *Germany and the First World War*; Wolfgang J. Mommsen, "Domestic Factors in German Foreign Policy," *Journal of Central European History*, Vol. 6, No. 1 (March 1973), pp. 3–43; Michael Gordon, "Domestic Conflict and the Origins of the First World War," *Journal of Modern History*, Vol. 46, No. 2 (June 1974), pp. 191–226; Kaiser, "Germany and the Origins of the First World War."

40. Bethmann opposed a preventive war for this reason. Wolfgang J. Mommsen, "The Debate on German War Aims," in Walter Laqueur and George Mosse, eds., *1914: The Coming of the First World War* (New York: Harper and Row, 1966), p. 60.

Table 1. The Preferences of the Great Powers in 1914.

Austria-Hungary:	LW > CW > NP > WW
Germany:	LW > CW > NP > WW
Russia:	NP > WW > CW > LW
France:	NP > LW > WW > CW
Britain:	NP > LW > WW ? CW
Serbia:	NP > WW > CW > LW

NOTES: These are the preferences of the central decision-makers in each state; there were significant differences within each state, as noted in the text.
NP = a *negotiated peace* based on significant but not unconditional Serbian concessions
LW = a *localized Austro-Serbian war* in the Balkans
CW = a *continental war* where Germany allies with Austria, and Russia and France ally with Serbia
WW = a general European war or *world war*, with Britain joining the war against the Central Powers
> = "was preferred to"
? = a definitive preference cannot be established

CONFLICTING SCHOOLS OF INTERPRETATION. The primary differences among the "inadvertent war" school, Fischer, and myself and others can be summarized by our respective views of German preference orderings:

"Inadvertent war school":	NP > LW > CW > WW
or	LW > NP > CW > WW
Fischer school:	CW > LW > NP > WW
Levy:*	LW > CW > NP > WW

* Konrad Jarausch and Stephen Van Evera would share my preference order for Germany, but not my overall interpretion of the causes of the war. See Jarausch, "Illusion of Limited War," p. 75; and Van Evera, "Why Cooperation Failed in 1914," p. 100.

primarily from the diplomatic, military, bureaucratic/organizational, and domestic constraints on the choices of political elites, and only secondarily from their mismanagement of the crisis.

Critical Decision Points

Political leaders were confronted, not with a single decision whether to go to war in 1914, but instead with a series of decisions at a succession of critical decision points as the crisis unfolded over time. Their preferences as to outcomes were stable over time, but their international and domestic constraints, available information and expectations, and policy options and strategies were constantly changing. Each decision altered the constraints existing at the next critical juncture, and further narrowed political leaders' freedom of maneuver.[41]

The choices made at several of these critical points follow directly from the preferences of leading decision-makers, along with their expectations regarding the probabilities of various actions and the consequences of those actions. This was certainly true for the Austrian decision to attack Serbia rather than accept negotiated Serbian concessions, given Austrian confidence in German support; for the German decision to support Austria, given German assumptions of British neutrality; for Serbia's refusal to accept unconditionally all Austrian demands; for the Russian decision to intervene in support of Serbia rather than allow it to be crushed by Austria; and for the German decision to come to the aid of Austria once Russia made its intentions clear.[42] But all of these choices hinged on the German assumption of British neutrality, which was the critical link in the escalation of all stages of the crisis. I argue that Bethmann and other key German political leaders were quite confident of British neutrality, that they based their policy on that expectation, and that only with the shattering of their assumption on July 29 did they reverse their policy and attempt, briefly, to manage the crisis to avoid war. I explain why Germans clung to this erroneous assumption for so long, focusing both on the British failure to give a clear commitment and on the German failure to recognize warnings that did exist. I then return to three other sets of critical decisions in the July crisis: Austria's failure to move immediately after the assassination; the failure of the Halt-in-Belgrade proposal; and the interlocking sequence of mobilization decisions.

THE GERMAN ASSUMPTION OF BRITISH NEUTRALITY
Kaiser Wilhelm II and Foreign Secretary Jagow were convinced from the beginning of the crisis that Britain would stand aside from a European

---

41. Thus the attempt to model the 1914 case as a 2 X 2 game in normal form (e.g., Glenn H. Snyder and Paul Diesing, *Conflict Among Nations: Bargaining, Decision Making, and System Structure in International Crises* [Princeton: Princeton University Press, 1977], p. 207) is flawed on several counts: the situation cannot be reduced to two homogeneous coalitions, to two strategic options for each actor, to the simple dichotomy between war and peace, or to a single choice in a one-play game.
42. Each of the first three decisions (by Austria, Germany, and Serbia) was a necessary condition for a local war, and thus for any larger war. Russian intervention was a necessary and sufficient condition for a continental war; it was not sufficient for a world war.

conflict.[43] Although Bethmann recognized the uncertainties involved and sometimes wavered in his estimates of British intentions, the bulk of the evidence suggests that he was generally confident of British neutrality.[44] He based his entire policy on this assumption, and undertook several diplomatic initiatives to secure a formal commitment of non-intervention from Grey. German leaders believed, however, that British neutrality was contingent on the British perception that Germany was fighting a defensive war in response to Russian aggression.[45] Thus Bethmann went to great lengths to ensure that Germany did not mobilize before Russia, in an attempt to shift the onus for starting the conflict onto Russia.[46] He believed that by blaming Russia he could also secure the support of the Social Democrats in Germany, which he thought to be politically necessary.[47] The military were generally less confident of British neutrality, but, given their short-war assumptions, they were confident that any intervention would come too late to influence the outcome of the war against France.[48] There is no doubt

43. Jagow said on July 26, "We are sure of English neutrality." Albertini, *Origins*, Vol. 2, p. 429. Later in the war the Kaiser exclaimed, "It only someone had told me beforehand that England would take up arms against us!" Tuchman, *Guns of August*, p. 143.

44. Fischer, *Germany's Aims*, pp. 50–92; Fischer, "The Miscalculation of English Neutrality," in Solomon Wank, et al., eds., *The Mirror of History: Essays in Honor of Fritz Fellner* (Santa Barbara, Calif.: ABC-Clio, 1988), pp. 369–393; Albertini, *Origins*, Vol. 2, pp. 502–520; Lebow, *Between Peace and War*, pp. 129–133; Lynn-Jones, "Détente and Deterrence," pp. 142–145. The confidence of the German political leaders in British neutrality is suggested by Chief of Staff Helmuth von Moltke's remark that "our people still expect a declaration from Britain that it will not join in." Fischer, *War of Illusions*, p. 400. On Bethmann's doubts see Steiner, *Britain and the Origins of the First World War*, p. 126.

45. As early as winter 1912–13, Bethmann expressed confidence that Britain would stand aside "if the *provocation* appeared to come directly from Russia and France," and Moltke insisted that "the attack must come from the Slavs." The German bid for British neutrality failed because it required that German *involvement* in war be sufficient for neutrality, whereas Britain insisted that it could offer neutrality only in the event of an *unprovoked* attack on Germany. Fischer, *Germany's Aims*, pp. 27, 31–33 (quotation), 63, 70–85; Fischer, "Miscalculation," pp. 373–382; Geiss, *July 1914*, pp. 269, 350; Jarausch, "Illusion of Limited War," pp. 63–68; Joll, *First World War*, pp. 20–29, 116; Albertini, *Origins*, Vol. 2, p. 502.

46. Fischer, "Miscalculation," pp. 373–375, 380, 382.

47. Bethmann believed that it was essential to maintain a united front at home, and was uncertain of the intentions of the Social Democrats, who had vacillated between a socialist-internationalist and a social-patriot position (supporting the Army Bill in 1913). Fischer, *War of Illusions*, p. 494; Geiss, *July 1914*, p. 269; Jarausch, "Illusion of Limited War," pp. 67–68. I thank Daniel Garst for ideas on this point.

48. L.L. Farrar, Jr., *The Short-War Illusion* (Santa Barbara, Calif: ABC-Clio, 1973). Gerhard Ritter, *The Schlieffen Plan: Critique of a Myth*, trans. Andrew and Eva Wilson (New York: Praeger, 1958), pp. 71, 161–162; Fischer, *Germany's Aims*, p. 49. Tirpitz and some others wanted to do everything possible to delay British entry, which reinforced German determination not to mobilize first. Sagan, "1914 Revisited," pp. 170–171. Military views were not crucial, however, for they had limited influence on German foreign policy decisions prior to July 30, and by that time civilian

that Bethmann, even in his most pessimistic moods, accepted this minimum assumption.[49]

The importance of the German assumption of British neutrality is also demonstrated by the reaction in Berlin to reports (beginning July 25) from Prince Lichnowsky, German ambassador to Britain, that Grey had changed his position toward opposition to Germany. The Kaiser was the first to take these warnings seriously (July 27), and within a day made his compromise Halt-in-Belgrade proposal, which was delivered to Austria on the morning of July 29.[50] Late on July 29 Bethmann received Lichnowsky's telegram with an unequivocal warning from Grey that Britain could not stand aside in a continental war involving France.[51] The response in Berlin was immediate and quite revealing. As Fischer argues, Bethmann and other German political leaders were "shattered" by the telegram, for "the foundation of their policy during the crisis had collapsed." Bethmann responded with a flurry of increasingly urgent telegrams that night. He proposed that Vienna accept mediation and the Halt-in-Belgrade proposal, and warned that Germany would not allow itself "to be drawn wantonly into a world conflagration by Vienna."[52] Thus in a desperate attempt to avoid the one outcome that he

expectations had shifted. See Kaiser, "Germany and the First World War," p. 469; Lynn-Jones, "Détente and Deterrence, " p. 144; Trachtenberg, "Meaning of Mobilization," pp. 137–144.

49. Bethmann's statement to the Kaiser (July 23), that "it was improbable that England would *immediately* enter the fray," implies that the expected delay was critical. (Jarausch, "Illusion of Limited War," p. 62.) He stated that "England's interest in the preservation of a European balance of power will not allow a complete crushing of France," assumed this was the British threshold for intervention, and was confident that intervention could be avoided by promising that Germany would "demand no territorial concessions from France." Germany's primary war aims, after all, were to support Austria and defeat Russia. Fischer "Miscalculation," p. 382. Thus, civilian and military leaders shared the assumption that if the British intervened at all, they would do so too late to influence the outcome of the war against France. Even if Trachtenberg ("Meaning of Mobilization," pp. 134–137) and others are correct that Bethmann did not expect British neutrality *per se*, that would not undermine the essence of my argument: German political and military leaders were confident that, at a minimum, Britain would not intervene until France was about to be crushed, that this would be too late to influence the outcome of the war in the west, and that Germany could influence the British decision by providing guarantees that it sought no territorial annexations from France. Bethmann would not risk a continental war in the absence of these assumptions. Thus my earlier proposition, that the German assumption of British neutrality was a necessary condition for war of any kind, holds if "neutrality" is interpreted broadly to mean "no immediate intervention."

50. Albertini, *Origins*, Vol. 2, pp. 431–445; Lebow, *Between Peace and War*, pp. 131–132, 140–141.

51. *German Documents Relating to the Outbreak of the World War*, collected by Karl Kautsky and edited by Max Montgelas and Walther Schucking (New York: Oxford University Press, 1924), No. 178, pp. 321–322. Grey indicated that Britain could remain neutral if France were not involved.

52. Bethmann to Tschirschky (2:55 a.m., 3:00 a.m.), July 30, 1914, in Kautsky, *German Documents*,

had always feared, but only on the 29th had recognized was likely, Bethmann suddenly reversed the policy that had guided Germany throughout the July crisis.[53]

Had Bethmann initiated this pressure any earlier, particularly before the Austrian declaration of war on the July 28, it would have been extremely difficult for Austria to resist, as I discuss below. First, however, why were German political leaders were so confident of British neutrality? It is easy to say that Germany should have known that Britain would intervene in any continental war involving its French and Russian allies, particularly if Belgian neutrality were violated. A German victory in a two-front war would give it a position of dominance on the continent and control of the critical Channel ports, leave Britain without strong allies on the continent, and provide Germany with a strategic and industrial base from which to mount a global

---

Nos. 192, 193, pp. 344–346. Fischer, *Germany's Aims*, pp. 78–82; Albertini, *Origins*, Vol. 2, pp. 504–527; Bernadotte Schmitt, *Coming of the War*, Vol. 2, pp. 156–172; Jarausch, "Illusion of Limited War," pp. 65–68; Lynn-Jones, "Détente and Deterrence," pp. 143–144. Fischer (*Germany's Aims*, pp. 79–82), and to a lesser extent Geiss (*July 1914*, p. 269) argue that Bethmann's policy shift on July 29–30 was temporary, and that "peace moves" later that day were simply tactical expedients to deceive Britain and ensure that the blame for the conflict could be shifted onto Russia. Lebow (*Between Peace and War*, pp. 135–139) emphasizes the importance of psychological stress, emotional turmoil, exaggerated confidence and pessimistic fatalism, and hypervigilant coping behavior in Bethmann's shifts in policy on July 29–31. For an alternative interpretation of these events see Trachtenberg, "Meaning of Mobilization."

The critical impact of British intentions is also demonstrated by the German response to Lichnowsky's August 1 report of Grey's offer that if Germany "were not to attack France, England would remain neutral and guarantee the passivity of France." Albertini, *Origins*, Vol. 3, pp. 380–381. With the Chancellor's eager support, the Kaiser announced "now we can to war against Russia only. We simply march the whole of our army to the East." Tuchman, *Guns of August*, p. 98. Moltke objected but was overruled, and Germany telegraphed its acceptance of what was thought to be the British proposal, only to learn that Lichnowsky's report had been erroneous. Albertini, *Origins*, Vol. 3, pp. 380–386. For more on the German response to Lichnowsky's August 1 report, see Jack S. Levy, "Organizational Routines and the Causes of War," *International Studies Quarterly*, Vol. 30, No. 2 (June 1986), pp. 199, 213–214.

53. Trachtenberg ("Meaning of Mobilization," pp. 136–137) argues that it was the news of the Russian partial mobilization, rather than the warning from Grey, that was the primary cause of Bethmann's sudden policy shift. He argues that Lichnowsky's telegram with Grey's warning, which was received at the German Foreign Office at 9:12 p.m., could not have been decoded in time to explain Bethmann's subsequent behavior. There is enough evidence, apart from Bethmann's behavior that night, of the German expectation of British neutrality in a continental war, that Trachtenberg's argument, if correct, would not undercut my assessment of German preferences or my overall interpretation of the causes of the war. But my own review of the sequence, timing, and content of Bethmann's outgoing telegrams on the night of July 29–30 suggests that Trachtenberg is not correct in these conclusions. Bethmann was late in getting the news from Russia, as well as from England, and the telegrams (dispatched at 2:55 and 3:00 a.m.) in which he first referred to the warning from Grey exhibited a much greater sense of fear and urgency than a slightly earlier telegram containing his first reference to the Russian mobilization.

challenge to Britain.[54] Moreover, there had been numerous warnings that Britain would not be able to stay neutral in a continental war.

Although the German political leaders' dismissal of these warnings and their failure to appreciate Britain strategic interests can be explained in part by motivated psychological biases and wishful thinking,[55] their assumption of British neutrality was not entirely unreasonable. Not all of the signals coming out of London were consistent with the warnings from Lichnowsky.[56] Though Grey repeatedly refused to give Berlin an unconditional commitment of neutrality, he also refused to give France and Russia a commitment to come to their defense. That German "misperceptions" derived as much from the inherent uncertainty of the incoming signals, as from any motivated biases, is suggested by the fact that officials in France and Russia, whose motivated biases would have led in the opposite direction from Germany's and who had constantly pressured Britain for a clear commitment, were also uncertain of British intentions.[57] Indeed, the British themselves were unclear as to what they would do. Cabinet members David Lloyd George and Winston Churchill were both skeptical regarding whether the government would intervene on the continent, and Grey himself was uncertain.[58]

---

54. First, naval agreements with France, ot which the Germans had some knowledge, created an additional British obligation. Second, British reputational interests were also at stake. Third, British policies in the two Moroccan crises indicated that no British government was likely to stand aside while Germany increased its influence at the expense of France. Moltke had argued in a 1913 memo that Britain would intervene in a Franco-German war "because she fears German hegemony, and true to her policy of maintaining a balance of power will do all she can to check the increase of German power." Tuchman, *Guns of August*, p. 144; Trevor Wilson, *The Myriad Faces of War: Britain and the Great War, 1914–1918* (Oxford: Basil Blackwell, 1986), chap. 1; Sir Llewellyn Woodward, *Great Britain and the War of 1914–1918* (Boston: Beacon, 1967), pp. 19–20.
55. See Lebow, *Between Peace and War*, pp. 130–131.
56. Lebow, ibid., p. 129, argues that Lichnowsky was out of favor in Berlin and that his early warnings were discounted for that reason.
57. French Chief of Staff General Joffre was so uncertain of British intervention that he did not assume it in forming the French army's war plan. Sazonov warned the Russian Council of Ministers on July 24 that any escalation of war would be dangerous "since it is not known what attitude Great Britain would take in the matter." Samuel R. Williamson, "Joffre Shapes French Strategy, 1911–1913," in Paul M. Kennedy, ed., *War Plans of the Great Powers, 1880–1914* (London: Allen and Unwin, 1979), p. 146; Sagan, "1914 Revisited," pp. 169–170.
58. On July 29, Grey told French Ambassador to Berlin Jules Cambon that "if Germany became involved and France became involved, we had not made up our minds what we should do." On August 1 the British Cabinet rejected a proposal to dispatch the British Expeditionary Force to the continent and forbade Churchill to order the full mobilization of the Navy. Wilson, "The British Cabinet's Decision," pp. 149–150; *British Documents*, Vol. 11, No. 283, p. 180; Joll, *First World War*, pp. 19–20. On the difficulty of identifying misperceptions and the usefulness of the "third party" criterion, see Robert Jervis, *Perception and Misperception in International Politics* (Princeton: Princeton University Press, 1976), p. 7; Sagan, "1914 Revisited," p. 170; Jack S. Levy,

Britain's failure to give a clear and timely commitment in support of her allies was a critical step in the processes leading to an Austro-Serbian war and its expansion into a world war, for it eliminated the one threat that would have led German political decision-makers to restrain their counterparts in Vienna. Yet British leaders were faced with serious diplomatic and domestic political constraints, and it is not clear that they could easily have acted differently. Their strategic dilemma was that while a clear commitment would reinforce deterrence against Germany, it might at the same time encourage Russia to pursue a riskier course against Austria-Hungary. Many British leaders assumed that by leaving their commitment ambiguous they could maximize the likelihood that they could restrain Russia without alienating her, and deter Germany without provoking her.[59] Grey's policy of diluting and delaying Britain's deterrent threat against Germany was reinforced by the British perception that Anglo-German relations had improved over the previous three years and his belief that a more accommodative strategy toward Germany might induce a cooperative solution to the July Crisis, as it had in the Balkan Wars.[60] The fear of provoking Germany was undoubtedly less compelling after July 27–28, however, for the German rejection of Grey's proposal for a four-power conference and the Austrian declaration of war greatly reduced any remaining doubt regarding the intentions of the Central Powers.

By July 27, if not before, the primary factor preventing Grey from issuing a clear warning to Germany was cabinet politics in England. About three-quarters of the Liberal cabinet were opposed to British involvement in war, and Grey knew that it would be difficult to secure any commitment from them.[61] Grey's objectives were to prevent a continental war if at all possible,

"Misperceptions and the Causes of War," *World Politics*, Vol. 36, No. 1 (October 1983), pp. 76–89.

59. Grey's attempted balancing act has been described as a "straddle strategy" by Glenn H. Snyder, "The Security Dilemma in Alliance Politics," *World Politics*, Vol. 36, No. 4 (July 1984), pp. 461–495. This strategy was based on the assumption that uncertainty would induce caution in both Russia and Germany, but the assumption that states are risk-averse is debatable. On "risk orientation," see Bueno de Mesquita, *The War Trap*, pp. 33–40, 60–64.

60. Lynn-Jones, "Détente and Deterrence," pp. 125–140. This argument is reinforced by evidence suggesting that Grey perceived that Berlin was divided between a peace party (headed by Bethmann) and a war party, feared that pressure against Germany would only strengthen hardline elements in Berlin, and believed that conciliatory actions might strengthen Bethmann in his internal political struggles with the military. See Michael Eckstein, "Sir Edward Grey and Imperial Germany in 1914," *Journal of Contemporary History*, Vol. 6, No. 3 (1971), pp. 121–131.

61. At a meeting of the cabinet on July 27, Grey asked if Britain would intervene were France attacked by Germany. Five ministers warned that they would resign if such a decision were

but if war occurred, to bring Britain into the war united. An early warning to Germany might advance the first aim but generate a domestic reaction that threatened the second. With regard to warning Germany that Britain would declare war if Germany attacked France or violated Belgian territory, Churchill later wrote:

I am certain that if Sir Edward Grey had sent the kind of ultimatum suggested, the Cabinet would have broken up, and it is also my belief that up till Wednesday (29th) or Thursday (30th) at least, the House of Commons would have repudiated his action. Nothing less than the deeds of Germany would have converted the British nation to war.[62]

It is significant that Churchill refers to *German* deeds. Austrian action against Serbia was not sufficient to bring Britain in, for if a settlement were not possible, Britain preferred a localized war in the Balkans, whatever its outcome, to a continental or world war. But what specific German deeds would be necessary or sufficient to bring Britain into the war?[63] Although one cannot know for sure how the cabinet would have acted under various contingencies, it appears that the critical trigger for cabinet approval of British intervention in the early stages of the war was the German violation of Belgian neutrality, which was an integral part of the German Schlieffen Plan.[64] For years the radicals had refused to be swayed by balance of power

---

taken. On July 29 the cabinet refused to specify the conditions under which it would decide for war. On August 1 Grey stated that "we could not propose to Parliament at this moment to send an expeditionary military force to the continent"; *British Documents*, Vol. 11, No. 426. See also Steiner, *Britain and the First World War*, chap. 9; Wilson, "The British Cabinet's Decision," pp. 148–159; Woodward, *Great Britain and the War*, pp. 21–22.

62. Albertini, *Origins*, Vol. 2, p. 515, quoting Churchill, *The World Crisis* (London: Butterworth, 1923–31), Vol. 1 (1929), p. 204.

63. To Grey, any Franco-German war sufficiently threatened British interests that it required intervention. For the cabinet, severe military setbacks to France and the threat of German continental hegemony was probably prerequisite to intervention; this was the German "weak neutrality assumption," described above. Grey was also worried about parliamentary support. Mayer, "Domestic Causes," pp. 298–299.

64. The Schlieffen Plan was based on the assumptions that any continental war would be a two-front war for Germany, that the offensive was the dominant form of warfare, that France and Russia had to be dealt with sequentially and in that order, that France could be defeated only by an enveloping movement through Belgium, and that this required the preemptive seizure of Liège early in the mobilization process itself (no later than the third day). Ritter, *The Schlieffen Plan*; Snyder, *Ideology of the Offensive*, chap. 4–5. Without the German violation of Belgian neutrality, British intervention in a continental war would have been considerably less likely, or at least delayed, for British radicals probably would not have been convinced of the strategic necessity for military action short of severe military setbacks to France. Thus the Schlieffen Plan and the envelopment of France through Belgium not only precluded the effective management of the crisis by Germany to avoid the world war they feared, but it also ensured

arguments, and in the end they needed the moral justification provided by the 1839 guarantee of Belgian neutrality.[65]

Grey's domestic political constraints still permitted him some means of influencing Germany. Although a formal threat to Berlin was probably precluded by cabinet politics, an informal warning was not. Although Grey's warning of July 29 had not been approved by the cabinet, that warning had a tremendous impact on Germany, and a similar informal warning could have been issued much earlier. Had a warning been issued prior to the Austrian ultimatum on the 23rd, or perhaps even as late as the 27th, it would have been sufficient to alarm Germany and to provoke successful German pressure against Austria-Hungary, and war could have been averted, at least for a time. But Grey was, in that period, constrained by strategic considerations. Although we now know that Germany was more in need of restraint than was Russia, and that earlier British pressure against Berlin probably would have averted war, it is more difficult to say that Grey should have known this in July 1914.

Although the erroneous assumption of British neutrality was a necessary condition for German support of an Austrian invasion of Serbia, and consequently for a continental or world war (at least until the Austrian declaration of war on July 28), it was not a sufficient condition. It is conceivable that a continental war could have been avoided if Austria had undertaken military action immediately following the assassination, if Austria had agreed to the Halt-in-Belgrade plan for limited military action against Serbia, or if diplomatic efforts to force Austria's acceptance of this plan and manage the crisis had been given more time to work. Below I consider each of these "roads not taken," and identify the strategic and domestic constraints that made these options too costly in the eyes of statesmen.

THE DELAY OF AUSTRO-HUNGARIAN MILITARY ACTION

Austria pursued a *fait accompli* strategy, but delayed military action against Serbia for a month after the assassination of the Archduke. The timing was

---

that the British would enter the war at an early stage and thus maximize their impact. Thus part of the explanation for the erroneous assumption of British neutrality by political decision makers must be traced to their miscalculation of the consequences of the Schlieffen Plan, to which I return below.

65. Steiner, *Britain and the First World War*, p. 237. Thus the significance of Belgium, particularly for the radicals in the cabinet, was more political than strategic; the balance of power on the continent and the future of Belgium and its channel ports would ultimately depend upon the outcome of a Franco-German war, regardless of whether Belgian neutrality was violated at its outset.

critical, for the combination of universal outrage against Serbia, the widespread belief that a limited Austrian response in defense of its honor would be legitimate, the fear of a wider war, and German threats against Russia might have been sufficient to localize the war. A.J.P. Taylor concludes that "the one chance of success for Austria-Hungary would have been rapid action."[66]

Most German political and military leaders assumed that a larger war might be avoided through immediate action, and this was a primary factor underlying their pressure on Austria to move as quickly as possible.[67] The greater the delay, however, the more the punishment of Serbia would be decoupled from the assassination that might have provided it some legitimacy, and the more the Tsar would shift his concerns from the principle of monarchial solidarity to his strategic and reputational interests in the Balkans. A major consequence of the delay was to transform the possibility of an early punitive strike into a larger local war that was more likely to escalate.

How do we explain the delay? Nothing could be done before the blank check from Germany July 5–6. Among the reasons for the extensive delay after this, one was military. Berchtold, who initially wanted to attack Serbia without first mobilizing, was distressed to learn from Conrad on July 6 that an invasion could not begin until two weeks after mobilization.[68] The delay was exacerbated by domestic structural and political constraints. The goal of a unified monarchy precluded any further action (including an ultimatum or

---

66. Taylor, *Struggle for Mastery,* pp. 522–223. Ritter concludes that "swift action would have been politically much more effective and less dangerous to the peace of Europe than the endless delay that did take place." Ritter, *Sword and the Scepter,* Vol. 2, p. 236. Samuel R. Williamson, Jr., writes that "what had appeared in early July to be a calculated, acceptable risk—a local war with Serbia—would loom more dangerous and provocative two weeks later." Williamson, "Theories of Foreign Policy Process and Foreign Policy Outcomes," in Paul Gordon Lauren, ed. *Diplomacy* (New York: Free Press, 1979), pp. 151–153. See George, *Avoiding War,* chap. 5, for a theoretical discussion of the *fait accompli* strategy.
67. Grey also accepted this assumption. Butterfield, "Sir Edward Grey," pp. 10–11; Fischer, *Germany's Aims,* pp. 53–61.
68. Albertini, *Origins,* Vol. 2, p. 455. The critical questions are whether Austria could have taken limited military operations (a punitive strike) against Serbia, independent of a general invasion; whether contingency plans for this option existed in early July (or later, with the Halt-in-Belgrade proposal); and whether such an action would have interfered with a subsequent mobilization against Serbia or Russia. See Levy, "Organizational Routines," p. 200; Pierre Renouvin, *The Immediate Origins of the War (28th June–4th August 1914),* trans. Theodore Carswell Hume (New Haven: Yale University Press, 1928), p. 128; Holsti, *Crisis, Escalation, War,* pp. 157, 216. But A.J.P. Taylor argues that Serbia had decided not to defend Belgrade; Taylor, "War by Timetable," in *Purnell's History of the Twentieth Century* (New York: Purnell, 1974), p. 445. If so, Austria could easily have occupied Belgrade without interfering with later operations.

declaration of war) until July 14, when Hungarian Prime Minister Tisza agreed to war, in return for the willingness of the Austro-Hungarian Council of Ministers to accept his demand for the renunciation of territorial annexations (excepting minor frontier "adjustments") at Serbia's expense.[69]

Two additional factors explain the nine-day delay in the ultimatum after July 14. Organizational constraints imposed by the timetable of the harvest leaves for the army complicated the recall of troops before their scheduled return on July 21–22, for that might disrupt the harvests and possibly the railroad-based mobilization plans, and eliminate the possible benefits of surprise.[70] In addition, Austrian decision-makers did not want to deliver the ultimatum to Serbia until after the state visit of Poincaré and Viviani to St. Petersburg on July 23, fearing that they might encourage a stronger Russian response.[71] But by this time, the cloak of legitimacy for an Austrian military action resulting from the royal assassination would have dissipated. Moreover, once the unprecedented terms of the ultimatum became known, European political leaders began to see Austria, not Serbia, as the primary violator of international norms. At this point, it is more likely that the best hope for peace lay in a *delay* of the Austrian declaration of war.

Although Conrad wanted to delay a declaration of war and a crushing *fait accompli* against Serbia until August 12, when military operations could begin, Berchtold insisted (July 26) on an early declaration of war to pacify Germany and an increasingly vocal press and domestic public.[72] Berchtold now welcomed the lapse between the declaration of war and the invasion, and hoped it would provide time for additional coercive pressure to secure Serbia's "unconditional submission."[73] The timing was critical, first, because the Aus-

---

69. Tisza wanted to reassure the Tsar and minimize the likelihood of Russian intervention. But even this action may have come too late, and it is not certain that Austria-Hungary planned to fulfill this promise. Albertini, *Origins*, Vol. 2, p. 175; Schmitt, "Coming of the War," Vol. 1, pp. 345–57; Norman Stone, "Hungary and the Crisis of July 1914," *Journal of Contemporary History*, Vol. 1, No. 3 (1966), pp. 147–164; Williamson, "Origins of World War I," p. 10.
70. See Williamson, "Theories of Foreign Policy Process," pp. 152–153; Levy, "Organizational Routines," p. 202.
71. Tschirschky to Bethmann, July 14, in Geiss, *July 1914*, pp. 114–115. The ultimatum was delivered on July 23.
72. Germany was pressing for immediate action. Turner, *Origins*, p. 98; Albertini, *Origins*, Vol. 2, pp. 453–458.
73. Thus Berchtold apparently shifted his preferred strategy from military victory over Serbia to coercive diplomacy. After designing the ultimatum so that its inevitable rejection would provide a justification for the war that he wanted, and then recognizing that Austria lacked the means for an immediate *fait accompli*, Berchtold switched to a coercive strategy but did not combine it with the diplomatic measures that might have made it effective. He did not soften

trian declaration of war and concurrent mobilization against Serbia led directly to the partial Russian mobilization, which initiated a rapid and nearly irreversible sequence of threats and mobilizations over the next four days. Second, it made it much more difficult for Vienna to give in to German pressures for restraint, which began during the night of July 29–30 after Lichnowsky's warning from Grey.

It is important to recognize that Vienna's declaration of war and military mobilization were driven by political rather than military considerations, as a brief examination of Austria's mobilization plans and its strategic dilemma suggests. Facing the prospect of a two-front war against both Russia and Serbia, Austrian military planners incorporated a degree of flexibility into their mobilization and war plans. They allowed for partial mobilization against either Serbia or Russia, and for offensive action against one and defensive action against the other, depending on the specific threat. But once a partial mobilization was initiated against Serbia, the troops involved could not easily be shifted back to the Galician front to meet a major Russian attack.[74] Although this created an incentive for Vienna to speed up the flow of events rather than slow them down once mobilization had begun, it also created a military incentive to delay mobilization as long as possible, while Russian intentions were uncertain. Mobilization was, for Berchtold, an essential element of a strategy to force Serbia's submission by coercive diplomacy if possible and by war if necessary. But mobilization was not essential to Conrad's preparation for war, and in fact was damaging to it.[75]

---

the degrading terms of the ultimatum to provide Serbia with a face-saving way out of the crisis, and he compounded matters further with a premature declaration of war that only strengthened the resolve of Serbia and the Entente, and contributed to the further escalation of the crisis. I thank Alexander George for suggesting this line of argument.

74. This rigidity was due to the inherent difficulties of fighting a two-front war, the poor quality of the Austro-Hungarian railway system, and to the inability and unwillingness of the Germans to provide significant help against Russia in the early stages of a war because of the requirements of the Schlieffen Plan. Conrad's defense plan called for minimal defense forces in both Galicia (*A-Staffel*, thirty divisions) and in the Balkans (*Minimalgruppe Balkan*, ten divisions). An additional twelve divisions (*B-Staffel*) could be sent either to the Balkans (where they would add sufficient strength to destroy Serbia) or to Galicia (where they would combine with *A-Staffel* to provide for a powerful offensive against Russia). But once committed, *B-Staffel* could not be shifted to the other front easily or quickly. Stone, "Moltke and Conrad," pp. 225–226, 243–244.

75. Conrad insisted that he had to know by the fifth day of mobilization whether the Russians were planning to intervene; else his plans would go awry. He described a delayed Russian intervention as "the most difficult yet most probable case." Moltke concurred. Stone, "Moltke and Conrad," pp. 228–235; L.C.F. Turner, *Origins of the First World War* (New York: Norton, 1970), pp. 92–93; Turner, "The Russian Mobilisation in 1914," in Kennedy, *War Plans*, p. 258; Albertini, *Origins of the War*, Vol. 2, p. 482; Fischer, *Germany's Aims*, p. 74.

In retrospect, Conrad's preference for a delay in the declaration of war until the onset of military operations may have increased the probability of a peaceful settlement, but not by much. Russian interests were threatened far more by the Austrian mobilization than by the declaration of war *per se.* Given the acceleration of events unleashed by the Russian mobilization, it is unlikely that a delay in the Austrian declaration of war would have bought much time for crisis management. On the other hand, Russian leaders might have been somewhat less certain of Austrian intentions in the absence of the declaration of war, and therefore slightly less inclined to mobilize, which would have provided a little more time for efforts to manage the crisis through the Halt-in-Belgrade proposal.[76] In addition, the Austrian declaration of war may have been more difficult to reverse, in the eyes of its decision-makers, than was mobilization.[77] A delay in the declaration of war alone would therefore have reduced the reputational, domestic political, and psychological costs to Austrian leaders of reversing course, and thus increased somewhat the likelihood that they might have accepted the Halt-in-Belgrade proposal under German pressure.[78] But it is impossible to say whether the magnitude of these changes would have been large enough to delay, even temporarily, a world war that none of the great powers wanted.

THE "HALT-IN-BELGRADE" PROPOSAL

After hearing of Austria's ultimatum on July 24, Russian leaders concluded that it was designed to provoke war. The next day the Tsar authorized preparatory military actions (short of mobilization) in order to deter an Austrian move against Serbia, and, if that failed, to facilitate military intervention in Serbia's defense.[79] Grey began exploring the possibility of British mediation

---

76. This is particularly true had the Russians understood the opportunities created by technical rigidities in Austrian mobilization plans, as I argue below.
77. The Austrians, unlike the Germans, did not perceive that mobilization necessarily meant war. See Schmitt, *Coming of the War*, Vol. 2, pp. 215.
78. This assumes that Grey would have seen the combination of the ultimatum, Bethmann's rejection of the proposal for a four-power conference, and Russia's early preparations for war as threatening enough—even in the absence of a Austrian declaration of war—to issue a strong warning to Germany. Nothing less than such a warning would have induced Germany to pressure Austria for restraint.
79. Russia's initiation of the "The Period Preparatory to War" on July 26 is best seen as the first stage of mobilization. Turner, "Russian Mobilisation," pp. 261–262; Baron M.F. Schilling, *How the War Began in 1914: The Diary of the Russian Foreign Office* (London: Allen and Unwin, 1925), pp. 62–66; Albertini, *Origins*, Vol. 2, pp. 565–572; Snyder, *Ideology of the Offensive*, chap. 6–7; Van Evera, "Cult of the Offensive," pp. 72–79.

on the same day, and on July 26 invited France, Germany, and Italy to send their ambassadors to a conference in London. Austria refused; so did Germany, which continued to press for immediate military action as a means of localizing the war.

By July 27–28 the Kaiser began to fear British intervention, and at the same time believed that after the conciliatory Serbian reply "every cause for war has vanished." He instructed Jagow to request that Vienna accept a "temporary military occupation" of Belgrade pending successful great power mediation.[80] This "Halt-in-Belgrade" proposal aimed to manage the escalating crisis and to localize it in the Balkans, by allowing Austria to gain a significant diplomatic victory and demonstrate its military prowess and prestige without damaging Russia's reputation.

Bethmann's pressure on Austria for restraint, induced by his changed perceptions of British intentions, came less than a day after the Kaiser's Halt-in-Belgrade proposal was delivered to Austria. Although Berchtold's formal response was delayed and deliberately evasive, he immediately told German Ambassador Heinrich Tschirschky that it was too late to change course. Strategically, Berchtold believed that the temporary occupation of Belgrade would not be sufficient to achieve Austria's initial objective of eliminating the threat from Serbia and the southern Slavs. He feared that although a temporary occupation of Belgrade would provide leverage against Serbia, it would also generate diplomatic pressure on Vienna to soften its demands. Moreover, even if Russia were willing to tolerate an Austrian occupation of Belgrade, it would be "mere tinsel," for the Serbian army would remain intact and see Russia as its savior, and Serbia would provoke another crisis in two or three years under conditions much less favorable to Austria.[81]

Berchtold was also concerned about the reputational and domestic political costs of reversing course after an earlier declaration of war. After considerable pressure from Germany to move quickly against Serbia, Austro-Hungarian leaders had taken the politically difficult decisions to issue the ultimatum,

---

80. *German Documents*, pp. 273–274. Grey made a similar proposal the next day. He requested that Russia suspend military operations against Serbia, while Austria "hold the occupied territory until she had complete satisfaction from Servia . . . [but] not advance further." *British Documents*, No. 286, p. 182.

81. Austro-German negotiations were also complicated by disagreements over how much to concede to their Italian ally to keep it in line. Schmitt, *Coming of the War*, Vol. 2, pp. 217–222; Fischer, *War Aims*, p. 73; Albertini, *Origins*, Vol. 2, pp. 656–57. It has also been argued that Vienna was constrained because it had no contingency plans for the occupation of Belgrade. Holsti, *Crisis, Escalation, War*, pp. 157, 216. See sources cited in note 68 above.

declare war, and begin mobilization. Once taken, these actions were very difficult to modify and redirect. This would have undermined Austrian credibility, upset a coalition of domestic political interests that had been very difficult to construct, and broken a serious psychological commitment.[82]

This episode demonstrates the importance of the timing of actions designed to reinforce crisis management. Had Germany initiated this pressure against Austria *prior* to the declaration of war on the 28th, it would have been far more difficult for Vienna to resist. Austria would have been even more likely to acquiesce had the German pressure come before the ultimatum was delivered on July 23, and there is every reason to believe that an earlier warning from Grey would have been sufficient to trigger a German warning to Vienna. Albertini concludes that, "if Grey had spoken before 23 July, or even after the 23rd but not later than the afternoon of the 27th, as he spoke on the 29th, Germany would very likely have restrained Austria from declaring war on Serbia and the European war, at least for the time being, would have been averted."[83]

Even as late as July 30, however, it is still conceivable that war could have been avoided, though the margin for maneuver was admittedly thin. Berchtold continued to delay a response to Bethmann's proposal, and Bethmann continued his pleas for peace but without increasing the pressure against his Austrian ally.[84] This was critical, for stronger German pressure, including an explicit threat to withdraw support from Austria, probably would have been sufficient to compel Vienna to accept the Halt-in-Belgrade plan and thus avoid more extensive military action, at least for the time being. Despite the costs of reversing course after a declaration of war, the prospect of being left to fight Russia and Serbia alone was even less desirable. In addition, Hungarian Prime Minister Tisza might have seized on German pressure as an excuse to back out of a decision that he had undertaken only with the greatest reluctance, and his defection would have undermined the internal unity necessary for a successful war effort. Thus David Kaiser argues, "the Vienna

---

82. Lebow, *Between Peace and War*, p. 136, argues that "having finally crossed their psychological Rubicon, the Austrian leaders obviously felt a tremendous sense of psychological release and were hardly about to turn back willingly."
83. Albertini, *Origins*, Vol. 2, p. 514; Vol. 3, p. 643. See also Lynn-Jones, "Détente and Deterrence," pp. 139, 144; Kaiser, "Germany and the First World War," p. 471.
84. Lebow emphasizes Bethmann's increasing fatalism and perception of narrowing options and loss of control, induced by psychological stress; *Between Peace and War*, pp. 136–147.

government could not possibly have held out against united pressure to accept some variant of the Halt-in-Belgrade plan."[85]

But German pressure on Vienna was only moderate in intensity, accompanied by mixed signals, and withdrawn early. The Kaiser's proposal was ready for delivery early on July 28, before the declaration of war, but Bethmann delayed sending it to Ambassador Tschirschky in Vienna for twelve hours and distorted its content in significant ways to reduce its impact.[86] Tschirschky delayed further and in fact may have encouraged Austrian belligerency.[87] The ambiguous signals from Berlin continued even after Bethmann reversed course on July 29 and began pressing Vienna to accept Grey's Halt-in-Belgrade proposal. At the same time that Bethmann was urging Berchtold to consider the Halt-in-Belgrade proposal, Chief of the German General Staff Moltke was urging Conrad, his Austrian counterpart, to press forward with mobilization, and warning that any further delay would be disastrous. This led Conrad to complain, "Who actually rules in Berlin, Bethmann or Moltke?"[88]

Berlin's pressure, too weak to impress Austrian leaders with the potentially serious consequences of their failure to accept the peace proposal, was not sustained. Bethmann reversed his position and effectively withdrew German support from the Halt-in-Belgrade proposal on the evening of July 30, after fresh reports that Russia was about to begin mobilization, that Belgium had

85. Kaiser, "Germany and the First World War," p. 471. Albertini (*Origins*, Vol. 2, pp. 659, 669–673) concludes that "Berchtold was assailed by doubts and hesitations [about general mobilization on July 31], so that it remains an open question whether he would actually have put the order into execution if he had received further strong pressure from Berlin in favor of the Halt-in-Belgrade and mediation."
86. Whereas the Kaiser insisted only that Austria had to have a "guaranty that the promises were carried out," the chancellor emphasized in his telegram (No. 174) to German Ambassador Tschirschky that the aim of the temporary occupation was "to force the Serbian Government to the complete fulfillment of her demands"; Bethmann deleted the phrase about war no longer being necessary. He also told Tschirschky "to avoid very carefully giving rise to the impression that we wish to hold Austria back . . . [we must] find a way to realize Austria's desired aim . . . without at the same time bringing on a world war, and, if the latter cannot be avoided in the end, of improving the conditions under which we shall have to wage it." *German Documents*, pp. 288–289; Fischer, *Germany's Aims*, p. 72.
87. Tschirschky also delayed notifying Berlin of the Austrian declaration of war. Albertini concludes that Tschirschky and Berchtold "were in league" to deceive Berlin and deflect German pressure for restraint. *Origins*, Vol. 2, pp. 653–661.
88. Albertini, *Origins*, Vol. 2, pp. 673–674. Moltke may have acted with the approval of the Kaiser. Schmitt, *Coming of the War*, Vol. 2, pp. 198; Albertini, Vol. 3, pp. 11–13; Trachtenberg, "Meaning of Mobilization," p. 139. Ritter (*Sword and the Scepter*, Vol. 2, p. 258) states that Moltke's telegram arrived on July 31, after the Austrian decision for general mobilization.

begun preparations for war, and that Austria was concentrating its forces against Serbia.[89] These reports led to an abrupt shift in Moltke's position, an uneasiness among the military, an increase in military influence in the political decision-making process,[90] greater inclination toward a preventive war, and intense pressure for the declaration of a "state of imminent war."[91] The consequences were enormous. Albertini concludes that, "if on the 30th Bethmann had not let himself be overruled by Moltke, had insisted with Berchtold, on pain of non-recognition of the *casus foederis*, that Austria should content herself with the Anglo-German proposals, and had then waited for Sazonov to follow suit, the peace of the world might have been saved."[92]

The Russian mobilization was particularly important in the shift in German policy and escalation of the crisis,[93] careful examination reveals that the structure of Russian mobilization plans provided an opportunity for Russia to slow down the accelerating pace of events without threatening its vital interests. Nevertheless, the likelihood of war was already quite high by this point.

THE RUSSIAN MOBILIZATION

Russian leaders hoped that mobilization, in conjunction with diplomatic pressure from the other powers, would deter Austria from an all-out military attack against Serbia, limit the concessions Serbia would have to make, and improve Russia's ability to defend Serbia in the event of war.[94] Russia did

---

89. Belgian preparations might bottle up the German invasion of France, and therefore disrupt the entire war effort based on the Schlieffen Plan. Ulrich Trumpener, "War Premeditated? German Intelligence Operations in July 1914," *Central European History*, Vol. 9, No. 1 (March 1976), p. 77. Austrian concentration against Serbia would leave inadequate strength in Galicia for an offensive against Russia. Albertini, *Origins*, Vol. 2, p. 500; Turner, "Schlieffen Plan," p. 215.
90. The military did not exert much pressure on Bethmann prior to July 30. See note 48, above.
91. At 9 p.m. on July 30 Bethmann sent Telegram 200 to Vienna, requesting that Austria accept the Halt-in-Belgrade plan. But this request was not accompanied by the coercive pressure that was necessary for its success, and in any event it was followed in two hours by another telegram suspending the first. Albertini (*Origins*, Vol. 3, pp. 21–24) interprets this as evidence of the increasing influence of the military, but Trachtenberg ("Meaning of Mobilization," p. 139) dissents.
92. Albertini, *Origins*, Vol. 3, p. 31.
93. It led political and military decision-makers to believe that a continental war was inevitable and that they had lost control of events. These perceptions began to acquire a self-fulfilling character. Decision-makers became more willing to let events run their course, and efforts to deter war gave way to preparations for an unavoidable war. Joll, *First World War*, pp. 21, 107, 203; Lebow, *Between Peace and War*, pp. 134–139, 254–256.
94. Russian leaders also hoped that mobilization might help diffuse internal unrest. Fay, *Origins*, Vol. 2, p. 305; Hans Rogger, "Russia in 1914," Laqueur and Mosse, *1914*, pp. 229–253.

not need to mobilize to achieve these goals, however; it only needed to *threaten* to do so. The Austrian mobilization against Serbia posed no immediate military threat to Serbia, for an Austrian invasion could not begin until August 12. Neither did it threaten Russia. The longer Russia delayed, the more Austrian mobilization against Serbia would progress, and the more difficult it would be for Austria to mount a successful defense against any Russian offensive from the east, which would ultimately determine Austria's fate. As L.C.F. Turner concludes, "it was very much to Russia's advantage to delay any mobilization until a substantial part of the Austrian Army was entangled in operations against Serbia."[95]

Thus Russia could have delayed a partial mobilization for several more days without harming Russian interests in the Balkans. Such a delay would presumably have delayed the alarm felt by Moltke and the German generals, eliminated the need for a German mobilization or even preparatory military action, and thus provided more time for Bethmann to continue to press Vienna to accept the Halt-in-Belgrade plan. The Russian decision to mobilize was taken in part, wrote L.C.F. Turner, because "Sazonov and the Russian generals failed to grasp the immense diplomatic and military advantages conferred on them by the Austrian dilemma."[96]

The Russians' belief that mobilization against Austria was necessary had serious consequences, however, because for technical military reasons it would be costly to initiate a partial mobilization against Austria and then wait before mobilizing against Germany. A partial mobilization would disrupt railway transport and delay for months a systematic general mobilization against Germany. Russia would be dangerously exposed to a hostile and war-prone Germany, and unable to come immediately to the aid of France.[97] But Russian leaders perceived that speed was of the essence, that a few days' delay would put France in an increasingly precarious position, that war had become inevitable,[98] and consequently that they must mobilize as quickly as

---

95. Turner, *Origins*, p. 92; Turner, "Russian Mobilisation," p. 258, 266; Albertini, *Origins*, Vol. 2, p. 482; Vol. 3, p. 31.

96. Turner, *Origins*, p. 93; Turner, "Russian Mobilisation," pp. 258, 266; Kennedy, *War Plans*, p. 15. Sazonov's original plan was to wait until Austria invaded Serbia before initiating partial mobilization. Albertini, *Origins*, Vol. 2, p. 538.

97. Albertini concludes that the Russian choice was, "either general mobilization or none at all." Albertini, *Origins*, Vol. 2, p. 543. Russian General Danilov wrote a decade later that the military, given a choice, might have preferred no mobilization to partial mobilization. Turner, *Origins*, p. 92; Schilling, *How the War Began*, p. 117.

98. Trachtenberg, "Meaning of Mobilization," pp. 125–126. This belief was reinforced by Russia's

possible. Thus the Tsar, convinced that he lacked military options that would allow him to stand firm against Vienna without threatening Berlin, and beset by increasing pressure from the Russian military and from Sazonov, decided to order general mobilization for July 31 rather than a partial mobilization against Austria-Hungary alone.[99] This was tragic, because the Russian mobilization was the decisive act leading to the war,[100] and because Russian leaders failed to appreciate the diplomatic advantages and time for maneuver they derived from technical rigidities in Austrian mobilization and war plans.[101] Additional opportunities for Russia, rarely noted in the literature, were provided by German mobilization plans, discussed next.

THE GERMAN MOBILIZATION

Because German political and military leaders believed strongly that for diplomatic and domestic political reasons it was essential that Russia be perceived as the aggressor, they had a strong incentive *not* to be the first to mobilize. Thus some form of Russian mobilization was for all practical pur-

---

fear that Germany was looking for an opportunity to launch a preventive war against Russia. Van Evera, "Cult of the Offensive," pp. 86–89.

99. A general mobilization had been ordered and cancelled on July 29, and a partial mobilization was ordered that day.

100. Kennedy, *War Plans*, p. 15; Turner, "The Russian Mobilisation"; Albertini, *Origins*, Vol. 3, p. 31; Levy, "Organizational Routines," p. 210.

101. Russian political leaders' lack of comprehension of the meaning and consequences of mobilization also affected decision-making earlier in the crisis, though it is hard to assess its importance. Until fairly late in the crisis, Russian Foreign Minister Sazonov perceived partial mobilization as a usable and controllable instrument of coercion, and did not realize that it would precipitate a general mobilization by Austria, which would invoke the Austro-German alliance, trigger a general mobilization by Germany, and therefore lead to war. Nor did Sazonov realize that a Russian partial mobilization would seriously interfere with a subsequent general mobilization. His ignorance is explained in part by the fact that Janushkevich had been chief of staff for only five months, was not familiar with the details of mobilization, and therefore failed to warn Sazonov of the implications of partial mobilization. The situation was compounded further by Germany's failure to warn Russia of the risks involved. In fact, on July 27 Jagow had assured both the British and then the French ambassadors to Berlin that "if Russia only mobilized in the south, Germany would not mobilize." Albertini concludes that if Sazonov had understood this, there is "no doubt" that he would have acted differently. He would have attempted to delay mobilization, rather than press for it from July 24, or proclaim it on July 29, and the Tsar probably would have gone along. Albertini, *Origins*, Vol. 2, pp. 294, 480–482 (quotation), 624; Vol. 3, p. 43; Turner, "The Russian Mobilisation," p. 260; Van Evera, "Cult of the Offensive," p. 76. This would have slowed down the momentum of events in Germany and provided additional time for political leaders to find a diplomatic solution to the crisis through the Halt-in-Belgrade plan. But whether this would have made a significant difference is open to question, for in the absence of an early partial mobilization by Russia it is unclear whether Grey would have issued the warning that induced Germany to restrain Austria. See Trachtenberg, "Meaning of Mobilization," for a critique of this line of argument.

poses a necessary condition for German mobilization. Russian *general* mobilization was a *sufficient* condition for German mobilization; but was a Russian *partial* mobilization a sufficient condition? Although Albertini and others may be correct that a partial mobilization by Russia "would have led to war no less surely than general mobilization,"[102] the causal linkage was delayed and indirect rather than immediate and direct: a Russian partial mobilization would eventually lead to a German mobilization because of the Russian threat to Austria, not because of the direct threat to Germany. In fact, the Russian threat to Germany would have been lessened somewhat as Russian partial mobilization measures against Austria progressed, because they would have delayed a subsequent Russian general mobilization.[103] If Russian leaders had known of these diplomatic and domestic political constraints on Germany, and recognized that rigidities in the Russian mobilization plans gave Germany incentives to delay mobilization, Russia could have avoided its fateful mobilization without undermining its coercive pressure against either Austria or Germany.

This argument is supported by evidence that German military and political leaders were cautious in reacting to Russian military actions prior to the Russian general mobilization. Germany did not respond in kind to Russia's pre-mobilization measures, as evidenced by Moltke's refusal to support War Minister von Falkenhayn's July 29 proposal for a proclamation of *Kriegsgefahrzustand*, or "threatening danger of war."[104] Later that evening Bethmann refused to order an immediate German mobilization, on the grounds that Germany must wait for a state of war between Russia and Austria-Hungary,[105] "because otherwise we should not have public opinion with us either at home or in England."[106] The German military began pressing hard for

---

102. Albertini, *Origins*, Vol. 2, pp. 292–293, 485n. See also Turner, *Origins*, pp. 92, 104; Snyder, *Ideology of the Offensive*, p. 88; Kennedy, *War Plans*, pp. 16–17; Van Evera, "Cult of the Offensive," p. 88; Levy, "Organizational Routines," p. 198.
103. An early partial Russian mobilization would also have allowed Austria to avoid a premature partial mobilization against Serbia.
104. Note that Falkenhayn did not believe that a preemptive mobilization by Germany was necessary. Albertini, *Origins*, pp. 496–497, 502; Trachtenberg, "Meaning of Mobilization," p. 138.
105. Moreover, Austria must not appear as the aggressor. Late on July 29, Moltke, with unanimous support, instructed Conrad: "Do not declare war on Russia but wait for Russia's attack." Fischer, *War of Illusions*, p. 496.
106. Moltke objected to this only slightly. Fischer, *War of Illusions*, pp. 495–496; Fischer, *War Aims*, p. 85. Although Russia had initiated partial mobilization by this time, it is not clear that Bethmann was aware of it. Albertini, *Origins*, pp. 502–503.

Kriegsgefahrzustand only at noon July 30, after receiving new information regarding the intensity of Russian military preparations, but Bethmann rejected this demand.[107] Only with the news of the Russian general mobilization at noon the following day did Bethmann agree to a German mobilization.[108]

Once both sides had mobilized, however, Germany had a strong incentive to strike first because of the demands of the Schlieffen Plan. Because the capture of Liège, with its vital forts and railroad lines, was necessary before the invasion of France could proceed, the Schlieffen Plan required that German armies cross the frontier and advance into Belgium as an integral part of mobilization. The perception that even small leads in mobilization would have significant military benefits and that small delays could be catastrophic created additional military incentives to move as quickly as possible.[109] Thus once Russia moved to a general mobilization, the German decision for war would immediately follow because of the structure of the alliance system and existing mobilization plans. Military requirements of preparing for war took precedence over political requirements for avoiding one, and a continental war was inevitable. Because the Schlieffen Plan involved movement through Belgium, a world war was almost certain to follow.[110]

The Schlieffen Plan made it inevitable that *any* war involving Germany would necessarily be a two-front war in which Britain would be forced to intervene, independently of the particular issues at stake or the political conditions under which it occurred. This worst-case outcome for Germany derives in part from the separation of military planning in the previous decade from the political objectives which it was presumably designed to serve, and from the disproportionate emphasis given to *winning* a war, as

---

107. *Kriegsgefahrzustand* would make mobilization more likely but not automatic. Albertini, *Origins*, Vol. 2, pp. 491, 599; Vol. 3, pp. 6–18; Trachtenberg, "Meaning of Mobilization," p. 138n. Bethmann did promise the military a decision by noon on July 31.

108. At this point Berlin sent a 12-hour ultimatum to St. Petersburg demanding that all military preparations be stopped. The Russian rejection of this demand was followed by the German declaration of war on August 1. Albertini, *Origins*, Vol. 2, pp. 494–503 and Vol. 3, pp. 6–18; Fischer, *Germany's Aims*, pp. 85–86.

109. Van Evera, "Cult of the Offensive," pp. 71–79; Turner, "Schlieffen Plan," p. 216; Levy, "Organizational Routines," pp. 195–196. See Trachtenberg's critique in "Meaning of Mobilization."

110. Albertini, *Origins* Vol. 2, p. 480; Turner, *Origins*, p. 63; A.J.P. Taylor, *War by Time-table* (London: Macdonald, 1969), p. 25; Levy, "Organizational Routines," pp. 197–198. For analyses of the feasibility of a German offensive in the East while Germany maintained a defensive holding action in the West, see Snyder, *Ideology of the Offensive*, pp. 116–122.

opposed to deterring it in the first place.[111] The Schlieffen Plan was constructed exclusively by the military, who consulted only minimally with civilian leaders, and on the basis of technical military considerations rather than political ones.[112] The sweep through Belgium, for example, did not take into account the political impact on England of the violation of Belgian neutrality.[113]

The narrow military orientation of the Schlieffen Plan, and the rigidities that made it difficult to modify by political leaders in response to changing political circumstances, was compounded by the limits on political leaders' knowledge of the nature of mobilization and how existing plans might constrain their strategy of coercive diplomacy.[114] The mobilization plans, which they thought provided an instrument for an admittedly risky strategy of coercive diplomacy, had in fact been constructed as a strategy which was to be implemented only when war was perceived to be inevitable. Bethmann might very well have acted differently had he realized that his attempts to neutralize Britain would be defeated by the demands of the Schlieffen Plan.[115]

These and related points have led numerous analysts to conclude that the mobilization plans of the European great powers were themselves one of the leading causes of World War I.[116] However, though it was hardly insignifi-

---

111. Technical military planning and military influence in political decision-making in the final stages of the July crisis are also evident in Russia, less so in France and Britain. Lieven, *Russia and the First World War*, pp. 63, 122. Steiner, *Britain and the First World War*, p. 220; John V. Keiger, *France and the Origins of the First World War* (New York: St. Martin's, 1983), chap. 7; Kennedy, *War Plans*, p. 7.
112. Thus Taylor argues that the mobilization plans "aimed at the best technical results without allowing for either the political conditions from which war might spring or the political consequences which might follow." Taylor, *War by Time-table*, p. 19; Ritter, *Schlieffen Plan*; Ritter, *Sword and the Scepter*, Vol. 2, chap. 9; Turner, "Schlieffen Plan," pp. 205, 277; Snyder, *Ideology of the Offensive*, chap. 4; Kennedy, *War Plans*, p. 17.
113. Jagow's request in 1912 that the plan for violation of Belgian neutrality be re-evaluated was rejected by Moltke, and until 1913 there was not even an inquiry into the feasibility of alternative operational plans than might carry fewer political risks. Snyder, *Ideology of the Offensive*, p. 121; Ritter, *Sword and the Scepter*, Vol. 2, p. 205.
114. Albertini (*Origins*, Vol. 2, p. 479) argues, "they had no knowledge of what mobilization actually was, what demands it made on the country, what consequences it brought with it, to what risks it exposed the peace of Europe." See also Levy, "Organizational Routines," pp. 209–210.
115. Albertini, *Origins*, Vol. 3, p. 249. Bethmann knew of plans to seize Liège, but he did not learn until July 31 that the invasion of Belgium must begin on the third day of mobilization (Turner, *Origins*, p. 213). Jagow, Tirpitz, and the Kaiser had even less knowledge about the Schlieffen Plan.
116. Ritter (*Schlieffen Plan*, p. 90) argues that "the outbreak of war in 1914 is the most tragic example of a government's helpless dependence on the planning of strategists that history has ever seen." Albertini (*Origins*, Vol. 3, p. 253) concludes that the primary reason that Germany

cant, the causal importance of this factor should not be exaggerated. These mobilization plans were part of the overall structure of constraints on the strategic choices of each of the great powers at several critical junctures in the July crisis, but we must keep in mind that these military mobilization and war plans were in place long before. They were the products of diplomatic alignments, strategic beliefs about the offensive nature of warfare, bureaucratic compromises among political and military leaders, and political and cultural assumptions about the interests of each of the great powers and the fundamental dynamics of international politics.[117] Although the mobilization plans, and the confusion surrounding them, clearly contributed to the spiral of escalation in the July crisis, the inference that the plans themselves were the primary cause of the war would be spurious.

Conclusions

I have argued that political leaders in each of the great powers in the July crisis preferred a peaceful settlement to a world war. The primary explanation for the outbreak of the world war, which none of the leading decision-makers of the European great powers wanted, expected, or deliberately sought, lies in the irreconcilable interests defined by state officials, the structure of international power and alliances that created intractable strategic dilemmas, the particular plans for mobilization and war that were generated by these strategic constraints, decision-makers' critical assumptions regarding the likely behavior of their adversaries and the consequences of their own actions, and domestic political constraints on their freedom of action. Thus the causes of World War I are to be found primarily in the underlying economic, military, diplomatic, political, and social forces which existed prior to the onset of the crisis. These forces shaped the policy preferences of statesmen and the strategic and political constraints within which they had to make extraordinarily difficult decisions. Thus the probability of war was already quite high at the time of the assassination.

"set fire to the powder cask" lay in "the requirements of the Schlieffen Plan, which no doubt was a masterpiece of military science, but also a monument of that utter lack of political horse-sense which is the main cause of European disorders and upheavals." See also Taylor, *War by Time-table,* p. 19; Turner, *Origins;* Levy, "Organizational Routines," pp. 209–210.

117. Van Evera, "Cult of the Offensive," pp. 58–63; Snyder, *Ideology of the Offensive;* Sagan, "1914 Revisited"; Kennedy, *War Plans,* pp. 18–19; James Joll, *1914: The Unspoken Assumptions* (London: Weidenfeld and Nicolson, 1968); Levy, "Organizational Routines," pp. 203–218.

To say that war was likely, however, is not to say that it was inevitable. At several critical points in the July crisis, political leaders took actions that increased the probability of war, and failed to take others that might have bought additional time for crisis management without seriously threatening their vital interests. No war would have occurred in the absence of the German assumption that Britain would stay neutral in a continental conflict, or at least not intervene until France was on the verge of being crushed, but that assumption was not entirely unreasonable given the information available at the time. Britain's allies and in fact Grey himself were uncertain of what Britain would do. An earlier explicit warning from Grey might have been sufficient, but he was faced with a strategic dilemma and severe domestic constraints.

An earlier punitive strike by Austria might have avoided a larger war, but that was delayed by political pressures related to the domestic structure of the Dual Monarchy and by cumbersome mobilization plans that precluded immediate action. The ultimatum and the acute international crisis that followed transformed the minimum military option from a punitive strike to a more substantial invasion and therefore increased the likelihood of Russian intervention. The Halt-in-Belgrade plan was the only remaining hope for peace, but this required strong and perhaps highly coercive pressure on Vienna from Berlin. However, such pressure could not be forthcoming until Grey's actions induced a change in German expectations. The Halt-in-Belgrade plan was undercut by Vienna's premature and politically motivated declaration of war, which increased the reputational and domestic costs to Austrian leaders if they subsequently reversed course; by insufficient pressures on Vienna from Berlin; and by the premature Russian mobilization. The Russian partial mobilization on July 29 was the crucial action of the escalating crisis. It occurred because Russian leaders feared that war was inevitable, and because they failed to recognize German diplomatic and domestic incentives not to mobilize first and Russian military incentives to refrain from responding immediately to the Austrian mobilization against Serbia.[118]

Some of these miscalculations and failures of judgment might have been avoided, and some of the domestic and bureaucratic pressures might have

---

118. It is perhaps not surprising that decision-makers in 1914, with limited information and under tremendous pressure, may have missed some opportunities for crisis management. Indeed, after seven decades of research and reflection, scholars continue to debate the consequences of the mobilization plans.

been finessed, but it is extraordinarily difficult to assess the causal impact of these missteps and missed opportunities. Europe in 1914 was a highly inter-dependent and chaotic system in which small changes could have enormous and therefore unpredictable effects, and it is impossible to validate counter-factual propositions with any degree of confidence. But my judgment is that the causal effects of these miscalculations and oversights were modest relative to the structure of incentives and constraints which were already in place; the miscalculations were, in part, the product of those incentives and con-straints and the underlying strategic assumptions that helped shape them. The windows of opportunity for the management of the July crisis by political leaders were narrow and constantly changing, at different rates and different times for each of the great powers in response to its own political dynamics. This placed enormous demands on the intellectual, diplomatic, and political skills of leading decision-makers. It is certainly possible that the July crisis might have ended differently if other individuals had been in positions of power at the beginning of July 1914.[119] But even the most successful cases of crisis management are characterized by numerous misperceptions and per-haps some good luck as well. Thus, it is problematic to infer a causal rela-tionship between war and misperceptions and missed opportunities, or to validate the counterfactual proposition that better crisis management would have resulted in a more peaceful outcome, particularly when the strategic and political constraints on central decision-makers are this severe.[120]

Moreover, even if Austria had agreed to the Halt-in-Belgrade proposal, and even if that bought enough time for the negotiation of a peaceful settle-ment, it is far from certain that this settlement would have been sufficiently stable to survive the next crisis that would inevitably arise in the next few months or the next few years—particularly in light of Germany's continued concern about its ability to prevail in a future war against an increasingly powerful Russia, and the likelihood of continued domestic political instability in the Austro-Hungarian, Russian, and German empires.

---

119. Of course, different individuals (a Bismarck, for example) might have attempted to prevent the European state system from developing into a rigid two-bloc system prior to 1914.
120. The crisis mismanagement hypothesis would be more compelling if it were validated by some type of comparative research design that controlled for context—for example, one that identified other crises with equally incompatible preferences and equally constraining strategic and domestic pressures, but that turned out differently because of skillful crisis management.

Clio Deceived

Holger H. Herwig

Patriotic Self-Censorship in Germany after the Great War

$\mathbf{J}$oseph Fouché, a man for all seasons who served the Directory, Consulate, Empire, and Restoration as minister of police, was once reputed to have stated that any two lines from any *oeuvre* would suffice to have its author hanged. Indeed, the efforts of various Germans, both in official and private capacities, to undertake what John Röhl has termed "patriotic self-censorship" with regard to the origins of the Great War reflect the sentiment expressed by the great French censor a century earlier.[1] For nearly fifty years, until Fritz Fischer's *Griff nach der Weltmacht* appeared in 1961, which in many ways offered German readers the findings of the Italian author Luigi Albertini, the German interpretation of the origins of the First World War was dominated in large measure by the efforts of "patriotic self-censors," and particularly by the historical writings of Alfred von Wegerer.[2]

Let me state at the outset that I accept the basic tenets of Fischer's research—with the notable exceptions of the allegedly decisive "war council" of December 8, 1912 and the so-called "bid for *world* power" in 1914. The Hamburg historian, assisted by a coterie of talented students, has convincingly documented that Vienna and Berlin opted for war in July 1914 in the belief that time was running out for both of them. In the case of Austria–

I am indebted to Professors Werner T. Angress at the State University of New York at Stony Brook and Melvyn P. Leffler of the University of Virginia for their sage advice in the preparation of this article.

Holger H. Herwig is Professor of History at Vanderbilt University.

1. John Röhl, ed., *1914: Delusion or Design? The testimony of two German diplomats* (London: Elek, 1973), p. 37. The literature on this topic is truly immense—there are no fewer than 3,000 books extant on the events at Sarajevo in June 1914 alone. For two recent updates, see Ulrich Heinemann, *Die verdrängte Niederlage: Politische Öffentlichkeit und Kriegsschuldfrage in der Weimarer Republik* (Göttingen: Vandenhoeck & Ruprecht, 1983); and Wolfgang Jäger, *Historische Forschung und politische Kultur in Deutschland: Die Debatte 1914–1980 über den Ausbruch des Ersten Weltkrieges* (Göttingen: Vandenhoeck & Ruprecht, 1984).
2. Fritz Fischer, *Griff nach der Weltmacht: Die Kriegszielpolitik des kaiserlichen Deutschland 1914/18* (Düsseldorf: Droste, 1961); Luigi Albertini, *The Origins of the War of 1914* (London: Oxford University Press, 1952–57), 3 vols. (Italian edition, *Le origini della guerra del 1914* [Milan: Fratelli Bocca, 1942–43], 3 vols.); Alfred von Wegerer, *Der Ausbruch des Weltkrieges 1914* (Hamburg: Hanseatische Verlagsanstalt, 1939), 2 vols.

International Security, Fall 1987 (Vol. 12, No. 2)
© 1987 by the President and Fellows of Harvard College and of the Massachusetts Institute of Technology.

Hungary, only a military strike against Serbia could retard the centrifugal forces of nationalism within the Dual Monarchy; for Germany, only preventive war with Russia would allow the Reich to secure continental hegemony before the Russian "Great Program" of rearmament was completed by 1917. Statesmen and soldiers in both Vienna and Berlin in July 1914 assumed a "strike now better than later" mentality. In both capitals, they accepted the "calculated risk" of a general European war in order to shore up—and, if at all possible, to expand—Otto von Bismarck's position of semi-hegemony in Europe.

This article will trace the genesis and course of the official campaign in the Weimar Republic (and beyond) to counter Allied charges of German war guilt (Article 231 of the Treaty of Versailles), and offer some suggestions concerning its impact upon subsequent German affairs. The inquiry will show that the German government as early as 1914, and especially during the period from November 1918 to June 1919, sought to "organize" materials in order to answer questions concerning the origins of the war. Further, it will show that from June 1919 through the Third Reich, key elements of the German bureaucracy mounted a massive and successful campaign of disinformation that purveyed false propaganda through a wide range of channels. These included the War Guilt Section (*Kriegsschuldreferat*) of the Foreign Ministry, which disseminated its official stance on war guilt most notably through two agencies which it recruited to this end—the Working Committee of German Associations (*Arbeitsausschuss Deutscher Verbände*) and the Center for the Study of the Causes of the War (*Zentralstelle zur Erforschung der Kriegsschuldfrage*)—as well as a parliamentary Committee of Enquiry (*Untersuchungsausschuss*). Writers were also engaged either directly or indirectly by the Foreign Ministry to propagate its views, to organize translations of foreign studies sympathetic to the German cause, and to channel the Wilhelmstrasse's official line to German schools and diplomatic missions via newspapers and radio. Finally, some comments will be directed toward several important memoirs which were either "ordered" by patriotic editors or watered down in their final published versions in an attempt to preserve a national–conservative version of history.

By selectively editing documentary collections, suppressing honest scholarship, subsidizing pseudo-scholarship, underwriting mass propaganda, and overseeing the export of this propaganda especially to Britain, France, and the United States, the patriotic self-censors in Berlin exerted a powerful influence on public and elite opinion in Germany and, to a lesser extent, outside Germany. Their efforts polluted historical understanding both at home and abroad well into the post-1945 period. Indeed, the acrimonious debate since 1983 concerning the originality of Kurt Riezler's diaries especially during the critical July crisis is but the most outward symptom of this ongoing historical conundrum.

The significance of the campaign of official and semi-official obfuscation and perversion of fact extends well beyond the history of Germany or the origins of the Great War. It raises basic questions concerning the role of the historian in society, scholarly integrity, decency, and public morality. It further illustrates the universal problem of establishing the critical record of events that are sufficiently vital to the national interest to become the objects of partisan propaganda. What is the present generation, for example, to make of the collective and concerted efforts of eminent German scholars purposefully to distort their countrymen's study of history and sociology of knowledge? Does a perverse law operate whereby those events that are most important are hardest to understand because they attract the greatest attention from mythmakers and charlatans? And is a nation well-served when its intellectual establishment conspires to obstruct honest investigation into national catastrophes, upon which past, present, and future vital national interests can be reassessed? The far-reaching effects of the resulting disinformation are incalculable.

Several other, related issues require to be addressed tangentially. Nazi expansionism clearly fed upon the fertile intellectual basis laid down for it by the patriotic self-censors in the 1920s. In other words, Adolf Hitler's radical "revisionism" was already well-rooted in public and elite opinion under the Weimar Republic. Finally, the export of this propaganda to Britain, France, and the United States did its part, however major or minor, to undermine the moral and eventually the strategic terms of the settlement of 1919. No less a statesman than Gustav Stresemann clearly recognized that patriotic self-censorship served to buttress his policy of rapprochement with the West as a necessary precondition for revision of what most Germans considered to be the most onerous clauses of the Versailles *Diktat*.

Last but not least, my investigation bears directly upon the nature and meaning of the "1914 analogy," which continues to influence political science thought on the possible causes of a third world war. I suggest that the history upon which that analogy was based has been distorted. It serves no purpose to continue to believe that Europe "slid" into war unknowingly in 1914, that no nation harbored aggressive tendencies during the July crisis, and that fate or providence alone designed this cruel course of events. Indeed, the "1914 analogy" ought to be rethought and reworked in light of the actual mindset of German political, diplomatic, and military leaders in 1914.

To sum up: Clio was, in fact, deceived in Germany as early as 1914. It is not my purpose to indict either individuals or nations. We might do well to keep before us the words of the epitaph that the historian Hans Delbrück chose for his gravestone:

Veritatem colui

Patriam delixi.[3]

Deployment of Illusions

On August 3, 1914, the day before the Great War officially began, the Imperial German government published a "colored book" to explain its stance on the origins of the conflict. Entitled the *Deutsches Weissbuch*, the tome represented a hasty sifting of the archives of the Foreign Office. On the last day of that month, Foreign Secretary Gottlieb von Jagow directed his Under Secretary, Arthur Zimmermann, to entertain a more "comprehensive publication" of documents for what Jagow was certain would become a heated debate. He instructed Zimmermann to take as his *Leitmotiv* the following: "The ring of entente politics encircled us ever more tightly."[4] The most knowledgeable authority on the war-guilt question, Imanuel Geiss, has suggested that this was already the germ cell of the postwar documentary editions. In fact, Legation Secretary Bernhard Wilhelm von Bülow, who for much of the war oversaw the holdings of the Wilhelmstrasse as political archivist and who would head its attempts at patriotic self-censorship after 1919, probably undertook already during the Great War a first "ordering" of the documents concerning the July crisis of 1914.[5] Whatever the truth of the matter, it was only after the trauma of defeat and revolution—first in Russia, and then in Germany—that official documents saw the light of day.

---

3. "I sought the truth; I loved my country." Cited in Arden Bucholz, *Hans Delbrück & The German Military Establishment: War Images in Conflict* (Iowa City: University of Iowa Press, 1985), p. 174.
4. Cited in Imanuel Geiss, ed., *Julikrise und Kriegsausbruch 1914* (Hanover: Verlag für Literatur und Zeitgeschehen, 1963), Vol. 1, p. 29.
5. Ibid., pp. 29–30. See also Bernhard W. von Bülow, "Die Behandlung der Schuldfrage," *Deutsche Nation*, Vol. 3 (1921), pp. 334–337; Bülow, *Die Grundlinien der diplomatischen Verhandlungen bei Kriegsausbruch* (Charlottenburg: Deutsche Verlagsgesellschaft für Politik und Geschichte, 1919); as well as Bülow and Max Montgelas, eds., *Kommentar zu den Deutschen Dokumenten zum Kriegsausbruch* (Berlin: Deutsche Verlagsgesellschaft für Politik und Geschichte, n.d.).

Indeed, only the Independent Socialists (USPD) demanded that Germany reveal the truth concerning the origins of the war, regardless of where the blame lay. On November 21, 1918, Kurt Eisner, Minister–President of the revolutionary government in Bavaria, instructed his envoy in Berlin to press the Provisional Government of Friedrich Ebert to publish all documents pertinent to the outbreak of the war. Two days later, Eisner provided Munich newspapers with excerpts from the reports of the Bavarian plenipotentiary at Berlin in July/August 1914 to show that the war had been orchestrated by what Eisner termed "a small horde of mad Prussian military" men as well as "allied" industrialists, capitalists, politicians, and princes.[6] At about the same time in Berlin, Karl Kautsky, who had recently joined the USPD, had suggested as early as November 13 that the Provisional Government publish documents relating to July 1914. The Provisional Government, composed of Independent as well as Majority Socialists (SPD), formally entrusted him with this task on December 9. Not surprisingly, given the sensational nature of Eisner's actions and perhaps fearing that documents might be destroyed, the Berlin regime on November 26 placed all former imperial archives under its protection.[7]

While Kautsky labored at his editorial task, the German Socialist movement in December 1918 tore itself apart in Berlin: the Independent Socialists left the Cabinet on December 29, and on the last day of the year the most radical socialists formed the Communist Party (KPD). Kautsky was now politically isolated. It was to be a harbinger of things to come that when he completed his task in March 1919, the Foreign Ministry, desiring to brand the highly critical work with the "stigma of treasonable socialism," opposed and delayed its publication. Kautsky was denied access to the Wilhelmstrasse's archives, and all secret documents in his possession were recalled. In July 1919, the Cabinet of Chancellor Gustav Bauer, now devoid of any Independent Socialists, went one step further and entrusted a second documentary publication to the more conservative duo of Count Maximilian von Montgelas and Walter Schücking. And while it could not formally censor and obstruct Kautsky's efforts for fear of thereby alienating the still dominant SPD, the Foreign Ministry nevertheless did all within its power to prevent the timely publi-

---

6. Jäger, *Historische Forschung*, pp. 22–23.
7. Erich Matthias, ed., *Die Regierung der Volksbeauftragten 1918/19* (Düsseldorf: Droste, 1969), Vol. 1, pp. 139–140. For the genesis of Kautsky's orders to publish the documents, see ibid., pp. 102, 243, 258.

cation of Kautsky's volumes. The campaign of what Erich Hahn has termed "preemptive historiography" was in full swing.[8]

That campaign was directed by what one historian has called the "general staff of the war-guilt struggle": the "Special Bureau v. Bülow" at the turn of the year 1918–19, and its successor in 1920, the War Guilt Section of the Foreign Ministry. Chief of this "general staff" was Legation Secretary Bernhard W. von Bülow, a future state secretary of the Wilhelmstrasse (1930–36).[9] Aided by five special assistants, Bülow set out to catalog the Foreign Ministry's holdings for ready reference: by May 1919, a special *Kartothek*, or card index of 7,000 documents, both in chronological and subject order, was ready. A special register of names to expedite further the Bureau's work was also prepared.[10] By and large, the final result of these endeavors is today's *Politisches Archiv* of the Foreign Ministry at Bonn, West Germany.

Bülow was appointed to this special post by Foreign Minister Count Ulrich von Brockdorff–Rantzau, who commenced his assignment at the peace negotiations in Paris by assuring the French that one of his ancestors had indeed been the father of Louis XIV, and that in his family the Bourbons had been considered "bastard Rantzaus for the past three hundred years." The unctuous Matthias Erzberger, head of the Catholic Centre Party and of the German armistice commission, also favored Bülow's appointment as he feared the damage that a possible publication of the Kautsky documents might do abroad. In fact, Bülow's most immediate task in 1919 was to do the spade work for the upcoming "negotiations" with the victorious Allies in Paris. An ardent nationalist and zealous bureaucrat, Bülow began to comb the recently published Soviet documents concerning the Tsar's foreign policy before July 1914 for incriminating materials that could be used against the Allies at Paris, and next studied and published critiques of the various

8. Geiss, *Julikrise*, Vol. 1, pp. 30–32; Erich J.C. Hahn, "The German Foreign Ministry and the Question of War Guilt in 1918–1919," in Carole Fink, Isabel V. Hull, and MacGregor Knox, eds., *German Nationalism and the European Response, 1890–1945* (Norman and London: University of Oklahoma Press, 1985), pp. 47, 49; and Heinemann, *Die verdrängte Niederlage*, pp. 75–77. The Berlin project appeared in 1919 in two versions: Karl Kautsky, *Wie der Weltkrieg entstand: Dargestellt nach dem Aktenmaterial des Deutschen Auswärtigen Amts* (Berlin: P. Cassirer, 1919); and Max Montgelas and Walter Schücking, eds., *Die Deutschen Dokumente zum Kriegsausbruch 1914* (Berlin: Deutsche Verlagsgesellschaft für Politik und Geschichte, 1919), 5 vols. The latter series was reprinted in 1922 and 1927. For the Cabinet's decision to recall Kautsky's project and to add Montgelas and Schücking as editors, see Anton Golecki, ed., *Akten der Reichskanzlei: Weimarer Republik. Das Kabinett Bauer* (Boppard: H. Boldt, 1980), pp. 137–138. Session of July 21, 1919.
9. Jäger, *Historische Forschung*, p. 47.
10. Heinemann, *Die verdrängte Niederlage*, p. 38.

"colored books" put out by Belgium, Britain, France, and Rumania to show that they were incomplete and inaccurate.[11] Yet his greatest task was to prepare the case against the Allied charge that Germany (and Austria–Hungary) was solely responsible for the Great War, and the accompanying demand for the surrender and trial of major "war criminals" (later, Article 228 of the Versailles treaty)—a demand that threatened to reach into the very chambers of the Wilhelmstrasse.

On January 7, 1919, Erzberger convened a special meeting with representatives of the Foreign Office and the erstwhile Supreme Command of the Army (O.H.L.). It was decided that Bülow would undertake research in the diplomatic records on the issue of war guilt; Major Bodo von Harbou, a former assistant to General Erich Ludendorff, was entrusted with similar work in the military records. On January 22, a second meeting was called to hammer out what was to become the official German position on the issue of war guilt. The documentary collections of Bülow and Harbou were to contain materials specifically designed to show that the entente had "for a long time systematically and jointly prepared for a war against Germany," that they, rather than Germany, were to be accorded "immediate guilt" for provoking war in 1914. Specifically, the researchers were instructed to amass materials that would document France's ever-increasing armaments outlays before 1914, Britain's intensive training of its "continental army" for deployment in Europe, Italy's provocations of Austria–Hungary and, above all, Russia's long-term stockpiling of financial means with which to conduct war against Germany.[12] These views were formally adopted by the Foreign Ministry's Office for Peace Negotiations (*Geschäftsstelle für die Friedensverhandlungen*) in February 1919. Moreover, the Office's head, Count Johann Heinrich von Bernstorff, the former German ambassador to the United States, asked Jagow, who had been Foreign Secretary in 1914, to prepare the pivotal position paper on the July crisis—along with the former head of his political section, Wilhelm von Stumm. At the express request of General Detlof von Winterfeldt of the General Staff, Jagow was asked to highlight therein "France's *revanche* policy" especially with regard to the reconquest of Alsace–

---

11. Ibid., p. 38; and Hahn, "German Foreign Ministry," p. 62. The so-called "colored books" were hastily assembled in the wake of the July crisis and included genuine as well as falsified materials; among the major powers, there were the Austro–Hungarian *Red Book*, the British *Blue Book*, the French *Yellow Book*, the German *White Book*, and the Russian *Orange Book*. See the Introduction to Albertini, *The Origins of the War of 1914*, Vol. 1.

12. Heinemann, *Die verdrängte Niederlage*, pp. 38–39.

Lorraine. Finally, the participants agreed to contact the former Great General Staff, Prussian War Ministry, and Imperial Navy Office to compile materials designed not only to refute the expected charge that Germany had started the war, but also to demonstrate Allied transgressions against international law both before and during the war.[13]

Bülow, who had gone to assist Brockdorff–Rantzau at Paris, was of course fully aware of the delicate nature of his task. As he returned official diplomatic records to Berlin, he instructed the later head of the *Kriegsschuldreferat*, Hans Freytag, to lock them up in a special safe so that "in case the entente should demand them"—as they apparently intended to reserve the right to do (later, Article 230 of the Versailles treaty)—"they can be got out of the way easily."[14] And in assembling his documents, Bülow might well have been aware of Fouché's *bon mot* cited at the beginning of this article: the legation secretary in an uncharacteristically candid moment informed Freytag that "any nation can be charged successfully" on the basis of its documents; "I would undertake 'to prove' conclusively from the archives of any nation that it, and it alone, is responsible for the war—or for whatever else you like."[15] In keeping with this spirit of selection, Bülow divided the documents that he assembled into two categories, marked "defense" and "offense."

The immediate result of these efforts was the "professors' memorandum" of May 27, 1919. Submitted to the Allies by Hans Delbrück, Max von Montgelas, Albrecht Mendelssohn–Bartholdy, and Max Weber, all members of the Heidelberg Association for a Policy of Justice, the document asserted that Germany in 1914 had conducted a "defensive war against Tsarism," "the most dreadful system of enslavement . . . ever devised before the present peace treaty." The memorandum certainly was based upon documents from the "Special Bureau v. Bülow" (today, "Weltkrieg, Vols. 1–16, Juli–August 1914" at Bonn); most likely, it was also penned by Bülow, well before the professors ever arrived at Paris. The academicians managed to agree to it in less than a week—probably a record of sorts. Their "prestigious autographs" lent the political document "the hallmark of independent scholarship."[16] All four undoubtedly signed it for patriotic reasons. Weber in his heart of hearts

---

13. Ibid., p. 39.
14. Cited in Hahn, "German Foreign Ministry," p. 63, n. 48.
15. Cited in ibid., p. 67. Bülow to Freytag, May 31, 1919.
16. Ibid., pp. 64–65; Geiss, *Julikrise*, Vol. 1, pp. 30–31; and Heinemann, *Die verdrängte Niederlage*, p. 45. See also Hagen Schulze, ed., *Akten der Reichskanzlei: Weimarer Republik. Das Kabinett Scheidemann* (Boppard: H. Boldt, 1971), pp. 384–385, n. 10.

at least knew better, and privately confessed to Delbrück that he "shuddered" at the thought of "what might be in our documents."[17]

The initial efforts to address Allied charges of war guilt described above had been largely inspired by the belief that Germany could hope to gain moderate peace terms on the basis of President Woodrow Wilson's Fourteen Points only if it could "prove" either that others had also harbored aggressive notions in July 1914 or that it had merely reacted to external threats. Specifically, the Hamburg banker Max Warburg had made it plain in March 1919 that Germany could not hope to obtain much-needed credits unless it could effectively reject war-guilt accusations. Moreover, the entire question of reparations, at least to the Germans, seemed to be legally based upon their acceptance of moral responsibility for the start of the war. In addition, there existed the possibility that the Allies might go ahead with their demands that German "war criminals" be handed over for trial, and that German records likewise be surrendered to serve as the basis of such proceedings.

The crisis situation in this respect reached fever pitch on two occasions: May 7, 1919, when the Allies handed the Germans the text of the proposed peace accord; and June 16, 1919, when Premier Georges Clemenceau presented Berlin with an ultimatum either to accept the offered terms or to renew the fighting. The Germans reacted on May 28 by submitting to the Allies a second *White Book*, which Brockdorff–Rantzau concurrently released for publication; its core was the famous professors' memorandum previously mentioned. Of course, these German efforts at "revision," as the campaign to overturn war-guilt charges was now labeled, had virtually no effect on the Allies. The Reich had no choice but to accept the *Diktat* on June 28, 1919. Therewith, the immediacy of the revisionist campaign momentarily passed.

The Wilhelmstrasse now changed tactics. It devised a long-term project to publish its records from before 1914 in order to buttress its rejection of Article 231—and possibly to force the Allies to open their archives as well. In fact, Count von Bernstorff, head of the Foreign Ministry's Office for Peace Negotiations, had suggested to the Cabinet as early as March 1919 that 1870 was the place to start.[18] That suggestion gained impetus on December 10, 1919, when British and Dutch newspapers leaked excerpts pertinent to the

---

17. Wolfgang J. Mommsen, *Max Weber und die deutsche Politik 1890–1920* (Tübingen: Mohr, 1974), p. 340. Weber to Delbrück, October 8, 1919.
18. Schulze, *Das Kabinett Scheidemann*, pp. 86–87, session of March 22, 1919; and Hahn, "German Foreign Ministry," pp. 67, 68.

July crisis from Karl Kautsky's collection of documents. Such a broad investigation offered the additional prospect of shifting attention from the immediate causes of the Great War to a less sensitive debate about European affairs in general over the past four decades. Consensus to proceed with this project was reached by the Cabinet on July 21, 1919.

The editors for the project—initially estimated to run for four months and to three volumes—preferably would have to be "respectable" scholars not immediately attached to the Foreign Ministry. Two candidates were quickly approved: Albrecht Mendelssohn–Bartholdy, a specialist on international law, was hired to investigate Germany's relations with Britain and its Empire; and Johannes Lepsius, a theologian and specialist on the Turkish treatment of Armenians, was entrusted with Balkan and Middle East issues. After considerable wrangling and upon the recommendation of the historian Friedrich Meinecke, Friedrich Thimme, the former director of the libraries of, first the Prussian Upper House, and subsequently of the entire Prussian Parliament, was selected as third editor, and made responsible for all issues not assigned to Mendelssohn–Bartholdy and Lepsius. Thimme and Lepsius were paid 2,000 Mark per month and provided with research and technical staff by the Foreign Ministry. In time, Thimme became managing editor of the mammoth project. The Wilhelmstrasse, for its part, not only directed the three editors on how to prepare the materials for publication, but also attached to them a special supervisor who was to evaluate possible public reaction to the documents selected for publication. Its War Guilt Section exercised final veto power over all volumes. The Foreign Ministry officially treated the documentary project as "secret" and "confidential" in order to camouflage its involvement therein.[19]

The end result was simply staggering in terms of labor and productivity: in just over six years, the three editors brought out forty volumes (in 54 parts) of documents pertaining to European affairs before 1914. Published between 1922 and 1927, *Die Grosse Politik der Europäischen Kabinette, 1871–1914*, in the words of Herman Wittgens, "established an early dependence

---

19. Annelise Thimme, "Friedrich Thimme als politischer Publizist im Ersten Weltkrieg und in der Kriegsschuldkontroverse," in Alexander Fischer, Günter Moltmann, and Klaus Schwabe, eds., *Russland—Deutschland—Amerika: Festschrift für Fritz T. Epstein zum 80. Geburtstag* (Wiesbaden: F. Steiner, 1978), pp. 225–229. See also the East German accounts, largely based upon the works of Imanuel Geiss: Fritz Klein, ed., *Deutschland im Ersten Weltkrieg* (East Berlin: Akademie–Verlag, 1971), Vol. 1, pp. 33–34; and Hans Schleier, *Die bürgerliche deutsche Geschichtsschreibung der Weimarer Republik* (East Berlin: Akademie–Verlag, 1975), pp. 141–144.

of all students of prewar diplomacy on German materials."[20] Obviously, this is not the place either to trace the reception accorded the documents in the 1920s or to analyze their selection in detail. Much of the critique has come about only in the past two decades on the basis of exhaustive research in Austrian, British, French, and German records by Fischer, Geiss, and others. On the other hand, since the series is still widely used today and since many of the standard works on the origins of the Great War were based upon it, a few comments on the materials collected therein are nevertheless in order.

The most obvious shortcoming of *Die Grosse Politik* stemmed from its very nature as a publication from the files of the former Foreign Office. In other words, the collection does not include the highly important, indeed critical, materials of several other, powerful planning agencies: the General Staff, the War Ministry, the Navy Office, and the bureaus responsible for economic preparations for the war.[21] This is especially unfortunate in the case of the General Staff and the War Ministry as their files were almost totally destroyed by that greatest of "censors," the Anglo–American Bomber Command, in February 1942 and April 1945. Of course, not all materials could be published even in a forty-volume series, and there is little doubt that many documents were suppressed or even destroyed. Moreover, some of the documents published were shortened, with potentially damaging sections deleted. Fritz Klein, for example, undertook a sample probe of volume sixteen of *Die Grosse Politik*, comparing Thimme's edition of a report on October 5, 1900 by Chancellor Bernhard von Bülow to Kaiser Wilhelm II concerning Germany's policy toward China. While Thimme shortened the report considerably and added a footnote stating that Imperial Germany had absolutely no territorial designs on China, the entire document—now available at Potsdam after the return to East Germany of the records of the former imperial embassy at Peking by the People's Republic after the Second World War—shows that quite the opposite was true. Klein reached the devastating conclusion that of the eleven

---

20. Herman J. Wittgens, "War Guilt Propaganda Conducted by the German Foreign Ministry During the 1920s," Canadian Historical Association, *Historical Papers* (1980), p. 231. The project appeared as Johannes Lepsius, Albrecht Mendelssohn–Bartholdy, and Friedrich Thimme, eds., *Die Grosse Politik der Europäischen Kabinette, 1871–1914: Sammlung der Diplomatischen Akten des Auswärtigen Amtes* (Berlin: Deutsche Verlagsgesellschaft für Politik und Geschichte, 1922–27), 40 vols. in 54.
21. For the shortcomings of *Die Grosse Politik*, see especially Geiss, *Julikrise*, Vol. 1, pp. 33–34; Heinemann, *Die verdrängte Niederlage*, p. 82; Schleier, *Die bürgerliche deutsche Geschichtsschreibung*, pp. 146–151; Klein, *Deutschland im Ersten Weltkrieg*, Vol. 1, p. 34; and Thimme, "Friedrich Thimme," p. 230.

points of the original memorandum, six were "prejudicially falsified," three entirely omitted, and a mere two faithfully reproduced by the editors of *Die Grosse Politik*.[22] Above all, the Kaiser's incriminating marginal comments on official documents, which Kautsky gleefully stated showed the monarch in his "underwear," remained largely unpublished; those included were usually given apologetic explanations by Thimme.

At another level, materials that might have jeopardized the Weimar Republic's relations with prominent neutrals were often not published. As a result, the "arrogant reports" of the former German Ambassador to Italy, Count Anton Monts, were suppressed on the advice of former Chancellor von Bülow. Japan formally requested that Germany not print the documents pertaining to its East Asian policies. Materials potentially embarrassing to Berlin through its former dealings with Denmark, Norway, and Sweden were also omitted. Not even the earliest period remained immune to "ordering" as fear of contemporary "Bismarck admirers" prompted the editors carefully to sift materials from the stewardship of the Iron Chancellor. Finally, the organization of the 15,889 documents into 300 subject areas rather than chronological order—again, at the express demand of the Foreign Ministry—tended to "sanitize" the material and to make it difficult for scholars to follow the day-to-day workings of the Wilhelmstrasse.

Imanuel Geiss has shown with specific reference to the July 1914 crisis that the editors failed to include (perhaps destroyed) a number of utterly critical documents: the discussions on July 5 and 6 at Potsdam not only among German leaders but also with Austro–Hungarian representatives; the detailed analysis of the Viennese ultimatum to Serbia, missing in *Die Grosse Politik* but handed to the Baden plenipotentiary on July 2; virtually any and all talks held by the Chancellor or the State Secretary and Under Secretary of the Foreign Office with representatives of foreign powers in July 1914; any and all contacts between Wilhelm II and his political as well as military leaders after the monarch's return from his northern cruise on July 27; and, last but not least, any and all notes pertaining to important telephone calls, telegraphs, or other verbal communications.[23] And according to Annelise Thimme, Mendelssohn–Bartholdy managed to defuse some potentially in-

---

22. Fritz Klein, "Über die Verfälschung der historischen Wahrheit in der Aktenpublikation 'Die Grosse Politik der Europäischen Kabinette 1871–1914,'" *Zeitschrift für Geschichtswissenschaft*, Vol. 7 (1950), pp. 319, 321, 328–329. Compare *Die Grosse Politik*, Vol. 16, pp. 143–146.
23. Geiss, *Julikrise*, Vol. 1, pp. 33–34.

criminating statements by Chancellor Theobald von Bethmann Hollweg simply by decreeing that the materials in question be returned to the family as "private" correspondence.[24] The chancellor's two-volume memoirs offer no clues concerning the July crisis, and his personal papers were either destroyed during the Second World War or captured by the advancing Soviet armies. Of course, we will never know how much was destroyed or returned to former players as "private" papers. Certain is that the present records of the *Politisches Archiv* of the Foreign Ministry at Bonn contain none of the documents listed by Geiss. They can be assumed lost forever.

His considerable efforts at patriotic self-censorship notwithstanding, Thimme later was to experience the wrath of academia. He was denied not only an honorary doctorate for *Die Grosse Politik*, but even the Leibniz medal from the Prussian Academy—despite a strong recommendation from Meinecke. The noted historian Erich Brandenburg, who had penned a book on Bismarck at the behest of the Foreign Ministry, claimed that these denials were based on the fact that Thimme was a "creature" of the Wilhelmstrasse and as such could not be "placed on an equal level with an independent scholar." By contrast, Alfred von Wegerer's efforts on behalf of the war-guilt campaign were rewarded with an honorary doctorate from Giessen University.[25] The labors of Bernhard Schwertfeger and Hans Draeger for the national cause—which will be taken up shortly—were likewise crowned with honorary doctorates. It is quite probable that the national-conservative German historians refused to honor Thimme for two reasons: his support of the "defeatist" policies of Chancellor von Bethmann Hollweg during the war, and his sharp attacks on Admiral Alfred von Tirpitz during the latter's campaign for the Presidency in 1924–25.

With the publication of its mammoth forty-volume project, the Foreign Ministry adopted the stance that all important documents were therewith available to scholars and that access to its files was not to be granted freely. Indeed, in 1929 the Wilhelmstrasse decreed that all materials of the past thirty years were to be closed to historical investigation—an unfortunate

---

24. Thimme, "Friedrich Thimme," p. 230.
25. Ibid., p. 235; Schleier, *Die bürgerliche deutsche Geschichtsschreibung*, pp. 146–147; Alfred von Wegerer, *Die Widerlegung der Versailler Kriegsschuldthese* (Berlin: R. Hobbing, 1928); Friedrich Thimme, "Die Auswertung der Aktenpublikation des AA für die Kriegsschuldfrage," *Die Kriegsschuldfrage*, Vol. 5 (1927), pp. 387–395; Thimme, "Das Ausland und die deutsche Aktenpublikation," *Weg zur Freiheit*, Vol. 20 (1927), pp. 314–319; and Thimme, *Die Aktenpublikation des Auswärtigen Amtes: Beiträge zu ihrer Entstehungsgeschichte* (Berlin: Deutsche Verlagsgesellschaft für Politik und Geschichte, 1924).

precedent that the current rulers at Bonn seem bent on repeating with their policy of *Datenschutz*. The widely acclaimed story that the Foreign Ministry marked several of its files "not to be shown to William Langer" may be apocryphal, but the case of George Hallgarten is documented. In 1931, Hallgarten was denied access to the foreign relations records as his work might "compromise" Germany's "present or future interests in China." Refusing to take no for an answer, Hallgarten reapplied for permission to use official materials, and was finally let in. By chance, he was handed the files on German policy with regard to Delago Bay—files that Thimme had assured scholars did not exist. Moreover, upon returning after the Second World War to reexamine the dossiers on China that he had been given in the early 1930s, Hallgarten discovered that potentially damaging documents had been removed before he was handed the materials, and later returned to their folders.[26] It is also interesting to note that the Federal Republic of Germany entrusted the supervision of the archival records in the *Politisches Archiv* of the Foreign Office at Bonn to Heinz–Günther Sasse, who had worked during the 1920s in the Center for the Study of the Causes of the War, one of the numerous organizations funded by the Foreign Ministry to rebut the "war-guilt lie."[27] Therewith, the patriotic self-censors established continuity from the Weimar Republic to the Federal Republic via the Third Reich.

Dissemination of Illusions

After the publication of *Die Grosse Politik*, the Foreign Ministry sought to assure the widest possible dissemination of the series' findings, both at home and abroad. Legation Secretary Freytag of its War Guilt Section had suggested as early as December 1919 a massive propaganda campaign to propagate the official German position on war guilt, but Bülow did not deem the moment right as the indiscriminate use of propaganda during the First World War had rendered large segments of the populace skeptical of any government-

---

26. George W.F. Hallgarten, *Imperialismus vor 1914: Die soziologischen Grundlagen der Aussenpolitik europäischer Grossmächte vor dem Ersten Weltkrieg* (Munich: C.H. Beck, 1963), Vol. 1, p. vii; and Schleier, *Die bürgerliche deutsche Geschichtsschreibung*, pp. 147–148. In a letter to Thimme on February 25, 1925, Mendelssohn–Bartholdy spoke of "destroying," "suppressing," and "ordering" certain potentially damaging documents. He asked Thimme to destroy his letter. Ibid., p. 149.
27. Wittgens, "War Guilt Propaganda," p. 244.

directed information. Nevertheless, Freytag clung to his plan to make certain "that this propaganda never be allowed to die."[28]

After various unsuccessful attempts to recruit patriotic organizations willing, able, and suitable to conduct its propaganda, the Foreign Ministry eventually decided to establish several independent bureaus under the umbrella of its *Kriegsschuldreferat*. These eventually functioned on both an overt and a covert level; at the public level, they disseminated the official view on the origins of the war, while behind the scenes they sought to promote those who followed the official line and to silence—indeed, eventually to hound out of office—those who put forth independent and/or unacceptable interpretations. And while much of the nation gradually had gotten over the initial shock of the harsh terms handed down at Versailles, the Allied demand in January 1921 for reparations in the amount of 226 billion Mark, with annual payments over the next 42 years, once again came to the aid of the Foreign Ministry's "revisionist" endeavors.[29] Foreign Minister Walter Simons and Finance Minister Joseph Wirth were quickly able to agree to make available 1 million Mark for propaganda purposes to the Center for the Study of the Causes of the War; an additional 200,000 Mark was released to support the efforts of German diplomatic missions abroad to distribute materials supportive of the Foreign Ministry's war-guilt stance. Mendelssohn–Bartholdy, now at Hamburg, was able to tap into this cash flow in 1923 in order to establish an Institute for Foreign Policy, publish a journal, *Europäische Gespräche*, and a "popular" four-volume abridgment of *Die Grosse Politik*.[30]

With governmental funding secure—augmented on occasion by private contributions—the "patriotic self-censors" were ready to spearhead the revisionist drive through a triad of dependent organizations. The "general staff" remained the War Guilt Section of the Foreign Ministry. It was headed by Hans Freytag in 1919–20, Professor Richard von Delbrück in 1921–22, and Friedrich Stieve from 1922 until 1928. The bureau made the basic decisions as to which publications critical of the official German line were to be attacked, by whom, and in which journals; or whether they simply were to be ignored. Moreover, the *Kriegsschuldreferat* acted as internal censor for all publications either of the Foreign Ministry or of the parliamentary investi-

---

28. Cited in Heinemann, *Die verdrängte Niederlage*, p. 56.
29. Ibid., p. 62.
30. Ibid., p. 66; and Schleier, *Die bürgerliche deutsche Geschichtsschreibung*, pp. 144, 151. See also Albrecht Mendelssohn–Bartholdy, ed., *Die auswärtige Politik des Deutschen Reiches 1871–1914* (Berlin: Deutsche Verlagsgesellschaft für Politik und Geschichte, 1928), 4 vols.

gations. Moreover, it composed the numerous official statements of German chancellors and President Paul von Hindenburg on the war guilt question.[31] At least under Stieve, the War Guilt Section openly conceded that historical elucidation was not its primary concern; rather, its purpose was "aggressive polemics." Above all, the War Guilt Section brooked no competition in its campaign of revision; when the Potsdam *Reichsarchiv* in 1923 threatened to compile its own documentary collection on the outbreak of the war, the Foreign Ministry secured a decree from President Ebert that it, and it alone, was entitled to undertake such endeavors.[32]

The *Kriegsschuldreferat* was also active in attempting to influence the publication of archival materials in other countries. In 1924, Stieve produced a four-volume collection of the reports of the erstwhile Russian Ambassador in Paris, A.P. Izvolsky, designed to show that these two entente powers had nurtured "imperialistic war aims" against Germany. The core of the publication consisted of 500 secret documents, purchased by the Wilhelmstrasse for 48,000 Mark—in reality, a bribe paid to the archivist of the Soviet embassy at Paris to smuggle the materials out.[33] To be sure, the Foreign Ministry had long encouraged the Ballhausplatz at Vienna to publish its documents on the July crisis "in the interests of greater Germany," and by 1923 had even hired the former editor of the Austro–Hungarian *Red Book* on the war's origins. Legation Secretary Roderich Gooss, in fact, was now sent to Vienna to assist the Ballhausplatz in sorting its documents—in the process passing copies of the most important materials on to his employers at Berlin. In the end, Stieve provided the editors of the Austrian documents, the *Kommission für neuere*

---

31. An example of the sort of speech penned by the War Guilt Section's staff was President von Hindenburg's eulogy at the unveiling of the Tannenberg memorial in September 1927: "The charge that Germany is responsible for this greatest of all wars, we and the German people at all levels reject with one voice. Not envy, hatred, or lust to conquer forced us to take up arms. Rather, the war was the ultimate . . . means with which to sustain ourselves in a world of enemies all around." Cited in Heinemann, *Die verdrängte Niederlage*, p. 227.

32. Wittgens, "War Guilt Propaganda," pp. 229–230; and Imanuel Geiss, "The Outbreak of the First World War and German War Aims," *Journal of Contemporary History*, Vol. 1 (1966), p. 77. This article was reproduced in German in Geiss, *Das Deutsche Reich und die Vorgeschichte des Ersten Weltkriegs* (Munich: C. Hauser, 1978), pp. 204ff.

33. Heinemann, *Die verdrängte Niederlage*, p. 89. See also Friedrich Stieve, ed., *Der Diplomatische Schriftwechsel Iswolskis 1911–1914: Aus den Geheimakten der Russischen Staatsarchive. Im Auftrag des Deutschen Auswärtigen Amtes in deutscher Übersetzung* (Berlin: Deutsche Verlagsgesellschaft für Politik und Geschichte, 1924), 4 vols.; Stieve, *Iswolski und der Weltkrieg: Aufgrund der neuen Dokumenten-Veröffentlichung des Deutschen Auswärtigen Amtes* (Berlin: Deutsche Verlagsgesellschaft für Politik und Geschichte, 1924); and Stieve, *Iswolski im Weltkriege: Der diplomatische Schriftwechsel Iswolskis 1914–1917* (Berlin: Deutsche Verlagsgesellschaft für Politik und Geschichte, 1926).

Geschichte Österreichs, 50,000 Mark to facilitate their work—as well as the services of Gooss and, for good measure, Friedrich Thimme.[34] And when it appeared in 1925 that the United States, at the prompting of Senator Robert L. Owen of Oklahoma, might undertake an official publication of documents pertaining to the outbreak of war in 1914, the Wilhelmstrasse instructed its embassy at Washington to make *Die Grosse Politik* readily available; Alfred von Wegerer was dispatched to the United States in order to exert "decisive influence" on the planned American publication, which never reached fruition.[35]

To expedite this hectic activity, the War Guilt Section in 1921 had established a pseudo-scholarly bureau, the Center for the Study of the Causes of the War. Headed until August 1923 by a Swiss doctor, Ernst Sauerbeck, and thereafter until its dissolution in 1937 by Major Alfred von Wegerer, it became "a clearinghouse for officially desirable views on the outbreak of the war."[36] The Center possessed only a small staff of "politically trained" scholars, but its directory included such notables as Count von Montgelas, Bernhard W. von Bülow, Hans Delbrück, and Hermann Lutz. The prolific Wegerer, who had come aboard in 1923 from the *völkisch* "Liga für deutsche Kultur," churned out no less than 300 articles to buttress the revisionist cause. The Foreign Ministry, at the height of the economic crisis of 1923, financed a monthly journal for the Center entitled *Die Kriegsschuldfrage, Monatsschrift für Internationale Aufklärung*, which in 1929 changed its title to *Berliner Monatshefte*. Its circulation hovered between 2,500 and 3,000 copies in 1925, then climbed to between 3,500 and 4,000 by 1931. Both journals of the *Zentralstelle zur Erforschung der Kriegsursachen* appeared with the "Quader–Verlag," a publishing house financially controlled by the Foreign Ministry—much in the man-

---

34. Heinemann, *Die verdrängte Niederlage*, pp. 90–91. The Viennese collection appeared as: Ludwig Bittner, Alfred Francis Pribram, Heinrich Srbik, and Hans Uebersberger, eds., *Österreich–Ungarns Aussenpolitik von der Bosnischen Krise 1908 bis zum Kriegsausbruch 1914: Diplomatische Aktenstücke des Österreichisch–Ungarischen Ministeriums des Äussern* (Vienna: Österreichischer Bundesverlag für Unterricht, Wissenschaft und Kunst, 1930), 8 vols.
35. Heinemann, *Die verdrängte Niederlage*, p. 91. See also Herman J. Wittgens, "The German Foreign Office Campaign Against the Treaty of Versailles: An Examination of the Activities of the Kriegsschuldreferat in the United States" (Ph.D. dissertation, University of Washington, 1970).
36. Wittgens, "War Guilt Propaganda," p. 233. See also Ernst Sauerbeck, *Der Kriegsausbruch: Eine Darstellung von neutraler Seite anhand des Aktenmaterials* (Stuttgart: Deutsche Verlags–Anstalt, 1919); and Alfred von Wegerer, "Die Zentralstelle für Erforschung der Kriegsursachen und die freien Kriegsschuldfrageorganisationen," in *Die Liga: Mitteilungsblatt der Liga zum Schutze der deutschen Kultur*, Vols. 7/8 (1921), pp. 90ff.

ner in which the latter kept the "Deutsche Verlagsanstalt für Politik und Geschichte" solvent by having it publish the works that the Wilhelmstrasse contracted out to Bülow, Lutz, Mendelssohn–Bartholdy, Montgelas, Schücking, Schwertfeger, Stieve, and Thimme. Again, Wegerer and his Center appeared on the surface to be independent; in reality, Wegerer remained in the pay of the Foreign Ministry in the position of *Ministerialrat*, and the War Guilt Section "supervised" the Center's publications.[37]

Unfortunately, there is no concise accounting of the subsidies paid out by the Foreign Ministry for its campaign of revision. Ulrich Heinemann has shown that Wegerer's Center received official support in the amount of 23,400 Mark in 1924–25, 34,400 Mark the following year, and 84,000 Mark by 1929–30; private contributions amounted to 5,200 Mark, 19,000 Mark, and 24,000 Mark for those respective years. These sums can best be gauged against the 120 Mark monthly wage of an average German industrial worker. Of course, these monies formed only a very small part of the overall outlays of the Foreign Ministry to the "war-guilt lie."[38] Nor is it possible to gain any accurate insight into the number of independent scholars and journalists engaged by the Wilhelmstrasse in a similar function. While Geiss speaks of a small army of such publicists, Heinemann tends toward a much smaller number. In the main, these writers were paid modest honorariums of perhaps several hundred Mark in order to pen three or four articles per month for leading newspapers, which, in turn, passed them on to the provincial press. Most prominent among this group were the Munich journalist Hermann Lutz and the army's specialist on Belgium, Colonel Schwertfeger; the latter was also paid by the Foreign Ministry to compile an eight-part guide to *Die Grosse Politik* for the nonprofessional reader.[39] One of the few foreign writers directly

---

37. Wittgens, "War Guilt Propaganda," pp. 233–234; Heinemann, *Die verdrängte Niederlage*, pp. 83, 96, 98; Geiss, "Outbreak of the First World War," p. 76; and Schleier, *Die bürgerliche deutsche Geschichtsschreibung*, p. 153.

38. Heinemann, *Die verdrängte Niederlage*, p. 97. German wage statistics are from Gerhard Bry, *Wages in Germany 1871–1945* (Princeton: Princeton University Press, 1960), pp. 51–55.

39. Heinemann, *Die verdrängte Niederlage*, pp. 98–99; Geiss, "Outbreak of the First World War," pp. 76–77; Schleier, *Die bürgerliche deutsche Geschichtsschreibung*, pp. 151–152; and Thimme, "Friedrich Thimme," p. 235. See also Bernhard Schwertfeger, *Die Diplomatischen Akten des Auswärtigen Amtes 1871–1914: Ein Wegweiser durch das grosse Aktenwerk der Deutschen Regierung* (Berlin: Deutsche Verlagsgesellschaft für Politik und Geschichte, 1923/27); *Der Fehlspruch von Versailles: Deutschlands Freispruch aus belgischen Dokumenten, 1871–1914* (Berlin: Deutsche Verlagsgesellschaft für Politik und Geschichte, 1921); "Geschichtswerdung und Geschichtsschreibung," *Archiv für Geschichte und Politik*, Vol. 1 (1923), pp. 385–408; and *Der Weltkrieg der Dokumente: Zehn Jahre Kriegsschuldforschung und ihr Ergebnis* (Berlin: Deutsche Verlagsgesellschaft für Politik und Geschichte, 1929).

subsidized by the Wilhelmstrasse appears to have been Miloš Boghitschew-itsch, the former Serbian *chargé d'affaires* to Germany, who wrote articles for the Foreign Office during the 1920s and who apparently was paid in that most rare of commodities at Berlin, gold.[40] Again, there is no indication of how many of these pieces were purchased by the Foreign Ministry and distributed gratis at home and abroad; Geiss speaks vaguely of "several hundred."

Since the Center for the Study of the Causes of the War viewed itself as a scholarly bureau, it is interesting to note the absence of German university professors—with the exception of that "outsider," Hans Delbrück. By and large, eminent scholars such as Hans Herzfeld, Paul Herre, Siegfried Kaehler, Wilhelm Mommsen, and Hans Rothfels viewed the origins of the Great War as current events rather than history, and thus hardly worthy of serious scholarly inquiry. Moreover, they continued in their fascination with the ancient world. It is striking that not a single eminent historian of the 1920s bothered to undertake serious research and publication on the origins of the war. In contrast to the post-1945 period, they left the debate by default in the hands of the Foreign Ministry and its minions. Many of the "German mandarins" announced at their annual convention at Göttingen in 1932 that they rejected the very term "war guilt" as being imprecise and not belonging to the vocabulary of a professional scholar; rather, the terms "origins" and "consequences" of war were deemed fit and proper for the *Zunft*.[41] And on the few occasions on which the senior historians addressed the issue of war guilt in popular magazines and newspapers, they basically followed Hermann Oncken's verdict that Imperial Germany had been driven by a genuine desire for peace, while France had been obsessed with the spirit of revenge, England with the encirclement of Germany, and Russia with hostility toward Berlin.

If the Center for the Study of the Causes of the War sought to conduct the revisionist campaign on a scholarly level, the Working Committee of German Associations was quite the opposite—namely, an organization committed to spreading the Foreign Ministry's message to as many agencies and papers as possible. The *Arbeitsausschuss Deutscher Verbände* (ADV) was quietly

---

40. Geiss, "Outbreak of the First World War," p. 77; and Wittgens, "War Guilt Propaganda," p. 239. See also Miloš Boghitschewitsch, *Die Auswärtige Politik Serbiens 1903–1914* (Berlin: Brück-enverlag, 1928–31), 3 vols.
41. Jäger, *Historische Forschung*, pp. 69ff; and Heinemann, *Die verdrängte Niederlage*, pp. 106–107.

founded by the Foreign Ministry in April 1921 without public knowledge or participation, and within a year claimed ties to between 500 and 600 member organizations, a figure that skyrocketed to between 1,700 and 2,000 by 1931. In the main, the member organizations were patriotic clubs such as *Rettet die Ehre* and the *Deutsche Frauenausschuss zur Bekämpfung der Kriegsschuldlüge*, but they also included the *Caritas–Verband*, the World Council of Churches, and the German City League. The Working Committee chose as its first president Legation Secretary Kurt von Lersner, a former head of the Foreign Office's legal section; he was succeeded in 1923 by Dr. Heinrich Schnee, the former governor of German East Africa. A special business office in Berlin, initially managed by Wilhelm von Vietsch and from 1923 until 1937 by Hans Draeger (who joined Joseph Goebbel's Propaganda Ministry in 1933), conducted the day-to-day business operations of the ADV.[42]

Perhaps because of its nature as an overt mass propaganda distribution center, the ADV was rather well financed. Official support came from the parent War Guilt Section and the Press Section of the Foreign Ministry as well as from the Ministry of the Interior, the Chancellery, and the State of Prussia. Private contributions flowed in from large industrial concerns such as IG-Farben, the northwest group of the Iron and Steel Cartel, and the Hamburg Board of Trade, with smaller amounts being raised by government-endorsed lotteries and public solicitations. While it is generally agreed that private contributions never amounted to more than the actual costs of printing the materials, the direct subsidies from the Wilhelmstrasse alone rose from 20,000 Mark in 1924 to 72,000 Mark by 1928/29.[43] With this money, the ADV organized speaker's seminars, conventions, exhibitions, rallies, and special information weeks to spread the gospel according to the Foreign Ministry. It is estimated, for example, that in 1925 alone, the Working Committee conducted 1,456 such undertakings in behalf of the revisionist campaign. Moreover, it effectively penetrated the daily press, maintaining contacts to no less than 1,500 newspapers through the 35 major news agencies in Berlin. A random sample of the Weimar press during any given week

---

42. Ibid., pp. 120–121; and Wittgens, "War Guilt Propaganda," p. 235. See also Hans Draeger, *Der Arbeitsausschuss Deutscher Verbände 1921–1931* (Berlin: Arbeitsausschuss Deutscher Verbände, 1931).

43. Wittgens, "War Guilt Propaganda," p. 235; Heinemann, *Die verdrängte Niederlage*, pp. 122–124; Dieter Fricke, ed., *Die bürgerlichen Parteien in Deutschland 1830–1945: Handbuch der Geschichte der bürgerlichen Parteien und anderer bürgerlicher Interessenorganisationen vom Vormärz bis zum Jahre 1945* (East Berlin: Das europäische Buch, 1968), Vol. 1, pp. 48–55.

revealed that it was not at all unusual for about 300 German papers to publish between 1,600 and 1,700 articles distributed by the ADV.

The latter was particularly active in providing literature sympathetic to the Foreign Ministry's "revisionist" stance to German schools. Not only was its journal *Der Weg zur Freiheit* much more popular than Wegerer's *Kriegsschuldfrage*, but the Working Committee carefully cultivated close ties to teacher organizations and schools. Among the literature that it provided for the schools were 67,000 free copies of Friedrich Stieve's highly revisionist *Deutschland und Europa, 1890–1914* as well as popular pamphlets such as Karl Bröger's "Versailles" (800,000 copies), a "Merkblatt zur Kriegsschuldfrage" (500,000 copies), a calendar "Für Freiheit und Ehre" (100,000 copies), and the all-time best-seller "Schuld am Kriege" (2.5 million copies). Assured of Foreign Ministry backing, the ADV placed its publications free of charge in hospitals, reading rooms, libraries, reception rooms of doctors and lawyers, and lounges at industrial plants. Nor was the foreign press ignored: the Working Center maintained ties to at least eleven major German–American newspapers, placing about 400 articles with them just in the few months between January and August 1922. It was aided in these endeavors not only by the Hamburg Board of Trade (Max Warburg, Wilhelm Cuno), but also by the World Council of Churches, and the *Vereine des Auslandsdeutschtums*. And after 1924, the ADV began to turn its attention to radio, broadcasting its views over the "Berliner Funkstunde"; its leaders prized this new medium because of "the strong participation of the workers in radio."[44]

The Wilhelmstrasse was especially interested that the Working Committee of German Associations and the Center for the Study of the Causes of the War establish contacts with foreign scholars who either were sympathetic to its official line or who were critical, for whatever reason, of their own government's role in the outbreak of the war or its settlement. In 1925, for example, the Foreign Ministry convinced Chancellor Hans Luther to provide 500,000 Mark for this purpose. Apart from distributing gratis 5,000 copies of Hermann Lutz's *An Appeal to British Fair Play* to addresses in England, the Foreign Ministry and ADV either provided research materials to or subsidized the translations and/or distribution of such sympathetic works as Alfred Fabre–Luce, *La Victoire*; Alcide Ebray, *La Paix Malpropre*; Victor Margueritte,

---

44. Heinemann, *Die verdrängte Niederlage*, pp. 126–129; and Wittgens, "War Guilt Propaganda," pp. 236–237. See also Friedrich Stieve, *Deutschland und Europa 1890–1914: Ein Handbuch zur Vorgeschichte des Weltkrieges mit den wichtigsten Dokumenten* (Berlin: Verlag für Kulturpolitik, 1926).

Les Criminels; Georges Demartial, *La Guerre de 1914*; and Edmund D. Morel, *Pre-War Diplomacy, Diplomacy Revealed, The Secret History of a Great Betrayal*, and *The Poison that Destroys*.

Perhaps of interest to the readers of this journal is the care lavished upon certain American scholars by the Foreign Ministry and its agents. As previously noted, Wegerer had been sent to the United States in 1925 to assist the Senate in a possible documentary series on the origins of the war; he also used the occasion to contact eminent historians such as Sidney B. Fay, Bernadotte E. Schmitt, William Langer, Carlton J. Hayes, and Ferdinand Schevill. The immediate upshot was that the Foreign Ministry purchased 250 copies of Fay's sympathetic two-volume *The Origins of the War* and had its diplomatic representatives overseas distribute the books free of charge. The Harvard historian was invited to visit the Center for the Study of the Causes of the War in 1923, and was asked regularly to contribute to its journal, *Kriegsschuldfrage*. In time, the Foreign Ministry funded both a German and a French translation of Fay's study. By contrast, Bernadotte Schmitt's critical *The Coming of the War 1914* was never translated into German, and when the Reich's consul at Chicago in 1928 arranged a visit by Schmitt to Germany to discuss his research, Wegerer strenuously objected to a tour by this "incorrigible" historian.[45]

The greatest attention and support was showered upon Harry E. Barnes of Smith College. In articles that appeared in *Current History, Nation, Christian Century*, and especially in his *Genesis of the World War* (1927), Barnes depicted France and Russia as the villains, Germany and Austria–Hungary as the victims of the July crisis. Wegerer's Center moved with alacrity after 1924. It provided Barnes with research materials, propagated his writings, and funded his visits to Berlin, Munich, and Vienna in 1926. The German embassy at Washington presented him with all forty volumes of *Die Grosse Politik*. Lutz put him into contact with the Serb, Boghitschewitsch, who was in the pay of the Foreign Ministry. Wegerer had Barnes's articles translated into German and published in his journal. The ADV translated Barnes's *Genesis* into German, and with the help of the Foreign Ministry not only distributed

---

45. Wittgens, "War Guilt Propaganda," pp. 240–244; Heinemann, *Die verdrängte Niederlage*, pp. 113, 115; and Fritz Fischer, *Krieg der Illusionen: Die deutsche Politik von 1911 bis 1914* (Düsseldorf: Droste, 1969), p. 670. See also Bernadotte E. Schmitt, *The Coming of the War* (New York and London: C. Scribner's Sons, 1930), 2 vols.; and Sidney B. Fay, *The Origins of the World War* (New York: Macmillan, 1928), 2 vols. The latter appeared in Germany as *Der Ursprung des Weltkrieges* (Berlin: A. Scherl, 1930), 2 vols.

it to Germany's overseas missions but even arranged a French translation. And while the Wilhelmstrasse saw Barnes's usefulness primarily as that of a popularizer, the eminent historian Hans Herzfeld went so far as to proclaim the American scholar's work "a document in the struggle for the war guilt thesis whose noble spirit cannot be appreciated enough."[46]

It is impossible to pinpoint the effect of this propaganda, either in Germany or overseas. Needless to say, the cumulative effect of ten years of continuous activity in this area must have taken its toll. Several German states, such as Baden, Bavaria, Sachsen–Anhalt, Württemberg, and Waldeck, openly adopted ADV materials for classroom instruction. In 1922, the Weimar federation of teachers agreed to serve the ADV, as did the federation of university professors. The administrative guardians of German universities, the rectors, also agreed to bring the Working Committee on board. The ADV, for its part, routinely organized talks at high schools and seminars at universities on the issue of the "war-guilt lie," and this mobilization especially of the youth could only have paved the way for their favorable reception of Adolf Hitler's "revisionist" ideas. Likewise, the overseas distribution of materials combating Article 231 of the Versailles treaty must have had its effects, however imprecise they may be to define. At least one generation of university students was raised on the apologias presented them by historians such as Sidney B. Fay and Harry E. Barnes in the United States, and writers such as Edmund Morel in England as well as Victor Margueritte and Alfred Fabre–Luce in France. This pollution of American, British, and French historical understanding of the origins of the Great War must have helped to undermine faith in the need to maintain the irenic clauses of the 1919 treaty. It remains an open question whether it also contributed to isolationism in the United States and pro-appeasement thinking in England in the 1930s.

The activities of both the Center for the Study of the Causes of the War and the Working Committee of German Associations lost much of their impact and political value after January 1933. Celebrating the fourth anniversary of his appointment as Chancellor, Hitler on January 30, 1937 informed the Reichstag that he was officially "revoking" the German signature on the document wherein a "weak government" had been "pressed" to accept Ger-

---

46. Wittgens, "War Guilt Propaganda," pp. 238–239, 242–243, 245. See Harry E. Barnes, *The Genesis of the World War: An Introduction to the Problem of War Guilt* (New York: Alfred A. Knopf, 1927); and *In Quest of Truth and Justice: De-Bunking the War Guilt Myth* (Chicago: National Historical Society, 1928). Barnes's *Genesis* appeared in Germany as *Die Entstehung des Weltkrieges: Eine Einführung in das Kriegsschuldproblem* (Stuttgart: Deutsche Verlags–Anstalt, 1928).

many's guilt for the First World War.[47] Therewith, the semi-official revisionist campaign was stripped of its reason to exist—or, more precisely, it was subsumed by the state. Two years later, Wegerer published his standard apologia, *Der Ausbruch des Weltkrieges*, which was to shape so many of the post-1945 histories of the July crisis. Arguing that no single nation was responsible for the outbreak of the war, Wegerer instead ingeniously suggested that a fatal entanglement of circumstances—perhaps even providence—had afflicted Europe with this curse. This convenient position was thereafter adopted by the majority of Germany's national-conservative historians, such as Karl Dietrich Erdmann, Hans Herzfeld, Hermann Oncken, Gerhard Ritter, Hans Rothfels, Theodor Schieder, and Egmont Zechlin, to name but a few. Moreover, it also made its way into the writings of Harry E. Barnes and Sidney B. Fay as well as their students in the United States, and is to be found in countless general histories and surveys still used in American universities. An inability or unwillingness to delve into the German sources—or at least the writings of Fritz Fischer and his students—perhaps accounts for this.

Furthermore, while the Second World War for many non-German scholars merely served once more to "prove" Berlin's responsibility for the First, the tone in what emerged as the Federal Republic of Germany (1949) was set again by historians such as Erdmann, Herzfeld, Ritter, Rothfels, and Zechlin, who now adopted the line that while Hitler (rather than Germany) was to blame for the Second World War, no such blame could be attributed for the First. In reaching this stance, they seconded Wegerer, ignored Albertini, and vilified Fischer.[48] Largely overlooked in the debate—both before 1933 and after 1945—was the work of the Reichstag investigation into both the origins and conduct of the Great War. This investigation was completely independent of the activities of the Foreign Ministry discussed previously; it came fully under the purview of the Reichstag, which had decided in 1919 to investigate the sudden and seemingly inexplicable reasons for the German collapse. While the Left thereby sought to lay the blame for the collapse at the feet of German admirals and generals and generally to delegitimate the old order, the Right joined the investigation in order to tar the major supporters of the Weimar Republic—Democrats, Liberals, and Socialists—with the brush of defeatism and betrayal.

---

47. See Jäger, *Historische Forschung*, p. 65.
48. Geiss, "Outbreak of the First World War," p. 78.

Parliament and the Campaign of Obfuscation

Thus united in policy if not in motive, the various political parties in the Reichstag had decided on the basis of Article 34 of the new constitution to convene a special parliamentary Committee of Enquiry to investigate the origins of the war, its possible prolongation, and the causes for defeat in 1918. The 28-member *Untersuchungsausschuss* was formally constituted on August 21, 1919 as the 15th Committee of the German Constitutional Assembly; it conducted its work until Hermann Göring in his capacity as president of the Reichstag dissolved it after the elections of August 30, 1932, and ordered the destruction of all available published volumes of its findings. There evolved four subcommittees of enquiry: the first was to investigate Germany's responsibility for the start of the war; the second to assess whether there had been any possibility for a negotiated peace before the military collapse; the third was to tackle Allied charges that the Reich had violated international law; and the fourth was to discern the causes behind the collapse both at the front and at home in 1918. Finally, a special tribunal (*Staatsgerichtshof*) composed of high-court judges and parliamentary deputies was to hear cases submitted to it by the four subcommittees. The cumbersome nature of the investigative process was due, in part, to the Foreign Ministry's desire to keep documents tied up in committee and thus from public scrutiny for an indefinite period. Indeed, the eminent jurist Otto von Gierke quickly pointed out that the special tribunal was not only contrary to German law, but that its decisions would constitute *ex post facto* justice.[49]

The story of the *Untersuchungsausschuss* is one of official obfuscation, interminable delays, and eventual failure. Only one subcommittee investigation, namely, that dealing with Germany's role at the Hague peace conferences in 1899 and 1907, was ever completed and printed—and then only in 1927, after the Foreign Ministry had repeatedly barred its publication as being detrimental to the national interest.[50] The Wilhelmstrasse in general and

49. The Cabinet decision to establish the Committee of Enquiry and the special tribunal is in Golecki, *Das Kabinett Bauer*, p. 199; session of August 16, 1919. See also W. Kahl, "Untersuchungsausschuss und Staatsgerichtshof," *Deutsche Juristenzeitung*, Vol. 25 (1920), pp. 2–7; Hahn, "German Foreign Ministry," pp. 54, 55; Schleier, *Die bürgerliche deutsche Geschichtsschreibung*, pp. 154–156; and Heinemann, *Die verdrängte Niederlage*, p. 156.
50. Eugen Fischer–Baling, "Der Untersuchungsausschus für die Schuldfragen des ersten Weltkrieges," in Alfred Herrmann, ed., *Aus Geschichte und Politik: Festschrift zum 70. Geburtstag von Ludwig Bergsträsser* (Düsseldorf: Droste, 1954), p. 137; and Klein, *Deutschland im Ersten Weltkrieg*, Vol. 1, p. 25. See also *Das Werk des Untersuchungsausschusses der Deutschen Verfassunggebenden*

Alfred von Wegerer of its War Guilt Section in particular not only decided
which documents were to be submitted to the Committee of Enquiry, but
also exercised veto power over the publication of its findings. Not unexpectedly, the various military bureaus refused from the start to participate in the
investigations or to make any of their materials available.[51] And as the shock
of defeat and revolution wore off, the composition of the Reichstag slowly
shifted to the right of the political spectrum, thereby altering the proportional
composition of the various subcommittees in favor of more conservative and
nationalist elements.

The most sensational investigation was that of the second subcommittee,
charged with evaluating the possibility of a negotiated peace in 1917–18.
Former Vice Chancellor Karl Helfferich set the tone of the investigation by
charging that those political parties that had supported the Reichstag's peace
resolution in July 1917 had, in effect, "stabbed the unrestricted submarine
war in the back." In addition, Helfferich accused the Social Democrats of
having accepted Soviet funds in order to "revolutionize Germany." But the
most dramatic effect was reserved for Field Marshal von Hindenburg. Having
been invited by Fritz Warmuth of the German National People's Party
(DNVP)—without the consent of the rest of the subcommittee—the former
Chief of the General Staff arrived in Berlin to "testify" on November 18,
1919. It was a triumphant farce. The army provided an honor guard at the
train station, two officers served as adjutants, and a guard detail was sta-
tioned at the Villa Helfferich where the field marshal resided while in the
capital. When Hindenburg, in full dress uniform, arrived to testify on November 18, the chamber was packed. All rose to their feet as he strode in to
take his chrysanthemum-bedecked chair. There were no questions, no cross-
examination. Instead, the field marshal read a brief prepared statement
wherein he blamed the military defeat on the material and numerical superiority of the Allies especially after April 1917, and on the "planned demor-
alization" of the High Sea Fleet by "revolutionary elements," presumably the

---

Nationalversammlung und des Deutschen Reichstages 1919–1930 (Berlin: Deutsche Verlagsgesellschaft
für Politik und Geschichte, 1927ff.), 19 vols. in 25. The first subcommittee published three
volumes in 1929 and 1930; the second brought out none; the third published four volumes in
1927; and the fourth managed twelve volumes between 1925 and 1929.

51. Fischer–Baling, "Untersuchungsausschuss," pp. 124, 129, as late as 1954 still claimed, despite
his intimate association with the workings of the Committee of Enquiry throughout the 1920s,
that the documentary materials of "all bureaus" had been made available and that it was simply
inconceivable that the "correct bureaucrats" of imperial Germany could have "suppressed or
ordered" any evidence. See also Heinemann, *Die verdrängte Niederlage*, p. 158.

Independent Socialists (USPD). Hindenburg ended his soliloquy by announc-
ing that the "good core" of the army, that is, its officer corps, could not be
blamed for the defeat; rather, it had been "stabbed in the back" (*von hinten
erdolcht*) by certain pacifist and socialist elements at the home front. Therewith, a legend was officially born, one that was to have fatal consequences
for the Republic. Unsurprisingly, the patriotic self-censors in the Foreign
Ministry barred publication of even a single volume of the findings of the
second subcommittee for fear of adverse reaction both overseas and among
the German clergy; further, they assured that even the unpublished material
would not see the light of day by indiscriminately stamping "secret" on 28
of the 37 folders of documents. The second *enquête's* work concluded in
1924.[52]

The third subcommittee, dealing with possible German violations of international law, was most closely supervised by the Foreign Ministry, which
provided as "expert" none other than Dr. Johannes Kriege, the erstwhile
head of the legal section of the Imperial Foreign Office. In fact, Kriege
undertook numerous visits to the exiled Kaiser Wilhelm II at Haus Doorn in
the Netherlands, ostensibly to keep the emperor informed of his efforts.
Whatever the case, Kriege, in the words of Ulrich Heinemann, quickly developed into "a master of juridical pettifoggery" (*Rabulistik*). With regard to
the use of poison gas, Kriege argued that whereas French weapons were
illegal under the Hague convention of July 29, 1899 because their intent was
solely the dissemination of gas, German equivalents were legal because they
also served as ordinary artillery shells. In particular, Germany's first use of
gas at Ypres on April 22, 1915 had been perfectly legal because the Reich
had not used "gas shells" but rather "gas clouds." Unrestricted submarine
warfare was likewise deemed legal as it had been adopted strictly as an
antidote to the illegal British "hunger blockade." And German air attacks on
London and Paris were ruled legal insofar as France, Germany, and Russia
on October 18, 1907 had not renewed the original Hague conditions for air
warfare of July 29, 1899. The admittedly brutal deportation of Belgian workers
was attributed solely to the inadequate organization of German transports.
When the Belgian government formally protested these mental gymnastics

---

52. Ibid., pp. 162–163; and Werner Hahlweg, "Das hinterlassene Werk des Parlamentarischen
Untersuchungsausschusses," in Rudolf Vierhaus and Manfred Botzenhart, eds., *Dauer und
Wandel der Geschichte: Aspekte Europäischer Vergangenheit, Festgabe für Kurt von Raumer zum 15.
Dezember 1965* (Münster: Aschendorff, 1966), p. 544.

at Berlin in 1927, the German military reacted by suggesting that the government buy up all remaining volumes of the findings of the third subcommittee and distribute them gratis at home. The plan was eventually realized in 1934, when Foreign Minister Konstantin von Neurath and Defense Minister General Werner von Blomberg persuaded the Finance Ministry to earmark 10,000 Mark for the purchase of all remaining volumes in the series. Of more immediate impact was that Hans Draeger of the ADV published Kriege's findings in 10,000 copies of his *Taschenbuch zur Kriegsschuldfrage*.[53]

Whereas the Foreign Ministry had refused to hand over only potentially incriminating documents to the *Untersuchungsausschuss*, the army and navy between 1924 and 1928 proved adamant in their refusals to assist in any way the work of the fourth subcommittee dealing with the collapse in 1918. In 1920, both services agreed jointly to plan their strategy in this regard—in sharp contrast to their inability either before or during the war to coordinate their military and naval strategies. Major Otto von Stülpnagel of the Defense Ministry bluntly warned that any opening of army archives would have "long-range consequences" for German policies not only domestically but also with regard to the Reich's "future world standing." Hence it was decided that official affidavits on the strategic ramifications of the great spring offensive in France in 1918 would be handled by the former general staff chief of Army Group Crown Prince Rupprecht, General Hermann von Kuhl, and on the political and military implications of "Operation Michael" by Colonel Schwertfeger, one of the Foreign Ministry's paid publicists; Professor Hans Delbrück was asked to submit a counter-affidavit. Kuhl, as was to be expected, reiterated Hindenburg's brazen "stab-in-the-back" theory, and argued that the army had been quite prepared to continue the war into 1919—had it not been for the systematic revolutionary planning of the Socialists. Delbrück countered by arguing that General Erich Ludendorff's "total war" strategy, which had gambled all on a decisive military victory in 1918, had grievously overestimated German resolve as well as resources, and thereby had directly contributed to the collapse. By reversing the relationship between goals and means, Ludendorff had displayed a shocking degree of

---

53. Fischer–Baling, "Untersuchungsausschuss," p. 135; and Heinemann, *Die verdrängte Niederlage*, pp. 193–194, 199–203. Kriege's numerous journeys to Doorn are chronicled in Sigurd von Ilsemann, *Der Kaiser in Holland: Aufzeichnungen des letzten Flügeladjutanten Kaiser Wilhelms II.* (Munich: Biederstein, 1967–68), 2 vols. On the Hague conventions, see Jost Dülffer, *Regeln gegen den Krieg? Die Haager Friedenskonferenzen von 1899 und 1907 in der internationalen Politik* (Berlin: Ullstein, 1981).

"unbridled egoism, megalomania, and lack of responsibility." When Del-brück's statements found their way into the press in 1924, Schwertfeger, Colonel Wolfgang Foerster of the *Reichsarchiv* at Potsdam, and the historian Hans Herzfeld viciously attacked Delbrück for his "unfounded, superficial, and misleading" interpretation. The so-called "Ludendorff controversy" reached its climax in November and December 1924, when the Cabinet twice agreed to sustain General Hans von Seeckt's veto of the planned publication of the findings of the fourth subcommittee for fear that this might harm "the moral fiber of the army."[54]

With regard to the navy's role in the collapse of 1917–18, tempers reached the flash point early in 1926, when the former USPD deputy Wilhelm Ditt-mann repeated his charges that the fleet "unrest" of October 1918 had, in fact, been precipitated by an "admirals' rebellion" against the government of Prince Max von Baden. Coming close on the heels of the sensational Munich "stab-in-the-back" press "investigation," Dittmann's charges sparked a vi-triolic exchange with the navy's official representatives, Vice Admiral Adolf von Trotha and Lieutenant–Commander Wilhelm Canaris, as well as with its parliamentary champion, Botho–Wendt zu Eulenburg of the DNVP. Eu-lenburg and Canaris especially applied the *Dolchstoss* thesis to the navy, arguing that both the SPD and the USPD in 1917–18 had delivered "the last fatal stab into the back of the fighting front." Had the admirals not refused to provide the fourth subcommittee with the war diary of the Supreme Command of the Navy (*Kriegstagebuch der Seekriegsleitung*)—which clearly revealed that naval leaders in October 1918 had planned a "suicide sortie" against the combined Anglo–American fleets in order to uphold the honor of the officer corps as well as to assure future naval funding—the so-called "Dittmann controversy" might well have been defused, if not resolved, right there and then.[55]

The most controversial investigation, of course, was that of the first sub-committee, charged with assessing Germany's role in the July crisis. There,

---

54. Heinemann, *Die verdrängte Niederlage*, pp. 179–187. For the Cabinet reaction, see Günter Abramowski, ed., *Akten der Reichskanzlei: Weimarer Republik. Die Kabinette Marx I und II* (Boppard: H. Boldt, 1973), Vol. 2, pp. 1160–61, 1213, 1222; sessions of November 7, December 4 and 12, 1924. See also Hermann von Kuhl, *Der Weltkrieg 1914–1918* (Berlin: W. Kock, 1929), 2 vols.; Bucholz, *Hans Delbrück*, pp. 121ff.; and Annelise Thimme, *Hans Delbrück als Kritiker der Wilhel-minischen Epoche* (Düsseldorf: Droste, 1955).
55. Heinemann, *Die verdrängte Niederlage*, pp. 188–189. The first scholarly evaluation of the navy's war diary was by Wilhelm Deist, "Die Flottenpolitik der Seekriegsleitung und die Re-bellion der Flotte Ende Oktober 1918," *Vierteljahrshefte für Zeitgeschichte*, Vol. 14 (1966), pp. 341–368.

after all, was the heart of Article 231 of the Versailles treaty. The Foreign Ministry was acutely sensitive to possible Allied charges that this committee was stacked with its minions, and hence the Wilhelmstrasse encouraged the Reichstag to engage "neutral" experts. The choice fell upon the Munich publicist Hermann Lutz and the Freiburg jurist Hermann Kantorowicz. Despite the fact that Lutz was closely associated with the revisionist campaign conducted by the Foreign Ministry, his affidavit, completed in 1924, proved embarrassingly balanced. Lutz placed Serbia and Russia at the top of the list of those responsible for the war, closely followed by Austria–Hungary, and then by the rest of the parties involved. Lutz's evaluation of the Habsburg policy of brinkmanship in July 1914 at once drew the ire of fellow investigators Max von Montgelas and Richard von Delbrück, both intimately involved with the Foreign Ministry's revisionist endeavors. Indeed, the Wilhelmstrasse "encouraged" Lutz to "revise" his affidavit; in its second form, the *Gutachten* placed Vienna in a more favorable light. Nevertheless, the Foreign Ministry again used its veto power to delay publication of Lutz's affidavit for half a decade (until 1930).[56]

The case of Hermann Kantorowicz in many ways symbolizes the entire campaign of "preemptive historiography." Charged with investigating the legal parameters of the war's origins, Kantorowicz submitted his affidavit in December 1923; revisions for publication were completed by the spring of 1925, and galleys were set to go to press two years later. Final publication came in 1967. Kantorowicz's original manuscript was destroyed when the Reichstag was bombed in 1945, but Imanuel Geiss managed to obtain a copy from the family's archive.

Kantorowicz attributed responsibility for the war primarily to the Central Powers: Austria–Hungary for the aggressive manner in which it had launched the Balkan war with Serbia, and Germany not only for supporting the Habsburg initiative but also for rejecting all peace efforts undertaken by England and Russia after the assassination at Sarajevo. Jew, Anglophile, pacifist, republican, and democrat, Kantorowicz was accused of "fouling his own nest" *(Nestbeschmutzung)* and soon experienced the wrath of official Germany. In January 1927, Prussian Cultural Minister Carl Becker informed the German Foreign Ministry of widespread opposition to Kantorowicz's

---

56. Heinemann, *Die verdrängte Niederlage*, pp. 212–213. See also Max von Montgelas, *Leitfaden zur Kriegsschuldfrage* (Berlin: W. de Gruyter, 1923); and Hermann Lutz, *Die europäische Politik in der Julikrise 1914* (Berlin: Deutsche Verlagsgesellschaft für Politik und Geschichte, 1930).

recent selection to a chair *(Ordinarius)* by Kiel University on the grounds that the jurist's affidavit "would severely damage German policies" in the eyes of the world. Foreign Minister Gustav Stresemann, who had not read Kantorowicz's *Gutachten*, concurred, basing his attempted veto of the appointment upon an evaluation of the affidavit submitted to him by none other than Johannes Kriege, the former imperial official who had headed the legal section of the Foreign Office during the Great War—in other words, the very bureau that Kantorowicz had investigated. According to Friedrich Thimme, editor of *Die Grosse Politik*, Stresemann at the end of 1927 had clearly indicated the interconnection between the nagging "war-guilt" issue and his policy of rapprochement with the West by arguing that publication of Kantorowicz's affidavit "would render my entire Locarno policy impossible."[57]

Yet, in one of those rare moments when academicians are willing to place the principle of academic freedom above personal interest, the law faculty at Kiel insisted on and won Kantorowicz's appointment as professor. But the Foreign Ministry was not yet done. After September 1928, Stresemann consistently delayed publication of Kantorowicz's affidavit—at first through appeals to Chancellor Hermann Müller, and thereafter by various delaying tactics involving additional counter-affidavits. In fact, Chancellor Müller and Paul Löbe, president of the Reichstag, at the height of the national furor over the Young Plan in 1929, conspired in further delays, despite threats by Kantorowicz that he would "privately" publish his findings. Stresemann, shortly before his death in October 1929, entrusted yet another counter-affidavit to the ever-available Kriege. Concurrently, the Wilhelmstrasse denied Kantorowicz private publication of his findings; the parliamentary Committee of Enquiry seconded this decision in February 1930. Kriege, for his part, informed Thimme that he intended to draw out his investigation as long as possible in order to stall Kantorowicz. The Finance Ministry at this point rejoined the revisionist campaign by refusing to make available to the fourth subcommittee the agreed-upon printing subsidy of 40-50,000 Mark—while at the same time the Foreign Ministry agreed fully to fund Kriege's counter-affidavit. In the meantime, Kantorowicz's career suffered irreparable damage. In 1933, his name was on the list of the first 25 professors to be

---

57. Cited in Schleier, *Die bürgerliche deutsche Geschichtsschreibung*, p. 157. Stresemann's papers were also carefully "ordered" after his death. See Gustav Stresemann, *Vermächtnis, der Nachlass*, ed. by Henry Bernhard (Berlin: Ullstein, 1932–33), 3 vols.; and Hans W. Gatzke, "The Stresemann Papers," *Journal of Modern History*, Vol. 26 (1954), pp. 49–59.

dismissed from university posts by the Hitler regime. Kantorowicz's earlier work on "The Spirit of English Policy and the Phantom of Germany's Encirclement," published in 1929, was among the books burned on the Nazi's pyre of ignorance in May 1933.[58]

To be sure, the vendetta conducted against Kantorowicz would not remain an isolated case. In 1932, several German historians, led by Hermann Oncken, Hermann Schumacher, and Fritz Hartung, conspired to deny the young radical scholar Eckart Kehr the Rockefeller Fellowship that Charles A. Beard had helped Kehr secure for study in the United States.[59] And as recently as February 1964, West Germany's Foreign Minister, Gerhard Schröder, acting upon the recommendations of Gerhard Ritter and Karl Dietrich Erdmann, formally rescinded Goethe Institute travel funds awarded Fritz Fischer for a planned lecture tour of the United States, a tour that Ritter equated with "a national tragedy." Apparently, the Foreign Ministry was quite prepared once more to take on the role of patriotic self-censor. It was only through the efforts of a dozen American scholars, led by Klaus Epstein, that Fischer's visit came about.[60] Ritter not only spoke of what he decried as Fischer's penchant for "political masochism," but poured out all his bitterness in a letter to Klaus Epstein's father, Fritz, a scholar also hounded out of German academia after 1933, by referring to Fischer as "an old Nazi, who had so quickly managed to convert to democracy" after 1945.[61] Ritter's real

---

58. See Hermann Kantorowicz, *Gutachten zur Kriegsschuldfrage 1914*, ed. by Imanuel Geiss (Frankfurt: Europäische Verlagsanstalt, 1967), pp. 7–42; Erich Eyck, *A History of the Weimar Republic* (London: Oxford University Press, 1964), Vol. 2, pp. 105–106, note; and Heinemann, *Die verdrängte Niederlage*, p. 215. Kantorowicz's earlier book was entitled *Der Geist der englischen Politik und das Gespenst der Einkreisung Deutschlands* (Berlin: E. Rowohlt, 1929).
59. See Schleier, *Die burgerliche deutsche Geschichtsschreibung*, p. 519; and Eckart Kehr, *Der Primat der Innenpolitik: Gesammelte Aufsätze zur preussisch-deutschen Sozialgeschichte im 19. und 20. Jahrhundert*, ed. by Hans–Ulrich Wehler (Berlin: W. de Gruyter, 1965), pp. 18–19.
60. Klaus Schwabe and Rolf Reichardt, eds., *Gerhard Ritter: Ein politischer Historiker in seinen Briefen* (Boppard: H. Boldt, 1984), pp. 587–589. Ritter to Schröder, January 17, 1964.
61. Ibid., pp. 559, 576. Ritter to Herzfeld, October 30, 1961; and Ritter to Epstein, February 15, 1963. On another occasion, Ritter denounced his Hamburg colleague as a "student of the arch-Nazi Erich Seeberg" and accused him of having gained his chair at Hamburg University in 1942 through the influence of Walter Frank, head of the *Reichsinstitut für Geschichte des neuen Deutschlands*. Bernd F. Schulte, *Die Verfälschung der Riezler Tagebücher: Ein Beitrag zur Wissenschaftsgeschichte der 50iger und 60iger Jahre* (Frankfurt, Bern, and New York: Peter Lang, 1985), p. 145. Fischer's defenders are conspicuously silent on the matter of his alleged Nazi past; it is inconceivable, of course, that any scholar could have attained an important academic post in 1942 without the official sanction of the Nazi regime. See Karl–Heinz Janssen, "Historischer Realismus," *Die Zeit*, March 2, 1973, p. 15. In any case, it is illuminating that an "old Nazi" such as Fischer should have been able to come to the position on the origins of the war that he did in *Griff nach der Weltmacht*, while a self-proclaimed anti-Nazi such as Ritter continued to tout the position of the patriotic self-censors from the 1920s.

grudge against Fisher was that the Hamburg historian with his *Griff nach der Weltmacht* had reopened the entire war-guilt issue, an issue *"that one had believed belonged to a distant past."*[62] In that one sentence to his colleague Theodor Schieder at Köln, Ritter expressed his generation's horror that perhaps the "patriotic self-censorship" of the Weimar Republic had not succeeded after all. It was a fitting eulogy for this unfortunate chapter of German historiography. And the passions engendered by the "Fischer controversy" certainly paralleled those of the Kantorowicz and Kehr scandals both in substance and in acrimony. Careers both before and after the Second World War all too often hinged upon one's stance on the issue of "war guilt."

Memoirs and Historical Falsification

Last but not least, attention should be drawn to several attempts to suppress or to "revise" memoirs after the First World War. One of the most celebrated cases involved General Helmuth von Moltke the Younger. The former Chief of the General Staff had died in 1916, and his widow with the assistance of Rudolf Steiner, the founder of anthroposophy, had prepared by the spring of 1919 a detailed memoir that promised to shed light on Moltke's role before and during the July crisis. Before the book could go to press, however, Eliza von Moltke was paid a visit by "certain persons" who advised her not to publish her husband's papers. Steiner, in turn, was informed by the Prussian envoy at Stuttgart, Legation Secretary Hans–Adolf von Moltke (!), that "Berlin did not desire" General von Moltke's memoirs in print; an unnamed general, who had served both Wilhelm II and Moltke, also sought out Steiner to caution against publication of the book.[63] These efforts were successful, and the *Erinnerungen* eventually put out by Eliza von Moltke in 1922 proved devoid of any information on the origins of the war. Moreover, Moltke's papers thereafter were so carefully "ordered" by self-appointed patriotic censors that, in the words of John Röhl, "they contain not a single document worth reading from the pre-War period."[64] The same is rumored about the

---

62. Ibid., p. 562. Ritter to Schieder, December 4, 1961. Emphasis added.
63. Helmuth von Moltke, *Erinnerungen. Briefe. Dokumente 1877–1916. Ein Bild vom Kriegsausbruch, erster Kriegsführung und Persönlichkeit des ersten militärischen Führers des Krieges*, ed. by Eliza von Moltke (Stuttgart: Der Kommende Tag, 1922), pp. vii–viii; and Roman Boos, ed., *Rudolf Steiner während des Weltkrieges: Beiträge Rudolf Steiners zur Bewältigung der Aufgaben die durch den Krieg gestellt wurden* (Dornach: Verlag der Sozialwissenschaftlichen Vereinigung am Goetheanum, 1933), pp. 99–100.
64. Röhl, *1914: Delusion or Design?*, pp. 37–38.

papers of Field Marshal von Hindenburg, which allegedly were "ordered" by the late nationalist historian Walther Hubatsch; the Hindenburg family to date has refused to deposit them with the Federal Military Archive at Freiburg.[65]

Three important collections of papers barely escaped destruction. Those of Admiral Georg Alexander von Müller, Chief of the Navy Cabinet to 1918, were earmarked for destruction upon the officer's death—an order fortunately not executed by his son, Sven. Yet when published by Walter Görlitz after the Second World War, the diaries incredibly appeared in a "carefully expurgated version," although the authentic text is highly readable.[66]

Likewise, in the case of Kurt Riezler, Chancellor von Bethmann Hollweg's *intimus*, the papers were slated for destruction. The conservative historian Hans Rothfels both during the Second World War and thereafter advised Riezler against publication in order not to reopen the debate concerning the origins of the Great War. After Riezler's death in 1965, his brother destroyed what he termed "private" parts of the *Nachlass*, and neither the Foreign Office at Bonn nor the Federal Archive at Koblenz could persuade Walter Riezler to turn the papers over to them. It was only through the repeated pressures of historians both in Germany and abroad to secure the critical memoir that Riezler's sister, Mary White, eventually consented to publication. Not surprisingly, the Riezler materials were carefully "ordered" by Karl Dietrich Erdmann in book form; thereafter, they remained closed to scholars at the Bundesarchiv at Koblenz for another eight years. Upon becoming available, the very originality especially of Riezler's notes during the July crisis was challenged in 1983. Gerhard Ritter, in the meantime, had persuaded the Bonn regime's *Bundeszentrale für politische Bildung* to print 10,000 copies of his apologetic account of the origins of the war, to be distributed primarily to West German schools and libraries. Eugen Gerstenmaier, the head of the West German Bundestag, thanked Ritter for his "brilliant clarification" and expressed the satisfaction that "therewith Fischer should really be finished off."[67] It was all in the best tradition of the patriotic self-censors of the 1920s.

---

65. Hubatsch used these papers, which remain with the field marshal's grandson, Hubertus von Hindenburg, in *Hindenburg und der Staat: Aus den Papieren des Generalfeldmarschalls und Reichspräsidenten von 1878 bis 1934* (Göttingen: Musterschmidt, 1966).

66. See Röhl, *1914: Delusion or Design?*, p. 37; Walter Görlitz, ed., *The Kaiser and His Court: The Diaries, Note Books and Letters of Admiral Georg Alexander von Müller Chief of the Navy Cabinet, 1914–1918* (New York: Harcourt, Brace & World, 1961), p. xiii. The papers are now at the Bundesarchiv–Militärarchiv (BA–MA) at Freiburg, West Germany: N 159, *Nachlass* Müller.

67. Karl Dietrich Erdmann, ed., *Kurt Riezler: Tagebücher, Aufsätze, Dokumente* (Göttingen: Van-

Finally, in the case of Admiral Alfred von Tirpitz, the family in the late 1960s released the papers of the former state secretary of the Navy Office to the Federal Military Archive at Freiburg only in exchange for a substantial fee. In fact, Tirpitz had caused a national scandal in 1924–25 when he published a two-volume set of documents designed to show that "navalism" had been the right course and that others had failed to do their part to realize it. The Wilhelmstrasse had even released Friedrich Thimme from his labors on *Die Grosse Politik* so that he could attack Tirpitz's publication "in the national interest."[68]

A final curiosity is the case of Prince Philipp zu Eulenburg–Hertefeld. A trusted advisor to the last Hohenzollern before his tragic involvement in a national scandal in 1907–09, Eulenburg had entrusted his voluminous correspondence to Professor Johannes Haller. The latter's handling of the matter of publishing Eulenburg's materials sheds light upon the vagaries of postwar politics and scholarship. Haller at first advised against publication of the *Nachlass* after what he termed his "dreadful" study of the diplomatic documents published by Karl Kautsky. In 1920, the aborted right-wing Kapp *Putsch* further convinced Haller that the time to publish the papers had not yet arrived. Especially the Kaiser's marginal comments on diplomatic documents and his juvenile letters to Nicholas II of Russia had shocked the Tübingen historian. Yet by the late 1920s, Haller was ready to edit the memoirs, arguing that by "clearing" Eulenburg's honor with regard to the homosexual scandal, he could lay the basis for the restoration of Wilhelm II.[69] In other words, scholarship was to be used as a tool in the fight against the Weimar Republic. The papers were not published until 1976.

It would be tedious to continue to list similar cases of suppression or revision of memoirs and diaries. Suffice it to say that these examples should

---

denhoeck & Ruprecht, 1972), pp. 8–12. The originality of especially Riezler's notes (*Blockblätter*) for the period from July 7 through August 14, 1914 has been contended: Bernd Sösemann, "Die Tagebücher Kurt Riezlers: Untersuchungen zu ihrer Echtheit und Edition," *Historische Zeitschrift*, Vol. 236 (April 1983), pp. 327–369. Karl Dietrich Erdmann, "Zur Echtheit der Tagebücher Kurt Riezlers: Eine Antikritik," ibid., pp. 371–402, maintains that the notes for the period in question stem from Riezler's hand. See also Schulte, *Die Verfälschung der Riezler Tagebücher*, pp. 9, 146.

68. Thimme, "Friedrich Thimme," p. 235; Annelise Thimme, "Der 'Fall Tirpitz' als Fall der Weimarer Republik," in Imanuel Geiss and Bernd–Jürgen Wendt, eds., *Deutschland in der Weltpolitik des 19. und 20. Jahrhunderts. Fritz Fischer zum 65. Geburtstag* (Düsseldorf: Droste, 1973), pp. 463–482; and Schleier, *Die bürgerliche deutsche Geschichtsschreibung*, p. 152. The papers are now at the BA–MA: N 253, *Nachlass* Tirpitz.

69. John C.G. Röhl, ed., *Philipp Eulenburgs Politische Korrespondenz* (Boppard: H. Boldt, 1976), Vol. 1, pp. 64–65.

provide an insight into the business of patriotic self-censorship during the Weimar Republic and thereafter. What has been entirely omitted in this article are the cases where editors were engaged to ghostwrite memoirs—such as those of Admirals Karl Dönitz and Erich Raeder—in order to preclude public debate on vital issues of national interest.

The Revisionist Syndrome: Conclusions

The foregoing discussion of the German war-guilt campaign raises the twin issues concerning its effect, both in the short and in the long term, and the motivations that prompted the self-censors. Of course, many German publicists simply saw it as their patriotic duty to defend the fatherland against Allied charges that it had caused the war. Few, indeed, had been in position in July 1914 to know what had transpired. Especially Bismarck-admirers could hardly be expected to believe that the men of the summer of 1914 had been so unrealistic as to risk a European war against a powerful coalition with only one ally—moribund, at that—in tow. Others simply wanted to maintain the old order under the guise of a Republic that continued to call itself a Reich and to fly the imperial black-white-red colors along with the democratic black-red-gold. It was simply too hard to break with the past; the old order, right or wrong, needed to be defended against outside attacks. Nor should it be overlooked that the men who conducted the revisionist campaign had been servants of the old imperial order. Their actions during the 1920s showed clearly that they cared little for the principles of a democratic foreign policy, and hardly at all for such "disturbing" institutions as political parties and parliaments.

Continuity, of course, could be maintained only if the senior civil servants of 1914 could demonstate that Allied charges of war responsibility were without foundation. In short, the high bureaucracy was not interested in personnel purges in 1919. Nor were the dominant Social Democrats. In fact, the SPD never demanded that the senior statesmen and diplomats of the empire be held accountable. The resulting irony was that the Republic's Committee of Enquiry, for example, relied for many of its "expert" affidavits upon the very men who had been in positions of power and responsibility in July 1914, men such as Gottlieb von Jagow and Johannes Kriege. By failing to clean house in 1919, by failing to confront the matter of Germany's role in the origins of the First World War brutally and honestly, and, above all, by failing to chase the patriotic censors from their temples of influence, the first leaders of the Weimar Republic did their country a great disservice. And for much of the 1920s, the lack of political experience under the empire of the parties of the center and left, compounded by their lack of republican self-confidence, rendered them ineffective not only against the self-censors but also in uncovering the causes for the war especially through the *Untersuchungsausschuss*.

Conversely, the patriotic censors with their campaign of obfuscation, delay, preemptive historiography, and mass propaganda made quite certain that the issue would never be allowed to die, as Hans Freytag had foreseen as early as 1919. Max Weber, despite his signature on the "professors' memorandum" of May 1919, in time came to lament this turn of events. "Every document that comes to light after decades," he sadly noted, "revives the undignified squabbling, the hatred and anger, instead of at least *decently* burying the war and its end."[70] As Michael Salewski has put it, the constant obsession with war guilt eventually mired the Republic in a "revisionist syndrome."[71]

Unsurprisingly, some of the self-censors were driven by reasons of personal interest. As Erich Hahn has suggested, the traditional elite of the Wilhelmstrasse fought for its political survival by defending its credibility— be it in 1914 or 1919—both at home and abroad. The war-guilt issue thus served its purpose much in the way that the "stab-in-the-back" legend served the army: as an escape from the political consequences of defeat. In other words, the consequences of the miscalculated risk of July 1914 could be avoided only by keeping the anti-war-guilt campaign alive after the peace. And since the Republic very much depended on the cooperation of former imperial officials, it naturally had an interest in establishing their "innocence." Yet the war-guilt game was dangerous because, as Karl Kautsky had put it in 1919, it was "not only a scholarly question for historians," but "an eminently practical question for politicians." For the authors of the war, the

---

70. Max Weber, "Politik als Beruf," in *Gesammelte politische Schriften*, ed. by Johannes Winckelmann (Tübingen: Mohr, 1971), p. 549.
71. Michael Salewski, "Das Weimarer Revisionssyndrom," in *Aus Politik und Zeitgeschichte: Beilage zur Wochenzeitung "Das Parlament"*, B2/1980 (January 12, 1980), pp. 14–25.

answer to the question of who was responsible amounted to a "death sentence" as they surely would be "cast among the politically dead . . . , stripped of all power."[72] It was to be part of the genius of the patriotic self-censors that they managed through their collective efforts at preemptive historiography to escape that "death sentence."

In retrospect, the revisionist campaign conducted by men such as Bülow, Draeger, Freytag, Montgelas, Schücking, and Thimme, among others, retarded critical appraisal of the origins of the war until the 1960s. A certain orthodoxy on the war-guilt issue developed; Europe, in the immortal words of David Lloyd George, had simply "slid" into the war in 1914 with roughly equal amounts of ignorance and naiveté. It simply cannot be stressed enough that by linking the war-guilt issue very early on to the campaign to "revise" the Versailles treaty, the patriotic censors virtually precluded sober and rational investigation into the matter. Hermann Kantorowicz's affidavit might have been accepted as an academic treatise; it was political dynamite for a Gustav Stresemann pursuing rapprochement at least with the West at Locarno. Only by rejecting Article 231 outright could German leaders hope to convince the Allies that the harsh terms of the *Diktat* were, in fact, based upon a misconception. In other words, if they could undermine the charge of war guilt, these Germans felt, they could press on with treaty "revisions" such as evacuation of occupied territories, redress of borders above all in the East, and lowering of reparations payments. Indeed, it had been Stresemann's onetime hope that the publication of *Die Grosse Politik* would serve precisely such national interests.[73] Put differently, the Wilhelmstrasse hoped that by undermining the moral foundations of Allied charges of war guilt, it

---

72. Hahn, "German Foreign Ministry," pp. 56, 69; and Kautsky, *Wie der Weltkrieg entstand*, p. 13.

73. Heinemann, *Die verdrängte Niederlage*, p. 224. On the foreign policy implications of the issue, see Andreas Hillgruber, "Unter dem Schatten von Versailles—die aussenpolitische Belastung der Weimarer Republik: Realität und Perzeption bei den Deutschen," in Karl Dietrich Erdmann and Hagen Schulze, eds., *Weimar. Selbstpreisgabe einer Demokratie. Eine Bilanz heute. Kölner Kolloquium der Fritz Thyssen Stiftung Juni 1979* (Düsseldorf: Droste, 1980), pp. 51–67. On May 7, 1932, the former head of the War Guilt Section, Legation Secretary Karl Schwendemann, crowed to Alfred von Wegerer of the effectiveness of the anti-war-guilt campaign: "You see, dear Herr von Wegerer, how important our enlightenment in the war-guilt question is for the disarmament negotiations here [at Geneva in 1932]. Had the disarmament conference taken place six years ago, then certainly the French would have brought the war-guilt question into debate and perhaps still with the prospect of success." National Archives Record Group 242, Records of the German Foreign Office Received by the Department of State, Microfilm Series T120: 3220/E547299-301, p. 300. I am indebted to Professor Don Emerson of the University of Washington for this citation.

could restore the diplomatic freedom that the Reich had enjoyed before 1914 as an equal and sovereign member of the community of European nations.

Last but not least, both Bülow and Stresemann realized that the Wilhelmstrasse's campaign against Article 231 of the Versailles treaty also served a highly useful domestic purpose: the "national alibi" constituted a convenient integration factor by rallying the political spectrum from *Vorwärts* to *Völkischer Beobachter*, that is, from Social Democrat to National Socialist, round this one great patriotic issue. In a land that had enjoyed a mere seventy years of nationhood and that remained deeply divided socially, politically, and regionally, such an integration factor was not to be overlooked. An additional domestic benefit was that the vigorous pursuance of "revisionism" on the part of the Wilhelmstrasse might take some of the thunder out of the charges of "defeatism" and "softness" constantly leveled against the Republic by its right-wing detractors over the issue of "fulfilment" of the Versailles treaty, and thereby benefit Stresemann's flexible and moderate revisionist diplomacy.[74]

Unfortunately, the events of 1932–33 were to show that this national consensus was tenuous at best; the seemingly diametrically opposed poles of extreme nationalism and national inferiority (engendered by the war-guilt charge) were to be brutally but effectively exploited by the extreme right, the real "winners" of the revisionist campaign. In short, by delaying an open and honest discussion on the origins of the First World War for four decades, the self-censors did their part to bring about a political climate receptive to the radical "revisionist" ideas of Adolf Hitler and his supporters.

At the risk of belaboring the obvious, I will conclude this overview of how Clio was deceived in Germany by suggesting that the moral and institutional lessons to be learned have not lost any of their crispness and validity over the decades. It serves no national interest to obfuscate and derail intellectual inquiry. Miscalculated risks are rarely glossed over simply by selectively editing pertinent documents and by having paid publicists tout the desired line through government-controlled presses and publishers. "Preemptive historiography" may succeed in the short run; over time, it is likely to be uncovered as the sham that it is. In the final analysis, it was nothing short of a tragedy that, in the words of Hermann Hesse, "90 or 100 prominent men" conspired in the supposed interests of the state "to deceive the people

---

74. Jäger, *Historische Forschung*, p. 68; and Heinemann, *Die verdrängte Niederlage*, pp. 226, 241.

on this vital question of national interest."[75] Nor was Hesse in doubt as to the effectiveness of the campaign of "patriotic self-censorship," informing Thomas Mann in 1931 of his opinion that "of 1,000 Germans, even today 999 still know nothing of [our] war guilt."[76] Little wonder, then, that Fritz Fischer's *Griff nach der Weltmacht* had such an explosive impact precisely thirty years later.

---

75. Eckart Klessmann, "Als politischer Zeitkritiker neu entdeckt: Hermann Hesse," in *Die Zeit, Zeitmagazin,* Vol. 15 (April 14, 1972), p. 10. Hesse to Wilhelm Schäfer, 1930.
76. Ibid., p. 10.